BASEBALL'S GREATEST COMEBACK GAMES

★ GAMES ★

Edited by Bill Nowlin

Associate editors Len Levin and Carl Riechers

Society for American Baseball Research, Inc.
Phoenix, AZ

Baseball's Greatest Comeback Games
Edited by Bill Nowlin
Associate editors Len Levin and Carl Riechers

Copyright © 2021 Society for American Baseball Research, Inc.
All rights reserved. Reproduction in whole or in part without permission is prohibited.
ISBN 978-1-970159-47-9
(Ebook ISBN 978-1-970159-46-2)

LOC # 2021901964

Front cover art and design by Ronnie Joyner.
Book design: Rachael Sullivan
Society for American Baseball Research
Cronkite School at ASU
555 N. Central Ave. #416
Phoenix, AZ 85004
Phone: (602) 496-1460
Web: www.sabr.org
Facebook: Society for American Baseball Research
Twitter: @SABR

CONTENTS

BASEBALL'S GREATEST COMEBACK GAMES

There were 8,000 fans at the ballpark. The temperature was 93 degrees. Monday, June 15, 1925, was celebrated as Flag Day in Philadelphia. The Cleveland Indians seemed to have the game in hand. They led 15-3 at the seventh-inning stretch, and the Athletics eked out only one run in the bottom of the seventh. After seven full innings, it was 15-4, Indians. There wasn't a lot of reason for any but diehard Athletics fans to stick around.

Then the A's exploded for 13 runs in the bottom of the eighth, taking a 17-15 lead, a lead that held. Those who had slunk out before the onslaught no doubt wished they'd stayed. There's a reason many fans stay to the bitter end – and there was every reason to think the game at Shibe Park was going to have a bitter ending. Those who stuck with it were rewarded in witnessing one of the greatest comebacks in baseball history.

Every comeback, of course, features a winner and a loser. And sometimes it's the visiting team that prevails. These days, more people watch games on television than at the ballpark. There is still often a deep emotional investment in one's team, and watching a great comeback might be either deeply deflating or truly exhilarating.

What are baseball's greatest comeback games? This book set out to look at these games. Rather than throw together an anecdotally-determined collection of games, we decided to see if there was an objective measure, a way to determine which was *the* greatest comeback game of all time, and to rank the games.

I asked Retrosheet's Tom Ruane. The question intrigued him.

Working with the Retrosheet database, he created a master list that totaled 630 games. And he ranked them mathematically in terms of how unlikely the win was (how great the comeback had been).

Shortly after doing so, Tom wrote up the approach he took and presented it on Retrosheet. It can be found here: retrosheet.org/Research/RuaneT/retro_fun5.htm#A190513

THE GAMES IN THIS VOLUME

The games in this volume are presented in rank order from the list Tom created, number 1 through number 64. There was no particular reason to stop at 64. It just seemed like a good place. The last two games were both Twins wins, but that's really neither here nor there.

One can notice a few interesting things in the list. The Phillies lead the list with six comeback wins in the top 64. Tied for second for most comebacks are four American League teams – the Red Sox, Indians, Tigers, and Yankees.

There's no particular pattern in the number of comebacks per decade that made the top 64:

- 1901-10   2 *(both of the games from this decade occurred in 1901, one in April and one in May)*
- 1911-20   6
- 1921-30   6
- 1931-40   8
- 1941-50   5
- 1951-60   4
- 1961-70   3 *(all three occurred in June 1961)*
- 1971-80   9
- 1981-90   3 *(all three of these games rank in the top 13 of all comeback games)*
- 1991-2000 7
- 2001-10   8
- 2011-19   2

After assembling that list, we added two additional elements. First, we decided to look at the greatest postseason comeback games. There are seven games presented in a separate section devoted to postseason games.

I wanted a fan of any of the 30 major-league teams to be able to find his or her team's greatest comeback. There were nine current teams that did not turn up as winners in the 64 ranked games. For this purpose, I treated – for instance – the Los Angeles Dodgers and San Francisco Giants as different from the Brooklyn Dodgers and New York Giants.

I looked at the list of additional games and selected the greatest comeback for each of these current teams. The games, and their ranking in the overall list, are:

- Colorado Rockies – their July 26, 2010, win ranks number 73 on the master list.

- San Francisco Giants – their game selected ranks number 93 on the master list

- Tampa Bay Rays – their greatest comeback ranks number 95

- Oakland Athletics – their greatest comeback ranks number 96

- Texas Rangers – their greatest comeback ranks number 117

- Seattle Mariners – their greatest comeback ranks number 133

- Arizona Diamondbacks – their greatest comeback ranks number 173

- Los Angeles Dodgers – their greatest comeback ranks number 205

- Washington Nationals – their greatest comeback ranks number 454

The future will hold other great comeback games. Here is a look at some of the greatest comeback games from years gone by.

—Bill Nowlin

TIGERS ROAR BACK WITH WIN

JULY 7, 1922:
DETROIT TIGERS 11,
WASHINGTON SENATORS 9
(SECOND GAME OF DOUBLEHEADER),
AT GRIFFITH STADIUM, WASHINGTON

BY KEVIN LARKIN

What follows is a narrative on the greatest comeback in baseball history.[1]

Since they began in the American League in 1901, the Washington Senators as of 1922 had finished fourth or better just six times. In 1915 and 1921 they were fourth, in 1914 and 1918 they were third, and in 1912 and 1913 they had two second-place finishes. Detroit, on the other hand, had won three pennants (1907-09) but had failed to win a World Series.

As of the first game of the July 7 Friday afternoon doubleheader with the Tigers at Griffith Stadium, the 1922 Senators were in fifth place with a record of 35-37 and they trailed the first-place St. Louis Browns by 8½ games. Detroit was a game and a half ahead of Washington, trailing the Browns by seven games.

Detroit squeaked out a 7-6 win in the first game of the twin bill, led by Bobby Veach, who was 3-for-4 with two RBIs, and Ty Cobb (triple, double, two runs scored), Topper Rigney, and Johnny Bassler, all of whom had two hits. The Senators' Walter Johnson suffered the loss in the game, giving up all of the Tigers' 13 hits.

To try to keep the Tigers from getting a sweep, the Senators sent George Mogridge to the hill to face Detroit's Red Oldham. Mogridge had spent the first two years of his major-league career with the Chicago White Sox (1911-12); from 1915 to 1920, he was with the New York Yankees. On April 24, 1917, Mogridge pitched the Yankees' first no-hit game, defeating the Red Sox, 2-1, at Fenway Park in Boston.

On December 31, 1920, the Yankees traded Mogridge and outfielder Duffy Lewis to the Senators for Braggo Roth.

Ty Cobb at bat, 1921. In the year 1922, he hit. 401 – the third year in which he hit above .400.

Oldham had just one winning season in the majors before 1922: in 1915 with the Tigers, when he had a record of 3-0 in 17 games. (He had just one other winning season in the majors, that coming in 1925 when he was 3-2 for the Pittsburgh Pirates.)

In the second game, Washington scored first when Roger Peckinpaugh reached first base with a single. Sam Rice grounded out to Detroit first baseman Lu Blue and Peckinpaugh went to second.

Joe Judge, who entered the game batting .296, worked the count to 3-and-2 and then hit a pitch to center field for a double that scored Peckinpaugh with the game's first run.

To quote a Detroit sportswriter: "Nothing of an exciting nature occurred until the Washington third that saw the Nationals getting a single with three doubles for three runs."[2]

Neither team scored in the second inning, and the Tigers did not score in the third. In the bottom of the inning, Clyde Milan singled to right field with one out. Peckinpaugh got his second hit of the day, a double. Rice hit the inning's second double, and then Judge hit the third. Three more runs added to the Senators' side of the scoreboard for a 4-0 Washington lead.

In the fourth inning a triple by Bucky Harris and a sacrifice fly by Patsy Gharrity gave the Senators a 5-0 lead.

With one out in the fifth inning, Chick Gagnon batted for Oldham and singled to left field. Lu Blue doubled with Gagnon holding at third base. A single by Fred Haney scored Gagnon. Blue thought the ball might be caught so he remained at second base. On Cobb's hit to left field, Blue left second homeward-bound. He beat the throw and Gharrity dropped the ball. Everybody in the ballpark saw that happen, except the one man whose opinion counted: home-plate umpire Ed Walsh, who called Blue out.[3]

Bobby Veach singled to score Haney and send Cobb to third base. But Harry Heilmann flied out. The Tigers had scored a pair and Washington's lead was now 5-2.

In the bottom of the fifth inning, Peckinpaugh walked and stole second base. With two men out, Frank Brower, batting for Senators right fielder Ed Goebel, singled off Carl Holling, who had relieved Oldham to the start of the bottom of the inning. Brower's hit scored Peckinpaugh and gave the Senators a 6-2 lead.

Two more runs came Washington's way in the seventh inning. Peckinpaugh started it off with a single to left field. He scored on a triple to center by Rice. Judge walked. Brower forced Judge while Peckinpaugh remained at third. Brower stole second base as Howie Shanks struck out, as Peckinpaugh scored on the bad throw.[4] Brower also tried to score but was out on Cobb's throw to catcher Clyde Manion.

The Senators got two more runs in the seventh inning and scored one in the eighth, when Mogridge doubled and scored on Clyde Milan's single to center field. Washington now led 9-2 going to the top of the ninth inning. "The haughty Griffmen, finding themselves leading by seven runs with the start of the ninth, smiled," wrote the *Washington Times's* scribe. "Possibly more than half of them were perishing from sheer hunger. They had been toiling today since high noon and it was time for ease and refreshment."[5]

A *Washington Herald* account said, "Everything happened in the ninth inning. And it all broke like an unexpected storm over a Sunday school picnic."[6]

With the game seemingly in hand, the Senators took to the field needing just three outs to add a win to their season total. "Can you picture a ballclub taking its last turn at bat seven runs down and emerging from it two to the good?"[7]

A single by pinch-hitter Larry Woodall, a walk to Blue, and a single by Haney loaded the bases with Cobb stepping into the batter's box. Cobb singled to center field to score Woodall and Blue with Haney going to second base A fly ball by Ira Flagstead was the first out of the inning. Heilmann, who entered the game with a .361 batting average, worked a walk to fill the bases again. George Cutshaw singled, scoring Haney and leaving the bases full. The Tigers now trailed 9-5.

Peckinpaugh's throw on Topper Rigney's groundball was late and Cobb scored the Tigers' fourth run of the inning. Howie Shanks missed a tag on Cutshaw on a groundball by Clyde Manion, allowing Heilmann to score. The Senators were now leading by just two runs, 9-7, and the bases were still loaded.

Woodall got his second hit of the inning, a single, and both Cutshaw and Rigney scored. The game was tied, 9-9.

The Tigers weren't through. They took the lead on a single by Blue that scored Manion and put Woodall safely at third base. Haney beat out a bunt that scored Woodall and the Tigers led, 11-9.

Tom Zachary took over for Mogridge and secured the second out. The scoring orgy ended when the second reliever of the inning, Jim Brillheart, struck out Heilmann with the bases still full.

The Tigers' Hooks Dauss came in to face the Senators in the bottom of the ninth. He got Peckinpaugh to foul out to catcher Manion. Shortstop Topper Rigney threw out Sam Rice and tird baseman Fred Haney threw out Joe Judge. The game was over after 2 hours and 40 minutes, and the Tigers had a thrilling (if a Detroit fan) or stunning (if a Washington fan) come-from-behind win. A Detroit writer described the scene: "You have seen a beaten fighter reeling from a beating for a place of refuge. That is the way the Nationals after going into the ninth inning happy at the thought of impending victory, staggered in broken order before the compelling influences of the Bengal drive."[8]

One Washington writer opined: "Ty Cobb and his Tigers won that game because they kept at it."[9]

Said another: "But the Griffs lost more than just two ball games. They lost also the whole-hearted support of approximately 17,000 fans who watched the Tigers perform the 'Impossible' in their last time at bat, watched them score nine runs on nine hits and three walks after the Griffs had gone into the last frame with a seven-run lead and appeared to have the game nailed in the win column."[10]

Carl Holling got the win, and Tom Zachary, who retired only one of the six batters he faced, bore the loss.

Nearly a century has passed as of this writing, and the game represents the greatest comeback in major-league history.

Sources

In addition to the game story and box-score sources cited in the Notes, the author consulted Baseball-Reference.com and Retrosheet.org.

Notes

1　Tom Ruane, "Perhaps the Most Improbable Comebacks From 1901 to 2018," Retrosheet.org, May 13, 2019, at retrosheet.org/Research/RuaneT/retro_fun5.htm#A190513.

2　Harry Bullion, "Bengals Open Final Seven Runs in Rear," *Detroit Free Press*, July 8, 1922: 12.

3　Bullion.

4　Bullion.

5　Louis Dougher, "Ferocious Jungle Cats Go After Griffs Again in Two Clashes Today," *Washington Times*, July 8, 1922: 10.

6　Ray Helgesen, "Detroit Wins Twice, Massacring Nationals in Second Game," *Washington Herald*, July 8, 1922: 9.

7　Bullion.

8　Bullion.

9　Dougher.

10　Helgesen.

HOPELESS DEFEAT TURNED INTO GLORIOUS VICTORY

MAY 23, 1901:
CLEVELAND BLUES 14,
WASHINGTON SENATORS 13,
AT LEAGUE PARK III, CLEVELAND

By Jean-Pierre Caillault

Chicago Daily News photograph.

Cleveland outfielder Jack McCarthy kicked off the two-out, ninth-inning rally with a single, then won the game with another single the second time he came up in the inning.

The newly-minted American League was barely a month old on May 23, 1901, when the Cleveland Blues rallied for one of the greatest ninth-inning comebacks in baseball history.

Cleveland's previous major-league team, the National League Spiders, had achieved ignominy two years earlier, in 1899, when they infamously lost 134 games, a record that may never be broken. When the National League reduced its roster of franchises from 12 to eight in 1900, the Cleveland team was, not surprisingly, one of the four teams that were disbanded.

A minor-league version of the American League was born in 1900 and Cleveland, with a completely revamped roster of players, was awarded one of the eight franchises. When American League President Ban Johnson declared the AL a major league in 1901 (major league because the league added franchises in the "major" cities of Baltimore, Boston, Philadelphia, and Washington), the Cleveland franchise was one of the four retained from the 1900 minor-league version. (Chicago, Detroit, and Milwaukee were the others.)[1] This time, though, a handful of the hometown players stayed in Cleveland, most notably veteran first baseman Candy LaChance, right fielder Ollie Pickering, and pitcher Bill Hoffer.

The 1901 Cleveland team came to be known as the Blues because of their all-blue uniforms,[2] and they played their games in League Park, the same wooden ballpark in which the Spiders had played.[3] The ballpark was at the northeast corner of what was then Lexington and Dunham Streets (now Lexington and East 66th Street) in Cleveland's Hough neighborhood. It had a capacity of about 9,000.[4]

The start of the Blues' season was bleak, as the team endured an 11-game losing streak in mid-May that resulted in their dropping into last place. By the time the Washington Senators came to Cleveland for their first visit of the season, the Blues had lost 18 of their first 24 games. Washington, meanwhile, had opened the season well, winning 12 of its first 19 and sitting comfortably in the first division.

In their first meeting, on Wednesday, May 22, the Blues surprised the Senators, grabbing a 6-4 lead midway through the game and holding on for a 6-5 victory.[5]

The next game, played on Thursday, May 23, looked as though it would end in the more expected result of Cleveland losing yet again. By the middle of the fifth inning, the Senators were leading 9-0. The Blues came back a bit in the bottom of the fifth, scoring four runs, but by the middle of the ninth and final inning, the Washington lead had ballooned to 13-5.[6]

Starting pitcher Hoffer, who had been the ace pitcher of the famous NL champion Baltimore Orioles of the mid-1890s (winning 78 games over a three-year span),[7] but then faded into relative obscurity, had been pounded by the Washington batters, giving up 14 hits in his nine innings on the mound. Seemingly set up to add insult to injury, Hoffer led off the bottom of the ninth. The few remaining fans could be heard making such sarcastic remarks as "Hit her out, Hoffer, and run around nine times – then you'll win."[8] Continuing his miserable day, Hoffer struck out.

Leadoff hitter Pickering was next. Although he is now unknown by most fans, Pickering actually had quite a few claims to baseball fame. He was the starting center fielder for the NL Louisville Colonels for the first half of the 1897 season, but on July 19 of that season he sat on the bench to make room for the major-league debut of all-time great Honus Wagner.[9] Pickering never again played center field for the Colonels and was sold to the minor-league Syracuse team two weeks later.[10]

Another claim to fame of Pickering's is that a month before this game against Washington, back on April 24, in the American League's first-ever game, when Cleveland visited Chicago to play the White Sox, Pickering was the first batter in American League history. (He flied out to center field.)[11]

And finally, Pickering is credited with making famous the Texas Leaguer-type hit, back in his debut with Houston in the Texas League in 1892.[12] Pickering's career in baseball spanned 30 years, from his debut as a player in 1892 until his last year as a manager in 1922.

Pickering followed Hoffer by grounding to Washington second baseman Joe Quinn for the second out.

With only one out remaining before the Blues would be put out of their misery, veteran left fielder Jack McCarthy came to the plate for Cleveland. McCarthy had been the starting left fielder the previous season for the NL's Chicago Orphans and for the Pittsburgh Pirates in the 1898 and 1899 seasons, as well. McCarthy hit a clean single to right field. "The spectators were offended. It seemed like a useless delay."[13]

Up-and-coming 23-year-old third baseman Bill Bradley, who like McCarthy had also played for the Orphans the previous year (and would end up playing more than 1,000 games for the Cleveland franchise), then got another hit.

Next up was cleanup hitter LaChance, who had begun his major-league career nearly a decade earlier, in 1893 with the Brooklyn Bridegrooms. He swung and missed on Senators left-handed pitcher Casey Patten's first pitch, then missed the second one, too. Down to his last strike, LaChance pounded a single to deep left, scoring McCarthy and Bradley to make the score 13-7. Thirty-five-year-old catcher Bob Wood, who had previously played for Ohio's other major-league team, the Cincinnati Reds, was then plunked by a tiring Patten.

Shortstop Frank Scheibeck, at 5-feet-7 and 145 pounds the shortest and lightest of Cleveland's players, was next in the order. Scheibeck had begun his major-league career with the old American Association version of the Cleveland Blues, way back in their inaugural 1887 season. The 36-year-old journeyman, whose career batting average was only .235, came through, though, when he doubled off Patten to drive in a couple more runs, cutting the deficit to four runs, 13-9.

Center fielder Frank Genins, then 34 and playing his last season of major-league ball (but who would continue to play minor-league ball into his early 40s) followed with a sharp single, sending Scheibeck home: 13-10. "The crowd became frantic. Hats and coats were thrown up in the air, and the Cleveland players were dancing all around the field. LaChance, working like a Trojan on the coaching lines, kept the crowd yelling so as to rattle the pitchers."[14]

Washington's manager, Jim Manning (who would never manage in the major leagues again after the 1901 season), told his team captain, Bill Everitt, former star infielder of Cap Anson's Chicago team, to remove Patten from the game. Everitt told right-handed veteran Win Mercer to take Patten's place, "but Mercer would not go in, claiming that he had not warmed up."[15] Young southpaw Watty Lee, who along with manager Manning, pitcher Patten, and half a dozen other Washington players had moved from the 1900 AL Kansas City franchise to the 1901 Senators, was called on instead.

The first batter Lee faced was Blues second baseman Truck Eagan. Eagan had been signed only a week earlier, after Pittsburgh released him two weeks into the season.[16] Eagan would then be released by the Blues a week later, terminating his major-league career with a total of only nine games played. (He did play in the California minor leagues for another decade, though.) Lee walked Eagan on four pitches to put men on first and second and bring the tying run to the plate.

With pitcher Hoffer scheduled to bat again, Cleveland's manager, Jimmy McAleer, who began playing professionally in 1883, including a decade for the local Cleveland major-league teams in the National League and the Players' League, and had also been the manager of the 1900 Cleveland Blues, didn't hesitate for a second to pinch-hit for his beleaguered pitcher.

Young Erve Beck, who would play only one more season in the major leagues, was called off the bench and smashed a hit so close to the left-field fence that Senators left fielder Pop Foster, "who stood on his tip toes to reach for it, but could only touch the ball,"[17] could not catch it and Beck ended up on second base with a double, having driven in two more runs to cut the lead to one, 13-12.

Pickering came to bat again and was hoping he would fare better than he had so far, having made outs in each of his first five plate appearances against Patten. This time, though, he was facing Lee, and he hit a clean single just outside of shortstop Billy Clingman's reach, scoring Beck from second, tying the game at 13 runs apiece.

"By this time the audience gave a life-sized picture of pandemonium let out for recess. A crowd of Indians on a red-hot warpath could not have been more demonstrative. They roared, they jumped, they shouted. They threw everything within reach in the air. Hats, umbrellas, canes, cushions went up as if a cyclone had struck that part of the landscape. They rushed on the field and came close to losing the game for Cleveland by forfeit."[18]

It took a few minutes to clear the field, then the game resumed, with McCarthy coming to bat once again. Lee's first pitch to McCarthy passed right by catcher Mike Grady, allowing Pickering to take second base. McCarthy then lined a clean single to left, allowing Pickering to race home ahead of Foster's throw with the unlikeliest of winning runs. The "crowd rushed onto the diamond"[19] and the "Cleveland players were carried to their dressing rooms by the jubilant crowd."[20]

The *Cleveland Press* began its report of this "remarkable"[21] game by quoting "from the proverbs of 'Rube' Waddell: 'A game of base ball hain't ever over until it is over. Don't ever forgit this.'"[22] (So it appears that Yogi Berra *wasn't* the one who coined this phrase!)

Both the *Cleveland Leader* and the *Washington Times* referred to the Blues' great comeback win as a "Garrison finish,"[23] a reference to nineteenth-century jockey Edward "Snapper" Garrison, known for his spectacular come-from-behind horse-racing wins.[24] The *Leader* called it "the greatest contest ever witnessed in this city."[25]

The *Cleveland Plain Dealer* said that the Blues' "sensational finish"[26] was like Sheridan arriving from Winchester, "a case of hopeless defeat turned into glorious victory."[27] This was a reference to the Civil War battle of Cedar Creek in the Shenandoah Valley, when Union Army Colonel (later promoted to general) Phil Sheridan dramatically returned from Winchester to rally his troops to defeat General Jubal Early's Confederate army on October 19, 1864.[28]

All of these descriptions were apt, as being down by eight runs with the bases empty and two outs in the bottom of the ninth inning, the probability of Cleveland winning the game was 0.0332 percent, the second most unlikely comeback in modern baseball history.[29]

Sources

In addition to the sources cited in the Notes, the author consulted Baseball-Reference.com and Restrosheet.org.

Notes

1 "The History of the American and National League, Part 1," Beyondtheboxscore.com, beyondtheboxscore.com/2008/11/18/664028/the-history-of-the-america, accessed November 29, 2019.

2 "Sports Team History," Sports Team History, sportsteamhistory.com/cleveland-blues, accessed November 29, 2019.

3 "League Park," League Park Info, leaguepark.info/facts.html, accessed November 29, 2019.

4 "League Park."

5 "Many Old Faces at League Park," *Cleveland Plain Dealer*, May 23, 1901.

6 "Never Too Late to Win," *Cleveland Plain Dealer*, May 24, 1901.

7 David Nemec, *Major League Baseball Profiles, 1871-1900, Volume 1* (Lincoln: University of Nebraska Press, 2011), 92.

8 "Never Too Late to Win."

9 "Louisville vs. Washington," *New York Clipper*, July 24, 1897: 340.

10 "Brief Ball Notes," *Rockford* (Illinois) *Daily Register-Gazette*, July 31, 1897: 3.

11 "Whitestockings Fly Flag," *Chicago Daily News*, April 24, 1901: 1.

12   "Texas Leaguers," *Sporting Life*, April 21, 1906: 2.

13   "Never Too Late to Win."

14   "Notes of the Game," *Cleveland Leader*, May 24, 1901.

15   "Notes of the Game."

16   "Never Too Late to Win."

17   "Nine Runs in Last Inning," *Cleveland Leader*, May 24, 1901.

18   "Never Too Late to Win."

19   "The Wily Spiders," *Evening Star* (Washington), May 24, 1901.

20   "Nine Runs in Last Inning."

21   "A Game to Remember," *Cleveland Press*, May 24, 1901.

22   "A Game to Remember."

23   "Nine Runs in Last Inning"; "In the Baseball World," *Washington Times,* May 24, 1901.

24   "Garrison finish," Merriam-Webster.com, merriam-webster.com/dictionary/Garrison%20finish, accessed December 1, 2019.

25   "Nine Runs in Last Inning."

26   "Never Too Late to Win."

27   "Never Too Late to Win."

28   "Union Colonel Phil Sheridan's Valiant Horse," Smithsonian.com, smithsonianmag.com/history/union-colonel-phil-sheridans-valiant-horse-124899830/, accessed December 1, 2019.

29   Tom Ruane, "Perhaps the Most Improbable Comebacks From 1901 to 2018," Retrosheet.org, retrosheet.org/Research/RuaneT/retro_fun5.htm#A190513, accessed December 1, 2019.

PHILLIES SCORE NINE IN THE NINTH AGAINST DODGERS, OVERCOMING A 10-RUN DEFICIT

AUGUST 21, 1990:
PHILADELPHIA PHILLIES 12,
LOS ANGELES DODGERS 11,
AT DODGER STADIUM, LOS ANGELES

BY STEVEN M. GLASSMAN

Entering the second game of a three-game series on August 21, 1990, the Phillies (57-62) were not playing well at Dodger Stadium. They had lost 12 of their 15 previous contests at Chavez Ravine, dating back to May 14, 1988.[1] This included a 2-1, walk-off loss on August 20 when Mike Sharperson hit a one-out, ninth-inning home run off starting pitcher Terry Mulholland.

Phillies rookie Jason Grimsley (0-0) was making his third start of the season (seventh in his major-league career) and first against the Dodgers (63-58). LA rookie Mike Hartley (4-1) was making his second major-league start after starting his career with 31 straight relief appearances.[2] Hartley was making a spot start in place of the injured Tim Belcher.[3]

The Phillies opened the scoring in the second. Tommy Herr walked with one out. He stole second as Carmelo Martinez struck out swinging and took third on catcher Mike Scioscia's throwing error. Dickie Thon's two-out, two-strike groundball single to left scored Herr. The Dodgers quickly tied it. Scioscia led off the bottom of the inning with a line-drive single to center and went to third on Sharperson's line-drive single to left, and scored on Alfredo Griffin's double-play grounder to second.

The Dodgers took the lead in the third. Lenny Harris led off with a ground single to center. Grimsley snared Kirk Gibson's liner and doubled off Harris at first. Kal Daniels walked. Eddie Murray's ground single to right sent Daniels to third. Hubie Brooks's walk loaded the bases. Scioscia's two-out, two-strike groundball single to center scored Daniels and Murray.

Grimsley was replaced by Bruce Ruffin after allowing three runs on six hits and three walks in three innings in 72 pitches.

Ruffin struck out Gibson swinging to lead off the fifth, but Darren Daulton's passed ball allowed Gibson to reach first. Daniels's line-drive single to center advanced Gibson to second. A walk to Murray loaded the bases. On third baseman Charlie Hayes's error on Brooks's groundball, Gibson scored, and Scioscia's line-drive ground-rule double to left-center plated Daniels and Murray and sent Brooks to third. Ruffin was replaced by Darrel Akerfelds after failing to retire a batter in the inning. Sharperson, the first batter Akerfelds faced, hit a groundball to Thon, who "made an unwise throw home when he should have gone to first."[4] Thon's throw to the plate was late, and Brooks scored.[5] Griffin's groundball single to right scored Scioscia.[6] Pitcher Hartley's bunt to the left side was dropped by Akerfelds.[7] The bases were loaded for the second time. Akerfelds, who failed to retire all three batters he faced, was replaced by Dennis Cook. Harris's fly-ball single to short center scored Sharperson and Griffin, and a similar single by Gibson loaded the bases for the third time. Pinch-hitter Stan Javier's groundout to Hayes scored Hartley. Ten straight batters had reached before Javier's at-bat. Cook got the side out, but the Dodgers had sent up 14 batters and scored eight runs (five earned) on five hits, two errors, and a passed ball. They led 11-1 after five.[8]

Dodgers manager Tom Lasorda began to empty his bench. Javier remained in the game in left field. Mickey Hatcher replaced Murray at first. Hartley retired the Phillies in order in the sixth for the third straight inning.[9] "The most pressure I've ever been in was a playoff game in the minor leagues," Hartley said. "But I enjoy it. This is the most fun I've ever had."[10] Lasorda pinch-hit rookie Jose Offerman for Hartley; Offerman flied out to right. Juan Samuel pinch-hit for Harris, striking out to end the sixth.

Don Aase started the seventh in relief for the Dodgers. Rick Dempsey replaced Scioscia at catcher. Jose Gonzalez replaced Gibson in center. Chris Gwynn replaced Brooks in right. Offerman remained in the game, playing shortstop. Samuel remained in the game, playing second. "Tommy started to take his starters out and then I began to take mine out," Phillies manager Nick Leyva said. "With the score 11-1 you want to think about tomorrow."[11]

The Phillies closed the deficit to 11-3 in the eighth. Rookie Dave Hollins, pinch-hitting for Joe Boever, led off with a line-drive single to left. Lenny Dykstra lined another single to left, advancing Hollins to third.[12] Daulton fouled out to Sharperson. Von Hayes's one-out, two-strike groundball double to right scored Hollins and Dykstra.

Roger McDowell started the eighth as the Phillies' sixth pitcher of the game. Tom Nieto replaced Daulton at catcher. Hollins remained in the game, replacing Charlie Hayes at third. Sil Campusano replaced Dykstra in center.

Rookie pitcher Dave Walsh started the ninth for the Dodgers.[13] Rod Booker, who replaced Herr at second in the seventh, led off with a walk. Martinez hit a potential double-play grounder to shortstop, but Offerman kicked the ball and the Phillies had runners on first and third.

Thon's line single to left scored Booker and sent Martinez to third. Hollins's ground single to center scored Martinez. Thon moved to second. Campusano flied out to right. Nieto's walk loaded the bases. Von Hayes's groundball to Offerman went off his glove for his second error of the inning, allowing Thon to score.[14]

Walsh was replaced by Tim Crews with the score 11-6, one out and the bases loaded. Dale Murphy lined a double to left, scoring Hollins and Nieto, and sending Von Hayes to third. "That," Leyva said, "is when I first thought we had a chance."[15] John Kruk, batting for pitcher McDowell, represented the tying run. "I had seen the way things were going," he said after

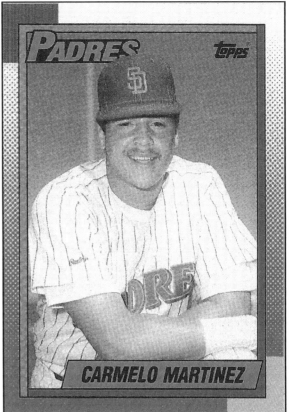

Courtesy The Topps Company.

Former Padre Carmelo Martinez signed with the Phillies in 1990. He doubled in the top of the ninth, to give the Phillies their 12th and winning run of the game.

the game. "So even though I was still four or five at-bats away when we were getting closer, I was getting ready to hit."[16] Kruk added, "You don't think about coming back and winning that game. When I came up, I looked at the scoreboard because I couldn't keep track."[17] He hit Crews's 2-and-0 pitch into the right-center-field seats to tie the game.[18] "Luck, that's what it was," he said. "I'm not a home-run hitter, so that's what it must be."[19] Booker, batting for the second time in the inning, reached on a groundball single to center. Crews was replaced by Jay Howell, the third Dodgers pitcher of the inning.[20] "I screwed up the game," said Crews, who gave up three runs and three hits and failed to retire a batter. "I can't give an explanation for it. All I know is, for my part, I didn't get the job done."[21] Booker hit a ground-ball single to center and stole his second base of the season with Martinez at the plate. Martinez's fly-ball double to left-center on a 1-and-1 pitch scored Booker with the tiebreaking run.[22] Altogether, the Phillies sent 14 hitters to bat, scoring nine runs (four earned) on six hits, and two Offerman errors.

The Phillies' nine runs equaled a season high; they had scored nine in an inning against Houston on July 14.[23] They were also the most runs the Phillies had scored in the ninth inning since July 6, 1918, against Cincinnati.[24] Their nine tallies were three short of the modern-day NL record of 12 by the 1961 San Francisco Giants.[25]

Don Carman started the ninth for the Phillies and Kruk replaced Martinez at first.[26] Carman made quick work of the Dodgers: Gonzalez fouled out to first, Javier hit a groundball single to left, Hatcher flied out to right, and Gwynn forced Javier at second to end the game. McDowell (5-6) won the game in relief.[27] Carman got credit for his first save of the season.[28]

"I'm shocked. ... I'm just shocked," Dodgers manager Tom Lasorda said. "I just don't believe it. I mean, we had them 11 to 1. Just to lose the game in itself is terrible."[29] He added: "I've never seen anything like this. It was the first time in my managerial career that something like this has happened."[30]

"I've never seen anything like it," Phillies manager Nick Leyva said. 'I've never even heard of it.

They kept making bad pitches, and we kept hitting them. My team played lousy early, (Lasorda's) team played lousy late. I went from wanting to fight everybody on my ballclub to wanting to hug everybody."[31]

Kruk said: "Let's be honest. We're losing by eight runs (11-3), and all I'm thinking about at that point is getting back to the hotel by midnight because that's when room service closes. All of a sudden we start getting hits, and I'm saying, 'I'm not going to make it.' If you're not going to get room service, you might as well win."[32]

Sources

In addition to the sources cited in the Notes, the author referred to Baseball-Reference.com, and Retrosheet.org for box scores, play-by-plays, and other pertinent information.

Notes

1   baseball-reference.com/play-index/head2head-games. cgi?team1=PHI&team2=LAD&from=1890&to=1990.

2   Hartley made four relief appearances against the Phillies in 1990, allowing two runs (both earned) in four innings.

3   Dave Cunningham, "Dodgers Build Big Lead, Then Blow It in 9th," *Long Beach* (California) *Press-Telegram,* August 22, 1990: C1.

4   Michael Bamberger, "Phils Roar Back With 9 in Ninth, Overtake Dodgers for a 12-11 Victory," *Philadelphia Inquirer,* August 22, 1990: F01.

5   Paul Hagen, "Phillies Turn a Debacle Into a Miracle/Phillies' 9-Run Ninth Beats LA, 12-11," *Philadelphia Daily News,* August 22, 1990: 80.

6   Griffin entered the game with the lowest on-base (.271) and slugging (.268) percentages in the NL,

7   Hagen.

8   This was the most runs the Dodgers scored in an inning since they scored nine in the first inning in St. Louis against the Cardinals on May 27, 1990.

9   Hartley retired the last 11 batters he faced and threw 90 pitches for the game. He made four more starts in 1990, posting a 2.52 ERA in 35⅔ innings pitched as a starter for the season. Hartley also limited opponents to the triple-slash line of .171/.250/.252 as a starter, but would not make any more major-league starts. After the 1990 season, all his 165 appearances were in relief.

10   Cunningham.

11   Associated Press, "Phillies Overhaul Dodgers," *Pittsburgh Post-Gazette,* August 22, 1990: E5.

12   Dykstra entered the game leading the NL in batting average (.342) and OBP (.439) and shared league lead in walks (71) and hit by pitch (7). He was second in the NL in doubles (32). Dykstra was third in the NL in hits (150) and runs scored (87).

13   Walsh was making his fifth major-league appearance. He twice previously finished games in losses (August 14, game one; and August 16). This was the first time he started the ninth inning in his major-league career.

14   The first error went through Offerman's legs. "Phillies Classic Comeback vs. Dodgers – August 21, 1990." youtube.com/watch?v=5d6lneeCN5s.

15   Hagen.

16   Sadowski.

17   "Phillies Overhaul Dodgers."

18   This was Kruk's third home run of the season and his first since May 1, 1990, at Cincinnati. It was also Kruk's third career pinch-hit home run and first as a Phillie, and his first career home run at Dodger Stadium.

19   Hagen.

20   Lasorda used 21 players in the game.

21   Sadowski.

22   This would be Martinez's last RBI as a Phillie. He played in four more games for the Phillies before being traded to the Pittsburgh Pirates on August 30 for outfielders Wes Chamberlain, Julio Peguero, and a player to be named later (outfielder Tony Longmire).

23   Sadowski.

24   Hagen.

25   "Big Rally In 9th Lifts Phils Over L.A. National League," *San Francisco Chronicle,* August 22, 1990: B3.

26   Leyva used 20 players in the game.

27   McDowell and Carman shared the team lead with six relief wins each in 1990.

28   Carman's save was the last in his Phillies career.

29   Sadowski.

30   "Phillies Overhaul Dodgers.'

31   Sadowski.

32   "Insiders Say," *The Sporting News,* September 10, 1990: 10.

TIGERS STAGE NINTH-INNING COMEBACK IN AL OPENER

APRIL 25, 1901:
DETROIT TIGERS 14,
MILWAUKEE BREWERS 13,
AT BENNETT PARK, DETROIT

By Dennis Pajot

More than a century ago, the Detroit Tigers staged the biggest ninth inning come-from-behind-victory engineered in baseball. It still stands.[1]

The inaugural 1901 American League season was scheduled to open in Detroit on Wednesday, April 24, but rain just before game time prevented play. The next day was sunny, warm for April, and "a day to make a well man glad to be alive, and a sick man feel the tingle of returning health."[2]

The largest throng to yet attend a ball game in Detroit overflowed Bennett Park. The players paraded to the park in carriages from the Russell House Hotel, and by the time they arrived, a mass of 10,023[3] had overflowed into the outfield. The overflow necessitated the imposition of a ground rule— any balls into the outfield crowd would be doubles.

The visiting Milwaukee Brewers[4] were introduced first to a polite reception. The Tigers, in red coats, then lined up, marched a few steps toward the grandstand, and removed their caps in a salute to the fans. After the teams warmed up, "Oom Paul," the canine Detroit mascot, made an appearance, and the local Elks club presented a loving cup to Tiger owner James Burns and manager George Stallings, both fellow Elks. A local legislator, Jacob Haarer, filled in for the mayor and threw out the first pitch to Charlie Bennett, a retired catcher and Detroit baseball legend for whom Bennett Park was named.[5]

After a band played a prophetic "There'll be a Hot Time in the Old Town To-night," Brewer lead-off hitter Irv Waldron hit a grounder to Kid Elberfeld at shortstop, who "made a gorgeous fumble."[6] Billy Gilbert followed with a base hit and Bill Hallman sac-rificed both runners up a base. Tiger third baseman Jim "Doc" Casey then forced Waldron at the plate on John Anderson's ground ball. Anderson and Gilbert attempted a double steal, but Elberfeld's return throw to catcher Fred Buelow caught Gilbert for the third out.

Casey led off for Detroit. Wearing the club's new uniform, with a small red tiger on the cap, he accepted a basket of flowers from the Elks on arrival at the batter's box. After he bowed in appreciation and handed off the flowers, he grounded back to the Milwaukee pitcher, Pink Hawley. The Tigers managed a hit and stolen base by Bill "Kid" Gleason, but didn't score.

Wid Conroy opened the Brewers' second with a single. He went to third on an out by playing manager Hugh Duffy, but first baseman Frank Dillon made a bad throw in an attempt to catch Conroy, who advanced and scored the first run of the game. With two outs Brewers catcher Tom Leahy reached second base on a wild throw by Elberfeld; he then scored as Tigers left fielder Ducky Holmes muffed a fly ball by Hawley when Holmes encountered the overflow crowd in the outfield. After another Elberfeld error, the Brewers were retired, but they had two runs. The four Detroit errors made it look to the *Detroit Tribune* reporter that the Tigers were hypnotized or suffering from an attack of stage fright. In any case they were playing "wretched ball."[7]

Detroit failed to score in its half of the second, and Milwaukee, already leading 2-0, added five more runs in the third on another error, four hits, a walk, and a sacrifice. Stallings replaced starting pitcher Roscoe Miller with Emil Frisk during the uprising. Milwaukee's seven-run lead held as the Tigers failed to score in their half of the third. Brewers captain and third baseman Jimmy Burke made the defensive play of the game here, stopping Buelow's hot grounder and throwing him out at first.[8]

Detroit managed to shut down the Brewers in the fourth, then scored their first run on an error, followed by Dillon's ground-rule double into the crowd. Elberfeld then knocked in Dillon with another ground-rule double. The Tigers pecked away with a run in the fifth, and after six innings it was 7-3, Milwaukee.

The Brewers, though, lengthened this to 10-3, plating three runs after two outs in the seventh. Duffy apparently considered the lead safe and replaced Hawley with Pete Dowling, a 24-year-old left-hander, who "had been Detroit's jonah all last season."[9] Dowling held form through the Detroit seventh, allowing only a walk.

Milwaukee padded its lead to 13-3 in the eighth, but the Tigers nicked Dowling for a run in their half, using another ground-rule double by Dillon. Still plugging away, Frisk got the Brewers one-two-three in the top of the ninth.

With their team down 13-4 and the Tigers not having shown them much, some Detroit fans had left by the bottom of the inning. But there were still enough for overflow in the outfield, and Casey led off with another ground-rule double. Jimmy Barrett beat out a slow grounder to third. Gleason then singled to center to score Casey. The crowd livened, as Holmes, Dillon, and Elberfeld all doubled. "The tremendous shouts that were sent up evidently unnerved Pitcher Dowling. As each hit went out a mighty cheer went up that was enough to make most any one lose his nerve."[10] Five runs were now in; it was 13-9.

By this time Duffy was feeling uneasy. He came in from center field and replaced Dowling with Bert Husting. Husting, who wasn't fully warmed up, uncorked a wild pitch, but settled down to retire Kid Nance for the first out.

As the inning progressed, the crowd had pressed closer to the diamond. Duffy protested, and umpire Jack Sheridan ordered the fans back. The game was delayed a few minutes as the Detroit players "ran out to push back the throng in order to afford the Milwaukee outfielders a chance to chase some of the terrific drives that were being sent out."[11] Although the delay gave Husting a chance to warm up, he walked the next batter, Buelow. Frisk followed with a single to left, scoring Elberfeld. 13-10.

Casey was next up and beat out a bunt down the third-base line to load the bases. Husting was able to

Detroit's Frank Dillon hit four ground-rule doubles (into the overflow crowd) to help lead the Tigers to victory.

fan Barrett for the second out. Gleason then hit a hard shot to Burke at third base. But Burke botched the play and Buelow scored to make it 13-11. It quickly became 13-12 when Burke couldn't get an out on Holmes' slow roller and Frisk scored.

Dillon was up again. The big first baseman already had three ground-rule doubles on the day, and made it a fourth when he ripped a 2-2 pitch into the crowd in left field. Casey and Gleason romped home with the tying and winning runs.

Pandemonium broke loose at Bennett Park. The crowd quickly overtook the field and "a dozen crazy fans picked [Dillon] up and carried him about the diamond on their shoulders, while everybody assured his neighbor that he had never in his life seen anything so

DETROIT TAKES THE FIRST GAME

Score 13 to 4 Against Them When Tigers Went to Bat in the Ninth.

Headline from the *Ste. St. Marie Evening News,* April 26, 1901.

wonderful."[12] The *Detroit Tribune* writer waxed rhapsodic: "The riotously jubilant vocalization of 10,000 throats let loose in one simultaneous sub-aerial explosion, [making] the old earth's enveloping atmosphere heave and billow clear to its surface 50 miles away, and no doubt it is tumultuous yet."[13]

And as of this writing in late 2015, the Tigers' feat on their first day of play in the brand-new American League is still the biggest ninth-inning game-winning comeback in major-league baseball history.

Across Lake Michigan in Milwaukee, there was astonishment as the wire reports rolled in. Brewer secretary Fred Gross was in the process of preparing a telegram recounting the victory to club president Matthew Killilea, who was in Arizona for health reasons. Before Gross could send the telegram he received a phone call telling him the Tigers had won the game. Gross assured the caller there had to be a mistake, as Detroit would have had to score 10 runs to win. When told this was exactly what had happened, Gross replied that he needed to hear from Duffy, then presupposed a reason for the apparent collapse: "The men all must be injured for a team to make ten runs in one inning. I will wire Duffy to take care of the men until they recover."[14]

Only the Brewers' pride had been injured by the epic Detroit rally. Although some in Milwaukee talked of a protest because of crowd interference, the *Evening*

Wisconsin was philosophical: "It was indeed hard for Duffy to lose a game in that manner, but such is baseball and will ever be that way. It only goes to prove once more that baseball is the one sport that is absolutely honest in every line of playing."[15]

Acknowledgments

I would like to thank fellow SABR members Marc Okkonen and Jonathan Frankel (and any others whose emails I might have accidentally deleted) for help in obtaining material for this article.

Notes

1   Carl Bialik, "Baseball's Biggest Ninth-Inning Comebacks," *Wall Street Journal*, July 28, 2008; blogs.wsj.com; "Tigers' Ten Greatest Games," This Great Game: The Online Book of Baseball History, thisgreatgame.com.

2   "Base Ball As A Barometer of Fans," *Detroit Tribune*, April 26, 1901: 5.

3   Scott Ferkovich, "Bennett Park (Detroit)," SABR Baseball Biography Project, sabr.org. Bennett Park was built in 1896 with a capacity of 5,000. Seats were added for the 1901 season to bring capacity to 8,500. Ibid.

4   The 1900 Brewers finished second in the then-minor-circuit American League. Over the 1900-01 offseason, however, league president Ban Johnson pushed the AL to at least nominal parity with the "senior circuit" National League, which had held major-league status since 1876. Brewers owner Henry Killilea was reluctant to spend the funds necessary to recruit National League players to Milwaukee; the team also lost 1900 manager Connie Mack to American League rival Philadelphia. With the game chronicled here typical of Milwaukee's competitiveness, the club stumbled to a last-place, 48-89 finish in 1901. Johnson moved the franchise, which became the Browns, to St. Louis for 1902. Major league baseball didn't return to Milwaukee until the arrival of the Braves from Boston for the 1953 season. Baseball-Reference.com; Donald Dewey and Nicholas Acocella, *The Ball Clubs* (New York: Harper Perennial, 1996), 307-08.

5   Ferkovich, "Bennett Park (Detroit)."

6   "Ten Runs Won in the Ninth," *Detroit Free Press,* April 26, 1901.

7   "Ten Runs in Ninth," *Detroit Tribune*, April 26, 1901: 1.

8   "Ten Runs . . .," *Detroit Free Press*, April 26, 1901.

9   "Between the Innings," *Detroit Free Press*, April 26, 1901.

10   "10,000 People See Great Batting Rally," *Detroit Free Press*, April 26, 1901.

11   "10,000 People See Great Batting Rally."

12   "Ten Runs in Ninth," *Detroit Tribune*.

13   "Base Ball As A Barometer Of Fans," *Detroit Tribune*, April 26, 1901: 5.

14   "Thirteen A Hoodoo," *Evening Wisconsin*, April 26, 1901.

15   "Thirteen A Hoodoo."

ATHLETICS OVERCOME 12-RUN DEFICIT TO KNOCK OFF CLEVELAND

JUNE 15, 1925:
PHILADELPHIA ATHLETICS 17,
CLEVELAND INDIANS 15,
AT SHIBE PARK, PHILADELPHIA

BY JOSEPH WANCHO

Al Simmons hit a three-run homer providing the final three runs of the 13-run outburst that gave the Athletics the win.

From 1910 through 1914, Philadelphia won four of five pennants in the American League. Included in this stretch were three World Series championships (1910, 1911, and 1913). But after losing to the Boston Braves in the 1914 fall classic, the Athletics fortunes' plummeted as they occupied the cellar of the junior circuit from 1915 to 1921. It was an incredible run of futility for the A's, but skipper Connie Mack was slowly bringing the team around to the caliber of the championship teams.

Conversely, the Cleveland Indians flew one solitary flag over Dunn Field. The Tribe polished off Brooklyn in seven games in the 1920 World Series. Although they remained competitive, the Indians could not claim a second pennant in the ensuing years. They slipped to a sixth-place finish in 1924. It was the first time the Indians had finished in the second division of the AL since 1916.

Philadelphia held a 1½-game lead over Washington in the American League standings when Cleveland arrived at Shibe Park for a four-game set beginning on June 14, 1925. The Indians were tied for fourth place with St. Louis, nine games off the pace.

Behind the pitching of right-hander Benn Karr, the Tribe blanked the A's, 3-0, on a five-hitter in the opener. Coupled with the Senators' 9-8 win over St. Louis, the Athletics lead shrank to a mere half-game over the Nats.

For the second game of the series, Cleveland manager Tris Speaker sent southpaw Jake Miller to the hill. In his first full season, Miller took the ball with a 3-3 record and an ERA of 2.25. Mack countered with right-hander Eddie Rommel. The Baltimore native toed the pitching rubber at Shibe Park with a 9-4 record and a rather robust ERA of 4.73.

After a scoreless first inning, Cleveland jumped on Rommel for four tallies in the top of the second inning. The first run crossed the plate on a base hit by Ray Knode. Rommel threw a wild pitch with the bases full of Indians, allowing Freddy Spurgeon to score from third base. In Spurgeon's haste to score, he collided with plate umpire Brick Owens. The impact sent Owens sprawling. He was subsequently carried off the

Courtesy of the Philadelphia Sports Hall of Fame.

ATHLETICS SCORE THIRTEEN RUNS IN ONE INNING TO BEAT TRIBE

Philadelphia Evening Tribune. June 16, 1925.

diamond and was delivered to a hospital for treatment. X-rays revealed that Owens had a torn muscle in his back, near his pelvis, and it was not believed to be serious. Bill Dinneen, who was umpiring at first base, took over for Owens behind the plate.

Mack had seen enough and lifted Rommel from the game in favor of Stan Baumgartner. A single by Charlie Jamieson and a double by Cliff Lee tallied the next two runs for Cleveland. Rommel's day was in the books. It was a short outing, as he went 1⅓ innings, and he was charged with four earned runs.

The A's scored a run in the bottom of the second inning when Jim Poole doubled and scored on a Chick Galloway single. But Cleveland came right back in the top of the third. Joe Sewell and Glenn Myatt each blasted a solo home run off A's reliever Fred Heimach to increase the Indians' advantage to 6-1. Myatt's homer left the yard, bounding over the right-field fence and onto Twentieth Avenue. Sewell's round-tripper was just that, of the inside-the-park variety. Again the Athletics scored a run in the bottom of the inning, but the Indians' lead was growing at 6-2 after three innings.

The middle innings were no better for the Athletics. Heimach surrendered two more runs in the top of the fourth on a triple by Lee and a double by Speaker. Heimach was replaced by Art Stokes. Cleveland reached Stokes for four runs in the fifth inning. The big hit was a two-run single by Jamieson.

After the Indians scored two more in the top of the sixth, they led Philadelphia, 14-2. The A's scored their third run in the home half of the sixth inning, to make the score look more like that of a football game, 14-3. The teams exchanged runs in the seventh inning, and it was 15-4.

The Tribe did not score a run in the eighth inning for the first time since the first. Miller was still on the mound as the bottom of the inning commenced. He was not having that great a day, but his offense was certainly carrying the day to this point as he walked four, struck out one, and gave up 10 hits. The Athletics stranded eight baserunners through seven innings.

Miller began the eighth inning by walking Galloway. Tom Glass flied out to right field and Max Bishop walked. Jimmy Dykes cleared the bases with a triple to cut the lead to 15-6. Speaker pulled

Miller from the game. By Speece emerged from the Cleveland bullpen.

But the relief pitcher was anything but, as he could not record an out. Instead, Speece gave up consecutive singles to Bill Lamar, Al Simmons, Frank Welch, and Charlie Berry. Southpaw Carl Yowell entered the game for Cleveland. The Indians lead was sliced to 15-9, and once again a pitcher from Cleveland's relief corps did not record an out. Yowell walked Poole to load the bases. Galloway followed with a single to left field and both Welch and Berry scored to make it 15-11. Yowell was given the hook by Speaker and George Uhle entered the game.

Sammy Hale, pinch-hitting for the pitcher, Glass, singled off Uhle to score Poole and send Galloway to third base. Hale promptly stole second base. Bishop singled to center field to plate both Galloway and Hale. The score was now 15-14.

Dykes grounded out to the shortstop, forcing Bishop at second base. Walter French entered the game to run for Dykes. But now there were two down. Uhle walked Lamar. Simmons came to the plate and unloaded a three-run shot over the roof in left field. That concluded the scoring for the Athletics, who crossed the dish 13 times in the inning to take a 17-15 lead. The *Philadelphia Inquirer* wrote, "As Al circled the bases … the din could be heard for blocks. It made madcaps of a big proportion of the 8,000, who jumped to their feet and shrieked and made wild gestures of joy. Scores sailed their straw skimmers down to the playing field."[1]

Rube Walberg entered the game to pitch the ninth inning. He closed the door on the Tribe to complete one of the most improbable comebacks in major-league history. Cleveland twice led by 12 runs, and the Athletics tied the record for biggest comeback in a major-league game. It had previously been accomplished by the Detroit Tigers on June 18, 1911. The Tigers trailed the Chicago White Sox, 13-1, heading into the bottom of the fifth inning at Bennett Park. Detroit scored five runs in the eighth and three more runs in the ninth to pull out the win.

For the Athletics, Tom Glass picked up his first win of the season. Uhle (7-5) took the loss. Jamieson had five hits for the Indians, while Sewell and Knode each had four. Lamar had four hits for the A's and Simmons and Galloway each drove in three runs.

With the win the A's now led Washington, which was idle, by a full game. But Washington eventually won the pennant. Philadelphia finished in second place, 8½ games back. The Indians finished in sixth place, 27½ games behind the Senators.

Sources

In addition to the Note, the author also consulted Baseball-Reference.com and Retrosheet.org.

Notes

1   James C. Isaminger, "Athletics Wonderful Finish Enables Them to Gain on Senators in American Race," *Philadelphia Inquirer*, June 16, 1925: 13.

ANGELS STUN TIGERS, 13-12

AUGUST 29, 1986:
CALIFORNIA ANGELS 13,
DETROIT TIGERS 12,
AT ANAHEIM STADIUM, ANAHEIM

BY RALPH CAOLA

The Angels came into the August 29 game with an AL West-leading record of 71-56. Three weeks before, they had lost three straight and saw their four-game lead shrink to 1½ games. But now they had won four games in a row and 15 of 22, and were back in front by 4½.

The Tigers, 38-41 and 13 games out of first in the AL East on July 5, went 21-9 to cut their deficit to 4½ games on August 7. They entered this game 68-61, losers of 11 of their last 20 and seven games behind the first-place Red Sox.

A decade before, Tigers starting pitcher Frank Tanana had been an Angels prodigy. In 1975, at the age of 21, he led the American League in strikeouts. Two years later he led the league in ERA. From 1975 through 1978 Tanana won 68 games and lost 40 and had a cumulative ERA of 2.79. But since then, his career had taken a turn for the worse. Over the next seven seasons, he lost 20 more games than he won and his ERA was more than a full run worse, at 3.84.

Second-year pitcher Kirk McCaskill started for the Angels. McCaskill had shown promise in his rookie season, starting 29 games and winning three in a row at the end of September. In one of those, he held Cleveland scoreless for eight innings, allowing only three hits. Now, having what would be the second-best season of his career, McCaskill came into the game with a record of 14-7 and an ERA of 3.33.

But this would not be his day. With one out in the top of the first, McCaskill walked Alan Trammell, Kirk Gibson singled to center, and Johnny Grubb cracked a home run, giving the Tigers a 3-0 lead. It seemed the Tigers might get more when, with two outs, Dave Collins singled and Darnell Coles doubled, but with

men on second and third, Chet Lemon flied out to end the inning.

In the bottom half, the Angels sliced a run off the Tigers' lead when Brian Downing hit one down the line in left for a solo home run.[1]

In the third Gibson led off with a double and one out later Darrell Evans hit a home run to right-center

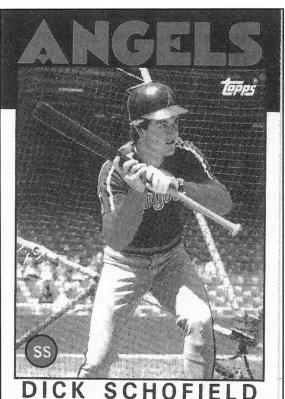

Dick Schofield Jr.'s grand slam in the bottom of the ninth capped an eight-run rally. A game-winning grand slam – the dream of every baseball-playing kid.

for a 5-1 Tigers lead. Collins followed with a triple and when Coles flied to right, Collins tried to score. But he was caught in a rundown and tagged out by third baseman Doug DeCinces.

In the fifth, McCaskill's replacement, Chuck Finley, walked the first two batters, Grubb and Evans. Collins sacrificed the runners up. After Grubb was out at home on a fielder's choice, Lemon doubled to center, scoring Evans and Coles. Mike Heath singled to left and Downing's throw home was too late to get Lemon, but when Heath tried to take second, catcher Bob Boone gunned him down to end the inning. The three runs stretched the Tigers lead to 8-1.

The Angels got two of the three back in the sixth. George Hendrick and Gary Pettis singled, putting runners on first and second with two outs. Boone's single to right drove in Hendrick, and when the ball got by Gibson, Pettis also scored, making the tally 8-3.

In the seventh, the Tigers continued their penchant for scoring in odd-numbered innings. With Vern Ruhle on the mound for the Angels, Evans singled, Collins reached on an error, and Lemon smashed a three-run homer, leaving him a triple short of the cycle and giving the Tigers an 11-3 lead.

In the bottom half, Randy O'Neal replaced Tanana and gave up a leadoff single to Rick Burleson. After Wally Joyner followed with another single, O'Neal uncorked a wild pitch, advancing the runners to second and third. With a force play no longer possible, consecutive groundouts by Downing and DeCinces scored Burleson and Joyner and left the score 11-5.

Doug Corbett came in for Ruhle in the eighth and yielded a leadoff home run to Trammell, giving the Tigers their fourth home run of the day and an even dozen runs. Two outs later, the Tigers got runners to second and third, but Corbett retired Coles and the score remained 12-5.

Neither team scored in its next at-bats before the Angels rallied in the bottom of the ninth. Dick Schofield Jr. started the inning with an infield single.[2] After Burleson lined out to center, Joyner walked and Downing blooped a single to center, loading the bases. Jack Howell, who had replaced DeCinces, ripped a two-run double to right-center to make the score 12-7.

Tigers manager Sparky Anderson brought in Willie Hernandez in relief, but Hernandez provided none. Hendrick singled in Downing, Bobby Grich singled in Howell, and the Angels had chopped the lead to 12-9. Pettis grounded into a force play at second, putting runners at first and third with two outs. Since his run didn't matter, the Tigers allowed Pettis to take second

on defensive indifference. Then pinch-hitter Ruppert Jones walked, loading the bases.[3]

The walk put the tying run on base and brought the winning run to the plate as Schofield batted for the second time in the inning. Hernandez was ahead in the count, 0-and-2, when he threw a screwball that stayed too high. Schofield lined it into the left-field seats[4] for a game-winning grand slam – the dream of every baseball-playing kid.

Angels coach Jimmie Reese said, "Never in 63 years in baseball have I seen anything like that. Two out, 0-and-2 on the hitter. … You see it once in a lifetime."[5]

For the Tigers, Darrell Evans and Chet Lemon each had three hits including a home run and Lemon drove in five runs. The Angels got three singles from George Hendrick.

Although Willie Hernandez was the losing pitcher, two years before, he won as many major trophies as a ballplayer can. In 1984 Hernandez became one of only three pitchers to win the Cy Young Award, Most Valuable Player Award, and a World Series championship in the same year. Sandy Koufax did it in 1963 and Denny McLain, in 1968.

In the next nine days, the Tigers lost 6½ games in the standings and fell 13½ off the lead. But they won their final five games to finish 87-75 and, after being in fourth place for 38 straight days, snuck into third place on the season's last day.

On June 15 the Angels were 31-31, 3½ games out, when they won eight of their next nine to vault into first place. There they remained for all but five days, stretching their lead to 10 games in September and winning the division title with a record of 92-70.

In the ALCS, the Angels lost a gut-wrenching series to the Boston Red Sox, four games to three. Angels fans were distraught because the Angels had been ahead three games to one, and had been one out in Game Five from going to their first World Series.

Worse, Gene Mauch, after 27 years of managing, had never led a team to the Series and had carried with him the misfortune of 1964 when, in one of the greatest collapses of all time, his Phillies lost a 6½-game lead with only 12 to play. This proved to be his last chance to win a pennant.

Worse yet, pitcher Donnie Moore never got over allowing the ninth-inning home run that cost the Angels Game Five and, less than three years later, committed suicide.[6]

From 1961 through 1985, the Tigers won more games than any AL team except the Baltimore Orioles and New York Yankees. The period included World Series championships in 1968 and 1984. The Tigers won the AL East again in 1987, but didn't get back to the playoffs until 19 years later, when, in 2006 they lost the World Series to the St. Louis Cardinals.

The Angels were big spenders in the early days of free agency; in 1977 they signed Grich, Don Baylor, and Joe Rudi. After they traded for Rod Carew in 1979, they won their first AL West title, but lost the ALCS to the Baltimore Orioles, from whom they raided Grich and Baylor.

The Angels won the division title again in 1982, but lost the ALCS to the Milwaukee Brewers after leading the best-of-five series two games to none. After 1986 the Angels experienced a playoff drought of 15 years, before winning the World Series in 2002.

Sources

In addition to the sources cited in the Notes, the author relied on Baseball-Reference.com.

Notes

1　John Weyler, "Schofield's Grand Slam in Ninth Wins It, 13-12," *Los Angeles Times,* August 30, 1986: III, 5.

2　John Lowe, "Angels Blessed, Tigers Shamed." *Detroit Free Press,* August 31, 1986: 7H.

3　Lowe.

4　Lowe.

5　Lowe.

6　Elliot Almond and Mike Penner, "Donnie Moore Dies in Apparent Suicide," *Los Angeles Times,* July 19, 1989: 31.

BRAVES SCORE SEVEN IN THE NINTH VERSUS THE PHILLIES, WIN IN 15

MAY 10, 1994:
ATLANTA BRAVES 9,
PHILADELPHIA PHILLIES 8
(15 INNINGS),
AT ATLANTA-FULTON COUNTY STADIUM, ATLANTA

BY STEVEN M. GLASSMAN

The Phillies (12-19) and Braves (19-11) were playing in their first series together since the NLCS the previous fall. Both teams were entering this series going in diametrically opposite directions. The defending NL champion Phillies had won their first three games of the season, but lost 19 of their next 28, including 13 of 15 on the road. This included a 7-2 loss to the Braves in the first game of their series. The Braves had won their first seven games and 13 of 14. Entering this game, the newest NL East member[1] was 7½ games ahead of the Phillies and only the Cincinnati Reds (20-11) had a better record. Only the Chicago Cubs (9-20) and San Diego Padres (10-21) had worse records than the Phillies.

The Phillies started the game with Shawn Boskie (0-1), who was making his third start and eighth appearance (one as a pinch-runner) since he was acquired in a trade with the Cubs on April 12 for pitcher Kevin Foster.[2] He was making his fifth career start (ninth appearance overall) vs. the Braves. The Braves started Kent Mercker (2-0), who was making his fourth start (seventh appearance overall). He was making his first career start versus the Phillies after 15 relief appearances.

The Phillies opened the scoring in the third. Lenny Dykstra led off with a line-drive double to right.[3] Mariano Duncan advanced Dykstra to third on a groundout to first. Ricky Jordan's one-out sacrifice fly to center scored Dykstra.

The Braves tied the contest in the fifth on Charlie O'Brien's leadoff home run, his second of the season. He was starting in place of rookie catcher Javy Lopez,

who had fouled a pitch off his left foot and been hit by pitches twice the night before.[4]

The Phillies took the lead again in the sixth. Jordan led off with his second home run of the season. Then

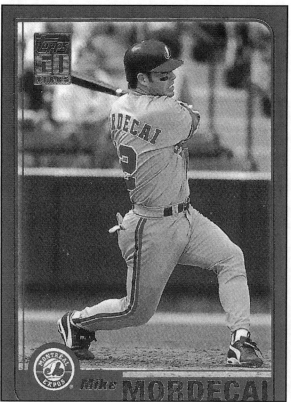

Courtesy The Topps Company.

In just the second game he ever played, Mike Mordecai's three-run homer was the biggest blow in the seven-run ninth that tied the game for the Angels and sent it to extras. He is pictured here with the Expos in this 2001 card.

Dave Hollins walked and Mercker was replaced by Mark Wohlers. Pete Incaviglia greeted Wohlers with a groundball single to left, sending advancing Hollins to third. Wes Chamberlain grounded to first, scoring Hollins.

The Phillies opened up the lead in the seventh. Dykstra led off with a line-drive triple to left-center and scored on Duncan's single to center. Jordan followed with a groundball double to left, advancing Duncan to third. Hollins walked for the third time in the game, loading the bases, and Wohlers was replaced by former Phillie Steve Bedrosian.[5] Incaviglia greeted Bedrosian with a grand slam to left, and the Phillies led 8-1.[6]

After a scoreless bottom of the seventh, top and bottom of the eighth, and top of the ninth, Boskie was prepared to close out the game.

He started the bottom of the ninth having allowed only the one run, two hits (both by O'Brien), and two walks (Mark Lemke and Mercker), while striking out two (Rafael Belliard and Ryan Klesko) and throwing 110 pitches in eight innings.[7]

Boskie allowed three straight singles (Klesko, Fred McGriff, and David Justice) to start the inning, loading the bases. He was replaced by Doug Jones.[8] Lemke's groundball single to right scored Klesko. O'Brien's single to left scored McGriff and Justice and advanced Lemke to second. Rookie Mike Mordecai, in his second major-league game, hit Jones's 1-and-2 pitch, a fastball inside, to left for a three-home run, his major-league career hit. Lemke and O'Brien scored. "I don't remember touching first base," said Mordecai. "If they had appealed it, I don't know what would have been called."[9] Jones was asked about coming into a non-save situation. "I think it might have been more concentration," he said. "We were ahead 8-1. I needed some work. My focus was just to make them swing the bat. Then, before you could turn your head, it had all blown up on me. But there's nothing I can do to make it come back."[10]

After retiring Bill Pecota on a grounder to first for the first out of the inning, Jones allowed a Deion Sanders pop-fly single to left, and gave way to Heathcliff Slocumb. Pinch-hitting for Mike Bielecki, Dave Gallagher grounded out to third as Sanders took second. Slocumb was replaced by David West. Lopez lined West's first pitch to right, scoring Sanders and tying the game, 8-8. The inning ended and the game went into extra innings when McGriff fouled out to third.

Altogether, the Braves sent a dozen hitters to bat in the ninth, scoring seven runs on eight hits. "I've been around this game a long time and I've never, ever seen anything like this," Phils manager Jim Fregosi said. "Not just that they scored seven runs in the ninth. The whole bleeping game, to be honest with you."[11]

The Braves came close in the 11th against Mike Williams, the Phillies' fifth pitcher of the game. Mordecai led off with a walk and moved to second on Pecota's sacrifice. Sanders was intentionally walked. However, Gallagher struck out looking and pinch-hitter Tom Glavine struck out swinging to end the rally.[12]

The Phillies came close in the 12th against Mike Stanton, the Braves' seventh pitcher.[13] With one out rookie Tom Quinlan hit a line-drive single to left and Todd Pratt walked.[14] But Stanton got Mickey Morandini on a foulout to third and John Kruk on a fly to left.[15] The Phillies had another opportunity in the 13th when Duncan singled to left with one out and stole second after Williams struck out swinging. Jim Eisenreich fouled out to left to end the inning.

The Braves also had a chance in the 13th. With one out Pecota singled to right and Sanders singled to center. But Gallagher grounded into a double play. They had another opportunity in the 14th. Stanton led off with a line-drive single to right and McGriff walked. Justice's double-play ball moved Stanton to third. After Lemke was intentionally walked, O'Brien's force-play grounder to shortstop ended the inning.

The Phillies' Kruk reached on a one-out line-drive single to right in the 15th. Dykstra struck out looking. Duncan walked with two out, but Kim Batiste, pinch-hitting for Williams, flied out to left to end another opportunity.

Andy Carter entered the game in the bottom of the 15th inning. He was the Phillies' sixth pitcher of the game and was making his fifth career appearance.[16] He got two outs on fly balls to center. But Deion Sanders lined a double to center. After Gallagher was intentionally walked, Sanders stole third with pitcher Stanton at the plate.[17] The *Philadelphia Daily News*'s Paul Hagen wrote: "Carter got two strikes on Stanton. Sanders danced off third. Stanton squared around to bunt. Instinctively, third baseman Tom Quinlan broke for the plate." Stanton's pop-bunt went over Quinlan's head and scored Sanders to win the game.[18] "It's the first time I've ever seen a bunt like that drop in," Fregosi said.[19] "Actually, to tell you the truth, [the bunt] was supposed to go to first," said Stanton, who earned the victory with four innings of three-hit shutout relief.

"But (Carter) ran it in on me and I got good wood on it."[20]

"There's really nothing you can say," the Phillies' Pete Incaviglia said. "(Boskie) pitched a gem. We had a seven-run lead. Pretty unbelievable. I'm at a loss for words."[21]

"Geez, this game, when things bad, boy! They just up and kick you," said Fregosi.[22]

"You never know in this game," said Incaviglia. "You might see a pitching matchup one night and think, 'This club's got no chance.' And then you look in the paper the next night and see they ended up winning the ballgame. This game is crazy like that."[23]

Sources

In addition to the sources cited in the Notes, the author referred to Baseball-Reference.com, and Retrosheet.org for box scores, play-by-plays, and other pertinent information.

Notes

1   After the 1993 season, the National League was divided into three divisions rather than two and the Braves moved from the West Division into the NL East.

2   Boskie ran for Morandini and scored a run two nights before, on May 8, against the Florida Marlins. This was his second career pinch-running appearance and his only one for the Phillies.

3   Dykstra entered the game among NL leaders in plate appearances (143, tied for first), doubles (13, third), walks (23, tied for fourth), and runs scored (30, tied for first).

4   Thomas Stinson, "Braves Notebook: Foul Off Foot Keeps Lopez Out of Lineup,' *Atlanta Journal and Constitution*, May 11, 1994: E/6.

5   Hollins walked four times in this game, at the time a personal high. He walked again four times on May 23, 1995, versus the San Francisco Giants.

6   This was Incaviglia's sixth career grand slam (second with the Phillies). It was the sixth grand slam Bedrosian allowed in his career.

7   Boskie pitched a complete game in his major-league debut, on May 20, 1990, against the Houston Astros.

8   Boskie pitched a complete game on June 27, 1994, versus the Florida Marlins. He started twice more for the Phillies before being traded to the Seattle Mariners on July 21 for minor-league first baseman Fred McNair.

9   Stinson.

10   Paul Hagen, "Laugher Dies in Sorrow/How Else Could It Have Ended?" *Philadelphia Daily News*, May 11, 1994: 90.

11   Hagen.

12   Batting for Greg McMichael, this was Glavine's only pinch-hitting appearance of the season. He had two career pinch-hits in 13 at-bats during his 22-year career.

13   Cox used 22 players in this game.

14   Pratt went hitless in six at-bats, striking out four times.

15   Morandini also was hitless in six at-bats.

16   Fregosi used 20 players in this game. Carter also pitched five innings in relief the night before when he replaced starter Juden in the third inning. Juden was ejected after hitting Lopez with a pitch after a Justice home run.

17   Sanders entered the game sharing the NL lead with 13 stolen bases and tied for second with five caught-stealings.

18   This was Stanton's first and only career walk-off hit and it was the only multi-hit game of his career. He began his career 6-for-11 with a double, a run scored and two RBIs. Stanton finished his career 8-for-24.

19   Hagen.

20   Stinson.

21   Hagen.

22   "Caught on the Fly," *The Sporting News*, May 23, 1994: 4.

23   Frank Fitzpatrick, "Phils Lose It After Leading Braves By 8-1," *Philadelphia Inquirer*, May 11, 1994: D01.

CLEVELAND OVERCOMES 12-RUN DEFICIT TO WIN

AUGUST 5, 2001:
CLEVELAND INDIANS 15,
SEATTLE MARINERS 14,
AT JACOBS FIELD, CLEVELAND

BY JOSEPH WANCHO

Perhaps the greatest story line during the 2001 season was the Seattle Mariners. Building on the previous season, when they took the New York Yankees to six games in the American League Championship Series, the Mariners waltzed through their 2001 schedule with grace and precision. They had a winning record against every AL opponent, and did not post double-digit losses in any month.

These were the new Mariners, as the Seattle faithful watched their favorite players depart from the Great Northwest. Gone were Ken Griffey Jr., Alex Rodriguez, Randy Johnson, and Tino Martinez. Only Edgar Martinez, Dan Wilson, and Jay Buhner, in a diminished role, were left from those great Seattle teams of the mid-1990s.

A rookie sensation, Ichiro Suzuki, joined Seattle from Japan. The presence of the 27-year old was immediately felt: He batted over .300 in the first three months of the season, including .379 in May. A left-handed batter who slashed line drives, he led off for manager Lou Piniella's squad and once on base he was a threat to steal at any moment.

Bret Boone, Mike Cameron, John Olerud, and Martinez backed Suzuki and the Seattle lineup was well-balanced between hitting for power and hitting for average.

The mound corps was led by a young hurler from Venezuela named Freddy Garcia. The third-year right-hander was joined by veteran pitchers Aaron Sele, Paul Abbott, and Jamie Moyer.

The Cleveland Indians were also a team in transition in 2001. Manny Ramirez had signed with Boston, and he was replaced by Juan Gonzalez. Marty Cordova

was the new left fielder and Einar Diaz replaced long-time backstop Sandy Alomar Jr. Their infield was still one of the best in the majors with third baseman Travis Fryman, shortstop Omar Vizquel, second baseman Roberto Alomar, and first baseman Jim Thome.

The pitching staff was led by a talented rookie, C.C. Sabathia. The big left-hander was the club's first-

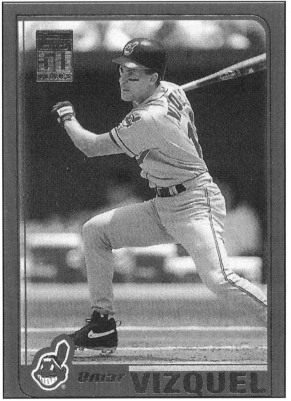

Omar Vizquel's bases-clearing triple tied the game in the ninth, to tie the game with three runs in a 12-run comeback.

round pick in 1998 and made a steady rise through the minor leagues before arriving in the big leagues. The Cleveland pitching staff offered few soft spots with veterans Dave Burba, Chuck Finley, and Bartolo Colon.

Both teams were in first place in their divisions as the Mariners invaded Cleveland for a four-game series in early August. Their battles for a division crown were polar opposites. The Mariners had a commanding 20-game lead over Oakland while the Indians held just a half-game advantage over second-place Minnesota.

Seattle defeated the Indians in the first two games, 2-1 and 8-5. The third game was a Sunday night affair with 42,494 fans stuffing Jacobs Field and a national TV audience looking on. The pitching matchup featured Sele (12-3, 3.41 ERA) for Seattle and Burba (9-8, 6.21 ERA) for Cleveland. Sele had won his first eight games of the season (April 4 to May 31), while Burba had a five-game winning streak (April 17 to May 8).

After a scoreless first inning, the Mariners tagged Burba for four runs in the top of the second. Back-to-back doubles by Al Martin and Cameron accounted for the first tally. With two outs, David Bell walked. Tom Lampkin doubled, driving in Cameron and sending Bell to third. Suzuki's single brought home the other two runs.

Seattle kept coming in the third. Consecutive singles by Martinez, Olerud, and Martin loaded the bases with nobody out. Cleveland manager Charlie Manuel went to his bullpen and brought in southpaw Mike Bacsik, who was making his major-league debut. Cameron smoked his second double, driving in two runs and sending Martin to third base. Carlos Guillen's single to left scored both runners, and the Mariners had doubled their advantage to 8-0.

They were not done. Bell singled to left field and Lampkin was hit by a pitch. Suzuki knocked in Guillen with a fly ball and Mark McLemore walked to load the bases again. Martinez reached on an error by the usually dependable Vizquel, allowing two more runs to score. Olerud singled home McLemore to complete the scoring. Seattle sent 12 men to the plate, and scored eight runs. They now led the Indians by 12-0.

Thome smashed his 35th home run of the season, a two-run shot, in the fourth inning. Seattle got two more runs in the top of the fifth inning, and their advantage was again 12 runs, at 14-2.

The Mariners held that lead through the middle of the seventh inning. The fans who stuck around broke into a half-hearted rendition of "Take Me Out to the Ballgame." Root, root, root for the home team sounded a bit silly at this point. It looked as if Manuel was waving the white flag when he removed starters Fryman, Gonzalez, Alomar, and Ellis Burks from the game.

Sele was sailing along but he surrendered a leadoff home run to Russell Branyan. Sele retired the next two batters, but then ran into trouble when Diaz singled and Kenny Lofton and Vizquel each walked. Piniella pulled the plug on Sele and brought in John Halama. The southpaw gave up a single to Jolbert Cabrera to score two more runs.

With the score 14-5, it seemed just a matter of time before Seattle would wrap up the game. But Thome socked his 36th homer in the bottom of the eighth. Halama then plunked Branyan and Cordova homered, and the score was now 14-8. Consecutive singles by Diaz and Lofton sent Halama to the showers and Norm Charlton emerged from the bullpen. Vizquel doubled, scoring Diaz. Lofton tried to score from third when a pitch got away from Lampkin, the Mariners catcher. But his throw to Charlton got Lofton, dousing the rally.

As the Indians came to bat in the bottom of the ninth, the five-run deficit seemed insurmountable. Ed Taubensee led off with a single. But Charlton retired Branyan and Thome and more fans took to the exits. Cordova doubled, and the Indians had runners at second and third with two down. Piniella again went to his bullpen and called on Jeff Nelson to shut the door. But the tall righty walked Wil Cordero to load the bases. Diaz followed with a single to left to score Taubensee and Cordova. It was 14-11.

Out went Nelson and in came Kazuhiro Sasaki, the Mariners closer, leading the team with 35 saves to this point in the season. Lofton singled to left to load the bases. Vizquel laced a 3-and-2 pitch down the right-field line, just past a diving Ed Sprague (who had entered the game as a pinch-hitter for Olerud) at first base. The ball caromed into the corner and Vizquel raced to third base. The three runners scored and unbelievably the game was tied, 14-14. "I told Omar that if Lofton got on base, and he was patient, he was going to hit a triple into the right-field corner," Manuel said later. "Sasaki is real gutty. I knew if Omar waited on his split-finger, he'd eventually come inside with a fastball to challenge him."[1] Said Vizquel, "No doubt it was my biggest hit of the year."[2]

The fans who were left broke out into bedlam. The 10th inning was scoreless. In the 11th Indians reliever John Rocker struck out the side, holding the Mariners scoreless for the sixth straight inning. Jose Paniagua entered the game in the bottom of the inning, Seattle's sixth relief pitcher. After he got the first out, consecutive singles by Lofton, Vizquel, and Cabrera ended the drama at 12:11 A.M. Cabrera's hit, a broken-bat single to left field, scored Lofton from second base for the winning run. Taubensee, who was on deck, lifted Lofton on his shoulders in a victory march to the third-base dugout.

"I got lucky," said Cabrera. "I put the ball on the bat, and it broke the bat. ... I think this can be the turning point of the season."[3]

"The biggest lesson this game teaches you is to never give up and to keep on swinging," said Manuel. "This may have been the best game I've ever managed. I took all my guys out and didn't have any moves left to make."[4]

It was the third time in the major leagues that a team came back from a 12-run deficit to win a game. The first time was on June 18, 1911, when Detroit came back to beat Chicago, 16-15. The second time, on June 15, 1925, Cleveland had the advantage over Philadelphia, but the Athletics came back to win, 17-15.

Seattle took the fourth game of the series to win three of four. Seattle won 116 games in 2001, setting a record for the most wins in a 162-game schedule.

Both teams won their division titles, and met in the Division Series. Seattle won the series in five games. The Mariners' season came to an end when they were again ousted by New York in the League Championship Series, this time in five games.

Sources

The author accessed Baseball-Reference.com for box scores/play-by-play information and other data, and Retrosheet.org.

Notes

1   Paul Hoynes, "WOW ABOUT THAT! Tribe Erases 12-Run Deficit to Stun Seattle," *Cleveland Plain Dealer*, August 6, 2001: D1.

2   Hoynes.

3   Tim Warsinskey, "Lofton Caps Comeback in Memorable Fashion," *Cleveland Plain Dealer*, August 6, 2001: D6.

4   Hoynes.

INDIANS SCORE NINE NINTH-INNING RUNS PUNCTUATED BY SIX CONSECUTIVE WALKS TO RALLY PAST PHILADELPHIA

AUGUST 21, 1934:
CLEVELAND INDIANS 12,
PHILADELPHIA ATHLETICS 11,
AT SHIBE PARK, PHILADELPHIA

BY GORDON GATTIE

The Philadelphia Athletics hosted the Cleveland Indians to complete their four-game series on a warm Tuesday afternoon. The third-place Indians (59-53) were percentage points ahead of the Boston Red Sox and 15 games behind the AL-leading Detroit Tigers. The seventh-place Athletics (47-63) were a half-game behind the St. Louis Browns and 26 games behind Detroit. The previous Saturday the ballclubs split a doubleheader, with Philadelphia winning the opener, 2-1, and Cleveland blanking the Athletics 10-0 in the nightcap.[1] Philadelphia won the Sunday afternoon matchup, 9-5, highlighted by a six-run second inning.[2]

The Indians were managed by Walter Johnson and led offensively by fellow future Hall of Famer Earl Averill in the outfield with breakout stars Hal Trosky and Odell Hale in the infield. The pitching staff featured Mel Harder, who had the lowest ERA (2.95) among qualifying (i.e., pitched at least one inning per team game played) pitchers in 1933, and youngster Monte Pearson, who won the 1933 AL ERA title with a 2.33 mark in 135⅓ innings.[3] The Indians were attempting to break their string of four consecutive fourth-place finishes; after a strong July, they were within 5½ games of first place, but struggled with a mediocre August.

The Athletics appeared in three straight World Series from 1929 to 1931, but slipped into second and third place in the American League in the ensuing two seasons. The team still boasted a formidable offense, finishing second in the major leagues with 139 homers and 875 runs in 1933, but their pitching staff issued the most walks (644) and had the second-highest team ERA (4.81) in the majors. Future Hall of Fame powerhouse first baseman Jimmie Foxx continued leading the team in most offensive categories, with catcher Mickey Cochrane, outfielder Bob Johnson, and third baseman Pinky Higgins significantly contributing to Philadelphia's strong offense. The Athletics struggled on the mound, as longtime staff ace Lefty Grove departed Philadelphia during the preceding offseason, and the Athletics ineffectively filled the void left in his absence.

Oral Hildebrand started for Cleveland. The tall right-hander was pitching in his fourth year with the Indians. In 1933 Hildebrand was selected to the AL squad for the inaugural All-Star Game, although he didn't appear in the game. He led Cleveland with 16 wins, 90 strikeouts, and 88 walks while finishing second on the staff with 15 complete games and 220⅓ innings. Entering the contest, Hildebrand was 9-7 with a 4.34 ERA in 149⅓ innings. He had lost his previous two decisions, though he defeated Philadelphia with a complete game after a shaky start on July 25.[4] Hildebrand was a late bloomer; he didn't play baseball until high school because his skills were needed on the family farm.[5] He threw a fastball and curveball; in the 1933 edition of *Who's Who in Major League Baseball*, Hildebrand was praised because "[h]e employs scarcely no windup yet specializes in a high-calibered fast ball that whistles past enemy batsmen. In addition he packs a baffling curve, but his chief stock in trade is a change of pace."[6]

Right-hander Al Benton, one of four rookies in the Athletics' rotation, started for Philadelphia. He was 7-8 with a 4.93 ERA in 140⅔ innings. Benton pitched the previous two seasons with minor-league Oklahoma City, winning 14 games and tossing over 200 innings each year. Benton primarily threw a fastball; later in his career, he developed a slider and curveball.[7] He faced Cleveland on July 23 when he slowed an Indians rally, allowing no runs in 1⅓ innings, and was the pitcher of record when Philadelphia scored three ninth-inning runs on back-to-back homers to win 11-9.[8]

The game started quietly; in the first inning, both pitchers issued a walk with two outs without either runner advancing. The Indians scored in the second inning when Hale walked and Bill Knickerbocker singled. With one out, Moe Berg plated Hale on a single to right field. A groundout moved Knickerbocker and Berg into scoring position, then Milt Galatzer singled both runners home to give Cleveland a 3-0 lead.

Doc Cramer led off the Philadelphia third inning with a triple to center field and scored on Dib Williams's sacrifice fly. Bob Johnson walked and Foxx doubled him home to trim Cleveland's lead to one run. Higgins deposited a two-run clout into the left-field seats,[9] his 12th homer of the season, to give the Athletics a 4-3 lead. Ed Coleman tripled, but a groundout and fly out prevented him from scoring.

Benton quieted Cleveland's bats over the middle innings. Hildebrand continued struggling; in the fifth inning, the Athletics loaded the bases on a walk to Higgins, Coleman's single, and an Eric McNair hit-by-pitch. With one out, Benton helped his own cause, beating out an infield hit and driving in Higgins. A fielder's choice stopped Philadelphia from increasing its lead.

The Athletics scored again in the sixth inning. Williams singled to left. Johnson hit into a fielder's choice, Foxx singled to center, and Higgins walked as Philadelphia loaded the bases for the second straight inning. Coleman ripped a single into right field, scoring two more runs. Hildebrand escaped further damage on a groundout and strikeout, but his day was finished with the Athletics leading 7-3.

In the seventh inning, Belve Bean relieved Hildebrand. Bean had pitched effectively in his recent outings, allowing three earned runs and winning three games in 18 innings pitched. Cramer greeted Bean with a double into the left-field gap but was thrown out trying to stretch his hit into a triple. Williams grounded out. Johnson and Foxx singled, but Higgins hit into a fielder's choice as Cleveland remained within striking distance.

In the Philadelphia eighth, Bean walked leadoff hitter Coleman, who then scored on McNair's double. After a strikeout, Benton singled, and McNair reached third. Cramer doubled to left field to score McNair. With two outs, pinch-hitter Lou Finney singled to left field, driving in Cramer and Benton. Foxx reached base on a hit-by-pitch, then left the game with a potential injury. The inning ended on a Higgins fly out. Philadelphia led 11-3 heading into the ninth inning.

Benton took the mound to finish off Cleveland in the ninth. Through eight innings, Benton had allowed three runs and five hits, including only two hits over the last six innings, and "there seemed no doubt that he would go to the finish."[10] But the Indians quickly loaded the bases on a single by Knickerbocker and back-to-back walks. Frankie Pytlak, pinch-hitting for Bean, walked, scoring Knickerbocker and ending Benton's day. Rookie reliever Joe Cascarella fared no better as he confronted the top of Cleveland's order. Cascarella walked the only two batters he faced; the Indians closed the gap to 11-6 with the bases still loaded and no outs. Sugar Cain relieved Cascarella and issued Philadelphia's sixth consecutive walk. Although the Athletics finally recorded an out when Trosky hit into a fielder's choice, Galatzer scored, and Cleveland brought the tying run to the plate. Hale hit an infield single and the bases were jammed yet again. Knickerbocker singled to score Trosky and advance Hale, who then scored on an error by third baseman Higgins on a relay from center field[11] as the Indians rebounded from an eight-run deficit to tie the score. Recording only one out, Cain was replaced by Roy Mahaffey. Willie Kamm, the first batter Mahaffey faced, singled to left field on the first pitch[12] to score Knickerbocker and Cleveland recaptured the lead. A double play mercifully ended the inning for Philadelphia, which allowed nine runs on four singles and six straight walks as the Indians batted around.

Willis Hudlin entered the game to save the game for Cleveland. Hudlin rushed to get ready for the bottom half; he had only started to warm up after Averill walked to bring in the Indians' fourth run in the top half.[13] Coleman popped out to the shortstop, and McNair grounded out to third base. Pinch-hitter Johnny Marcum replaced catcher Charlie Berry and flied out to left field, preserving the win for the Indians.

Cleveland scored nine unanswered runs to win the wild game in completely unexpected fashion. Knickerbocker led Indians hitters with three runs and four hits while Galatzer was the only Clevelander to drive home more than one run. All of Cleveland's nine hits were singles, and Knickerbocker was the lone Indian with a multi-hit game. Philadelphia hitters banged out 18 hits, led by Cramer and Coleman, who had four hits apiece. Although four different Athletics scored two runs apiece, Philadelphia stranded 15 runners. Bean won his fifth game, Hudlin earned his fourth save, and Cain was charged with the loss.

The Indians finished third in AL in 1934 with an 85-69 record, 16 games behind pennant-winning Detroit, breaking their streak of four consecutive fourth-place finishes. The Athletics finished in fifth place with a 68-82 record, 31 games behind the Tigers. The ballclubs faced off 22 times during the season with Cleveland winning 13 games.

Sources

Besides the sources cited in the Notes, the author consulted Baseball-Almanac.com, Baseball-Reference.com, Retrosheet.org, and the following:

James, Bill. *The New Bill James Historical Abstract* (New York: The Free Press, 2001).

Thorn, John, and Pete Palmer, et al. *Total Baseball: The Official Encyclopedia of Major League Baseball* (New York: Viking Press, 2004).

Oral Hildebrand on SABR BioProject: sabr.org/bioproj/person/6708ec71.

Notes

1 James C. Isaminger, "Macks Win, 2-1, Lose, 10-0; Phils Skid, 2-0," *Philadelphia Inquirer*, August 19, 1934: 1.

2 James C. Isaminger, "Macks Win 9-5; Phils Lose, 3-1, 4-2," *Philadelphia Inquirer*, August 21, 1934: 11.

3 Paul Mickelson, "In Upset Year, Grove Held His Hurling Title," *Dayton* (Ohio) *Daily News,* December 21, 1933: 15.

4 Gordon Cobbledick, "Indians Bombard 4 Mack Rookies For 8 to 3 Victory," *Cleveland Plain Dealer,* July 26, 1934: 14.

5 Dick Farrington, "Milch Cows and Milk Weed Turn Hildebrand, Cleveland Pitcher, Against Farm and Into Baseball," *The Sporting News,* January 11, 1934: 3.

6 Harold "Speed" Johnson, *Who's Who in Major League Baseball* (Buxton Publishing Co., 1933), 216, cited in Bill James and Rob Neyer, *The Neyer/James Guide to Pitchers: An Historical Compendium of Pitching, Pitchers, and Pitches* (New York: Fireside Books, 2004), 243.

7 James and Neyer, 132.

8 Associated Press, "A's Home Runs Sink Indians," *Wilkes-Barre* (Pennsylvania) *Record,* July 24, 1934: 15.

9 "Details as Indians' Mighty Rally Beats A's," *Cleveland Plain Dealer,* August 22, 1934: 13.

10 James C. Isaminger, "Macks Lose, Phils Win, Tigers Cash In," *Philadelphia Inquirer*, August 22, 1934: 13.

11 Isaminger, 13.

12 Gordon Cobbledick, "Indians' 9-Run Blast in Ninth Stuns A's, 12-11," *Cleveland Plain Dealer,* August 22, 1934: 13.

13 Cobbledick, "Indians' 9-Run Blast in Ninth Stuns A's, 12-11."

PHILLIES SLUGGER MIKE SCHMIDT HITS FOUR HOME RUNS AT WRIGLEY FIELD

APRIL 17, 1976:
PHILADELPHIA PHILLIES 18,
CHICAGO CUBS 16 (10 INNINGS),
AT WRIGLEY FIELD, CHICAGO

BY RICH D'AMBROSIO

The Philadelphia Phillies opened a two-game weekend series at Wrigley Field on Saturday, April 17, 1976, in a bit of a slump. Their record four games into the new season was an uninspiring 1-3, putting a damper on the enthusiasm surrounding a team that had been picked by many to win the National League East.

One player in particular had been struggling mightily. Third baseman Mike Schmidt, the two-time defending National League home-run king, entered the game batting a woeful .167 with just one homer, two RBIs, and nine strikeouts in 18 at-bats. His slump prompted manager Danny Ozark to drop Schmidt from third in the batting order to sixth that afternoon. Consequently, Schmidt sought some advice. "I had a long talk with Dick Allen before the game," Schmidt said. "I can't say I was hang-dog or down in the mouth, but he's a good friend and I needed a little boost. He got my mind right."[1]

The veteran slugger told Schmidt, "Mike, you've got to relax. You've got to have some fun. Remember when you were a kid and you'd skip dinner to play ball? You were having fun. Hey, with all that talent you've got, baseball ought to be fun. Enjoy it. Be a kid again."[2]

Schmidt had sustained a finger injury in the Phillies' series at Montreal a few days earlier, so he was having trouble gripping a bat. That afternoon in Chicago, Schmidt borrowed teammate Tony Taylor's bat, which was an inch shorter and an ounce lighter. He also wore reserve infielder Terry Harmon's tee shirt.

Taylor joked that it was guaranteed to be "loaded with hits."[3] Clearly, Schmidt was looking for something to get him back on track.

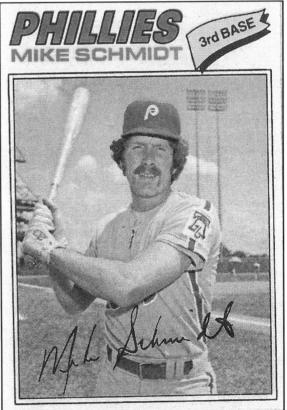

Eight runs batted on four home runs – including the game-winner in the 10th – made future Hall of Famer Mike Schmidt the big gun of the game.

A crowd of 28,287 settled into Wrigley Field on that warm, sun-splashed afternoon. The Phillies sent Steve Carlton to the mound against the Cubs' Rick Reuschel. Carlton was hit hard in his season debut against the Pirates on April 11 and struggled in this outing as well. After being staked to a 1-0 lead courtesy of a Garry Maddox home run in the second inning, Carlton was rocked for seven runs on seven hits in just 1.2 innings pitched. The Cubs continued to hammer a succession of Phillies' relievers and led the game 12-1 after three innings. When Rick Monday ripped his second homer of the game in the fourth inning, the Cubs' lead grew to 13-2. Another Phillies' loss seemed assured.

In the top half of the fifth inning, Jay Johnstone and Greg Luzinski knocked consecutive singles, but Allen hit into a double play, sending Johnstone to third. Schmidt came to bat and on a 1-1 curveball hit a long homer off Reuschel that landed on Waveland Avenue to make the score 13-4. The homer didn't seem like much at the time, but the Phillies' bats were coming to life. Good relief pitching by Ron Reed and Wayne Twitchell kept the Cubs off the scoreboard and helped the Phillies make this a competitive game.

Larry Bowa led off the Phillies' half of the seventh inning with a single to left and scored on Johnstone's triple. Luzinski then hit a sacrifice fly to score Johnstone. One out later, Schmidt hit his second homer of the day off Reuschel to make the score 13-7. In the Phillies eighth, Mike Garman came on in relief for the Cubs. Bobby Tolan, pinch hitting for Twitchell, greeted him with a single.

Dave Cash followed with another single, and Bowa walked to load the bases. With two outs, Allen singled to center to drive in Tolan and Cash. Then Schmidt came to bat and hit a ball up in the wind to right field for his third homer of the day, a three-run blast to get the Phillies to within one run, 13-12.

The Phillies went ahead in the ninth inning 15-13, courtesy of a Bob Boone homer and a triple by Bowa. Tug McGraw, though, couldn't hold the lead and surrendered a game-tying single by Cubs catcher Steve Swisher. In the 10th, Darold Knowles issued a lead-off walk to Allen. Paul Reuschel, Rick's older brother, replaced Knowles as Schmidt came to the plate once again. Schmidt drilled a Reuschel fastball into the left-center-field bleachers for his fourth consecutive homer of the day, a two-run blast that put the Phillies ahead 17-15. In a rare display of emotion, the normally cool Schmidt actually smiled as he crossed the plate.

Schmidt became the 10th player in major-league history to hit four homers in a game (and the first since Willie Mays in 1961), and just the fourth player to hit four consecutive homers in as many at-bats, joining Bobby Lowe (1894), Lou Gehrig (1932), and Rocky Colavito (1959).[4] His eight RBIs in the game tied a Phillies' club record. Philadelphia added another run that inning to make the score 18-15, but Tommy Underwood allowed an RBI double by Bill Madlock in the bottom of the tenth to keep the Cubs' hopes alive. Jim Lonborg came in to record the final out and seal the 18-16 Phillies' victory.

Schmidt finished the day with five hits in six at-bats and raised his average from .167 to .333. After the game, he shared his thoughts about his approach at the plate: "I wasn't thinking anything special when I went up there," he said. "I was feeling good and nice and relaxed. I don't think moving down to sixth (in the order) meant anything."[5] As for being dropped to the sixth position in the batting order, he added, "I don't care where I hit…third…sixth…ninth. There'll be people on base to drive in."[6]

When asked about his pre-game sit-down with Allen, Schmidt said, "I needed somebody to talk to and Allen is the perfect guy. He's been around a long time and he knows what to say and how to say it. I go to him a lot and so do some of the other players. In fact, I think more of us ought to do it."[7]

The fact that the Phillies were down 11 runs in the third inning may have affected Schmidt's approach that afternoon. When asked if he thought the Phillies had a chance to come back, he said, "Really, deep down, you don't think so. But maybe the lack of pressure helped. You just go up there and work on your swing. I need a game like this to take off some of the pressure."[8]

This game, one of the most memorable in Phillies' history, had a favorable effect on the team in general and Schmidt in particular. The young slugger went on to homer in six of the next eight games and finished April with 11 home runs, tying the record for round-trippers in the month (Willie Stargell in 1971 and Graig Nettles in 1974), and was featured on the cover of the May 3 issue of *Sports Illustrated*. By the end of May, Schmidt was hitting a robust .307 and in a tight race with the Mets' Dave Kingman for the National League lead in homers. Schmidt was named to the All-Star team and finished with 38 homers, good enough to win the NL home-run crown for the third straight season. One can argue that the 1976 season elevated

Schmidt to superstar status and paved the way for his Hall of Fame career.

Inspired by the great comeback in Chicago, the Phillies went on an incredible roll. Bill Conlin of the *Philadelphia Daily News* nicknamed the team "The Blitz Kids." The Phillies moved into first place in early May after winning 10 out of 11 games and never relinquished the lead. From April 17 to August 26, the Phillies' record was an amazing 81-39. By August 26, the Phils had built a commanding 15-game lead over the Pittsburgh Pirates.

A serious slump from late August to mid-September, combined with the Pirates playing their best baseball of the season, cut the Philadelphia lead to a mere three games by September 17. However, the Phillies rebounded and clinched the NL East title at Montreal's Jarry Park on September 26. Philadelphia fans were witnessing their team's Golden Era, which would culminate in a World Series championship in 1980.

Sources

In addition to the sources cited in the Notes, the author used the Baseball-Reference.com and Retrosheet.org websites for material pertinent to this article.

Notes

1   William Kashatus, *Mike Schmidt: Philadelphia's Hall of Fame Third Baseman* (Jefferson, Noth Carolina: McFarland, 1999), 34.

2   Kashatus.

3   Bill Conlin, "Schmidt Nails 'em," *Philadelphia Daily News*, April 19, 1976: 54.

4   Check out SABR's comprehensive list of all four-HR games in professional baseball history here: https://sabr.org/research/four-homers-one-game

5   Conlin.

6   Conlin.

7   Ray Kelly, "Schmidt HR Bat Works Overtime, 8 in 6 Games," *The Sporting News*, May 8, 1976: 7.

8   Allen Lewis, "Schmidt Hits 4 Home Runs," *Philadelphia Inquirer*, April 18, 1976: 1D.

ONE SUGARCOATED GAME

JUNE 30, 2009:
BALTIMORE ORIOLES 11,
BOSTON RED SOX 10,
AT ORIOLE PARK AT CAMDEN YARDS, BALTIMORE

BY THOMAS E. SCHOTT

There's no way of sugarcoating it: The 2009 Baltimore Orioles were a terrible baseball team. They finished last in their division, 39 games behind the eventual World Series champion New York Yankees, with the worst record in the American League, losing 98 games. An average-hitting team—with below-average power—when it came to pitching, the Orioles set the standard for wretched.[1]

Nick Markakis doubled in the tying and go-ahead runs for the Orioles in the bottom of the eighth.

Courtesy The Topps Company.

But for one glorious night game, which began in the sunshine on the last day of June, the woeful 34-42 Orioles looked like world-beaters against the powerful, division-leading Boston Red Sox. The 10-run rally in a nine-inning game the Orioles staged that evening remains the team record, but it wasn't the largest in the game's history. Three teams have come back from 11 runs behind to win in regulation. Nonetheless, in a game that lasted almost 3½ hours, including a 70-minute rain delay, the Orioles' rally remains an achievement, especially given the odds of it ever happening.[2]

The Boston visitors, actually cheered by "most of" the 31,969 attendees, virtually owned the Orioles, having beaten them in eight straight games (and 12 of 13), and boasted former, future, and present-day All-Stars, up and down: steady Dustin Pedroia at second, third baseman Kevin Youkilis, power-hitting DH David "Big Papi" Ortiz, outfielders Jacoby Ellsbury and Jason Bay, catcher Jason Varitek, plus All-Star pitchers in starter John Smoltz and closer Jonathan Papelbon, and a bullpen with a couple more standouts. Baltimore countered with little to boast of. Arguably the team's best player, center fielder Adam Jones, left the game with a shoulder injury after two innings and was replaced by youngster Félix Pié. Solid performers like first baseman Luke Scott had a 117 lifetime OPS+, and Nick Markakis in right was in his fourth year of a productive 14-year career through 2019. Rookies Nolan Reimold in left and catcher Mark Wieters rounded out a motley collection of veterans and a pitching staff of average journeymen.[3]

The contrast between the starting pitchers for this game couldn't have been starker. Boston's 42-year-old Cy Young Award winner and future Hall of Famer

Smoltz was in the final year of his distinguished career. Baltimore started 29-year-old southpaw Rich Hill, who in his undistinguished previous four years with the Chicago Cubs had gone 18-17 with a 4.37 ERA and 1.268 WHIP.[4]

The ensuing game divides neatly into three parts: the first four innings, all Boston, a short two-inning intermission, and the final three frames, the Orioles' comeback to win. The Red Sox wasted no time scoring. The leadoff guy, shortstop Julio Lugo, singled sharply to left, and after Pedroia popped out, Lugo stole second. Youkilis parked a ball to deep left-center: three hitters, two runs. The Sox put another two guys on—a screaming double to center by Big Papi and a walk to Varitek, but neither scored. The Orioles went three up, three down with two strikeouts. Boston stepped up the pressure in the second. After a bunt groundout, Hill walked first-sacker Jeff Bailey and surrendered another single to Lugo. Pedroia now stroked a line-drive double to the left-center wall, scoring two more runs. The Orioles got a runner on in their half of the inning (Scott walked), but the other three hitters went out.

The Red Sox went quietly in the third, strikeout, groundout, fly out, as if preparing for their next-inning onslaught. Meanwhile, the Orioles managed to score a run on a ground single by shortstop Robert Andino, a career utility infielder, and a line-drive triple to right center by Pié. They were trailing by three when the roof caved in in the top of the fourth. Ellsbury opened with a deep line-drive homer over the fence in center-right. Then with two on (Bailey via a single and Pedroia via a throwing error from third), Youkilis doubled down the left-field line, scoring Bailey. After intentionally walking Jason Bay to load the bases, Hill allowed Ortiz to bash a single to left, filling the bases again. Pedroia scored and the other runners moved up.

This ended Hill's ugly night; righty Matt Albers came in from the pen to quench the flames and plunked the first hitter he faced, forcing in Youkilis from third. After catching the next hitter looking at a third strike, Albers gave up a line-drive single to Ellsbury, his second hit and RBI of the inning. Mercifully, with the sacks still jammed, he got Bailey to ground out. Now with an eight-run lead, Smoltz made quick work of the bottom of the inning: he gave up a one-out single to Reimold, who was erased on a double-play ball by the next batter.[5]

Then came the rain, delaying the game for over an hour. When play resumed in the top of the fifth, Albers gave up an infield single to Youkilis (his third hit of the game), but nothing otherwise. Boston's new hurler—Smoltz was obviously done after the long delay—right-hander Justin Masterton, got three straight Orioles out, two on whiffs. In the top of the sixth, both teams went three up and three down. As the game entered its final three innings, the Red Sox, leading 9-1, were driving down Easy Street. Mark Hendrickson took over pitching for the Orioles. The Red Sox added another run in the top of the seventh: With one out Bailey tripled to center and Pedroia singled him home a batter later.[6]

From this point on, the game underwent an utter transformation. The home team, trailing 10-1, could not err, and the visitors' pitching simply cratered. As one disgusted Boston writer put it: "[T]he Orioles stripped and sold the Red Sox bullpen for parts."[7] First baseman Aubrey Huff singled to open the Orioles' half of the seventh. Reimold singled on the ground to right. DH Scott hit a line-drive double to center-right, scoring Huff. At this point Baltimore sent Óscar Salazar in to hit for Melvin Mora, and he cracked the second pitch he saw deep down the left-field line for a three-run homer. Inexplicably, Masterson stayed in for the next hitter, Wieters, who grounded a single to center. Manny Delcarmen replaced Masterson on the mound. He lasted three batters, getting two groundouts before Pié stroked a single to center, scoring Andino and sending Delcarmen to the showers. Boston's fourth pitcher, Hideki Okajima, finally extricated the Red Sox from their hellish inning. Boston 10, Baltimore 6.

The Red Sox took the field with a comfortable four-run lead in the bottom of the eighth with Okajima still on the mound. He surrendered hits to every batter he faced in the inning: the first four. Line-drive single by Reimold, long fly-ball double to right by Scott, Salazar's squibber in front of the plate, and a line-drive single to left by Wieters, scoring Reimold. Unsurprisingly, Boston decided to switch pitchers, and the home team sent a pinch-hitter to the plate. The new reliever Takashi Saito, a highly effective closer himself, wasn't comfortable in his role as a late-inning set-up man for Boston's All-Star closer Papelbon. Ty Wigginton stood in to hit for Andino and lofted a long fly to deep right that scored Scott. Second baseman Brian Roberts, hitless in four at-bats (indeed, suffering an 0-for-18 skid) followed that with a grass-cutting single to left, scoring Salazar and moving Wieters to second, where pinch-runner Jeremy Guthrie replaced him. Now ahead by only a single run, Boston manager Terry Francona brought Papelbon to the mound. Why not? He was a perfect 20-for-20 in save opportunities against Baltimore. Indeed, he promptly struck out Pié. Markakis, who at that point was 0-for-7 with four strikeouts against Papelbon, jumped on the first pitch and sent a rope to deep left-center for a double that scored both Guthrie and Roberts. The lowly O's had captured the lead from nine runs back![8]

Papelbon got out of the inning with no further damage. Boston made things scary for George Sherrill, the O's closer (and those fans who had hung around through the rain and previous horrors) in the ninth. Bailey led off with his third hit. Sherrill bore down to retire Lugo and Pedroia. But then on a 1-and-2 pitch, with the crowd ready to split the sky in celebration, he hit Youkilis with a pitch, putting the tying and go-ahead runs on base. But Sherrill fanned Jason Bay on four pitches to seal the historic victory. "[A]bsolutely tremendous," Orioles manager Dave Trembley exulted. "When you talk about playing all 27 outs, that's tonight." Smoltz, who had left the game thinking the Red Sox victory was practically in the bag, was amazed. "It's just one of those games . . . you can't believe what you just saw." Papelbon put it more tersely: "We pretty much imploded."[9]

Lest anyone think that this stirring victory ignited the Orioles, don't. They blew a four-run lead in the ninth inning the following evening. Counting the Boston series, the Orioles went on to lose 18 of their remaining 27 series, winning only six and splitting three.[10]

Sources

In addition to the sources cited in the Notes, my thanks to SABR members Gregory Wolf and Bill Nowlin who provided me with research assistance. I also used the statistical data and play-by-play information available at baseball-reference.com and retrosheet.com in preparing this article.

Notes

1   As a team, Baltimore allowed more runs per game (5.41), hits, runs, and home runs, and had the worst ERA (5.15) and WHIP (1.525) in 2009 than any other major-league team. Not to mention the highest number of losses and fewest opponent strikeouts in the AL.

2   David Ginsberg, "Orioles Cap 9-Run Comeback Over Bosox," *Porterville Recorder* (Porterville, California), July 1, 2009; Stacey Long, "June 30, 2009: A Night to Remember," *Orioles Buzz,* June 29, 2011, masnsports.com/orioles-buzz/2011/06/june-30-2009-a-night-to-remember.html, accessed December 29, 2019. Data on the best comebacks for both regulation and extra-innings games is at baseball-reference.com/friv/comeback-wins.shtml, accessed December 29, 2019. In the greatest comeback in a major-league game, the Cleveland Indians erased and surpassed a 12-run Seattle lead in an extra-inning game on August 5, 2001. Chris Jaffe, "10-Year Anniversary of Baseball's Greatest Comeback," *Hardball Times,* August 5, 2011, tht.fangraphs.com/tht-live/10-year-anniversary-of-baseballs-greatest-comeback/, accessed December 29, 2019. Three teams have come back from 11 runs down in a regulation nine-inning game: Philadelphia vs. Cleveland (1925), St. Louis Cardinals vs. New York Giants (1952), and Houston vs. Cardinals (1994).

3   Bill Wagner, "Stirring Surge Shakes Up Sox," *The Capital* (Annapolis, Maryland), July 1, 2009: A9, A11. Basically a career minor leaguer who occasionally dipped into the Big Show, Félix Pié, who broke into the game at 17, spent parts of six seasons in the big leagues over 12-plus years in Organized Baseball. He slashed .246/.295/.369 in the majors and had a -1.6 WAR and -14 RAR.

4   Hill was with the Orioles for only this season, achieving a 3-3 record in 13 starts with a 7.80 ERA and 1.873 WHIP. Amazingly, he hung on in the big leagues for 10 more years, approximately half the time as a starter and half as bullpen guy.

5   Matt Albers has through 2019 enjoyed a 14-year career solely as a relief specialist with eight different teams in both leagues; Baltimore was his second big-league club.

6   Stacey Long, see note 2.

7   Adam Kilgore, "Stunning Moment in the Rain," *Boston Globe,* July 1, 2009: C6.

8   Associated Press, *Herald* (Jasper, Indiana), July 1, 2009. Interestingly, this second of Papelbon's blown saves of the season came on the night after he tied Bob Stanley's record for career saves with the Red Sox.

9   Kilgore; Amalie Benjamin, "Old Bawl Game," *Boston Globe,* July 1, 2009: C1.

10   Dan Connolly, "Back to Reality for O's," *Baltimore Sun,* July 2, 2009.

BOB FOTHERGILL LEADS WHITE SOX IN 11-RUN EIGHTH-INNING RALLY TO BEAT YANKEES

JULY 28, 1931:
CHICAGO WHITE SOX 14,
NEW YORK YANKEES 12,
AT YANKEE STADIUM, NEW YORK

BY MIKE HUBER

In one of the greatest comebacks in major-league history, the Chicago White Sox "staged an eleven-run rally" in the eighth inning of a game against the New York Yankees, in front of the home crowd in the Bronx. The *New York Times* estimated that "twelve thousand fans, most of them Boys' Club guests of the Yankees seated in the left-field stand," witnessed the counterattack, which erased a nine-run New York advantage.[1] Edward Burns of the *Chicago Tribune* wrote that the White Sox, "those undermanned wanderers," scored 11 runs in the eighth inning "to nose out the powerful and affluent New York Yankees."[2] The *Brooklyn Daily Eagle* noted, "Fifteen Chicago batsmen came up and every one of them had a bat."[3]

By the end of July in the 1931 season, New York had been closing in on 60 wins, but they began a six-game series with Chicago stuck in third place in the American League. The Yankees were enjoying an extended homestand that saw them play only one game away from Yankee Stadium since the Fourth of July.[4] They had played 18-8 baseball, leading up to this game on July 28, yet managed to gain only three games on the League-leading Philadelphia Athletics. Chicago, on the other hand, was in the midst of a 22-game road trip. The seventh-place White Sox had gone 6-10 coming into this contest.

For Chicago, sixth-year right-hander Tommy Thomas was given the start. He was looking for his third straight win, but he brought an ERA of 4.24 with him. New York countered with Herb Pennock, pitching in his 19th season. He had lost his last decision (on July 17), and his ERA stood at 4.29.

After Pennock easily retired the White Sox in order to start the game, the Yankees jumped on Thomas. Samuel Byrd and Joe Sewell each singled. With runners on the corners, Babe Ruth rolled a grounder to first baseman Lu Blue, who threw home to get Byrd. Lou Gehrig plated Sewell with a single. Thomas struck Ben Chapman with a pitch, loading the bases. Lyn Lary hit a fly ball to center, driving in Ruth, and New York had a 2-0 lead.

A one-out double by Bob Fothergill got things going for the White Sox in the second. John Kerr followed with a single to right, and Fothergill scored. An inning later, Chicago struck again. Thomas helped his own cause with a leadoff double to deep left field. Blue's single resulted in an RBI and the game was tied.

Each pitcher settled down, working through the opposing team the second time through the order. Then, in the bottom of the fifth, Pennock drew a walk. An out later, Sewell reached on an error by shortstop

11-Run Attack In Eighth Wins For Chicago Nine

Fothergill Chases Pennock With Homer Then Hits Triple in Same Frame as Pale Hose Stage Exciting Comeback to Triumph, 14-12

The headline from the next day's *Springfield* (Massachusetts) *Republican* tells the story.

Bill Cissell. Ruth again pulled a grounder to first for an out, advancing the runners. Thomas intentionally walked Gehrig. This backfired when Chapman singled to left, driving in two runs and sending Gehrig to third. Then, with right-handed batter Lary in the batter's box, "Locomotive Lou Gehrig and Ben Chapman successfully put on a double steal,"[5] with Gehrig swiping home and Chapman adding his 41st steal of the season.

Chicago manufactured a run in the sixth. Lew Fonseca singled and went to third on Fothergill's second double of the game. Kerr hit a comebacker to Pennock, who threw to first for the out, but Fonseca scored.

The Yankees weren't done scoring, though. In the sixth inning, "the trouble Thomas encountered was of his own making."[6] After retiring the first two New York batters, the White Sox pitcher seemed to lose control. He walked Pennock for the second time in the game. Byrd slammed a ground-rule double. Sewell doubled to right, plating both runners. Ruth singled to center, and Sewell scored. Gehrig singled and Chapman tripled to deep center, driving in two more. Chicago manager Donie Bush made a pitching change, probably a few batters too late. Right-hander Biggs Wehde came on in relief. Wehde had appeared in four games in 1930 (all in the same September week) and this was his seventh appearance of 1931. In his previous outing (July 26), he had pitched six innings against New York and had been touched for nine runs on 10 hits and four walks.[7] Wehde walked Lary and gave up an RBI single to Bill Dickey.

Wehde walked Tony Lazzeri to start the bottom of the seventh. Pennock sacrificed Lazzeri to second and Byrd singled up the middle, making the score 12-3 in favor of the New Yorkers. Pennock and the Yankees were cruising.

Until the top of the eighth.

With one out, Chicago's Carl Reynolds came through with his first hit of the game, a double. Fonseca singled for a run batted in, and then Fothergill drove a homer into the left-field stands. Kerr singled and Pennock's afternoon was finished. Red Ruffing became the new Yankees hurler. Cissell greeted him with a single. Frank Grube also singled, with Kerr scoring. Smead Jolley batted for Wehde and doubled, scoring Cissell and sending Grube to third. Pat Caraway ran for Jolley. Blue launched a ball to Lazzeri at second that hit him in the chest and rolled across the foul line. Blue was credited with a triple and two runs batted in.

Ruffing was lifted for Lefty Gomez. Irv Jeffries, another pinch-hitter, hit a fly to right, and Blue scored. Gomez couldn't keep the bases empty, though. Reynolds doubled, his second two-bagger of the inning, which tied a record for most doubles in an inning. Fonseca drove him home with a single, and this brought up Fothergill for his second at-bat of the inning. He "poked a fly to right which became a triple when Ruth tried for a shoestring catch and failed to stop the ball."[8] Fonseca had crossed the plate with the go-ahead (13th) run for Chicago. According to the *Chicago Tribune*, "It scarcely could be figured that Fothergill, with two doubles and a homer already in his bag, was due, but plump Robert delivered a triple."[9]

Jim Weaver became the fourth New York pitcher of the inning, replacing Gomez, and gave up an RBI single to Kerr. Fothergill's run made it 14-12 in favor of the visitors. Cissell grounded out, but Chicago had sent 15 batters to the plate, scoring 11 tallies.

Reynolds, Fonseca, Fothergill, and Kerr each collected two hits in the big inning. Chicago did not discriminate, blasting Pennock, Ruffing, and Gomez with equal power, "as their rally roared and rumbled."[10] The White Sox had sent the three future Hall of Famers to the showers in the same frame.

Vic Frazier pitched the eighth and ninth innings for the White Sox, but the Yankees were obviously deflated and went hitless. The final score remained Chicago 14, New York 12. The top seven men in New York's order garnered all of their 13 hits, but it was not enough. Ten different Chicago batters had contributed to their 20-hit attack. Fothergill led the way in a 4-for-5 effort with 11 total bases, and his home run and triple in the eighth were the key blows. Blue, Fothergill, and Kerr each had three runs batted in.

Amazingly, Wehde picked up the victory, earning notice in the next day's papers with, "Wilbur Wehde may not remain long in the majors, but he can tell his grandchildren how his name went down as the winning pitcher the day the White Sox scored 11 runs in one inning against the Yanks."[11] This was somewhat prophetic, as Wehde appeared in only one more major-league game. That contest has a twist: Wehde came on in the eighth inning five days later, on August 3 against Detroit with two outs and runners at first and second. After a pitch to the batter, the runner at second was caught stealing for the final out of the inning. The White Sox were behind, so Detroit didn't bat in the ninth. Wehde's line was one-third of an inning pitched but he was not credited with facing a batter. Wehde's career in the majors consisted of 12 appearances (all in relief), 22⅓ innings pitched and a 1-0 record.

The *New York Times* told its readers that the White Sox "fell short by three runs of equaling the modern record for runs scored in an inning."[12] On September 6, 1883, the Chicago White Stockings exploded for 18 runs against the Detroit Wolverines. The modern record (since 1900) belonged to the 1920 Yankees (who scored 14 runs in the fifth frame against the Washington Senators on July 6, 1920) and the 1922 Chicago Cubs (who scored 14 runs in the fourth inning against the Philadelphia Phillies on August 25, 1922).

Sources

In addition to the sources mentioned in the Notes, the author consulted base-ball-reference.com, retrosheet.org, and sabr.org.

Notes

1 William E. Brandt, "11 White Sox Runs in 8th Beat Yanks," *New York Times*, July 29, 1931: 25. Neither baseball-reference.com nor retrosheet.org lists the official attendance.

2 Edward Burns, "Sox' 11 Run Rally in 8th Beats Yanks, 14-12," *Chicago Tribune*, July 29, 1931: 15.

3 "1-Frame Orgy of Hits Just Buries Yanks," *Brooklyn Daily Eagle*, July 29, 1931: 20.

4 The Yankees traveled to Washington on July 12 for a single game against the Senators.

5 *Brooklyn Daily Eagle*.

6 Burns.

7 Wehde had entered the July 26 game as a reliever, after starter Caraway had allowed 13 runs (10 earned), so Wehde did not get a decision.

8 Brandt.

9 Burns.

10 Brandt.

11 Burns.

12 Brandt.

DOWN 10-0, WHITT AND JAYS SLAM RED SOX

JUNE 4, 1989:
TORONTO BLUE JAYS 13,
BOSTON RED SOX 11,
AT FENWAY PARK, BOSTON

BY ADRIAN FUNG

While Neil Young began the year singing, "Keep on rockin' in the free world,"[1] millions around the globe were seeking freedom by the spring of 1989. One day before Toronto and Boston concluded their weekend three-game series, the Chinese government used lethal force to crush a seven-week pro-democracy protest in Beijing.[2] In Poland, citizens voted in multiparty elections for the first time since the end of World War II,[3] while East Germans curiously watched and cautiously dreamed of tearing down the Berlin Wall and also voting freely one day.[4]

Within the green walls of Fenway Park, Boston looked to avoid a series sweep against Toronto. After the Blue Jays went scoreless in the first inning, rookie hurler Alex Sanchez walked the Red Sox' Jody Reed and Ed Romero, and after Wade Boggs grounded out, Mike Greenwell and Dwight Evans both hit one-bounce, run-scoring singles to left field. Ellis Burks took two called strikes, then belted a hanging curveball over the Green Monster to give Boston a 5-0 lead. After Sanchez walked the next batter, his start was finished. It would be another long afternoon for the Toronto bullpen.

Both clubs had leaned heavily on their relievers on Friday and Saturday but the Red Sox got an early boost from tall right-handed starter Mike Smithson. The veteran pitcher blanked Toronto over six innings while his teammates doubled their lead.

Boston added single runs in the second, third, and fourth innings, then appeared to put the game out of reach in the sixth, thanks to a two-error play by Toronto first baseman Fred McGriff. After Boggs and Greenwell walked, Evans hit a bouncing ball that deflected off McGriff's glove to his right. McGriff grabbed the ball and threw toward first base but the ball sailed by pitcher Xavier Hernandez, allowing Boggs to score, Greenwell to move to third, and Evans to reach second. Burks then drove in his game-high fifth run on a sacrifice fly to deep center field. Toronto was now behind 10-0.

Courtesy The Topps Company.

Ernie Whitt's grand slam in the top of the ninth gave the Blue Jays an 11-10 lead, though it took 13 innings to seal the deal.

Facing a giant hill to climb, Lloyd Moseby and Ernie Whitt both walked to open the seventh inning. Boston manager Joe Morgan lifted Smithson, whose new pair of spikes had raised a blister on his right big toe, and brought in Bob Stanley, who walked Rance Mulliniks to load the bases. Nelson Liriano bounced into a 4-6-3 double play, scoring Moseby for Toronto's first run. Rookie Junior Felix, who hit a rare inside-the-park grand slam off Stanley two nights earlier, just the third ever at Fenway,[5] burned Stanley again, hitting a ground-rule double into the Boston bullpen to cut Boston's lead to 10-2.

Toronto further closed the gap in the eighth. After George Bell blooped a single to shallow center in front of a sliding Burks, McGriff lined a Stanley offering high off the left field wall, putting runners on second and third. Then Moseby singled to center to plate both runners. Whitt lined one to right field but Randy Kutcher, fielding his first chance of the game after replacing Evans, ran in and made a nice shoestring catch.

As Mulliniks stepped into the box, Canadian television viewers were informed on their screens that "one year ago today, the Blue Jays scored seven runs here in the top of the ninth inning to win 10-2." On this day, the Jays still needed six runs just to *tie* Boston. Mulliniks golfed a 2-and-1 pitch into left-center field, perfectly splitting the outfielders, and as the ball rolled to the wall, Moseby scored. Morgan slowly walked to the mound to relieve the ineffective Stanley, bringing in left-hander Rob Murphy.

Liriano kept things moving for Toronto, lining an opposite-field single to right to cash Mulliniks but Felix grounded out to end the inning. While Toronto was now within four runs, the Blue Jays were down to their last three outs.

Tony Fernandez led off the Toronto ninth with a high chopper that deflected off Murphy's glove for a leadoff infield single, prompting Morgan to call for his closer, Lee Smith. The hard-throwing veteran was struggling in 1989 with a 6.32 ERA in 15⅔ innings pitched.

Smith walked his first batter, Kelly Gruber, then left a fastball up to Bell, who ripped a double off the left-field scoreboard, driving in Fernandez and sending Gruber to third. Alarmingly for Boston, the best hitter in Toronto's lineup, McGriff, came to the plate representing the tying run. Smith threw mostly fastballs and struck out McGriff, but Smith continued to struggle with location, walking the next hitter, Moseby, on four pitches.

Whitt stepped in representing the go-ahead run. Despite the longshot odds, Whitt said, the whole team was confident: "For some reason, everyone on the bench felt that we were going to come back. Even in the eighth inning, being down by five runs, that we were going to win it."[6]

Smith started off with three pitches away. Ahead in the count 2-and-1, Whitt tried to keep things simple. "All I wanted was a base hit to keep the momentum going."[7] Smith came back with a fastball in the strike zone and Whitt, down on one knee, swung hard and launched the ball on a line just inside the right-field foul pole for a grand slam. "I wasn't thinking home run in that situation and Lee's their stopper and he's a power pitcher," Whitt said, explaining his approach. "I feel I'm a pretty good fastball hitter so I was looking [for a] fastball and he got it over the plate for me."[8]

As the ball disappeared into the crowd, Smith looked down at the ground, then looked up and sighed with a shocked expression of utter disbelief. The jeering crowd grew even louder as Smith walked off the field, relieved by former Toronto right-hander Dennis Lamp.

One hour ago, Boston was winning a laugher 10-0; now, in the ninth inning, the visitors were ahead 11-10. The Red Sox had never before, in their 89-year franchise history, frittered away a 10-run lead.[9]

In the bottom of the ninth, Toronto closer Tom Henke walked leadoff hitter Nick Esasky, who moved to second on a sacrifice. Esasky came home when Jody Reed fought off an 0-and-2 Henke fastball, dropping it into right-center field to tie the game. After Romero grounded out, moving the winning run to second, Henke intentionally walked Boggs, bringing reliever David Wells into the game to face pinch-hitter Marty Barrett.

Amazingly, Barrett battled Wells for 17 pitches, hitting 13 of them foul, including seven in a row, before grounding out to third, ending the inning. The throw from Gruber to McGriff took the first baseman into the baseline and as Barrett changed his running path, he suddenly tumbled in agony to the dirt with a ruptured right knee ligament. (Barrett later sued team doctor Arthur Pappas based on incomplete diagnostic disclosure.[10])

In extra innings, Lamp retired Toronto in order in the 10th and 11th while Boston got the winning run to third in the 10th before reliever Duane Ward struck out Esasky to end the threat.

Finally, in the 12th, Toronto went ahead again. Tom Lawless flared a leadoff single to right just past the infield dirt and advanced to second on a sacrifice. Felix drove Lamp's first pitch to him into a spectator walkway in the right-field seats for a two-run home run. Felix was 8-for-16 with 11 RBIs and three extra-base hits during the series. In the bottom of the 12th, Ward finished off the Red Sox with his third hitless inning, getting a generous called strike three on Kutcher to finish a wild and improbable comeback win.

Toronto manager Cito Gaston praised his team's perseverance. "You never want to give up," he said. "You never quit in this ballpark because you can score a lot of runs, and I tell you the truth, [my players] never quit."[1]

Incredibly, Toronto's victory was its 12th consecutive win in Fenway Park, a streak no other visiting club had ever achieved.[12]

The Red Sox were understandably stunned.

"This is the worst defeat of my managerial career in any league or city," said Joe Morgan succinctly.[13]

"That wasn't a pretty sight," said Smithson.[14]

"The ceiling just fell in," said Burks.[15]

Reed refused to fault the Boston bullpen and tipped his cap to Toronto's hitters. "Everything looked like it was under control then the floodgates broke. I'm not going to put the blame on anybody. You've got to give those guys credit. … They were battling for runs and then they got the big blow when Ernie hit the grand slam. … We lost as a team."[16]

Moseby was not surprised that Toronto rallied. "I can believe it, sure. I've lost ballgames like that. Baseball is a funny game. It's the turning point of our first half, I can tell you that."[17] Indeed, the series sweep elevated Toronto out of the division basement for good and the Blue Jays had added excitement heading home as they were due to open their new ballpark, SkyDome, the following night.

Sources

Besides the sources listed in the Notes, the author consulted Baseball-Reference. com, Retrosheet.org, and the following:

"Labatt's Blue Jays Baseball: Toronto Blue Jays at Boston Red Sox," CTV Television (Toronto, CFTO, June 4, 1989).

Notes

1   Andy Greene, "Flashback: Neil Young Unveils 'Rockin' in the Free World' at 1989 Seattle Gig," *Rolling Stone,* July 14, 2015. rollingstone.com/music/music-news/flashback-neil-young-unveils-rockin-in-the-free-world-at-1989-seattle-gig-158334/.

2   Thomas Usher, "Chinese Army Crushes Protest," *Toronto Star,* June 4, 1989: A1.

3   "Solidarity Confident on the Eve of Free Ballot," *Toronto Star,* June 4, 1989: A22.

4   Richard Gwyn, "Will the Wall Come Tumbling Down?" *Toronto Star,* June 4, 1989: A17.

5   Don Lenhardt (April 19, 1952) and Gary Geiger (August 8, 1961) both hit inside-the-park grand slams for the Red Sox at Fenway Park. Mike Greenwell hit the fourth inside-the-park grand slam at Fenway Park on September 1, 1990.

6   Larry Millson, "'Slamming' Jays Rise Up to Beat Sox," *Globe and Mail,* June 5, 1989: C1.

7   Dave Perkins, "What a Comeback by the Jays!" *Toronto Star,* June 5, 1989: D3.

8   *"Sky High! The Story of the 1989 Toronto Blue Jays,"* Major League Baseball Productions, 1989.

9   "Blow by Blow with the Red Sox," *Boston Globe,* June 5, 1989: 39.

10 Joseph Nocera, "Bitter Medicine," *Sports Illustrated,* 83, no. 20 (1995): 74-88.

11 Joe Burris, "Best Comes Last," *Boston Globe,* June 5, 1989: 39.

12 Burris. The 1954 Cleveland Indians won 11 consecutive games at Boston. Toronto swept another three-game series in Boston in August to run its streak to 15 straight wins at Fenway Park.

13 Mark Blaudschun, "From 10-0 to Nothing," *Boston Globe,* June 5, 1989: 35.

14 David Cataneo, "More Lore for Sox to Endure," *Boston Herald,* June 5, 1989: 92.

15 Cataneo.

16 Marvin Pave, "They Had a Sinking Feeling," *Boston Globe,* June 5, 1989: 39.

17 Mike Shalin, "Jays Prove No Lead Safe at Fenway," *Boston Herald,* June 5, 1989: 86.

ROUGH INNING FOR CARDINALS THIRD BASEMAN LEADS TO IMPROBABLE DODGERS COMEBACK

MAY 18, 1950: BROOKLYN DODGERS 9, ST. LOUIS CARDINALS 8, AT EBBETS FIELD, BROOKLYN

BY BRIAN M. FRANK

St. Louis third baseman Tommy Glaviano was having a solid start to the 1950 baseball season. Slotted in as the Cardinals' leadoff hitter, he was hitting .342 with an on-base percentage of .464. He'd made four errors in his 20 games at the hot corner, but no one could have foreseen the disastrous defensive inning that was about to befall him to help finish off one of the biggest comebacks in Brooklyn Dodgers history.

The Cardinals were looking to avoid being swept by Brooklyn, after well-pitched games by Preacher Roe and Don Newcombe led the Dodgers to victories in the first two games of the three-game series. What was about to transpire in the third game, is what Harold Burr of the *Brooklyn Daily Eagle* called "one of those games that might well be the making of one team and the ruination of the other."[1]

A pair of veteran southpaws battled in the series finale, as Brooklyn sent Joe Hatten, 1-2 with a 4.33 ERA, to the mound to face Howie Pollet, 3-3 with a 2.17 ERA, on a chilly, overcast 52-degree day at Ebbets Field.

Events did not go Hatten's way to start the game. Chuck Diering reached on an error by Dodgers third baseman Billy Cox with one out in the top of the first. He advanced to third when red-hot Stan Musial, who entered the game hitting .451, banged one off first baseman Gil Hodges' knee and into the grandstand for a ground-rule double. After Johnny Lindell was intentionally walked and Enos Slaughter popped out, Marty Marion singled Diering and Musial home to give St. Louis a 2-0 lead.

The Cardinals continued to chip away at Hatten as the game progressed. St. Louis scored another run on Diering's RBI double in the second inning. Hatten was

PEE WEE REESE
shortstop BROOKLYN DODGERS

Being shut out 8-0, the Dodgers scored four in the eighth and five in the ninth, with Pee Wee Reese involved during both innings.

fortunate to escape further damage when Slaughter lined out to left field with the bases loaded to end the frame. The Cardinals put together another rally in the fourth inning. Tommy Glaviano led off the inning with a home run. After the Redbirds put runners at first and third, Dodgers manager Burt Shotton pulled Hatten from the game and replaced him with right-hander Erv Palica. The first batter Palica faced, Marty Marion, hit a groundball that looked as though it would be the third out of the inning, but it got through Gil Hodges at first and two runs crossed the plate to put the Cardinals comfortably in front, 6-0.

St. Louis continued the onslaught in the sixth inning when Johnny Lindell blasted a two-run home run off Billy Loes, a 19-year-old reliever making his major-league debut. It was Lindell's first hit as a Cardinal after he had been purchased from the Yankees. The two-run shot gave the Cardinals a seemingly insurmountable 8-0 lead.

Meanwhile, Howie Pollet was making short work of the Dodgers. Through six innings, he'd allowed only two hits and three walks. However, in the seventh he began to show signs of tiring when he gave up singles to Duke Snider and Roy Campanella to start the inning. He was able to retire the next three batters and escape the inning without a Dodger crossing the plate. After seven innings, the Cardinals led 8-0, and as Dick Young wrote in the *New York Daily News*, "[T]he Brooks had nicked Howie Pollet for only four hits. They had looked more miserable than the weather. They hadn't hit, their pitching had been punk, and even their defense, which has been Brooklyn's matchless pride, had been butchered."[2]

The gloomy atmosphere for the Dodgers and their fans was amplified as rain started falling on Ebbets Field to start the eighth inning. Jim Russell led off the eighth with what looked to be a harmless single into left field. Jackie Robinson drilled a double to right and Carl Furillo sent a ball through the raindrops and into the left-field seats to cut the Cardinals' lead to 8-3. The Dodgers faithful rejoiced, as "the 17,579 fans, including Ladies Day guests and Knothole Kids started a mad clamor on a rising crescendo as the runs went clattering impossibly over the dish."[3] Hodges lined out to center field for the first out of the inning. Duke Snider singled and Campanella followed by drilling a ball that was caught by left fielder Lindell. Bruce Edwards, pinch-hitting in the pitcher's spot, lined a single to left and when the ball was bobbled by Lindell, Snider raced to third. That was the end of the line for Pollet. Dick Young wrote, "Seven straight

line drives flew off the Brooks bats. Rarely in his life has Pollet been hit so hard."[4]

The Cardinals' bullpen was shorthanded –as Ted Wilks was out with an elbow injury – so manager Eddie Dyer turned to Gerry Staley, who had a 5.35 ERA in seven games, to try to end the Dodgers' offensive outburst. Pee Wee Reese greeted the new hurler by rapping the ball through the left side of the infield, bringing home Snider and cutting the Cardinals' lead to 8-4. But with runners at first and second, Staley was able to avoid further damage by getting pinch-hitter Gene Hermanski to pop out for the final out of the inning.

Ralph Branca came out of the Dodgers bullpen in place of Rex Barney who'd thrown a shutout eighth, and retired the Cardinals in order in the ninth to keep the deficit at four runs heading into Brooklyn's final at-bat.

Rain was falling steadily as Jim Russell collected his third hit of the afternoon, a double into the right-field corner, to lead off the bottom of the ninth. Jackie Robinson cashed in Russell with another double into the right-field corner to cut the Cardinals lead to 8-5 and cause Dyer to pull Staley in favor of southpaw Al Brazle. Brazle retired Furillo on a popup for the inning's first out. Hodges then hit a bouncer to short and beat Marion's throw to first. Snider, after being behind 1-and-2 in the count, worked a walk to load the bases, and then catastrophe struck the Cardinals, specifically third baseman Tommy Glaviano.

Harold Burr wrote: "Fate decreed that the last three Dodgers should make (Glaviano) their target. It was raining steadily and hard, the ground under his spikes treacherous and the ball slippery, by way of excuse."[5] Roy Campanella stepped up to the plate representing the winning run. He hit a sharp ground ball to Glaviano, who fielded the ball cleanly and fired a wild throw to second base, forcing Red Schoendienst to come off the bag, and all hands were safe as Robinson scored to cut the lead to 8-6. Cloyd Boyer was brought in to replace Brazle and try to finish the game for St. Louis. He seemed to do his job when he induced pinch-hitter Eddie Miksis to hit a "high bouncer right at Glaviano."[6] Rather than throwing to second for what looked like "a certain force out at second and a probable double play," Glaviano fired home to try to force Hodges.[7] But the throw was once again well wide of the mark and catcher Del Rice had to "dive flat on his face for the save" as Hodges crossed the plate.[8]

Pee Wee Reese came up with the tying run at third and Campanella representing the winning run at second. Reese became the third consecutive batter to hit a grounder to Glaviano. Dick Young wrote: "This time, Tommy didn't throw wild. He didn't throw at all, because he never held the ball. He had planned to scoop it up, step on third, and fire to first – but in moving toward third, he let the ball zip through his legs and into left."[9] Ebbets Field erupted as the tying and winning runs crossed the plate. Roscoe McGowen reported in the *New York Times,* "The downpour of torn papers that fluttered down on the field when Campanella raced over the plate with that all-important run turned the drizzle into a snow storm."[10]

The improbable had happened as three straight balls hit to Glaviano ended up as errors, tying a major-league record for errors in a single inning.[11] Cardinals manager Eddie Dyer summed up his team's mood, saying: "That was the most bitter defeat of any I've had in the years I've managed."[12]

Brooklyn had managed only two hits through six innings, and trailed 8-0 through seven, but rallied for nine runs in the final two frames for an improbable victory. An afternoon that began slowly for the Dodgers suddenly changed in the eighth inning and ended with "a deluge of rain, runs, hits, and errors."[13]

Sources

In addition to the sources cited in the Notes, the author consulted Baseball-Reference.com and Retrosheet.org.

Notes

1 Harold C. Burr, "Glaviano Becomes Brooklyn's Man of the Week with 3 Bobbles," *Brooklyn Daily Eagle,* May 19, 1950: 19.

2 Dick Young, "Dodgers Overhaul Cards, 9-8, on 3 Glaviano Errors in 9th," *New York Daily News,* May 19, 1950: C20.

3 Burr.

4 Young.

5 Burr.

6 Young.

7 Bob Broeg, "Glaviano Goat of a Black Day," *St. Louis Post-Dispatch,* May 19, 1950: 10C.

8 Young.

9 Young.

10 Roscoe McGowen, "Dodgers Score 9 Runs in Last 2 Innings to Upset Cards," *New York Times,* May 19, 1950: 33.

11 McGowen.

12 Broeg: 8C.

13 Burr.

CLEVELAND BATTLES FROM 10-RUN DEFICIT TO DEFEAT RAYS

MAY 25, 2009:
CLEVELAND INDIANS 11,
TAMPA BAY RAYS 10,
AT PROGRESSIVE FIELD, CLEVELAND

BY JOSEPH WANCHO

The Tampa Bay Rays were the defending American League pennant winners in 2009. Just 11 years after their expansion season in 1998, the Rays ran through the gauntlet that is the American League East in the regular season, eclipsed Chicago and Boston in the playoffs, and were then crowned AL champs.

Cleveland catcher Victor Martinez hit a walkoff single to center producing the tying and winning run in a seven-run rally.

Courtesy The Topps Company.

The ultimate dream of a World Series championship ended with a thud as the Philadelphia Phillies defeated Tampa Bay in five games to win their first World Series since 1980.

The Rays started out the 2009 season with a 9-14 record in April and were relegated to cellar dwellers in the East. They won seven of 10 as they came to Cleveland for a four-game set beginning May 25 at Progressive Field. Tampa now stood at an even 23-23 but were only four games behind first-place Boston.

The Rays got some bad news when they got to Cleveland. Starting shortstop Akinori Iwamura was injured in a play the day before. Iwamura was taken out on a hard slide at second base by Florida's Chris Coghlan. The result was a ruptured ACL, and he would be lost for the season.

The Indians (17-28) were in the basement of the AL Central, 8½ games behind front-running Detroit. Cleveland lost three of four to Tampa Bay at Tropicana Field the previous week. It looked as if matters would be getting worse before they got better for manager Eric Wedge's Indians.

A Memorial Day crowd of 20,929 made its way into the ballpark. Perhaps they were not expecting much given their team's woes. But then again, that's why they play the games.

The pitching matchup for the evening affair matched Tampa Bay's David Price (first start) and the Tribe's Fausto Carmona (2-4, 5.74 ERA). Price, a southpaw, had been recalled from Triple-A Durham (1-4, 3.93 ERA). He had pitched well out of the bullpen for the Rays in the previous year's playoff run. But now he was thrust into the starting rotation, where expectations of his abilities were much higher. Carmona, who won 19 games in 2007 for the Indians, had a great sinker, but not much else, and once batters learned to lay off his meal-ticket pitch, he got knocked around. In 2008 he was 8-7 with a 5.44 ERA, and thus far the 2009 season was not treating him any better.

The Rays proved to be a rude guest. After a scoreless first inning, they hung five runs on the scoreboard in the second inning. Carmona walked the first four batters (Carlos Peña, Willy Aybar, Ben Zobrist, and Gabe Gross) in the second inning. Gross was credited with an RBI and the Rays led 1-0. But that was only momentarily. After Carmona struck out Dioner Navarro, Reid Brignac singled to right field, knocking in Aybar and Zobrist. Gross raced to third base.

Melvin Upton, the Rays' leadoff hitter, laid a bunt down the first-base line. Gross scored, Upton was safe at first base and Brignac moved to second. Carl Crawford singled to right field, Brignac scored, and Upton went to third. Carmona walked Evan Longoria, his fifth walk in the inning, and the bases were reloaded for the Rays.

With the Rays leading 5-0 and threatening to score more, Wedge removed Carmona. "He's been pitching for a long time," the manager said of Carmona. "He's got to be better than that."[1] Relief pitcher Jensen Lewis was summoned from the bullpen and he retired Peña and Aybar to end the frame.

The halt in scoring was only temporary, as Gross unloaded a two-run home run in the top of the third inning off Jensen. It was the third homer of the year for Gross as the Rays' lead grew to 7-0.

The Rays were far from finished: Lewis walked Crawford and Longoria to start the fourth inning. A single by Peña scored Crawford and sent Longoria to third. Wedge brought in Rich Rundles (his only appearance in the season) from the bullpen to relieve Lewis. After Aybar lined out, Zobrist doubled Longoria home. Gross walked to load the bases, and Navarro was hit by an errant pitch from Rundles to force in Peña. The Rays were up 10-0.

A two-run homer by Ryan Garko in the bottom of the fourth put the Indians on the board. The comeback trail was long as they trailed 10-2. But Price did not make it out of the inning; two consecutive walks followed Garko's bomb. Rays manager Joe Maddon brought in Lance Cormier. "It all starts with starting pitching," said Price. "I've got to do a better job than that. Averaging 10 pitches an out is not good enough."[2]

Jeremy Sowers entered the game for Cleveland in the top of the fifth inning. The southpaw kept the Rays

from tallying more runs. In the bottom of the eighth, the Indians inched a little closer. On the mound for the Rays was Dale Thayer. Shin-Soo Choo, Mark DeRosa, and Garko hit consecutive singles off Thayer. Matt LaPorta bounced into a 5-4-3 double play, and Choo scored. Ben Francisco followed with a single to plate DeRosa and the Rays' lead was six runs, 10-4.

Thayer was still on the hill in the bottom of the ninth. But he soon found himself in a jam. Grady Sizemore led off with a walk. After Victor Martinez popped out, Jhonny Peralta singled and runners were on first and third. Maddon went to his bullpen and brought in Randy Choate.

Choo hit a grounder to Brignac at short, but a throwing error scored Sizemore and the Indians now had runners on second and third. In came Grant Balfour for the Rays and he got DeRosa to line to third for the second out. But Garko smacked his second home run of the game, a three-run shot to left field, and the Rays' lead shrank to 10-8. Asdrubal Cabrera pinch-hit for LaPorta and walked.

Maddon trudged to the mound once more and called for Jason Isringhausen. But the one-time NL saves leader could not find the plate. Consecutive walks to Francisco, Jamey Carroll, and Sizemore forced in Cabrera and the Indians trailed by just a run, 10-9.

But not for long. Victor Martinez singled to center field to score Francisco and Carroll and the Indians came all the way back from a 10-0 deficit to win the game, 11-10. "I definitely was not going to be an easy out for him, especially when he's having trouble throwing strikes," said Martinez. "I went up with a plan and executed it. He gave me a pitch I was looking for."[3]

Sowers (1-2) pitched five innings of scoreless relief to record his first win. "Jeremy gave us a chance to get back in the game," said Wedge. "He pitched very well."[4]

"Just a bad night. I couldn't find the plate," said Isringhausen. "It's inexcusable to walk three guys like that: I can't remember the last time I did that. I'd rather give up three home runs than give them free passes. It's just a shame how well we came out and hit the ball and let it slip away from us."[5]

Cleveland swept the Rays in the four-game series. But neither club factored into their divisions' postseason races. Tampa Bay (84-78) finished in third place in the East, 19 games behind first-place New York. Cleveland (65-97) finished tied with Kansas City for fourth in the Central Division, 21½ games behind first-place Minnesota.

Iwamura's injured ACL turned out to be strained and not ruptured as originally thought. He did return to the Rays in late August. But he missed three months of the season.

Sources

In addition to the sources cited in the Notes, the author accessed Baseball-Reference.com and Retrosheet.org.

Notes

1   Dennis Manoloff, "Greeting Win with Open Arms," *Cleveland Plain Dealer*, May 26, 2009: D1.

2   Joe Smith, "Price Chides Self over Short, Wild '09 Debut," *St. Petersburg Times*, May 26, 2009: 4C.

3   Manoloff.

4   Manoloff.

5   Joe Smith, "Rays Reach Peak of Embarrassment," *St. Petersburg Times*, May 26, 2009: 1C.

PHILLIES STUN PIRATES, 12-11

JUNE 23, 1961:
PHILADELPHIA PHILLIES 12,
PITTSBURGH PIRATES 11,
AT FORBES FIELD, PITTSBURGH

BY RALPH CAOLA

The Pirates were fresh off winning the 1960 World Series in one of the most exciting games ever. The good feeling bled over for a while; on May 24, 1961, they were 20-13, in second place, only one game out of first. But then they lost five in a row, fell into fourth place, and entered the June 23 game with a record of 32-27, six games out.

The Phillies, on the other hand, were fresh off finishing in last place. Terrible as usual, they came into the game having lost seven in a row; earlier in the season, they had lost 10 straight. Their record was 18-40 and they were in last place, 19½ games out.

The Pirates attacked future Hall of Famer Robin Roberts in the bottom of the first. With one out, Dick Groat doubled to left[1] and scored when Bob Skinner tripled to right-center. Pittsburgh's cleanup hitter, Dick Stuart, reached on an error by third baseman Charley Smith as Skinner held at third. When Roberto Clemente doubled to right, Skinner scored and Stuart moved to third. With first base open, Roberts intentionally walked Don Hoak to load the bases. The strategy worked when Don Leppert grounded into a 5-4-3 double play. The Pirates led 2-0.

Bill Mazeroski opened the Pirates' half of the second with a single up the middle. Pitcher Joe Gibbon sacrificed Mazeroski to second and Mazeroski scored when Bill Virdon followed with a single up the middle to increase the Pirates' lead to 3-0.

The Pirates continued to pound Roberts in the third as Stuart and Clemente started the inning with doubles. Atypically, Stuart stopped at third on Clemente's two-bagger. Again Roberts intentionally walked Hoak to load the bases and face Leppert. Again the

move was successful as Stuart was forced at home on Lepper's grounder.

But the success was temporary as Phillies catcher Jimmie Coker allowed a passed ball that permitted Clemente to score and the other runners to advance. Mazeroski drove in Hoak with a sacrifice fly. When Roberts served up a run-scoring triple to pitcher Gibbon, Phillies manager Gene Mauch yanked Roberts

Charlie Lau entered the game in the sixth and hit the single that won it in the 11th, 7-6.

Courtesy The Topps Company.

57

and replaced him with Jack Baldschun. If allowing six runs in 2⅔ innings didn't seal Roberts's fate, giving up an extra-base hit to the opposing pitcher surely did. The inning ended with the Pirates ahead 6-0.

The Pirates were finally held scoreless in the fourth, but in the fifth, they jumped on Baldschun's replacement, Jim Owens, with three more runs to build a 9-0 lead. Clemente and Hoak started the inning with singles. After Leppert struck out, Mazeroski singled, scoring Clemente and moving Hoak to third. Gibbon reached on an error by Coker that scored Hoak. Virdon followed with a single to center to drive in Mazeroski. Owens got out of the inning when Groat grounded into a second-to-short-to-first double play.

Through five innings, the Phillies had mustered only three singles and two walks and the probability that they would win dropped below one percent.[2] But they fought back in the sixth. With two outs, Pancho Herrera singled to right and Don Demeter homered to left and the Phillies were on the scoreboard, albeit trailing 9-2.

But the Phillies gave those two runs back in the bottom of the seventh. With Dallas Green on the mound and one out, Walt Moryn, pinch-hitting for Gibbon, singled to center field and Virdon singled to right. After Groat was hit by a pitch, Skinner singled Moryn and Virdon home and Pittsburgh's lead was back to nine, 11-2.

The Phillies launched another effort at a comeback in the eighth. With the Pirates' Clem Labine pitching in relief of Gibbon, Tony Taylor led off with an infield single. Pinch-hitting for right fielder Ken Walters, Tony Gonzalez singled to center. Herrera walked, loading the bases, and Demeter ripped a double to left, scoring Taylor and Gonzalez.

Unhappy with Labine's short performance, Pirates manager Danny Murtaugh replaced him with Roy Face. But Charley Smith cracked a single to right-center, scoring Herrera and Demeter and cutting Pittsburgh's lead to 11-6. Face then faced three consecutive pinch-hitters – Johnny Callison, Elmer Valo, and Clay Dalrymple. He struck out Callison, walked Valo, and got Dalrymple to hit into a double play, escaping without any further scoring.

After the Pirates were retired in order in the bottom of the eighth, the Phillies were losing 11-6 and down to their last three outs. But Bobby Del Greco, Taylor, Gonzalez, and Herrera singled and suddenly the Phillies had closed to 11-8 and had the tying run at the plate. Earl Francis relieved Face and, coincidentally, the Pirates' defense fell apart.

Demeter hit a potential double-play grounder to shortstop Johnny Logan, but the ball got stuck in Logan's glove, leaving time only for the force at second as Gonzalez took third. Again the Pirates failed to execute a possible double play, this time a game-ending one, when Smith grounded to third baseman Hoak, who threw wildly to second as Gonzalez scored, Demeter took second, and Smith, first.

With no position players left to pinch-hit, pitcher Ken Lehman batted for himself and tapped the ball inches in front of home plate. Leppert tried to get the force at second, but heaved the ball into center field as Demeter scored the Phillies' 10th run and Smith went to third. When Bobby Malkmus hit a sacrifice fly, Smith scored and the game was tied, 11-11.[3]

With Lehman on first and two outs, the Pirates seemed on the verge of getting out of the inning when Dalrymple popped a lazy foul behind home. But their nightmare continued when Leppert dropped the ball. Given a second chance, Dalrymple got the count to 3-and-2 and singled to left-center with Lehman running on the pitch. Skinner fielded the ball, but slipped and fell as he threw, causing a wild peg to cutoff man Logan. By the time Logan's relay reached the plate, Lehman was sliding home, safe by an eyelash, and the Phillies took the lead, 12-11.[4]

When the shell-shocked Pirates went down without a fight in their half of the ninth, the Phillies had a stunning victory.

For the Pirates, Clemente and Virdon each had three hits and Skinner drove in three runs. The Phillies got three hits from Taylor and four RBIs from Demeter.

In the clubhouse, the Phillies enjoyed some long-awaited laughs. Lehman, who won his first major-league game in more than three years, poked fun at his batting and baserunning. "That ball I hit came back and was laying on home plate. I thought it was foul. Then the catcher picked it up and I thought, 'Lord, what if it winds up a double play to end the game? 'The slide? Well, that was a work of art. Anybody else would have been out, but I tiptoed in there."[5]

None of the last four runs scored by the Phillies were earned, due to four errors, two by Leppert. Leppert compounded the effect of his miserable fielding by going 0-for-5 and leaving 10 runners on base.

A 29-year-old rookie, Leppert reached the major leagues after six years in the minors. He had played his first game just five days before and, on the first pitch he saw, hit a home run. After two seasons with Pittsburgh, he was traded to the Washington Senators.

In 1963 Leppert got off to a great start, hitting .387 in late April and making the American League All-Star team. Leppert's early-season streak included a game in which he hit three home runs, leading to the distinction of being one of only five players since 1904 who hit three home runs in a game and as few as 15 in a career.[6]

After hitting only .156 in 1964, Leppert retired and later became a coach, for which most readers remember him. He enjoyed an 18-year career, coaching for the Pirates, Blue Jays, and Astros, from 1968 through 1985.

Despite their dramatic win, the Phillies' season was pathetic. Not only did they, for the fourth consecutive year, finish in last place, they spent all but 13 days there. They won only 47 games and ended up 46 games behind the first-place Cincinnati Reds and 17 behind the seventh-place Chicago Cubs.

The next season, the Phillies improved significantly, winning 81 games and increasing their winning percentage 198 points, the sixth most in major-league history.[7]

The Pirates played the rest of the season eight games below .500 and finished 75-79, in sixth place, 18 games out of first. Clemente, however, was brilliant: He led the NL with a batting average of .351 and finished fourth in voting for Most Valuable Player.

In the 12 years from 1946 through 1957, the Pirates finished above .500 only once. After winning the 1960 World Series, they spent the following decade as an above-average team, then won the Series again in 1971.

Sources

In addition to the sources cited in the Notes, the author relied on Baseball-Reference.com.

Notes

1 The box score and play-by-play of the game can be found at baseball-reference.com/boxes/PIT/PIT196106230.shtml.

2 See the Win Probability Chart at baseball-reference.com/boxes/PIT/PIT196106230.shtml.

3 Stan Hochman, "Everybody's Laughing but the Pirates," *Philadelphia Daily News*, June 24, 1961: 30.

4 Jack Hernon, "Phils' 'Nightmare Ninth' Nips Bucs, 12-11," *Pittsburgh Post-Gazette*, June 24, 1961: 9.

5 Hochman, "Everybody's Laughing but the Pirates."

6 The others are Merv Connors (of a career total of 8), Bill Glynn (career total 10), Tuffy Rhodes (total 13), and Jose Ortiz (total 14).

7 mcubed.net/mlb/bwimp.shtml. Accessed October 17, 2019.

A DOUBLE WALK-OFF DOUBLEHEADER

JUNE 18, 1961:
BOSTON RED SOX 13,
WASHINGTON SENATORS 12
(GAME ONE OF DOUBLEHEADER),
AT FENWAY PARK, BOSTON

BY BILL NOWLIN

Talk about a spree, in which one player had a huge impact in three consecutive games. The second of the three games was the greatest comeback in Red Sox history.

The Boston Red Sox entered the first game of the June 18, 1961, doubleheader with a dead-even record of 30-30. The sixth-place Washington Senators were right behind them at 30-32. After the first 4½ innings, Washington led 5-2. Red Sox starter Ike Delock was replaced by a pinch-hitter in the bottom of the fifth. Boston scored one more run, when Senators starter Carl Mathias hit Don Buddin with the bases loaded. Buddin homered his next time up, in the seventh. The score stood Senators 7, Red Sox 5 after eight innings. No one would have predicted how the rest of the Sunday doubleheader would unfold.

Red Sox reliever Ted Wills replaced Billy Muffett in the top of the ninth, coming in with runners on second and third and one out. Gene Woodling singled for Washington to give the Senators an insurance run. Pinch-runner Chuck Hinton stole second and Wills walked Dale Long. Willie Tasby then hit a grand slam into the Red Sox bullpen to put the game out of sight. It was Washington 12, Boston 5. The left-handed rookie, Mathias, was still pitching for the Senators. He had given up only five hits. Manager Mickey Vernon was likely feeling pretty good.

Vic Wertz led off the bottom of the ninth for the Red Sox. He grounded out to the first baseman, Mathias covering the bag. Buddin, having himself a decent day, singled to right field, but Billy Harrell pinch-hit for Wills and struck out. One more out and the game was over, leaving manager Pinky Higgins of the Red Sox hoping to win the second game for a split.

Chuck Schilling singled to center field, Buddin to second. Then Carroll Hardy singled to right-center, scoring Buddin while Schilling took third. It was 12-6, but there were still two outs. Gary Geiger walked, loading the bases. Vernon brought in Dave Sisler to close things out for Mathias.

Sisler, however, had trouble finding the plate. He walked Jackie Jensen, forcing in a run. 12-7. Then he walked Frank Malzone, forcing in another run. 12-8. Now, improbably, the tying run was at the plate, but it would take a grand slam for one batter to tie the game. Catcher Jim Pagliaroni was up. Maybe he'd draw a base on balls, too, and close the gap a little more? He was 0-for-4 so far, with a strikeout, two groundouts, and a liner to center field. He'd come into the weekend batting .230, but had hit a two-run pinch-hit home run the day before, on Saturday in the bottom of the sixth, providing the two runs that gave Boston a 6-5 win over Washington. Pagliaroni had 17 RBIs in mid-June and had hit five home runs. It was his first full season in the majors.

Sisler finally found the plate, pitching to Pagliaroni. He put one right over that Pags hammered (on a 2-and-1 count) into the net atop the wall in left field. The tying run that had been at the plate had indeed scored.

It was 12-12. Maybe headed for extra innings.

Sisler walked Wertz. Vernon had seen enough. Marty Kutyna was waved in from the bullpen. Buddin singled, Wertz to second. Then Higgins had a pinch-hitter bat for his pinch-hitter. He went with Russ Nixon, who pinch-hit for Harrell. And he had the fleeter Pete Runnels run for Wertz at second base. Nixon singled to right field, to the first-base side and two inches from second baseman Chuck Cottier's

Courtesy of the Boston Red Sox.

Jim Pagliaroni's grand slam tied the first game in the bottom of the ninth. Then he homered in the bottom of the 13th to win the day's second game.

glove; Runnels ran across the plate and the Boston Red Sox had wrapped up what remains the statistically greatest comeback game in team history. Or, as *Boston Record* sports cartoonist Bob Coyne dubbed it "one of the greatest comebacks since they invented the boomerang."[1] The Red Sox had been down by seven runs with two outs in the bottom of the ninth inning, and yet won the game.

Manager Higgins said, "It just doesn't happen, but it did. Have I ever seen anything like it before? Not that I can remember. Not with two out and one on. It's tough for them; it really is. I really feel for them. That just doesn't happen."[2]

"Sisler doesn't have much of a slider," Pagliaroni said after the game. "When I saw it coming, I just took a rip and hoped."[3]

THE DAY'S SECOND GAME

There was still another game to come. The Red Sox held a 3-0 lead after the first two innings and a 5-2 lead after the first five. But Sox starter Gene Conley gave up a pair of home runs – a two-run homer by Jim King in the seventh and a solo homer by Willie Tasby in the eighth – and the Senators tied it. Tom Sturdivant took over in relief for the Senators and pitched no-hit ball for the seventh, eighth, and ninth. The game went into extra innings.

Sturdivant continued pitching no-hit ball, in the 10th, 11th, and 12th. Mike Fornieles, who had relieved Conley, also worked six innings of long relief for Boston. He gave up a single in the eighth and a single in the 10th, but neither resulted in a run.

In the bottom of the 13th inning, Jim Pagliaroni was scheduled to lead off. At this point, Sturdivant had retired 11 batters in a row. Once again, Pag hit one into the netting. The pitch had been, he said, "a fast ball, little better than knee high and on the inside of the plate."[4]

Pagliaroni was 1-for-10 for the day when he came up to bat in the bottom of the 13th inning in the second game. Over the course of the two games, being 2-for-11, he had seen his batting average drop from .236 to .231. But he'd hit three key home runs in three consecutive games. Obviously thrilled, he cautioned a writer not to get too carried away. "Hey, don't get too excited. This may be only a spree."[5]

This was essentially the first year in two decades that the Red Sox were playing without Ted Williams. And Carl Yastrzemski hadn't established himself yet as a solid successor. Jim Pagliaroni's showing for three games in a row was a welcome tonic to Red Sox fans. Naturally, they hoped he would build a career that endured.

Pagliaroni joked with writers after the day's games: "The next time I bat against that team I'd better wear a coat of armor to the plate. They'll surely be looking to knock me on my haunches."[6]

Attendance was 17,645. Despite the 25 runs scored in the first game, the time of game was 2:47.

Additional items:

By season's end, Pagliaroni had 16 home runs with 58 RBIs. Over the course of his 11 seasons in the majors, he hit 90 homers. The mid-June 1961 burst was indeed a spree.

The two wins boosted the Red Sox into fourth place.

The team had nominally played three games on June 18, losing the first. In the annual Red Sox Father and Son Game which preceded the doubleheader, the Sons crushed the Fathers, 14-0. Pagliaroni was 23 at the time and had no children. He did not figure in the scoring.

Sources

In addition to the sources cited in the Notes, the author also consulted Baseball-Reference.com and Retrosheet.org.

Notes

[1] See the game story and accompanying cartoon. Murray Kramer, "PAG – Slam Wins First, 13-12; HR Tips Nats in 13th, 6-5," *Boston Record*, July 19, 1961: 20.

[2] Bill Fuchs, "Senators Wake Up in Sixth After Nightmare Weekend," *Evening Star* (Washington), July 19, 1961: 14.

[3] Larry Claflin, "Sox 7½ Off Top but Hit Road Hex," *Boston American*, July 19, 1961: 8.

[4] Henry McKenna, "Pag Belts Ruin Nats, 13-12, 6-5," *Boston Herald*, July 19, 1961: 25.

[5] Bill Liston," Pag Gets Top Mileage at Bat," *Boston Traveler*, July 19, 1961: 31.

[6] Clif Keane, "Vernon Out-Guessed Himself to Set Up 8-run Sox 9th," *Boston Globe*, July 19, 1961: 25.

ANGELS SCORE SEVEN IN NINTH AND BEAT BLUE JAYS IN 10TH

APRIL 15, 1994:
CALIFORNIA ANGELS 14,
TORONTO BLUE JAYS 13 (10 INNINGS),
AT ANAHEIM STADIUM, ANAHEIM

BY MADISON MCENTIRE

Those fans among the 20,413 at the Angels-Blue Jays game on April 15, 1994, who left after the seventh inning must have been shocked when they eventually heard the final score. Through seven innings, California led Toronto, 6-3, in what could be describe as a typical major-league game, but over the next two innings the teams combined for 17 runs before the Angels pushed a run across in the bottom of the 10th for a wild 14-13 win.

Four days earlier, the Angels had staged a wild rally in the bottom of the ninth against Cleveland in which, trailing 9-1 with two outs and no one on, they scored five runs and had the tying run at the plate only to fall short when Bo Jackson struck out swinging to end the game.

The Blue Jays and Angels were each playing their 11th game of the season when they met at Anaheim Stadium. California had captured the first game of the season between the teams the previous evening by a 6-4 score and entered this game with a record of 5-5, while Toronto was 6-4.

The game started slowly and was scoreless after two innings as veteran Dave Stewart, seeking his 161st career win and his third of the season, battled against 21-year-old Brian Anderson, who was after his second major-league win. In the top of the third, the Blue Jays scored first on a two-out single by Devon White that scored Ed Sprague, who had walked and advanced to third on a pickoff throwing error by Anderson.

Foreshadowing things to come, California responded with a rally in the bottom half of the frame. Greg Myers led off with a single to left and with one out Gary Disarcina walked. Both runners moved up when

Chad Curtis grounded out to the catcher, Pat Borders, and then a single by Dwight Smith gave the Angels a 2-1 lead. Tim Salmon followed with a homer to make it 4-1.

In the fourth, Eduardo Perez homered to increase the Angels' lead to 5-1.

Harold Reynolds scored the first run of the Angels, then came up to bat again and doubled in two to tie the game.

63

Toronto trimmed the lead in the sixth with RBI doubles from Paul Molitor and John Olerud. In the bottom half, Perez slammed his second homer of the game to put the Angels up 6-3.

After a scoreless seventh inning, the game became a high-scoring affair. Scott Lewis, who had pitched the seventh in relief of Anderson, allowed a double to White and a walk to Molitor to start the eighth. When Joe Carter reached on an error by third baseman Damion Easley with one out, Bob Patterson came in and gave up a single to Olerud before striking out rookie Carlos Delgado. Mike Butcher entered in relief and immediately gave up a two-run double to Sprague and an RBI single to Borders as the Blue Jays built an 8-6 lead.

In the top of the ninth, the Blue Jays seemingly put the game out of reach when they plated five more runs to increase their lead to 13-6. Butcher gave up singles to White and Alomar and, following Alomar's steal of second, a two-run single to Molitor. Bill Sampen relieved Butcher but didn't fare any better as he gave up a single to Olerud and a three-run home run to Delgado. The blast was part of a hot start for Delgado, his seventh homer and 15th RBI of the season in just his 40th at-bat, but he would homer just twice more before being sent down to Triple-A Syracuse in early June.[1]

With the Angels down six runs with three outs to go, Myers led off with a single to right, Harold Reynolds walked, and Disarcina singled to third to fill the bases against Mike Timlin, who had taken over for Stewart to start the eighth inning. After Curtis was called out looking, Jim Edmonds, who had replaced Smith in left field to start the eighth, slapped a single to left to score Myers. Salmon walked to force in Reynolds and bring Todd Stottlemyre into the game to pitch for Toronto. Chili Davis greeted the new hurler with a base hit to plate Disarcina, and Easley followed with a single to chase home Edmonds. Perez lined a sacrifice fly to left field for his third RBI of the game, to bring home Salmon and make the score 13-11.

Duane Ward, Toronto's closer and the AL leader with 45 saves in 1993, would normally have been called on to quash the Angels rally but he had been placed on the disabled list earlier in the month with tendinitis in his bicep and would miss the entire season.[2]

The Angels were down to their final out when Jackson was called on to pinch-hit for Myers and walked to reload the bases. The 11th batter of the inning was Reynolds, who hammered a ball over the head of Carter in right that bounced into the stands for a ground-rule double.[3] Davis and Easley scored to tie the game but Rex Hudler, running for Jackson, was forced by rule to stop at third base. Angels manager Buck Rodgers said later, "If Reynolds doesn't hit the ball so hard, we win it then and there."[4] With Reynolds on third as the winning run, Disarcina grounded out to shortstop and sent the game to extra innings.

Craig Lefferts took over on the mound for California to start the 10th and quickly retired Alex Gonzalez on a grounder to short and White on a close play on a grounder to third. Alomar and Molitor each singled to put the go-ahead run in scoring position but Lefferts kept Toronto off the scoreboard by getting Carter to line out to left field.

Scott Brow was the Blue Jays' choice to pitch the home half of the 10th. After striking out Curtis (who finished 0-for-6, the only Angels starter without a hit) and Edmonds, he gave up an infield single to Salmon and a walk to Davis. Easley stepped in the box and sent the crowd home happy when he lined a single to left field to score Salmon with the winning run and atone for his error in the eighth inning which allowed Toronto to score four unearned runs.

Toronto manager Cito Gaston would not be around to see the ending, having been ejected in the top of the 10th for arguing and making contact with first-base umpire Rick Reed after a close play at first base. He eventually served a three-game suspension.[5]

The winning pitcher was Lefferts, who picked up the 58th and final victory of his 12-year career, in which he appeared in 696 games. The loss went to Brow, the second of his four career losses.

Rodgers attributed the comeback in part to the Angels no longer being intimidated by the two-time-defending World Series champs, citing a bench-clearing brawl between the teams from the previous June 2 in which Easley was ejected. "Last year, we were a little intimidated by that club, and we had to have a brawl to get rid of it. But now, there's no way that we are intimidated by them. In fact, we enjoy playing them."[6]

"It was quiet in the dugout when we came up in the ninth," Easley explained. "Buck said, 'Let's have some good at-bats and let's see what happens.' Everyone had great at-bats, and this is the way it turned out."[7]

The comeback tied the largest in Angels team history, previously accomplished on August 29, 1986, when Dick Schofield capped an eight-run ninth inning against Detroit with a game-ending grand slam.[8] Schofield, now a utility infielder for Toronto, sat watching the Angels comeback from the opposing dugout.

The 14 runs scored by the Angels were the most runs Toronto allowed all season and the most runs California scored in a game in 1994. (They also scored 14 on July 30 at Texas.) It would be more than 14 years before the Angels would again allow 13 or more runs in game in which they won (in a 15-13 victory at Texas on September 19, 2008).[9]

The dramatic victory put the Angels a half-game up in the standings of the newly realigned American League West. Despite a record of 47-68, they were only 5½ games back when the season ended on August 11 due to the players strike. Toronto finished 55-60, but 16 games back in the stronger AL East.

Sources

In addition to the references cited in the Notes, the author consulted Baseball-Reference.com and Retrosheet.org.

Notes

1   *The Sporting News*, June 20, 1994: 32.

2   *Longview* (Washington) *Daily News*, April 16, 1994: 16.

3   John Weyler, "A Mission Impossible?: Not for Angels," *Los Angeles Times,* April 16, 1994: C1.

4   Weyler.

5   Associated Press, "7 Back, Angels Stage Team's Biggest Rally," *Washington Post*, April 16,1994: G4.

6   Associated Press.

7   Associated Press.

8   Weyler.

9   Bill Plunkett, "Angels Are Most Offensive in Win," *Orange County Register* (Anaheim, California), September 20, 2008.

BREWERS TREAT EX-MATE HENRY POORLY IN 10-9 COMEBACK WIN

MAY 22, 2000:
MILWAUKEE BREWERS 10,
HOUSTON ASTROS 9
(FIRST GAME OF DOUBLEHEADER),
AT MILWAUKEE COUNTY STADIUM, MILWAUKEE

By Michael Trzinski

Doug Henry returned to Milwaukee County Stadium's visitors locker room for the sixth time in late May 2000 since being traded from Milwaukee to the New York Mets six years earlier. He had pitched well in his previous outings as a visitor to County Stadium, compiling an ERA of 1.69 over 5⅓ innings against his former mates.

He would not be so lucky on May 22, 2000.

The California native had pitched for the Brewers from 1991 to 1994, racking up 61 saves during his tenure in Milwaukee, including 29 saves in 1992. Henry had saved 44 games in his first two seasons with the Brewers and appeared to be on his way to stardom.

But all good things must come to an end, and Henry was traded to the Mets before the calendar flipped to December in 1994 in exchange for players to be named later who turned out to be Fernando Vina and Javier Gonzalez. Vina showed that he was a good player for Milwaukee for five years, including an All-Star campaign in 1998.

Henry bounced around the majors after being traded to the Mets, playing for four teams in seven years, and finished his career with 82 saves, managing only 21 saves after his time in Milwaukee.

As Henry and his Houston teammates strolled into the visiting clubhouse on May 22, their team was dwelling in the cellar of the National League Central Division with a record of 15-26, riding a five-game losing streak.

The Brewers weren't much better, languishing in fourth place in the NL Central with a ledger of 17-25.

Fewer than 4,000 fans were on hand to watch the two squads play in the first game of the makeup doubleheader, caused by two rainouts the week before.

The doubleheader was announced with just three days' notice, leading to the tiny crowd and cheap ticket prices. Milwaukee sold bleacher seats for $1, and though the team was charging $10 for the best seats, fans who paid for any seat were allowed to move up to a better seat.[1]

It was a chilly, windy day, with the thermometer registering 58 degrees at the 1:05 P.M. start time, with winds blowing at a gusty 15 MPH from the right-field side toward the left-field line.

Normally, a day like this would be detrimental to offensive efforts, as batters don't like "bees in the handles" of the bats, as players will speak of hitting when the weather is less than optimal.

But the two teams combined for 19 runs on a crazy, raw, and windy day.

The Astros took a first-inning lead on a leadoff triple by Roger Cedeño and a sacrifice fly by Craig Biggio off Brewers starter Steve Woodard.

Not to be outdone, the Brewers came back with two runs in the bottom of the inning. After Jeromy Burnitz and Charlie Hayes reached with two-out singles, Lyle Mouton banged a double down the left-field line to make it 2-1.

Houston took a 4-2 lead in the top of the third on a three-run homer by Richard Hidalgo, his 13th of the season.

It remained 4-2 until the top of the eighth, and then the game got a little crazy.

Juan Acevedo took over for Woodard in the eighth and gave up a leadoff double to Ken Caminiti but got two quick outs.

Then the roof caved in: The Astros scored three runs on two singles, two walks, and an error to take a 7-2 lead.

Henry came into the contest in the bottom of the eighth, threw just 10 pitches to get three outs, and took his Houston squad to the top of the ninth still holding a 7-2 lead.

Hector Ramirez took the slab for the Brewers in the top of the ninth and mixed two outs with two walks before former Brewer Bill Spiers drove in both runners with a two-bagger to right-center, giving Houston a seemingly insurmountable 9-2 lead with just three outs left for the home team.

Henry sauntered to the mound for the home ninth with a seven-run lead. But he failed to claim the save and he didn't even finish the inning.

Burnitz walked and Hayes singled, then Mouton doubled to score Burnitz. José Hernandez doubled, scoring Hayes and Mouton, to make it 9-5. That blow chased Henry in favor of Jose Cabrera.

After a wild pitch, Marquis Grissom lined a single to left to score Hernandez.

Astros 9, Brewers 6.

At that point, ace reliever Billy Wagner came into to close out the contest. Wagner – who would see his season end in the middle of June with a torn flexor tendon in his pitching arm – walked Raul Casanova before striking out James Mouton and Ronnie Belliard to put the Brewers down to their last out.

With their backs truly against the wall, Milwaukee cut into the lead when Mark Loretta singled Grissom home to make it 9-7.

After a wild pitch, Burnitz pulled a single to right, scoring Casanova and Loretta and tying the contest, 9-9. Hayes grounded out to end the inning, which featured seven runs on six hits.

David Weathers came in to pitch the 10th inning for Milwaukee and put up a goose egg, allowing only a scratch leadoff single to Cedeño and an intentional pass to Caminiti with two outs.

It didn't take long for the Brewers to get on the board in the bottom of the 10th. Joe Slusarski took over on the mound for Houston and leadoff batter Lyle Mouton popped out to Jeff Bagwell near the tarp in foul territory on the first-base side for the first out, but then it was time for José Hernandez.

Courtesy The Topps Company.

His 10th-inning homer won the game for the Brewers, but Jose Hernandez also doubled in two during the seven-run ninth inning that tied the game.

On the first pitch he saw from Slusarski, Hernandez lined the ball over the left-field fence to give the Brewers a most improbable 10-9 comeback victory.

"On the home run, I just saw a good pitch and hit it," said Hernandez. "All the hard work was in the comeback."[2]

The rally was the fifth time the Brewers had come back in the ninth inning from a deficit of four runs or more, according to Elias Sports Bureau. The previous efforts were from leads of four runs (1977, 1980, 1991, 1999).[3]

"You don't expect it, not that you're giving up, but it's a highly unlikely probability of scoring seven runs in one inning, especially in the bottom of the ninth," said Brewers manager Davey Lopes, whose team had won five of its past six games.[4]

"But we did do it, and it was very gratifying, and this team is feeling a little excitement right now."

And in the other dugout, as expected, the exact opposite feelings were being expressed by the Astros.

"As soon as they tied the game, you could just feel the letdown," Houston manager Larry Dierker said. "I was not optimistic at that point. It's the worst I've seen in 35 years. It was terrible."[5]

The second game of the doubleheader had less drama but the same result, as the Brewers scored all their runs in the first four innings for a 6-1 victory and the twin-bill sweep.

In the final season at County Stadium, the Brewers provided some fireworks for the 3,913 fans who probably all sat in the "front row" on the chilly, windy day in late May.

Sources

In addition to the sources mentioned in the endnotes, the author consulted Baseball-Reference.com and SABR.org.

Notes

1   Greg Beacham, "Brewers Rally to Sweep Astros," *Texas City* (Texas) *Sun*, May 23, 2000: 9.

2   Beacham.

3   Eric Anderson, "Comeback Is Oh-So Sweep," *Wisconsin State Journal* (Madison), May 23, 2000: 3C.

4   Anderson.

5   Beacham.

ONE IS THE LONELIEST NUMBER

JUNE 17, 1936:
ST. LOUIS BROWNS 14,
PHILADELPHIA ATHLETICS 13,
AT SPORTSMAN'S PARK III, ST. LOUIS

BY KEVIN LARKIN

From 1925 until 1933 the Philadelphia Athletics finished in third place twice, second place four times, and first place three times (winning the World Series in 1929 and 1930). Beginning in 1934, however, the A's were on a downward spiral that saw them with just two fourth-place finishes between 1934 and 1968.

As for the St. Louis Browns, between 1930 and 1953 they had third-place finishes in 1942, 1943, and 1945, and in 1944 they won the American League pennant, but went on to defeat by the St. Louis Cardinals in the World Series. After 1953 the Browns moved to Baltimore and became the Baltimore Orioles.

Philadelphia was in St. Louis for a three-game series at Sportsman's Park III. The A's had taken the first game of the series, 9-4, on a six-hit, three-strike-out complete game by Harry Kelley. In the second game of the series, on June 17, St. Louis manager Rogers Hornsby sent Earl Caldwell to the mound to face Stu Flythe of the Connie Mack-led A's.

Caldwell was in his third major-league season and had a record at the start of 1936 of four wins and six losses. As for Flythe, he had made his major-league debut on May 31, a 2⅔-inning performance against the Washington Senators. His next appearance was on June 4 against the Detroit Tigers, when he went three innings. The start against the Browns was his first major-league start.

The attendance was given, but a *St. Louis Post-Dispatch* writer observed, "There weren't many fans out yesterday to watch the second game of the series between the Browns and the Athletics."[1]

Glen Waller of the *St. Louis Globe-Democrat* marveled at what those present had witnessed, wriing, "The old fighting spirit of never give up has been accredited to the Browns this year, regardless of their many weaknesses never paid better dividends than yesterday afternoon at Sportsman's Park when the men of Rogers Hornsby overcame a 10 run deficit to eventually defeat the Athletics, 14-13."[2]

The Athletics got on the scoreboard in the top of the first inning beginning with a leadoff double by Lou Finney. Rabbit Warstler was out on a sacrifice and Wally Moses tripled, scoring Finney. Moses scored when George Puccinelli singled. Pinky Higgins walked and a single by Bob Johnson scored Puccinelli

First baseman Jim Bottomley drove in four of the Browns runs – two in the seventh and two more in the eighth. Shortstop Lyn Lary also had four RBIs, including the game-winner

with the third run. There was no more damage done when Rusty Peters grounded into an inning-ending double play.

The Browns could not score in their half of the first and the only runners to reach base were Lyn Lary, who walked and Jim Bottomley, who was hit by a pitch.

Philadelphia added three runs in the second inning. With one out Fylthe and Finney singled, Warstler lined out to left field, and Moses hit a three-run home run to make the score 6-0. Hornsby replaced Caldwell with Russ Van Atta, who got Puccinelli to ground out, ending the inning.

St. Louis got a run back in the second inning without a hit. Sam West walked and went to second on a wild pitch by Flythe. After a passed ball put West on third base, Flythe walked Tony Giuliani and was replaced on the mound by Buck Ross, who allowed West to score on a fly ball by Van Atta.

After a scoreless third inning, Finney doubled and scored on a single by Warstler with two outs. The A's added two more runs in the fifth inning. Puccinelli singled and Higgins homered. The Browns countered with a single tally in the bottom of the fifth, and the Athletics were ahead 9-2.

The Athletics seemingly put the game away in the sixth inning, scoring four runs. Ross led off with a double against Roy Mahaffey, who had relieved Van Atta to start the inning. A single by Finney sent Ross to third base and he scored on Warstler's single. A single by Moses loaded the bases and a fourth straight single, by Puccinelli, scored Finney and Warstler. Mahaffey wild-pitched the runners up a base, and Moses scored the fourth run of the inning when Peters reached on an error by shortstop Lary. After the final out of the inning, the Athletics had a 13-2 lead.

The Browns scored a run in the sixth inning when Beau Bell singled, went to third base on an error by Finney at first base, and scored when Tom Carey flied out to center field. Now the Athletics' lead was 13-3.

An anonymous sportswriter described the remainder of the contest: "Cuffed around from pillar to post

Lary's Hit in 9th Gives Browns 14-13 Victory Over A's

Headline from June 17, 1936 *Tampa Tribune*.

and on the verge of despair as late as the sixth inning at Sportsman's Park yesterday, the local American Leaguers awakened their several hundred snoozing patrons by staging a hilarious rampage in the last three frames that wiped out a ten-run Philadelphia lead, won a hopelessly lost ballgame 14-13, and cut the margin between themselves and seventh place to a mere two and a half games."[3]

"Going into the seventh inning with the score 13 to 3 against them, the Grand and Didier athletes continued striving to batter down the defense of the visitors regardless of the apparent hopelessness of the situation," reported the *Globe-Democrat*.[4] Lary reached in that inning on a one-out single and Moose Solters doubled him home. Bottomley then hit a two-run home run to make the score 13-6, Athletics. Ivy Andrews relieved Mahaffey and retired Philadelphia one-two-three in the top of the eighth.

In the bottom of the eighth, the walls came tumbling down for Philadelphia. Sam West walked, Tom Carey singled, and Ross was replaced on the mound by Bill Dietrich. A single by catcher Giuliani scored West and, with Carey on second and Giuliani on first, Ed Coleman, pinch-hitting for pitcher Andrews, drew a walk, loading the bases. Lyn Lary's single drove in two runs. Harlond Clift singled, the bases were loaded again, and Dietrich was yanked in favor of Harry Kelley, who had pitched the A's complete-game victory the day before. Kelley got Solters on a called third strike, but Bottomley drove in his third and fourth runs of the day with a double. Even when the Browns made an out they scored: Beau Bell's groundout to third base knocked in Clift with the sixth run of the inning. Finally, Sam West singled and Bottomley came across with the run that tied the game, 13-13. Tom Carey's force-play grounder ended the inning.

The Athletics got a walk in the top of the ninth, but didn't score. For the Browns, Giuliani led off with a walk. Jack Knott, who had replaced Andrews on the mound in the top of the inning, sacrificed Giuliani to second base. The game ended when Lary singled to center field and Giuliani scored, giving the Browns a stirring 14-13 victory.

Together the teams totaled 30 hits (17 for Philadelphia and 13 for St. Louis). Lou Finney led the way for the A's with four hits (two doubles, four runs scored); Wally Moses (home run, triple, four RBIs), and George Puccinelli each had three. Philadelphia used a quartet of pitchers in the game – Stu Flythe, Buck Ross, Bill Dietrich, and Harry Kelley – with Kelley taking the loss.

Lyn Lary had four singles for St. Louis, with four RBIs, including the winner, and two runs scored. Jim Bottomley added a double, a home run and four RBIs. Each team used four pitchers. Jack Knott earned the win and Harry Kelley took the loss.

The *Post-Dispatch's* scribe summed up the game this way: "Only Roget's Thesaurus contains enough words to properly describe the contest, so take all the adjectives in the first 100 pages of Mr. Roget's well-known volume, add them together and mix well."[5]

Sources

In addition to the game story and box-score sources cited in the Notes, the author consulted the Baseball-Reference.com and Retrosheet.org websites.

Notes

1   James M. Gould, "Browns Overcome 11 Run Deficit and Defeat Athletics, 14 to 13," *St. Louis Post-Dispatch*, June 18, 1936: 22.

2   Glen L. Waller, "Hornsbymen Score Eleven Runs in Last Three Frames," *St. Louis Globe-Democrat*, June 18, 1936: 7.

3   "Browns Overcame 10-Run Handicap to Beat Mackmen, 14-13," *St. Louis Star and Times-Dispatch*, June 18, 1936: 34.

4   Waller.

5   Gould.

DOWN EIGHT AFTER SEVEN INNINGS, YANKEES RALLY TO WIN IN EXTRA INNINGS

AUGUST 20, 1947: NEW YORK YANKEES 14, DETROIT TIGERS 13 (14 INNINGS), AT BRIGGS STADIUM, DETROIT

BY ALAN RAYLESBERG

The ability of the New York Yankees to come from behind has long been part of baseball lore. Starting with the great 1927 team, the Yankees were associated with the slogan "Five O'Clock Lightning," for their many late rallies leading to comeback wins.[1] Of the many such wins in their storied history, August 20, 1947, stands out. At what was then known as Briggs Stadium,[2] the Yankees gave up nine runs in the seventh inning to fall behind by eight, only to rally with three in the eighth and five in the ninth to send the game to extra innings, where they won in the 11th by a score of 14-13.

The Yankees went on to win the 1947 World Series. After finishing a close third in 1948, the Yankees won the World Series the next five seasons (1949-53) and then won the American League pennant in nine of the next 11 (1954-64), along with another four World Series championships.

After they finished third or fourth in the prior three seasons, the latest edition of the Yankees dynasty was forming in 1947. On August 20 the Yankees were first with an 11½-game lead. Despite their sizable lead, the Yankees' recent play had been inconsistent, and first-year manager Bucky Harris was under fire from the New York press. From Harris's perspective, "there [was] too much World Series talk on this club. ... [w]e have got to do more ball playing and less talking."[3]

August 20 was the final visit of the season by the Yankees to Detroit, the second of a two-game series with the then third-place Tigers. As the Yankees took the field, their lineup featured stars of the past, present,

and future. The Yankees had won the pennant in seven of eight seasons from 1936 through 1943 and no star shined brighter during that time than Joe DiMaggio. DiMaggio was 32 years old but in the midst of another fine season in which he would hit .315 with 20 home runs and 97 RBIs. Tommy Henrich, at age 34, was another stalwart from those great 1930s Yankees teams. Behind the plate was a 22-year-old rookie named Lawrence Peter "Yogi" Berra, who went on to win 10 World Series with the Yankees and make the Hall of Fame. The shortstop was another Hall of Famer, 29-year-old Phil Rizzuto, in his prime and three years shy of his 1950 MVP season.

The 1947 Tigers were a team in transition. After winning the World Series in 1945, they finished second in 1946, 12 games behind. And while they ended up finishing second to the Yankees in 1947 (again 12 games out of first), the 1948 team would drop to fifth. In 1947 the Tigers had some good young talent, led by 24-year-old third baseman and future Hall of Famer George Kell. Vic Wertz, a 22-year-old rookie, was in right field and center was patrolled by 26-year-old Walter "Hoot" Evers, in his first full season with Detroit.

The starting pitcher for the Tigers was Virgil Trucks, who pitched 12 of his 17 big-league seasons with Detroit. Opposing him for the Yankees was a 39-year-old journeyman, Bobo Newsom, near the end of a 20-year career, having been acquired by New York only a month earlier from Washington.

On a hot, humid, day, those among the 23,508 fans in attendance who liked offense were about to see quite a show. The game began as a see-saw affair: The Yankees scored three in the first only to see the Tigers come back with three in the second and one in the third to take the lead and send Newsom to the showers. In the fifth the Yankees regained the lead when Berra hit his 11th home run of the season to make it 5-4. The seventh inning was not kind to the Yankees as relievers Frank "Spec" Shea and Joe Page were lit up by the Tigers for nine runs. When the dust settled, Detroit had a seemingly insurmountable 13-5 lead with only two innings to go.

Yet, even after giving up nine runs and falling way behind, the "Yankee spirit would not wilt,"[4] as they began to chip away against Trucks. DiMaggio singled in the eighth and, with the game seemingly lost, was removed for pinch-runner Bobby Brown. Brown took second on a single by first baseman George McQuinn, and the two runners scored on a triple by left fielder Johnny Lindell. That was it for Trucks. Rizzuto greeted reliever Al Benton with an RBI single to make it 13-8 in the middle of the eighth.

As the ninth inning began, with Benton on the mound, no one expected what came next. Allie Clark, a rookie who had replaced Henrich, singled leading off.[5] After Berra singled, Brown followed with another single, scoring Clark. The next two batters made out, with one run scoring and the Yankees were down to their last out, trailing 13-10. Down but not out, as Lindell singled to make it 13-11. Now things were getting interesting. And they got more interesting when Rizzuto singled to left with Lindell racing to third and Rizzuto taking second on the throw to the base. Now with runners at second and third with two out, three runs in and two runs down, Yankees reliever Randy Gumpert was due up.

With the drama building, and Hal White in to replace Benton, Harris sent Lonny Frey up to bat as a pinch-hitter. The 36-year-old Frey was another mid-season acquisition by the Yankees. Once a regular infielder in the National League, Frey was coming to the end of his career, in a season where he would bat .179 for the Yankees with only 28 at-bats. After joining the Yankees in June, Frey had been used mostly as a pinch-runner. He had only two plate appearances before this one, but the Yankees bench was nearly empty. Frey swung from the left side against the righty White.[6] With the game on the line and a classic comeback in the making, Frey came through with a single, scoring Lindell and Rizzuto with the fourth and fifth

PHIL RIZZUTO
shortstop NEW YORK YANKEES

Phil Rizzuto had three base hits and drove in two runs as the Yankees responded to a nine-run seventh inning by the Tigers, scoring eight of their own and sending the game to 11.

runs of the inning, and the Yankees had tied the game. For Frey it was his first hit as a Yankee and it is hard to imagine a bigger one. The speedy Frey stole second to put the winning run in scoring position but Snuffy Stirnweiss made the third out and the teams went to the bottom of the ninth tied at 13-13.

Rookie right-hander Karl Drews retired Detroit in the ninth and the game went to extra innings. Neither team threatened in the 10th. Then, in the 11th, with White still pitching for Detroit, Lindell singled with one out. Up stepped Rizzuto and he doubled, scoring Lindell from first. The Yankees had the lead, 14-13.

The Yankees took that lead to the bottom of the 14th but this game was not over yet. Doc Cramer batted for catcher Bob Swift and drew a walk from Drews. With Jimmy Outlaw running for Cramer, the Tigers sent a good-hitting pitcher (and future major-league manager), Fred Hutchinson, up to bat for White. He singled, sending Outlaw to third and now the Tigers had runners at the corners and nobody out. With the Yankees having already used five pitchers, this game was going to be for Drews to win or lose. At 6-feet-4 and nearly 200 pounds, Drews was "gigantic" for his time and, in his rookie season, no moment was more "gigantic" for the 27-year-old.[7] In need of clutch pitching, Drews provided it as he got out of the jam, getting Eddie Lake to hit into a fielder's choice with Outlaw being thrown out at home, and then retiring Jackie Mayo and Wertz to end the game. Eight runs down with two innings to go and the Yankees had come back to win it.

In 2005, four years before his death, Lonnie Frey was interviewed by the *St. Louis Post- Dispatch* and asked to name the one highlight of his career. He could not do it and responded that "every day was a highlight."[8] If pressed, Frey might have thought back to August 20, 1947, when his first hit as a Yankee completed an incredible two-out rally to tie the game in what would become one of the great comebacks in Yankees history.

Sources

In addition to the sources cited in the Notes, the author consulted Baseball-Reference.com and Retrosheet.org.

Notes

1   In 1927, there were only day games and those at Yankee Stadium started at 3:30 P.M. Games typically lasted about two hours, so it would be around 5:00 P.M. that the late Yankees rallies would begin. Shane Tourtellotte, "'Five O'clock Lightning': A Legend of the 1927 Yankees," *The Hardball Times,* August 1, 2018, available at tht.fangraphs.com/five-oclock-lightning-a-legend-of-the-1927-yankees/.

2   The ballpark, opened in 1912, was named Navin Field until it became known as Briggs Stadium in 1938. The name was changed to Tiger Stadium beginning in 1961 and remained that way through 1999, when the last game was played there.

3   Dan Daniel, "Too Much World Series Talk on Yankees, Says Uneasy Harris," *The Sporting News,* August 20, 1947: 10.

4   James P. Dawson, "Bombers Triumph in 11 Innings 14-13," *New York Times,* August 21, 1947: 28.

5   Henrich left after the seventh inning "when his injured ankle started acting up." Of course, with his team trailing 13-5, it did not make sense to leave him in. Dawson.

6   Prior to 1939, Frey was a switch-hitter before becoming exclusively a lefty batter.

7   Dawson.

8   James Forr, "Lonny Frey," sabr.org/bioproj/person/59f29784.

GIANTS STAGE SURPRISING COMEBACK TO BEAT PIRATES

SEPTEMBER 8, 1947:
NEW YORK GIANTS 10,
PITTSBURGH PIRATES 8,
AT FORBES FIELD, PITTSBURGH

BY JOHN J. BURBRIDGE JR.

The New York Giants and the Pittsburgh Pirates were to play the initial game of a three-game series at Pittsburgh's Forbes Field on Monday, September 8. The Giants had just concluded a four-game series against the Brooklyn Dodgers at the Polo Grounds. The Giants split the four-game set with more than 166,000 fans attending. After the last game with the Dodgers, the Giants' record was 68-64.

The Pirates were struggling, having lost six of their last seven games. Their record now stood at 55-79. The season had been disappointing after they acquired slugger Hank Greenberg in the offseason from the Detroit Tigers for $75,000.[1] In 1938 Greenberg had come close to breaking Babe Ruth's record of 60 home runs in a season, hitting 58. To aid his home-run exploits, the Pirates shortened the distance to the left-field foul pole from 365 feet to 335.[2] The area behind the left-field fence was now called Greenberg's Gardens.

While the Pirates had Greenberg and the young Ralph Kiner, the Giants had sluggers Johnny Mize, Walker Cooper, Willard Marshall, and Sid Gordon. Greenberg, Kiner, and Mize are Hall of Famers.

For this contest the Giants started upon Sheldon Jones and the Pirates started 39-year-old forkballer Fritz Ostermueller. The Giants were managed by their former star slugger, nice guy Mel Ott, who had hit 511 home runs in his career. Billy Herman managed the Pirates. Both are in the Hall of Fame. The umpires were Beans Reardon at home plate with Larry Goetz at first base and Al Barlick at third. Barlick was also enshrined at Cooperstown; some feel Reardon and Goetz also deserve the honor.

Ostermueller retired the Giants in the first inning with a walk to Bobby Thomson the only blemish. In the bottom of the first, a bizarre play resulted in the Pirates scoring an unearned run. Frankie Gustine doubled with one out. Billy Cox popped out for the second out, and Kiner walked. Greenberg hit a ground-ball to third baseman Jack "Lucky" Lohrke, whose throw to second to force Kiner pulled second base-man Bill Rigney off the bag. Kiner, thinking Rigney had dropped the ball, continued running to third base. Gustine, who had reached third, broke for home, drawing a throw from Rigney that went past Cooper, the Giants catcher. Gustine scored, with Greenberg and Kiner now at second and third.[3] Wally Westlake's grounder to shortstop ended the inning.

Neither team scored in the second, and the Giants were retired in order in the top of the third. In the bottom of the inning, the Pirates scored three runs. Gustine led off with a single and, after two strike-outs, Greenberg walked. Westlake was hit by a pitch, loading the bases, and a walk to Jimmy Bloodworth forced a run home. Joe Beggs replaced Jones and Clyde Kluttz greeted him with a two-run single.

The fourth inning was scoreless. So was the fifth, though two-out walks to Gordon and Lohrke broke a string of 12 consecutive batters retired by Ostermueller.

In the bottom of the fifth, Andy Hansen replaced Beggs for the Giants and Greenberg greeted him with a single. After an out, Bloodworth and Kluttz singled, loading the bases. Ostermueller's fly ball to center field sent Greenberg home. Gene Woodling ended the inning by grounding out. The Pirates now led 5-0.

In the top of sixth, Rigney led off and singled, the first hit off Ostermueller. Buddy Kerr also singled.

But Ostermueller struck out Thomson and Mize and got Cooper on a fly out to center. In the bottom half of the inning, Lloyd Gearhart replaced Thomson in center field for the Giants as Bobby's trick knee acted up.[4] The Pirates went out in order as did the Giants in the top of the seventh. In the bottom of the seventh, the Pirates' Greenberg led off with a walk and took second on Westlake's sacrifice. Bloodworth and Kluttz then walked. With the bases loaded, Ostermueller laid down another bunt. He was thrown out, but Greenberg scored and the other runners moved up. Both scored on Woodling's single. Gustine's fly out ended the inning with the Pirates ahead 8-0.

As the game entered the top of the eighth inning, the Pirates' Ostermueller had allowed just two hits. Leading off, Ernie Lombardi batted for Hansen and singled to left field. Buddy Blattner, running for the slow-footed Lombardi, was forced out at second on Rigney's groundball. But Kerr singled and Gearhart was safe at first when center fielder Woodling dropped his fly ball. The bases were loaded, and Mize's double off the screen in right field brought home two runs.[5] Cooper followed with a single, and Gearhart and Mize scored. Cooper went to second on a grounder by Marshall and scored on Gordon's single. After he walked Lohrke, Ostermueller was replaced by Jim Bagby Jr. The pitcher's spot, now occupied by pinch-runner Blattner, was next and Joe Lafata batted for Blattner. After a balk by Bagby moved runners to second and third, Lafata's hit scored Gordon and Lohrke. Lafata was thrown out by Woodling trying to get to second, and the inning was over. The Giants had scored seven runs and the Pirates eight-run lead had been trimmed to one run. The score was 8-7 entering the bottom of the eighth. Woodling's error had proved costly, leading to four unearned runs.

The Giants' Ken Trinkle faced the Pirates in the eighth and gave up just a two-out walk to Greenberg. In the top of the ninth, with Bagby still pitching, Rigney led off with a double and went to third on Kerr's sacrifice. Gary Gearhart, who had replaced Thomson, sent a drive into Greenberg Gardens, giving the Giants an improbable 9-8 lead. Bagby was replaced by Al Lyons, who was greeted by Mize's double. Cooper grounded out and Marshall was walked intentionally. Gordon followed with a single, knocking in Mize with the Giants' 10th run. Lohrke's grounder ended the inning with the Giants leading 10-8.

Ken Trinkle stayed on the mound to close out the game. The Pirates didn't go quietly. Kluttz singled with one out. After Bill Salkeld, pinch-hitting for Lyons, flied out, Woodling singled. With two runners on, Trinkle retired Gustine on a popup to shortstop, sending the small crowd of 3,936 home mostly unhappy.[6] The hitting hero for the Giants was Gearhart, who hit the two-run home run in the ninth. Kluttz had three hits and Woodling two for Pittsburgh. Trinkle was the winning pitcher and Bagby took the loss.

The Giants won the next two games of the series, and when it was over, the Pirates found themselves in the National League cellar. The Giants had a historic year, finishing 81-73 but setting a major-league record with 221 home runs.[7] The Pirates ended up sharing the cellar with Philadelphia, both in last place with 62-92 records. As the season was about to conclude, the Pirates fired manager Herman.

On an individual basis, Mize and Kiner tied for the home run lead in the major leagues with 51. Greenberg had a rather disappointing season, hitting only 25 home runs, even with the shortened fences. Greenberg retired after the 1947 season; Mize and Kiner continued to hit home runs, tying for the National League lead with 40 in 1948. In 1948 Leo Durocher replaced Ott as manager of the Giants. With Durocher at the helm, the Giants underwent significant roster changes, and won the 1951 pennant in their historic playoff in 1951 decided by Bobby Thomson's Shot Heard 'Round the World. The Pirates rebounded in 1948 and finished fourth under new manager Billy Meyer. However, they then floundered and Branch Rickey was hired as general manager in 1950. A long rebuild occurred which resulted in a 1960 World Series victory.

Sources

In addition to the sources mentioned in the Notes, the author consulted Baseball-Reference.com.

Notes

1 Scott Ferkovich, "Hank Greenberg," SABR BioProject, sabr.org/bioproj/person/64198864.

2 Curt Smith, "Forbes Field (Pittsburgh)," SABR BioProject, sabr.org/bioproj/park/forbes-field-pittsburgh.

3 Vince Johnson, "Bucs Blow 8-Run Lead to Giants, 10-8," *Pittsburgh Post-Gazette*, September 9, 1947: 14.

4 James P. Dawson, "Ottmen in Triumph at Pittsburgh," *New York Times*, September 9, 1947: 42.

5 Johnson.

6 Dawson.

7 The record as of 2020 was owned by the Minnesota Twins, who hit 307 homers in 2019. The New York Yankees were right behind them with 306. In the current homer-happy era, the Giants' 221 aren't even in the top 50.

"THE KIND OF A NIGHT YOU DREAM ABOUT"

SEPTEMBER 2, 1972:
NEW YORK METS 11,
HOUSTON ASTROS 8,
AT ASTRODOME, HOUSTON

BY IRV GOLDFARB

Every team has comebacks.

Miraculous rallies from seemingly insurmountable deficits litter the historical landscape in every major sport. Whether a club ultimately needs that special comeback on their way to a championship, or merely uses it as a springboard for success later in the season, it's often remembered in team lore as a landmark victory.

However, there are also those miracle games that occur during seasons that aren't quite as successful and whose outcomes don't mean as much in the big picture of a full season.

Historically, the New York Mets have experienced their share of the latter. So in a campaign that ended with an 83-73 record and a 13½-game deficit in the National League East standings, their game against the Houston Astros on September 2, 1972, should have been lost deep in the pages of baseball history.

Instead, it will be remembered as one of the biggest comebacks the team ever had.

The 1972 season began with major-league baseball's first strike, over a dispute regarding the players' pension fund. By the time the sides agreed on a $500,000 increase for the plan, 13 days at the start of the regular season had been lost. By September 2, the National League standings told a fairly dismal story for both teams: The Mets were already 14 games back of the eventual division-winning Pittsburgh Pirates, while the Astros still clung to a glimmer of hope for a strong finish: They were on a six-game winning streak and trailed the soon-to-be pennant-winning Reds by seven games. As a matter of fact, they knew they could

have gained another game that night, as Cincinnati lost to the Montreal Expos.

Houston had pounded the Mets in the Astrodome, 8-0, the night before, handing franchise pitcher Tom Seaver his 10th loss of the season while beating up on a beleaguered Mets bullpen. And amazingly on this

Courtesy: The Topps Company.

KEN BOSWELL

Losing 8-0 after seven innings, the Mets scored 11 times in the final two frames. Second baseman Ken Boswell homered to drive in three and then scored another run.

Saturday night, the Astros grabbed another 8-0 lead, sparked this time by Lee May's two-run homer in the first inning, his 28th of the year, a two-run double by Cesar Cedeño in the third inning, and Bob Watson's two-run single in the bottom of the seventh, as the Astros hammered starter Brent Strom and relievers Ray Sadecki and Bob Rauch, the latter a rookie hurler appearing in his only major-league season. Hence, the Mets entered the eighth inning hopelessly behind for the second consecutive game, as veteran right-hander Don Wilson had shut them down over the first seven innings, facing only 24 hitters and allowing just four hits.

But backup catcher Duffy Dyer, a holdover from the Miracle Mets of '69 (as was every starting position player in this game except right fielder John Milner), opened the inning with a single to left. Shortstop Bud Harrelson followed with another base hit and utility outfielder Dave Marshall, pinch-hitting for Rauch, walked to load the bases. Center fielder Tommie Agee hit a sacrifice fly to right for the Mets' first run of the game, which brought up second baseman Ken Boswell, another unheralded contributor to that 1969 team.

Though he had already been responsible for half his club's hits entering the inning (two singles in three at-bats), Boswell had come into the game batting a paltry .177. "I started out the season not hitting badly, but I always came up empty-handed," Boswell remarked after the game. "I kept trying to laugh it off, figuring things would straighten out but they didn't." They straightened out well enough in this at-bat, however, as Boswell launched his eighth homer of the season, a three-run blast that made the score 8-4. "I think it was a hanging slider," he guessed. "I was just trying to get it in the air."[1]

Though a home run in the midst of a big comeback is often dubbed a "momentum-killer" and the Mets were still down by four runs, a pitching change from Wilson to journeyman reliever Fred Gladding didn't stop the Mets' sudden offensive onslaught: Milner immediately collected a single, veteran Met first baseman Ed Kranepool followed with another, and left fielder Cleon Jones doubled in a run, with Kranepool stopping at third. Astros manager Leo Durocher then called for reliever Jim Ray to replace Gladding, but it made no difference as third baseman Wayne Garrett singled in Kranepool and Jones to make the score a suddenly tight 8-7.

Dyer made his second plate appearance of the inning and singled again, but Ray got Harrelson to pop out to the shortstop in foul territory and Marshall to fly out to end the Mets biggest inning of the season. They had scored seven runs on eight hits and were now down by only a single run.

To start the eighth, Mets manager Yogi Berra sent out legendary left-hander Jerry Koosman. Koosman, who had faced three batters in relief the night before, had been sent to the bullpen earlier in the season after three early-season losses because he had "lost his rhythm." "I literally forgot how to wind up," he said after his career.[2] Koosman got into some trouble, hitting Tommy Helms with a pitch, then giving up a two-out single to Roger Metzger. At that point, Berra called on Tug McGraw, who struck out Cedeño looking.

Now it was their turn again and the Mets offense didn't miss a beat: Agee walked to start the ninth and Boswell chimed in with another single, his fourth hit of the game. Durocher marched out reliever Tom Griffin, but the Astros' luck didn't change as a sacrifice attempt by Milner was fielded by the usually surehanded third baseman Doug Rader, who made a disastrous throw wide of first. The error scored Agee to tie the game, sending Milner to second and Boswell to third.

Durocher then ordered Kranepool walked intentionally to load the bases, but that strategy backfired as well: Jones singled to right to score Boswell and Milner and give the Mets a two-run lead. Kranepool was thrown out at third as Cleon Jones took second and Garrett singled him in. Dyer followed with a strikeout, but even more action followed – Harrelson singled and even McGraw got into the act as he walked to load the bases. Reliever George Culver got Harrelson on a fielder's choice, however, and the Mets took the field in the ninth with a three-run lead.

With Willie Mays now in center field in one of his last regular-season appearances, McGraw got the side in order in the ninth, closing out the 11-8 victory by getting Watson to ground out to the star of the game, Kenny Boswell.

Boswell, originally from Austin, Texas, said he usually had to have about 30 tickets available for friends and relatives who wanted to see him play when the came to Houston. "but I've never been able to do anything. Guess I was trying to impress them (tonight)," he said later.

For Houston manager Durocher it was just one of those games. "Everything they hit was right between somebody," he lamented after the nightmarish experience. "We got beat with the best we had, so what can you say?"

"It's about time we find a few holes," Berra declared.

For Boswell, who actually ended his career with the Astros five years later, it was the night of his life. "It's nice to know there's a little left," the 26-year-old veteran declared. "It's the kind of a night you dream about."

Sources

In addition to the sources cited in the Notes, the author also consulted Baseball-Reference.com, Retrosheet.org, and the following:

Strauss, Michael. "Mets Score 7 in 8th, 4 in 9th, Win, 11-8, *New York Times*, September 3, 1972: S1

Associated Press. "Mets Down Houston 11-8," *Austin Statesman*, September 3, 1972: D7.

Notes

1   "Boswell Finds a Little Left," *Newsday,* September 3, 1972: 5C. All quotations come from this article unless otherwise indicated.

2   Interview with the author, 2008, in Matthew Silverman and Ken Samelson, eds., *The Miracle Has Landed* (Hanover, Massachusetts: Maple Street Press, 2009), 141.

OUTBURST BY TIGERS' INERT OFFENSE STUNS ST. LOUIS

AUGUST 30, 1919:
DETROIT TIGERS 8,
ST. LOUIS BROWNS 7
(SECOND GAME OF DOUBLEHEADER),
AT SPORTSMAN'S PARK, ST. LOUIS

By Nathan Bierma

Time was running out for the Detroit Tigers to keep the Chicago White Sox from running away with the 1919 pennant. Ten years after manager Hughie Jennings took his Tigers to their last World Series, their third straight appearance and third straight loss in the fall

Howard Ehmke dug himself a huge hole, pitching and giving up seven earned runs – but he also kicked off the scoring with a leadoff double in the eighth and a single to lead off the ninth.

Courtesy The Topps Company.

classic, he knew his team had a narrow margin for error if they wanted to return.[1] The Tigers did their best, winning 15 of their first 19 games in August, getting as close as four games behind Chicago in the standings. But the torrid White Sox were just as steady, putting together a 10-game winning streak during the Tigers' tear.

By the time the Tigers (65-47) arrived in St. Louis to close out the month, they had lost four straight and seen the White Sox lead widen to eight games. They had to stop the bleeding in a four-game weekend series with the Browns (59-53) before returning to Detroit to face the league leaders in a Monday doubleheader.

The Tigers won their series opener with Jimmy Burke's Browns, then dropped the first game of a Saturday doubleheader, shut out by Allen Sothoron in a 4-0 loss.

St. Louis starting pitcher Dave Davenport began the second game on the right note, stranding Ty Cobb after his two-out first-inning single. Tigers starter Howard Ehmke was shakier out of the gate, walking his first two batters, Jimmy Austin and Joe Gedeon. Baby Doll Jacobson sacrificed to advance the runners, and Austin scored on a groundout by George Sisler.

The Tigers had a rare early chance in the top of the second, when Harry Heilmann walked and Chick Shorten bunted and beat Davenport's throw. But the threat vanished instantly with the next batter, Bob Jones, who hit into a double play, and Eddie Ainsmith sent a harmless groundball to Sisler at first to end the inning. The Tigers offense then went back into hibernation.

TIGERS SCORE EIGHT RUNS IN FINAL INNINGS AND SAVE GAME WITH ST. LOUIS BROWNS, 8–7

Headline from *Colorado Springs Gazette* August 31, 1919.

Josh Billings kept the Browns alive in the second inning with a two-out single, before Ehmke hit Davenport to put two runners on. That turned the lineup over to Austin, who hit a double to the right-field wall. Austin tried his luck after a faulty throw from Shorten but was thrown out at home plate. But Billings and Davenport had scored to make it 3-0.

St. Louis kept sizzling in the third on a two-run home run by Sisler after Jacobson's leadoff single and Gedeon's infield popup. Jack Tobin came "within an inch," the *Detroit Free Press* said, of matching Sisler's result, but Shorten retired him "on the edge of the sun gods' section."[2] Ray Demmitt became the third straight batter to send a fly ball in Shorten's direction, but it was the easiest to handle. That ended the inning, but the Browns were on top 5-0.

The fifth inning all but assured fans that the home team would win for the second time that day, and likely even more decisively. Austin and Gedeon led off with back-to-back walks for the second time. Jacobson tried to bunt them over but popped up to Ehmke. Sisler singled to right to score Austin, and Gedeon came home on a squeeze bunt by Tobin. The Browns led 7-0, and the game appeared to be out of reach.

While the Browns' bats battered Ehmke, Davenport "boomed along like a stake horse," the *Free Press* reported.[3] After Cobb's harmless first-inning single, the Tigers went six more innings without a hit from anyone other than Ehmke, who mustered two. As they entered the eighth, they had played 16 innings that long day without scoring a run.

"For seven innings of the second game, Dave Davenport held the Tigers about as Sothoron had in the first," the *Free Press* wrote. "No matter what the Bengals did the lean flinger of the Browns checked them and it looked like curtains for the second time with the enemy rolling along on a seven-run lead and no prospects of anything to relieve the situation."[4]

If anyone were to ignite an improbably rally, it would have to be Ehmke, who was having more success at the plate than on the mound. He answered the call by leading off the eighth inning with a double

to left field. Donie Bush followed with a single, and Ralph Young was safe at first on a fielder's choice that retired Bush but scored Ehmke. The Tigers had, at long last, changed their number on the scoreboard.

Then, in an unexpected outburst, they kept right on going. Cobb came up after Young and clobbered a ball over the fence for a two-run homer to make the score a more respectable 7-3. Davenport had utterly stymied the Tigers for seven innings, but now, the *Free Press* commented, "Everything he threw up the Tigers hit."[5] Veach and Heilmann followed Cobb with singles, and the starting pitcher, "clearly upset, wild-pitched the pair" to second and third, the *Free Press* reported. With Shorten in the batter's box and the tying run now, incredibly, on deck, Burke yanked his starter in favor of Ernie Koob.

Jennings responded by replacing Shorten with the right-handed Ira Flagstead to face the lefty reliever. Koob immediately made matters worse by plunking Flagstead to load the bases. Ben Dyer's groundball scored Veach but retired Heilmann on a force out at third. Ainsmith grounded back to the mound to end the inning. But the Tigers were within reach, with the score 7-4.

Ehmke completed the bottom of the inning and was due up once again to lead off the ninth. Jennings gave his starter a chance to tally his fourth hit of the game, and Ehmke did just that, nabbing an in-field single before being lifted for pinch-runner Babe Ellison. After Bush flied out to center, Young's single to left put runners on first and second for Ty Cobb. The league batting leader smacked a double to score Ellison. It was 7-5 with two runners in scoring position. Bobby Veach brought them both home on a single to right field, and scampered to second on the futile throw to home plate.

"This attack of the Tigers, in view of the way they had behaved prior to the eighth, struck the fans dumb and must have had a disheartening effect on the Browns," the *Free Press* wrote.[6]

Having trailed by seven runs with only the faintest of pulses, the Tigers had rallied to tie the game.

Desperate and dumbfounded, Burke made another call to the bullpen and brought in Bert Gallia.

"Heilmann's greeting to Bert was a smash to center," the *Free Press* reported.[7] Veach reached the dish and the Tigers took an 8-7 lead.

Flagstead kept the pressure on with a single, but Dyer struck out, and after Ainsmith reached first on an infield hit, Heilmann was out on the basepaths on the play and the inning was finally over. After nothing but goose eggs all day, the Tigers had scored four runs in consecutive innings. The stunned Browns now faced a do-or-die bottom of the ninth.

With Ehmke benched for the pinch-runner, Jennings called on Slim Love, and the new hurler slammed the door, striking out pinch-hitter Herman Bronkie, inducing a grounder to short from Austin, and getting Gedeon on strikes for the final out.

"That's the story of how the Browns let a seven-run lead slip away from them," wrote the *St. Louis Post-Dispatch*. "This contest was one of the toughest the Burkemen have lost this season."[8]

The Tigers, snatching victory from not just the jaws but the tonsils and windpipe of defeat, had earned a comeback win and a doubleheader split.

"There didn't appear to be a chance in the world for the Tigers, under the conditions, to save even a vestige of the afternoon," the *Free Press* wrote. "Only the most vicious attack that a Bengal club ever has administered a collection of rival pitchers averted a double beating at the hands of the Browns."[9]

Sources

In addition to the sources cited in the Notes, the author consulted Retrosheet.org and Baseball-Reference.com in writing this article.

Notes

1   Jennings' 1919 season would be his 13th and last with the Tigers. His 1,131 wins as Detroit skipper stood until Sparky Anderson eclipsed the mark in 1992.

2   Harry Bullion, "Tigers Win Second Game in Great Closing Rally; Shut Out in the Opener," *Detroit Free Press*, August 31, 1919: 13.

3   Bullion.

4   Bullion.

5   Bullion.

6   Bullion.

7   Bullion.

8   "12-Swat Shell from Detroit Artillery Gives Jungaleers an Even Break with Browns," *St. Louis Post-Dispatch*, August 31, 1919: 6.

9   Bullion.

"NO NO-HITTER FOR BOROWY AS THE PHILLIES RALLY AT WRIGLEY"

JUNE 10, 1946:
PHILADELPHIA PHILLIES 9,
CHICAGO CUBS 8,
AT WRIGLEY FIELD, CHICAGO

BY JAMES FORR

In a time when a pitcher's ability to finish games was thought to say something about his character, even his masculinity, Hank Borowy was developing a reputation as a man who couldn't finish what he started.

An All-Star with the New York Yankees, Borowy was considered one of baseball's best pitchers, but in 1945 the Yankees decided they'd had enough of him. In July they sold him to the Chicago Cubs in a shocking deal that made no sense to anybody. The best defense mercurial Yankees President Larry MacPhail could offer was Borowy's supposed lack of stamina. "This year he pitched four complete games for us after April, none after June 24. Last season he won only five and lost eight after July 15. In short, he has not been, for the Yankees, a pitcher who could be relied upon when pitching class was needed most."[1] In Chicago, the no-good bum promptly completed his first 10 starts, went 11-2 with a glittering 2.13 ERA, and propelled his new club to the National League pennant.

Borowy's 1946 season started equally well, but whether it was because the best hitters were back from World War II or because he had lost something, it quickly became apparent that the 30-year-old right-hander wasn't the same pitcher. In fact, each of his previous two outings had ended in spectacularly catastrophic fashion.

On May 30 Borowy entered the ninth inning with a 6-1 lead over Cincinnati but surrendered four runs as part of a six-run onslaught as the Reds rallied for a dramatic comeback win. In his next start, he took a three-hit shutout and a 6-0 lead into the eighth inning against the New York Giants before allowing three runs in the eighth and one more in the ninth. The Giants maintained their assault after he got the hook and sent the game into extra innings, although Chicago did storm back to pull out a win. Borowy, who came into the season with a career ERA of 2.66 and 64 complete games in 110 starts, was 1-3 with a 4.15 ERA and just one complete game in nine starts as he prepared to face the last-place Philadelphia Phillies on June 10.

Philadelphia starter Al Milnar had his own problems. He too had been an All-Star once but that was much earlier, before he tore up his shoulder, before two years in the US Army. By 1946, the 32-year-old left-hander was barely hanging on. This was his first appearance as a Phillie after the perpetually pitching-poor club purchased him from the St. Louis Browns two weeks earlier.

The Cubs were winners of seven in a row and their offense, though inconsistent, had shown itself capable of some significant outbursts – not the team you wanted to see if you were a pitcher with a job on the line. On this Monday afternoon, Milnar's worst nightmare came true. In the words of the *Chicago Daily News*, "[His] stay was short but turbulent."[2]

Milnar walked the first two men he faced in the bottom of the first, Eddie Waitkus followed with a single that scored Stan Hack, and Phil Cavarretta tripled in two more runs. Four batters, no outs – and that was it. Dick Mauney came in from the bullpen, only to be greeted by Marv Rickert's single that made it 4-0. (Immediately after the game, Philadelphia sold Milnar back to the Browns. The Phillies "gave no reason for the action," probably figuring his line against the Cubs was explanation enough.[3] He never appeared in the major leagues again.)

The weather provided a suitable backdrop for what became a surreal game. It was 84 degrees at game time but a late-spring cold front of almost biblical proportions rolled through Wrigley Field in the third inning, sending dust devils swirling across the infield and the temperature plummeting into the 50s. Those gusts, along with some defensive misadventures, gave a further boost to the Cubs. Mauney was pitching well but in the sixth he walked Borowy and later, with two outs, Phillies shortstop Skeeter Newsome booted Don Johnson's groundball. Waitkus then lofted a lazy fly ball to left field but the tricky wind carried it beyond the reach of Del Ennis. Borowy and Johnson raced home, while Waitkus found himself on second with a gift double. Cavarretta's single drove in Waitkus for another unearned run and a 7-0 Cubs lead.

That advantage appeared to be insurmountable because Borowy appeared to be unhittable. As he took the mound in the seventh inning, he had not allowed a hit and had retired 13 Phillies in a row. That, however, is when his problems began. He walked the first two batters, and then after two outs, Andy Seminick hit a sharp grounder to third that Hack misplayed. It was ruled an error, and Roy Hughes came in with an unearned run. But Borowy still had a no-hitter going and a 7-1 lead.

Chicago restored the margin to seven runs with a run in the bottom of the seventh, but then Borowy unraveled completely. Emil Verban led off the eighth with a single to right, ending the no-hit bid. Next came a walk to Oscar Judd, an exceptionally good hitting pitcher who was batting for Mauney. Johnny Wyrostek doubled in Verban to trim the lead to 8-2. Hughes's infield grounder brought home another run. Ron Northey singled in another. Two batters later, Ennis knocked in another. Just like that, it was 8-5.

Charlie Ripple retired the Cubs in short order, and then in the ninth, as the *Chicago Tribune* put it, "the party popped wide open."[4] With the pesky Verban on second and two away, Borowy had the Phillies down to their final out, but a walk to Wyrostek and a single to center by Hughes cut the lead to 8-6, as Wyrostek made it to third. With that, rookie Russ Meers came in to relieve Borowy.

Right-handed-hitting Lou Novikoff pinch-hit for Northey against the left-handed Meers and beat out a dribbler up the third-base line that scored Wyrostek.[5] Philadelphia was within a run. Meers exited for Hi Bithorn, who surrendered a double to Frank McCormick. That hit ended McCormick's 0-for-14

slump, drove in two runs, and gave the Phillies an improbable lead.

Philadelphia needed three pitchers to subdue a Cubs threat in the bottom of the ninth. With two outs and a man in scoring position by way of a walk and a stolen base, Charley Schanz got pinch-hitter Charlie Gilbert to ground out to second, preserving the 9-8 victory.

The win went to Ripple – his only major-league victory. Meers was tagged with a loss that he didn't really deserve, but the fingers all pointed toward Borowy. The *Chicago Daily News* described the defeat as "one of the late inning collapses that are becoming traditional with him," while the *Chicago Tribune* labeled it one more troubling case of "the Henry Borowy swoon."[6]

Borowy didn't start another game for almost two weeks. This one must have been tough to put behind him. "You can lose 18-0 or 1-0 and feel that you deserve it, but a defeat like we encountered today I wouldn't wish on my worst enemy," Cubs manager Charlie Grimm shuddered. "I've never seen anything like it and I hope I'm never part of anything like it again."[7]

Sources

In addition to the sources cited in the Notes, the author used Baseball-Reference.com and Retrosheet.org.

The author also reviewed the following sources for play-by-play and other information:

Munzel, Edgar. "Phillies Topple Cubs 9-8 on Late Outbursts," *Chicago Sun*, June 11, 1946: 18.

"Phils Get First Hit in 8th, Rally to Defeat Cubs, 9-8," *Philadelphia Inquirer*, June 11, 1946: 27.

"Phillies Crack Bruin Winning Streak By 9-8," *Sioux City* (Iowa) *Journal,* June 11, 1946: 10.

The author also would like to thank Jack Zerby for his assistance.

Notes

1   *New York Herald Tribune*, September 13, 1945, cited in Lyle Spatz, "Hank Borowy," SABR Baseball Biography Project, sabr.org/bioproj/person/ea042adc#_edn8, accessed September 27, 2019.

2   Howard Roberts, "Phils Upset Cubs 9-8: Rally in 9th Ends Streak," *Chicago Daily News*, June 10, 1946: 21.

3   "Milnar Returned to Browns by Phillies," *St. Louis Post-Dispatch*, June 13, 1946: 16A.

4   Irving Vaughan, "Borowy Fails Again; Phils Beat Cubs, 9-8," *Chicago Tribune*, June 11, 1946: 27.

5   As of this writing, the Retrosheet and Baseball-Reference play-by-play accounts state that Wyrostek scored from second base on Novikoff's single; however, contemporary newspaper accounts indicate he was on third.

6   Roberts; Vaughan.

7   Jack McPhaul, "Grimm Sends Wyse After New Streak," *Chicago Daily Times*, June 11, 1946: 41.

CONNIE RYAN RETURNS TO BOSTON, HELPS REDS FLIP STANDINGS

JUNE 4, 1951:
CINCINNATI REDS 10,
BOSTON BRAVES 7,
AT BRAVES FIELD, BOSTON

BY JACK ZERBY

In the days of two eight-team major leagues, "division" meant something quite different from the three regional designations currently used in the National and American Leagues. Back then, fans and writers alike tended to dwell at some length on which teams were in each league's "first division" – among the top four teams in the standings. To be a "second division club" tended to cast a pall on attendance and was a factor in the first franchise moves of the modern era.[1]

A monetary incentive was also in play – especially important in the days when many major-league players needed winter jobs to carry them through to spring training. A first-division finish meant the team would receive at least a small share of that season's World Series net revenue; fifth- through eighth-place teams missed out.[2]

As the 1951 calendar flipped into June, the Cincinnati Reds, standing sixth in the National League but only 2½ games behind three teams, the Giants, Cubs, and Braves, rolled into Boston for a two-day, three-game series starting with a doubleheader on Sunday, June 3. They won both of those games to pull their record to 21-22, still sixth but only a half-game behind the teams tied for fourth place, the Braves and Cubs, both 22-22. Although it was early in the season, positional jockeying, especially between the first and second divisions, was something that kept fans tuned to their radios, watching the out-of-town scoreboard when in the ballparks, and checking each new edition of their newspapers as games unfolded.

Cincinnati hadn't finished in the first division since 1944. By comparison, the Braves had enjoyed a post-World War II upswing, finishing fourth in 1946,

then third in 1947, then winning the 1948 National League pennant on the strength of strong pitching led by Johnny Sain and Warren Spahn. They had slipped back to fourth place in both 1949 and 1950, but still had five consecutive first-division finishes.

Despite this relative success, the 1951 Braves were drawing poorly in cavernous Braves Field. Just under 10,000 fans had turned out for the Sunday twin bill, and a paltry 1,577 showed up for the Monday afternoon series finale. Spahn and Sain were still bulwarks of the pitching rotation, but neither had appeared thus far in the Cincinnati series.

On Monday afternoon Boston manager Billy Southworth sent 29-year-old righty Max Surkont to the hill.[3] Cincinnati's Luke Sewell countered with another right-hander, Herm Wehmeier. The respective lineups featured a pair of players traded for each other in May 1950. Seven-time NL All-Star catcher Walker Cooper, 36, had come to the

Courtesy The Topps Company.

Second baseman Connie Ryan started the scoring for Cincinnati with a three-run homer in the eighth.

Braves in exchange for second baseman Connie Ryan, five years younger.[4] After breaking in with the New York Giants for 11 games in 1942, Ryan had played with Boston since 1943, with the 1945 season lost to military service. Except for that absence, he had been the club's starting second baseman through 1947.

But when Boston acquired Eddie Stanky prior to the 1948 season, Ryan lost his starting role. Then, when Stanky was traded to the Giants two years later, Southworth installed 24-year-old rookie Roy Hartsfield at second base despite an "ultimatum" by Ryan that "if I don't play regularly, I want to be traded."[5] Ryan was gone on May 10, 1950.

Cooper had the best of it the early going, as he opened the scoring in the Boston second inning with a home run off Wehmeier that scored Bob Elliott. In the fifth, he increased the lead to 3-0 with a run-scoring single, then scored himself when Sid Gordon homered to put Wehmeier further in the hole at 5-0. In the sixth, Sewell replaced Wehmeier with Eddie Erautt; he proved equally ineffective, yielding single runs in the sixth and seventh innings, the last one driven in by pitcher Surkont.

But as the Reds came to bat in the top of the eighth down 7-0, Surkont weakened. He walked Lloyd Merriman and then got an out before Grady Hatton hustled a tap in front of the plate into an infield single. Fate had placed Ryan, batting second in the lineup, next up. He chided Southworth and his former teammates with a three-run homer that, if nothing else at this point, ended Surkont's shutout bid, making it 7-3, Boston. *Boston Globe* beat writer Bob Holbrook even trod lightly in his game story: "Still no one was worried about the eventual outcome. This game looked like money in the bank," as Southworth kept Surkont in the game and he retired Johnny Wyrostek and Ted Kluszewski on fly balls to escape further damage.[6]

Holbrook, though, took care to add, later in his account: "This game meant too much. It meant the difference between the Braves landing back in third place or winding up in sixth place, behind the Cincinnati Reds."[7]

The Braves responded by loading the bases against reliever Bud Byerly in their eighth; the drama included a steal of second base by Cooper – his only one of the season – but Byerly avoided any scoring by getting second baseman Sibbi Sisti to roll out to shortstop to end the half-inning.[8]

Apparently liking what he had seen for the last two outs of the eighth inning, Southworth sent Surkont out for the ninth. The roof fell in. Surkont allowed two singles and a walk before Southworth pulled him and presented reliever Dick Donovan, pitching in just his 17th major-league game, with a bases-loaded, no-outs situation. Donovan walked Merriman, delivering Cincinnati's fourth run. He then threw three balls to pinch-hitter Johnny Pramesa. With the 3-and-0 count Southworth brought in Sid Schacht, who hadn't reached the majors until age 32 the year before; and even then, it had been with the hapless Browns. Just in from the pen and needing to throw a strike with something on it, Schacht remarkably got Pramesa to pop out in foul ground but then yielded a bases-clearing double to Hatton that tied the score, 7-7. Ryan walked, then Wyrostek finished Schacht's day with a single that scored Hatton with the lead run. "Young [26], untried [pitching in his only major-league season]" George Estock was Southworth's next mound choice.[9] He gave up a fly ball to Kluszewski that scored Ryan and a run-scoring single to Virgil Stallcup.[10]

The Reds' merry-go-round seven-run, ninth inning put them ahead, 10-7; manager Sewell used Frank Smith to retire Boston's Buddy Kerr, pinch-hitter Willard Marshall, and Sam Jethroe one, two, three, to wrap up the exhilarating comeback. Byerly got the win. Schacht took the loss for the now-sixth-place Braves.

Reds beat writer Lou Smith caught the early-season essence, noting near the top of his game story that "by defeating the Braves the Reds moved into the first division – a fourth place tie with the Chicago Cubs. They're only one-half game out of third, now owned by the New York Giants, with whom the Reds Tuesday night open a crucial three-game series."[11]

Southworth took criticism from the Boston press. "Many laid the blame for yesterday's loss smack in the lap of manager Billy Southworth," wrote Holbrook. "The general opinion was that he fouled up the relief pitching by sending children to do the work of men."[12] At the same time, Ryan, the former Brave, got some praise. "Ryan has blossomed into a fighting, hard-hitting second baseman with the Reds." Quoting Ryan, the story continued, "With the Reds I'm able to try different things. If they work it's all right and if they fail no one ever says anything about it." Sewell chimed in for the Cincinnati press: "Swapping Walker Cooper for Ryan was by far the best deal the Reds have made since I've been with them. He's developed into a 'take charge guy' for us on the field."[13]

As far as finishes were concerned, 1951 wasn't a pennant year for either the Reds or Braves. That decision went three days beyond the regular season with the Giants and Dodgers.[14]

After surging as high as second place on June 9, Cincinnati faded to sixth place at 68-86. Two weeks after this game, Southworth was replaced as Boston manager by Tommy Holmes, who had the club in third place, although 17½ games back, on September 3. The Braves did, however, manage a first-division finish, fourth, at 76-78. Even at two games under .500, they got a piece of the World Series pool revenue. But after a desultory seventh-place finish and average home attendance of only 3,652 in 1952 (they had averaged 6,630 in 1951), they became the first modern-era franchise to relocate – becoming the Milwaukee Braves in 1953.

Sources

In addition to the sources cited in the Notes, the author consulted Baseball-Reference.com and Retrosheet.org.

Notes

1   Witness the St. Louis Browns: In 31 American League seasons, commencing with a close second-place finish in 1922, the Browns finished in the first division only eight times through 1953. While most of these were distant third- and fourth-place finishes, the Browns did eke out a wartime pennant in 1944, only to lose the World Series in six games. By 1953 the team finished eighth, 46½ games out of first, drew an average of 3,860 fans for each of their 77 home games, and re-emerged as the Baltimore Orioles for the 1954 season.

2   The total pool for division shares after the 1950 World Series was $486,371 for the four-game Series played that year. (It increased to $560,562 in 1951, when the Series went six games.) Fourth place in the 1950 National League – as well as in the American League – meant a 2½ percent share of the Series pool, or roughly $14,000 for the fourth-place teams (Boston in the NL; Cleveland in the AL) to divide among personnel. Don Drysdale, whose major-league career spanned 1956 through 1969, once remarked,

"When we played, World Series checks meant something. Now all they do is screw up your taxes." World Series Gate Receipts item, Baseball Almanac. com, accessed July 12, 2019. baseball-almanac.com/ws/wsshares.shtml.

3   Sain had pitched a complete-game win on June 1 and next started on June 5, when he was hit hard over four innings. Spahn started on June 2 but was ineffective and lasted only 1⅔ innings. He started again on June 6 and went all nine innings in a win. Providing even minimal rest for these veterans may have factored into Southworth's decision not to use either of them in the crucial ninth inning of this game.

4   Cooper made his eighth NL All-Star team as a Brave after the 1950 trade. Ryan had been a wartime NL All-Star selection for Boston in 1944.

5   Associated Press, "Power-Hungry Braves Trade Cooper From Cincinnati for Connie Ryan," *Phoenix* (Arizona) *Republic*, May 11, 1950: 32.

6   Bob Holbrook, "Southworth Under Fire for Selection of Relievers," *Boston Globe*, June 5, 1951: 31.

7   Holbrook.

8   Over his 18-year major-league career, Cooper stole 18 bases in 29 attempts. Cooper may have "run well for a catcher," but legendary Pittsburgh broadcaster Bob Prince might have dismissed him as having "larceny in his heart but lead in his feet," as Cooper made his way around six of the eight National League outposts from 1940 through 1957. Author's recollection from Prince's game coverage on KDKA radio, Pittsburgh, circa 1953-1960.

9   Estock was pitching in his ninth major-league game. He had been ineffective two days previously in relief of Spahn against the Cubs.

10   Holbrook.

11   Lou Smith, "Greatest Red Rally in Years Wins, 10-7; Ryan, Hatton, Big Guns in Upsetting Braves," *Cincinnati Enquirer,* June 5, 1951: 22.

12   Holbrook.

13   Lou Smith column, "Sewell Praises Ryan; Adcock Eying Return," *Cincinnati Enquirer,* June 5, 1951: 22. Sewell managed the Reds for the last three games of the 1949 season through the first 98 games of the 1952 season.

14   On August 11, 1951, the New York Giants stood 13 games behind the Brooklyn Dodgers, then roared back to finish in a regular-season tie with Brooklyn on September 30. The three-game playoff series that ensued is forever etched in baseball history by Bobby Thomson's "shot heard 'round the world" home run on October 3 that won the National League pennant for the Giants. Scott Ferkovich, "The Giants Win the Pennant!" SABR Baseball Games Project. sabr.org/gamesproj/game/october-3-1951-giants-win-pennant.

FOR A DAY, NATS SLAM BRAKES ON YANKS' STEAMROLLER

AUGUST 18, 1953:
WASHINGTON SENATORS 10,
NEW YORK YANKEES 8,
AT YANKEE STADIUM, NEW YORK

BY ANDREW SHARP

The Yankees were cruising to their fifth straight AL pennant in 1953 when they took on the Senators in New York for a three-game series beginning on August 18. The Nats[1] had just split a doubleheader in Boston with the Red Sox, while the Yankees had won four straight after pummeling the sixth-place A's in both ends of a doubleheader in Philadelphia.

New York, a winner of 18 in a row beginning in late May, stood at 79-37, nine games ahead of second-place Chicago. Washington was 58-60 in fifth place. The Senators had lost seven of eight meetings at Yankee Stadium and had won just five of 17 games between the two teams thus far.

The Yankees could be merciless on second-division teams. After losing to the Nats in Washington, 2-1, on August 11, the Yanks crushed the Senators 22-1 the next night and beat them 6-1 the following night. After a 9-8 loss to the Athletics on August 15, the Yankees rode roughshod over the A's in doubleheaders the next two days (8-0, 7-3 and 10-3, 9-0).

A paid crowd of 24,599 came to the Tuesday night contest, which featured a pregame performance by the popular baseball acrobat Jackie Price.[2] Although baseball broadcasts had become a TV staple in New York, this game was blacked out.[3]

Left-hander Bill Miller, called up two weeks earlier from Kansas City, started for New York. Veteran lefty Johnny Schmitz, waived by the Yankees in May, was Washington's starter. Schmitz had beaten the Yankees with six innings in relief on July 5, but lost to them in a four-inning relief stint a week later. New York had scored only two runs against him in 10 innings.

The Nats' shoddy fielding led to the Yankees scoring twice in the first. With a runner on and one out, shortstop Pompeyo Davalillo[4] booted Mickey Mantle's double-play grounder. Schmitz then walked Yogi Berra. Hank Bauer grounded to Nats first baseman Mickey Vernon, who "made an indecisive play …

Jim Busby tripled in the top of the ninth, driving in two and giving the Senators the runs they need to take the lead.

finally tossing to Schmitz, who was charged with an error when he failed to touch the bag," the *Washington Post*'s Shirley Povich wrote.[5] Gil McDougald scored on the play. Gus Triandos hit a slow grounder that Davalillo also mishandled. Mantle scored on what was ruled an infield single, but Berra rounded third too far and was caught in a rundown and tagged out. Both runs were unearned.

Schmitz walked Phil Rizzuto to lead off the second. Miller tried to sacrifice, but Rizzuto was forced out. Singles by McDougald and Bill Renna scored Miller. Then Mantle again grounded to Davalillo. From second, Renna ran into the shortstop as he fielded the ball. Davalillo tagged Renna and threw on to first in time to get Mantle. A double play would have ended the inning, but Renna was called out for interference, and the ball was dead. The fielder's choice put Mantle on first. "A lucky break on an umpire's call helped the Bombers," Roger Kahn wrote in the *New York Herald Tribune*. It allowed Berra to bat with two men on. His line-drive homer into the right-field seats, Berra's 22nd and his eighth against Washington, put New York up 6-0.

Clyde Vollmer's homer to left with one out in the fourth was all the Nats could muster against Miller through seven innings. The Yankees, meanwhile, scored twice more in the fifth against Sonny Dixon, who had taken over for Schmitz.

Berra led off the fifth with a bloop double to center "on which (Jim) Busby did not distinguish himself," Povich wrote. Bauer followed with a homer to right, his eighth of the season, making the score 8-1. The homer extended Bauer's modest hitting streak to 13 games.[6]

"Soon afterwards, complacent Yankee fans started filing toward the exits to miss one of the most uproarious finishes seen at the Stadium in a long time," Kahn wrote.[7]

The Yanks threatened again in the sixth. Two lead-off singles put runners on the corners, but Mantle lined to Vernon, who turned it into a double play. A ground-ball double play helped keep New York off the board in the seventh after the first two batters reached.

Washington chipped away with two solo home runs in the eighth against Miller. With one out Vernon, 3-for-18 in the past four games, "hit a whistling homer into the right-field seats," Povich wrote. With two outs, Vollmer hit his second homer of the game, deep to left.

Righty Jerry Lane, a rookie called up in July, retired the Yankees in order in the eighth. The game went to the ninth with New York leading 8-3.

When Nats catcher Ed Fitz Gerald led off the top of the ninth with a single, Yankees manager Casey Stengel went to the mound to lift Miller, "to the annoyance of the crowd," Joseph M. Sheehan wrote in the *New York Times*.[8]

Stengel brought in Allie Reynolds, the Yankees' most effective late-inning reliever that season. It's likely that with a five-run lead, Reynolds had little time to warm up in the bullpen. He threw a wild pitch before walking pinch-hitter Gil Coan. Having used three pinch-hitters already, Nats manager Bucky Harris sent up ace starter Bob Porterfield to bat for Lane. Reynolds struck out Porterfield on three fastballs.[9]

Eddie Yost began the scoring onslaught with a single that brought in Fitz Gerald. A walk to Mel Hoderlein loaded the bases for Vernon, still the league's leading hitter at .330. Reynolds fell behind 3-and-1 before Vernon hit a ball off the wall in the right-field corner that caromed away from Bauer. Vernon cleared the bases and ended up with a triple, where he represented the tying run.

"Out dashed Stengel to the mound to a chorus of boos," Sheehan wrote.[10] Right-hander Tom Gorman came in and got two quick strikes on Jackie Jensen before walking him.[11] Vollmer's ground single to left scored Vernon and tied the game.[12]

"Casey came back on the field to the tune of even louder derisive hooting" and brought in veteran righty Johnny Sain.[13] Busby, his first batter, fouled off two pitches before hitting "a long drive to center that should have been caught," Sheehan wrote. Mantle, "back in the lineup after ten days … with a wrenched knee," had persuaded Stengel that he was well enough to return to center field.[14] Stengel "can now tell Mantle to save his suggestions," Kahn wrote.[15]

Busby's triple scored Vollmer and Jensen. Mantle recovered in time to relay to Billy Martin at second, who threw out Busby trying for an inside-parker, at home, but the damage was done.

Connie Marrero, a 42-year-old Cuban right-hander, retired Mantle and Berra in the bottom of the ninth.[16] Then Yost ended the game, diving to his left to snare Bauer's sharp liner. Lane was the winning pitcher, the first of his two major-league victories. Gorman was charged with the loss.

Between them, the Yankees' three relievers in the ninth finished the season with 26 saves. This was one that stunningly got away. Unfazed, however, the Yankees shut out Washington the next afternoon, 2-0. Berra homered yet again. On Thursday afternoon New York shut out Washington once more, 7-0.

The Senators finished at 76-76, the last time while in Washington that the team avoided a losing record. The Yankees ended the season with 99 victories and won the World Series. So if nothing else, this game kept them from winning 100 in the regular season.

Sources

In addition to the sources cited in the Notes, the author also consulted Baseball-Reference.com and Retrosheet.org.

Notes

1   Washington was still officially the Nationals, which accounts for the shorthand "Nats" and subsequent references to the team in game stories. Yet just about everybody called them the Senators. The name Nationals was not officially abandoned until after longtime owner Clark Griffith's death in October 1955.

2   Price, who played with the 1946 Indians, could do amazing things with baseballs in incredibly absurd positions. He could bat or throw strikes with his body upside down and, among other things, catch long fly balls in the outfield while riding a jeep. As it was said then, you had to see it (youtube.com/watch?v=_Jflun5CyIc) to believe it. But as fewer people attended the mostly minor-league games at which he would perform, he couldn't make a living. He took his own life in 1967.

3   Roger Kahn, "Senators Score 7 in 9th and Beat Yankees, 10-8," *New York Herald Tribune*, August 19, 1953: 20.

4   Davalillo, nicknamed Yo-Yo, stood just 5-feet-3. He had been called up and made his debut on August 1. The brother of Vic Davalillo, he appeared in 19 games in 1953, his only time in the majors.

5   Shirley Povich, "Nats RallyfFor 7 Runs in 9th to Beat Yanks, 10-8," *Washington Post*, August 198, 1953: 13.

6   Bauer was hitless the next day, as was Irv Noren, who extended his hitting streak to 11 games in this one.

7   Kahn.

8   Joseph M. Sheehan, "Washington Explodes for 7 Runs in Ninth to Stop the Bombers, 10-8," *New York Times*, August 19, 1953: 32.

9   Povich.

10   Sheehan.

11   Povich.

12   Kahn.

13   Sheehan.

14   Sheehan.

15   Kahn.

16   Marrero was almost 103 years old when died in Cuba in 2014, the oldest former player at the time. This was one of two games the 5-foot-5 right-hander saved in 1953 and the only two games in which he appeared in relief.

ORIOLES SCORE SEVEN RUNS IN NINTH TO THWART BLUE JAYS

JULY 2, 1995:
BALTIMORE ORIOLES 9,
TORONTO BLUE JAYS 7,
AT SKYDOME, TORONTO

BY MIKE HUBER

"Jays Turn Victory into Defeat" read the headline in the *Ottawa Citizen* the morning after the Baltimore Orioles beat the Toronto Blue Jays, 9-7, in a Sunday afternoon game at Toronto's SkyDome.[1] The home-team Blue Jays were three outs away from a 7-2 victory over the visiting Orioles when a terrible finish erased their terrific start.

The Blue Jays had suffered a devastating defeat on June 21, when a ninth-inning grand slam gave Milwaukee a 10-9 win. Toronto went into an eight-game losing streak and had dropped from third place in the American League East to fifth. Despite winning three of their last four games, the Blue Jays (23-35) were 10 games out of first place. The Orioles (27-33) had won four of six games on their most recent road trip, which wrapped up with this game in Toronto.

A Sunday crowd of 42,226 came out to root for the Jays. Manager Cito Gaston gave the start to third-year right-hander Woody Williams, making his first start in the big leagues after 88 appearances out of the Blue Jays' bullpen. Baltimore skipper Phil Regan countered with John DeSilva, a righty making just the second start of his career.[2] DeSilva had been called up from the minors to pitch on June 27, earning his first victory after pitching 5⅓ innings in a game against the Milwaukee Brewers.

Williams dominated from the umpire's "Play Ball!," striking out the side in the first. In the home half, Paul Molitor singled with one out and went to second on a passed ball. DeSilva walked Roberto Alomar, and Joe Carter hit the pitcher's first offering deep into the seats in left, giving Toronto a 3-0 lead.

Ed Sprague led off the Blue Jays' fourth with a homer to left. DeSilva retired Shawn Green but then walked Candy Maldonado, his fourth free pass of the game, prompting Regan to make a change. Mike Oquist relieved DeSilva and got out of the inning. However, an inning later Oquist was in trouble. He walked leadoff batter Alomar, who stole second on the first pitch to Carter. Carter popped out and then Oquist

Manny Alexander led off the ninth with a home run, then came up again and singled in two more runs.

intentionally walked John Olerud, who was riding a five-game hitting streak. This move backfired when Sprague lined a double into left field, driving Alomar and Olerud home.

In the bottom of the seventh, with Mark Lee now pitching for Baltimore, Domingo Cedeno tripled and scored on Molitor's sacrifice fly. The Blue Jays led, 7-0. Their pitcher Woody Williams turned in a "gutsy, seven-inning effort"[3] for his first start, a sportswriter observed. Harold Baines had doubled with one out in the second, and then Williams held the Orioles hitless through the seventh.

As the eighth inning opened, though, it all changed. Kevin Bass singled to lead off. After Jeff Huson fouled out, rookie catcher Gregg Zaun hit his first major-league home run, cutting the score to 7-2. After Curtis Goodwin grounded out to first, unassisted, Gaston decided to pull his starter. Williams had thrown 103 pitches. He walked off the field to a standing ovation. Reliever Danny Cox finished the inning, striking out Brady Anderson. Armando Benitez pitched the eighth for the Orioles, striking out the side on 16 pitches.

As the top of the ninth got underway, Toronto rookie Tomas Perez jogged out to play shortstop and Cedeno moved from his position at shortstop to second base, replacing Alomar. In a bizarre development, Alomar was taken off the field due to a death threat against him. The *Toronto Star* reported that "Metro Police arrested a 31-year-old Port Hope woman after she was held by [the SkyDome] hotel staff. A stolen, loaded .22-calibre handgun was found in her possession,"[4] and she had allegedly threatened to kill Alomar.[5] Taking no chances, Gaston changed his infield.

Manny Alexander led off and lifted a fly ball over the left-field wall to start the Orioles' offense. Rafael Palmeiro singled, as did Cal Ripken. (Palmeiro motored to third on the hit.) Ricardo Jordan replaced Cox on the mound. Jeffrey Hammonds batted for Baines and drove a fly ball into left, deep enough for Palmeiro to score Baltimore's fourth run. Jordan then struck out Bass for the second out. Again, Gaston made a move to the bullpen, bringing on rookie right-hander Tim Crabtree to face Bret Barberie, now pinch-hitting for Huson. Crabtree had been called up to Toronto from Triple-A Syracuse on June 23, bringing a 5.40 earned-run average with him. He had pitched to one Baltimore batter the day before. Barberie lined "a low fastball up the middle, past Crabtree"[6] to keep Baltimore's hopes alive. Ripken stopped at second base.

Chris Hoiles became the third pinch-hitter of the inning, batting for Zaun. Hoiles sent Crabtree's offering to right field for the potential final out, but it bounced off Shawn Green's glove for an error. (Green admitted, "I just took my eye off it.")[7] Both Ripken and Barberie scored, and Hoiles ended up on second base. Goodwin then grounded a ball to Perez, who glanced at third (Hoiles was running on the play) but threw to first. His throw was high, pulling Olerud off the bag, and Goodwin was safe on the throwing error. With runners at first and third, Gaston called for Crabtree to walk Anderson, loading the bases. Manny Alexander dug in a the batter's box for the second time in the inning. The Orioles had batted around.

Alexander said he realized that "Crabtree was a rookie who was struggling and couldn't afford to walk in the tying run."[8] So, figured Alexander, he was going to get a steady dose of fastballs. He reckoned correctly and lashed a 1-and-1 fastball up the middle for a single, driving in Hoiles and Goodwin. The Orioles had completed a miraculous comeback. Crabtree, surely frazzled by his team's shoddy defense, uncorked a wild pitch to Palmeiro, allowing Anderson to score Baltimore's ninth and final run. Crabtree retired Palmeiro on a fly ball to center for the only out he was credited with. He had faced six batters, allowing four runs, all unearned. Baltimore had scored seven runs (five unearned) in the final inning and now led, 9-7.

Doug Jones came on for the Orioles to close out the ninth. The Jays went quietly, three up and three down, with Jones fanning Carter for the final out. Several Orioles came running out of the dugout onto the field, "as if a bench-clearing brawl had broken out. Except there were handshakes all around, instead of punches."[9] Hoiles commented, "Any time you can come up with seven runs in the ninth inning and win, that's pretty impressive."[10]

This was the first time the Blue Jays had given up seven runs in the ninth inning. After the game, Sprague lamented, "It looked like it was in the bag, then the baseball gods took over."[11]

Baltimore sent 11 batters to the plate in the ninth inning. Two errors and a wild pitch kept the inning going, after Toronto had gotten two outs. Palmeiro said, "That's what's so good about baseball. If it was basketball or football, and there was a minute to go, it would've been over."

Orioles skipper Phil Regan told *Baltimore Sun* reporter Buster Olney, "It was a good day for San Pedro de Macoris. Manny got the big hits and Armando Benitez got his first big-league victory."[12] Both players were born in the same town, San Pedro de Macoris, Dominican Republic.

With the comeback, "a solid 4-3 road trip turned into a great 5-2 road trip and was a bit of a payback."[13] In the last six seasons, the Blue Jays had beaten the Orioles in the final at-bat 14 times, including 12 times at SkyDome. Toronto were 4-4 leading up to the 1995 All-Star Game. Afterward, they went 29-48, falling to last place in the division. Meanwhile, Baltimore won nine of its next 13 games and finished the 1995 campaign in third place, two games below .500.

Sources

In addition to the sources mentioned in the Notes, the author consulted base-ball-reference.com, retrosheet.org and sabr.org.

Notes

1   "Jays Turn Victory into Defeat," *Ottawa Citizen,* July 3, 1995: 3.

2   This game was DeSilva's last one in the majors. He was granted free agency by the Orioles at the end of the season but never made it back to the big leagues.

3   Mark Zwolinski, "Jays' Play for the Birds," *Toronto Star*, July 3, 1995: C1.

4   Zwolinski.

5   Alomar lived in the SkyDome Hotel during the regular season.

6   Buster Olney, "Orioles Roll Lucky 7, Rock Jays in 9th," *Baltimore Sun*, July 3, 1995: C1.

7   Olney, "Orioles Roll Lucky 7."

8   Olney, "Orioles Roll Lucky 7."

9   Olney, "Orioles Roll Lucky 7."

10   Olney, "Orioles Roll Lucky 7."

11   Zwolinski.

12   Buster Olney, "As Batman, Alexander Is Unlikely Hero," *Baltimore Sun*, July 2, 1995: 6C.

13   Olney, "Orioles Roll Lucky 7."

12 UNANSWERED RUNS LEAD TO A PADRE VICTORY

JUNE 14, 2019:
SAN DIEGO PADRES 16,
COLORADO ROCKIES 12,
AT COORS FIELD, DENVER

BY DAVID BLACK

The thin Rocky Mountain air, the enlarged outfield dimensions, and the standard of low humidity have long made Coors Field a ballpark where the improbable regularly happens, especially with its run-scoring environment. While the home of the Colorado Rockies has hosted many incredible comebacks in its tenure, few were as unlikely as the one the San Diego Padres experienced on the evening of Friday, June 14, 2019.

The Padres were visiting Denver for the second game of a four-game weekend series. The Rockies captured the Thursday night game, 9-6. Colorado entered the Friday game with a 36-32 record, having battled back from a dreadful season start. Optimism was growing for the club, with the hometown fans hoping the team could parlay its current surge into a competition for a third straight playoff berth. As for the fourth-place Padres, they trailed their second-place counterparts by 3½ games, holding a 33-36 mark.

Rookie right-hander Cal Quantrill took the mound for the Padres. He was faced by 26-year-old righty Jeff Hoffman, a pitcher for whom the Rockies had high hopes but who struggled regularly with his command during his young career. True to form, Hoffman grooved a high fastball to Hunter Renfroe of the Padres in the second inning, and Renfroe deposited a majestic shot deep into the Padres bullpen in right-center field. However, Hoffman settled in and pitched five innings, giving up only the single run, along with three hits and two walks. Hoffman's night was through after his 88-pitch outing.

Quantrill did not fare as well in his five innings of work. He gave up two runs in the third inning on left fielder David Dahl's opposite-field homer to left

field. Additionally, Quantrill was charged with two runs in the fifth inning. Right fielder Charlie Blackmon singled and shortstop Trevor Story doubled. Dahl and first baseman Daniel Murphy followed with productive outs, a groundout and sacrifice fly successively, to put the Rockies ahead 4-1 at the end of five innings. After both starting pitchers departed, the game was left to the efforts of the respective bullpens, who would struggle mightily on this evening.

While the Padres tallied twice in the sixth and once in the seventh, it was the Rockies who took control of the contest by scoring seven times in these two frames. A five-run sixth was highlighted by a three-run inside-the-park home run by Ian Desmond, who had entered the game on a double-switch, and a rally consisting of singles and Padres errors in the seventh, with Desmond earning another RBI on a single. The end of the seventh found the Rockies with a commanding 11-4 lead, and with – it seemed – just two innings to play.

The partisan crowd of 38,077 was dismayed by what followed. The Padres, beginning in the eighth inning, decimated the Rockies relief corps with 12 consecutive runs, tying the game in the ninth inning and seizing the lead and victory in the 12th. As they entered the eighth, the win expectancy for San Diego, according to Fangraphs, was a mere 0.3 percent.[1] Their odds of victory did not significantly improve after they scored a run in the inning on a two-out double by Austin Hedges that brought home Hunter Renfroe.

The Rockies, feeling confident of the outcome of the game with a six-run ninth-inning lead, turned to left-hander Mike Dunn to finish the game. Dunn, however, was able to secure only one out while being charged with four earned runs. Fernando Tatis Jr., as he did so many times during his rookie campaign, jump-started the Padres offense with a single to left. After Josh Naylor struck out, Manny Machado singled, and both he and Tatis advanced one base on Dunn's wild pitch. Eric Hosmer followed with a two-run single, and Hunter Renfroe clubbed his second home run of the night, this time to the left-field pavilion. Dunn's night was finished as the Rockies opted to bring in their closer, right-hander Wade Davis.

Davis's season had been a success thus far as he entered the game with a 2.55 ERA and eight saves. However, he was not able to hold down this victory for Colorado. With one out, Wil Myers and Ian Kinsler singled. Austin Hedges flied out, but pinch-hitter Manny Margot walked to load the bases. Then Tatis got his second hit of the inning, a solid single to center, and the game was tied. As the boos rained down in Coors Field, Davis managed to strike out Josh Naylor to end the inning.

The Rockies were retired one-two-three in the ninth and 10th, and managed only a single in the 11th. The Padres didn't score in either the 10th or 11th, themselves also limited to an 11th-inning single.

The game remained tied at 11-11 until the 12th inning. By this time fireballing right-hander Jairo Diaz was on the mound for Colorado. The Padres pounded him for five extra-base hits in the inning, the big blow being the third home run of the game by Hunter Renfroe, each one off a different pitcher. The Rockies, competing with a depleted bullpen at this point, allowed Diaz to remain in the game and take the abuse. Padres batters poured across five runs.

The Rockies did manage to score in the bottom of the 12th on a solo home run by leadoff batter Charlie Blackmon, but Padres relief specialist Kirby Yates was able to close out the contest and a 16-12 Padres triumph 5 hours and 4 minutes after the first pitch of the game.

It is not often a major-league team scores 12 consecutive runs, and the postgame quotes from the Padres noted this fact. "Went from about as ugly as we could possibly play to as unbelievable as it could possibly be," said manager Andy Green.[2]

Center fielder Wil Myers said, "I ain't seen nothing like that."[3]

Rockies manager Bud Black was more circumspect, simply sharing that the game was "a tough one … because it looked like we had it."[4]

While the Padres completed their astounding Friday evening comeback, this four-game series of baseball was not over. In fact, the 16-12 Padres win

Courtesy The Topps Company.

Hunter Renfroe homered three times (including a two-run homer in the ninth and a two-run homer in the 12th), driving in five runs.

was merely a part of a wild weekend in Denver, whose impact set the tone for the rest of the Rockies' season.

The Padres ended the set with a split, losing the Saturday evening contest, 14-8, and triumphing on Sunday, 14-13. The series set the major-league record for the most runs scored in a four-game series, 92, surpassing the previous record of 88 set by the Phillies and Dodgers in 1929. The Rockies and Padres also nearly broke the mark for the most hits in a four-game series, falling two short at 131.[5]

Many traced the start of the downfall of the 2019 Rockies to the June 14 game and the entire series versus the Padres. After their Thursday night victory, the Rockies went 35-59 the rest of the way, with much criticism levied against a faltering bullpen – one that was devastated in the games against San Diego.

On an individual note, Rockies right fielder Charlie Blackmon clubbed 15 hits in the series, also a major-league record for a four-game series, four of which were counted from Friday night. In addition, Blackmon became the first player since Rafael Furcal in 2007 to record four hits in three consecutive games. Blackmon, however, had a difficult time enjoying his achievements when the weekend ended. "The last three games were five hours, four hours, five hours," Blackmon said. "It's just really hard to go out there, play that much baseball at altitude. To end up a split, it's disappointing."[6]

While the Rockies briefly rebounded from this grueling game and series, they cratered in July with a 6-19 record, their beleaguered bullpen being a key source of the struggle. The Rockies ended the 2019 season with a disappointing 71-91 record, well out of playoff contention. The Padres fared even worse, ending the campaign one game below the Rockies in the standings at 70-92, but with vivid memories of an amazing comeback on a Colorado night in June.

Author's Note

The author attended this contest, remaining in his seat the entire 5:04 of the game and outlasting all but a thousand or so of the patrons that night.

Sources

In addition to the sources cited in the Notes, the author accessed Baseball-Reference.com, MLB.com and Retrosheet.org

Notes

1   fangraphs.com/wins.aspx?date=2019-06-14&team=Rockies&dh=0&season=2019.

2   Kevin Acee, "Padres Beat Rockies with Mile High Miracle, Rallying from Six-Run Deficit in Ninth," *San Diego Union-Tribune,* sandiegouniontribune.com/sports/padres/story/2019-06-14/padres-rockies-trade-deadline-eric-hosmer-fernando-tatis.

3   Nick Groke, "'I've Never Seen Anything Like It.' Looking Back at the Coors Field Series That Wrecked the Season," *The Athletic*, theathletic.com/1212946/2019/09/16/ive-never-seen-anything-like-it-looking-back-at-the-coors-field-series-that-wrecked-the-rockies-season/.

4   Patrick Saunders, "Rockies blow six-run lead in ninth inning in historic meltdown, lose in extra innings to Padres," *Denver Post,* https://www.denverpost.com/2019/06/15/rockies-historic-meltdown-padres-loss/.

5   The Pirates and Phillies combined for 133 hits (August 7-August 10, 1922 at the Baker Bowl in Philadelphia.

6   Jake Elman, "Rockies' Blackmon records 15 hits in four-game series," *UPI Sports,* June 17, 2019, accessed April 14, 2020, https://www.upi.com/Sports_News/MLB/2019/06/17/Rockies-Blackmon-records-15-hits-in-four-game-series/9241560779045/

THE FUTURE WORLD CHAMPION MARLINS REDEEM THEMSELVES FROM A 25-9 BLOWOUT THE NIGHT BEFORE

JUNE 28, 2003: FLORIDA MARLINS 10, BOSTON RED SOX 9, AT FENWAY PARK, BOSTON

BY BRUCE "WICKER" THOMPSON

This was a battle between two ballclubs that both played deep into the postseason in 2003. In June the Florida Marlins faced the Boston Red Sox for three interleague games. The Marlins were in fourth place in the NL East, already 12 games behind the Atlanta Braves. The Red Sox were second in the AL East, two games behind the New York Yankees.

After the year had fully played out, the Red Sox had been edged by the Yankees in an 11-inning Game Seven of the American League Championship Series. The Marlins won the 2003 World Series against the Yankees, taking the Series in six games.

In the three games in late June, the Red Sox outscored the Marlins, 45-25. The first of the three-game set at Boston's Fenway Park was a 25-8 blowout on Friday night, June 27, kicked off by a 14-run bottom of the first inning – 10 of the Red Sox runs scoring before the Marlins had even recorded the first out.

The Marlins were looking for some sort of redemption the next night, and they found it.

The matchup for the Saturday night game featured knuckleballer Tim Wakefield pitching for the Red Sox and left-hander Tommy Phelps going for the Marlins.

Marlins leadoff hitter Juan Pierre beat out a bunt. While Luis Castillo was batting, Pierre stole second base and then stole third. Castillo struck out, but Marlins catcher Iván Rodríguez hit into a 6-3 ground-out that enabled Pierre to score easily from third. The Marlins' Lowell, playing as the designated hitter in the American League ballpark, flied out to center.

In the top of the second the Marlins added a run. Juan Encarnación singled to left field, stole second, moved to third on Derrek Lee's single to right field, and scored when Miguel Cabrera hit into a 5-4-3

The Marlins overcame a 9-2 Red Sox lead, and Mike Lowell's three-run homer in the top of the ninth inning boosted the Marlins to a 10-9 lead.

double play. The Red Sox did little against Phelps and the score after two innings was 2-0, Marlins.

In the bottom of the fourth, the Red Sox tied the score when Bill Mueller drew a walk off Phelps and shortstop Nomar Garciaparra hit a two-run home run to deep left field.

The score remained 2-2 until the bottom of the sixth, when the Red Sox took advantage of a tiring Phelps, who had thrown close to 100 pitches. Gabe Kapler, making his Red Sox debut after his contract was purchased from the Colorado Rockies, drove in Kevin Millar from first with a triple to right field. Freddy Sanchez laid down a squeeze bunt to the pitcher, reaching safely and scoring Kapler. Johnny Damon singled to right, and Garciaparra drove in both runners with a double to center field, giving the Red Sox a 4-2 lead. That was it for Phelps; he ended the day with 112 pitches in 5⅔ innings.

Things got no better for Phelps's replacement, right-hander Nate Bump, who was making his big-league debut. He gave up a single to Manny Ramirez, walked David Ortiz, and hit Millar with a pitch. With the bases loaded, Kapler doubled to left field, driving in two runs. Millar, running from first base, rounded third, reversed course and scampered back to the bag but was tagged out. The Red Sox had scored seven runs on seven hits, led, 9-2, and the Marlins faced a big uphill climb.

In the eighth inning, with Tim Wakefield still on the mound for the Red Sox, the first three batters, Pierre, Castillo, and Rodríguez got hits; Rodríguez's infield hit to second drove Pierre home. After an out, Encarnación hit a home run to deep left field, driving Wakefield from the game after 93 pitches in 7⅓ innings. Mike Timlin retired the side, and the Marlins trailed, 9-6.

After Nate Bump retired the Red Sox in the eighth, Red Sox right-hander Brandon Lyon entered the game in search of his 10th save of the season. He had a 3.07 ERA coming into the game. Brian Banks and Pierre singled with one out, and when Castillo hit into a force play, the Marlins were down to their last out. Ivan Rodríguez staved off defeat when he punched a single to center field, scoring Banks.

Lyon got two strikes on the next batter, Mike Lowell. Lowell then launched a three-run home run into the Red Sox bullpen in deep right field, and the Marlins led, 10-9. It was his 25th home run of the season, leading the National League. The 3-4-5 batters in the Marlins order (Rodriguez, Lowell, and Encarnacion) now each had three RBIs. The Marlins had scored four in the eighth and four in the ninth.

The Red Sox had one last chance but couldn't capitalize. Batting against Braden Looper with one out, catcher Jason Varitek doubled off the wall in left-center field, but became the final out of the game when Johnny Damon lined out to center fielder Pierre, whose throw to shortstop Alex Gonzalez doubled up Varitek before he could get back to second base. Varitek admitted afterward that he had misread the ball and thought it was going to drop.[1]

The Marlins had overcome "the largest deficit for a victory in franchise history."[2]

Nate Bump recorded the win in his major-league debut.

The Marlins win shifted the spotlight from Gabe Kapler, who had been 4-for-5 with a triple, two doubles, and three runs batted in for his Red Sox debut.

Red Sox manager Grady Little said of Lyon, "It caught up to him tonight. The kid's been nearly perfect for us all season long and tonight it caught up to him. He's a human being, too, and that happens."[3]

The win brought the Marlins' record to 41-41. They were in fourth place in the National League East Division, 11 games behind the division-leading Atlanta Braves. The Red Sox fell to 46-33, in second place in the AL East Division, 3½ games behind the New York Yankees.

After the game Florida manager Jack McKeon, who complained the night before about Boston's 25-8 win, said, "We were embarrassed last night," and went on to say "they woke us up" and "this takes a little of the taste out of our mouths."[4]

After the season had fully played out, the Red Sox had been edged by the Yankees in an 11-inning Game Seven of the American League Championship Series. The Marlins won the 2003 World Series against the Yankees in six games.

Sources

In addition to the sources cited in the Notes, the author consulted Retrosheet.org, Baseball-Reference.com, and SABR.org.

Notes

1   Bob Hohler, "Marlins' Payback Really Hurts Sox," *Boston Globe*, June 29, 2003: C1.

2   Hohler.

3   Aaron Harlan, "Flop of the 9th for Lyon," *Boston Globe*, June 29, 2003: C10.

4   Associated Press, "Red Sox Blow 7-Run Lead, Fall to Marlins," *San Francisco Chronicle*, June 29, 2003: 37.

A LUCKY 13 ON THE 13TH

MAY 13, 1911:
BOSTON RED SOX 13,
DETROIT TIGERS 11,
AT BENNETT PARK, DETROIT

BY BOB LEMOINE

The crowd at Bennett Park in Detroit had come to see a slugfest, at least one produced by their hometown Tigers. You can't blame them for expecting this, even though today we refer to this game on May 13, 1911, as taking place in the Deadball Era. Their Tigers had produced a lot of "big innings" so far in the 1911 season, putting up eight-run and five-run innings against St. Louis (April 25 and May 6); and a five-run first inning, two four-run innings, and a 14-5 pounding against Cleveland (April 18, April 26, and May 1). And they had outscored their opponents 141-79. Outbursts were, in the words of F.A. Batchelor of the *Detroit Free Press*, "Tigeresque."[1] The crowd of just over 11,000 got what they came for as the Tigers pounced to a 10-1 lead over Boston. Their Tigers were ahead in the ninth, 10-4, and many "wended their way in mass formation toward the exits," and probably did not learn until the next day's paper that the Red Sox had stunned the Tigers with a dramatic, improbable comeback. Such an outburst was so Tiger-like that Batchelor wrote, "Manager [Hughie] Jennings ought to sue the Boston Red Sox for infringement of copyright."[2]

The Tigers had come roaring out of the gate to begin the 1911 season, starting 6-0 and finishing April 13-2. The Tigers continued their storm into May, winning nine in a row, including a 10-0 rout against the New York Yankees, then called the Highlanders. They actually "slumped" against those New Yorkers, splitting their four-game series, but stood at 22-4 as the Red Sox came to town.

Boston had also played well, though nowhere near as well as the soaring Tigers. Still, the Red Sox occupied second place at 14-10. They started slowly out of the gate and were 6-7 through April, but had been 8-3 since, taking three of four decisions at both New York and Cleveland.

Ed Willett took the mound for the hometown Tigers. His season had been a mixed bag so far. Willett shut out the White Sox and got a win in relief against the Browns, but also had short starts in his last two outings. He was 2-1. He was opposed by Boston's Ed Karger, who was 2-2 in a combination of starts and

Smoky Joe Wood had already pitched four complete games and two shutouts for the Red Sox that season. Today, they needed him to close out a slugfest.

RED SOX BEAT TIGERS IN 10-INNING CLASH

Riggert and Williams Are the Heroes With the Stick, Lewis's Drive for the Circuit Being a Mighty Aid In Defeating Detroits.

Boston Journal headline May 14, 1911.

relief appearances, which described much of his six-year career.

The Red Sox jumped on the scoreboard in the first inning. Harry Hooper led off with a single, took second on an out, and scored on Tris Speaker's single. The speedy Speaker stole second and third but was stranded to end the inning. On the steal of third, Speaker slid right into George Moriarty, who slammed the ball down in disgust, arguing with base umpire Jack Egan, who kicked him out of the game. Tommy Connolly was the plate umpire. Charley O'Leary replaced Moriarty at third. The 1-0 Red Sox lead held until a typical Tigers big inning in the bottom of the third.

Oscar Stanage smashed his second home run of the season over the screen in left. Willett singled to center and Delos Drake reached on a muffed grounder by Clyde Engle. Donie Bush pushed a bunt toward first and a fine one-handed pickup by Rip Williams was wasted when Karger didn't cover the bag. The bases were now loaded for Ty Cobb, who came into the game batting .408 (his .419 average would win the 1911 batting crown). Cobb "hit the ball into the next county," wrote Batchelor of the enormous grand slam over the right-field corner.[3] The newspapers in both cities mentioned this being the farthest Cobb had ever hit a ball. The *Boston Globe* called it, "undoubtedly the longest hit made in Detroit since the organization of the American League."[4] Batchelor said Cobb's clout soared over "the egg-shaped sphere clearing the palings just where Walker's sign is located. This sign is some 400 feet from the plate and the ball cleared it by a good 10 feet." This, he wrote, was "the first time in history that anyone has driven one over this particular fence. Never will (Cobb) club one any further than this."[5]

Sam Crawford followed with a single and bluffed going to second, fooling Speaker into making a wild throw. The crafty Crawford reached third. He scored on Jim Delahanty's sacrifice to give the Tigers a 6-1 lead.

Karger's day was done and Charley Hall came in from the bullpen, but couldn't stop the bleeding. The Tigers poured on more runs in the fourth and fifth. Stanage singled and scored on Drake's triple, and then Bush singled Drake home to extend the lead to 8-1. In the fifth Crawford tripled to right. Delahanty walked and stole second. O'Leary singled both runners in but was caught in a rundown. Jack Ness reached on an error by Heinie Wagner and later attempted to score on another error but was thrown out at the plate. The Tigers led 10-1. Hall's day was over just like that.

Singles by Lewis, Williams, Carrigan, and pinch-hitter Jack Thoney helped Boston get two runs back in the sixth. The Red Sox pushed another run across in the seventh to cut the lead to 10-4. Jack Killilay came in from the Boston bullpen and made his major-league debut. He tamed the Tigers for three innings, holding them scoreless on two hits. That's the way the game stood as Boston batted in the top of the ninth.

Hooper grounded out to Delahanty to start the inning. Larry Gardner reached on an infield hit, as did Speaker, which Delahanty could have turned into an out "with a little more speed on his part," Batchelor wrote.[6] Lewis sent a scorching liner past short that also skipped past Drake and also Cobb, who was backing up Drake. Lewis had an inside-the-park home run and Boston trailed 10-7.

Engle and Wagner punched back-to-back singles. Hughie Jennings was likely shaking his head in disbelief and summoned Ralph Works from the bullpen. Jennings often clashed with Works, but so far he had a victory in all of his five appearances, three of them starts. Williams singled to score Engle and the score was 10-8. Works induced Bill Carrigan to pop out for the second out of the inning. Detroit was still in control of this now nail-biting game.

Red Sox manager Patsy Donovan called upon rookie Joe Riggert to pinch-hit for Killilay. Riggert had his first major-league at-bats the day before in Cleveland, where he went 2-for-4 with a triple and four RBIs. Riggert scorched a sinking line drive to right. Crawford made a desperate attempt to end the game, but the ball skipped past him and Riggert had a game-tying triple. Delahanty kicked Hooper's grounder and Riggert scored the go-ahead run. Gardner grounded out to end the inning. Boston had scored seven runs to lead 11-10.

Even with the Tigers' offense, they now had to mount a comeback against Smoky Joe Wood, Boston's ace pitcher. Wood had thrown nearly 200 innings in

1910 with a minuscule 1.69 ERA. He had won five games so far in 1911 with two shutouts and four complete games. Davy Jones, batting for Drake, grounded out. Bush singled and scored the tying run on Cobb's double off the left-field screen. Wood intentionally walked Crawford. Both runners took off. Carrigan's throw was on target, but third baseman Engle appeared skittish with the approaching Cobb (perhaps sliding with spikes in the air) and the Georgia Peach slid in safely. Cobb represented the winning run. Wood wanted to pitch to Delahanty and was perturbed when Donovan called for an intentional walk to set up a force play. The strategy worked, however. Boss Schmidt, batting for O'Leary, struck out and Cobb was a dead duck, caught between third and home. Batchelor thought Cobb was trying to decoy Carrigan into a bad throw. Perhaps it was a busted squeeze play or hit-and-run. Whatever the reason, Wood welcomed the favor and got out of jail free.

In the top of the 10th, Jennings turned to reliever George Mullin. Speaker reached on second baseman Delahanty's error but slid into first base and sprained his ankle. He was replaced by Billy Purtell and Speaker missed the next eight games. Lewis sacrificed and Engle grounded out, sending Purtell to third. Wagner singled him home and he himself scored on a double by Williams. Boston was back on top, 13-11. Wood struck out two in the 10th and put the finishing touch on an amazing Red Sox comeback.

May 13, 1911 had been a peculiar day. The Red Sox scored 13 runs. The Pirates had 13 hits in their game. The Giants beat the Cardinals, 19-5, with both clubs knocking 13 hits each and New York scoring 13 runs in the first inning! Both the Senators and Athletics had 13 hits in winning their contests. "13? Oh, not so unlucky as it might be," the *Globe* quipped.[7]

The Tigers' offensive surge was not unique in 1911. Before the season major-league club owners agreed to the use of a new cork-centered ball, and many were discussing the new lively power numbers around the league, while others said the new ball was harder to grip for a curveball.[8]

Whatever the reason, the rapid increase in hitting from 1910-1911 is shown below. By 1914, offensive production looked more like 1910.

American League team totals 1910-1911, 1914

Year	BA	HR	2B	3B	RBI	R	SLG	ERA
1910	.243	147	1299	568	3659	4573	.313	2.52
1911	.273	198	1623	641	4623	5654	.358	3.34
1914	.248	148	1435	598	3796	4609	.323	2.73

"The ball may be lively," wrote Herman Nickerson in the *Boston Journal*, "but the Red Sox are livelier."[9]

At least they were on the 13th.

Sources

In addition to the sources cited in the Notes, the author consulted Baseball-reference.com and Retrosheet.org.

Notes

1   F.A. Batchelor, "Red Sox Get Seven Runs in Ninth and Win Overtime Tilt," *Detroit Free Press*, May 14, 1911: 17.

2   "Red Sox Get Seven Runs in Ninth and Win Overtime Tilt."

3   "Red Sox Get Seven Runs in Ninth and Win Overtime Tilt": 21.

4   "Red Sox Win Out in Sensational Finish," *Boston Globe*, May 14, 1911: 21.

5   "Red Sox Get Seven Runs in Ninth and Win Overtime Tilt": 17; The "Walker" of "Walker's Sign" is likely Walker & Co., a construction company. The sign was mounted on top of the billboards on the outfield wall. See a photo from the digital collections from the Detroit Public Library: "Billboards at Bennett Park," digitalcollections.detroitpubliclibrary.org/islandora/object/islandora%3A164933. Retrieved April 18, 2020.

6   "Red Sox Get Seven Runs in Ninth and Win Overtime Tilt": 21.

7   "Red Sox Get Seven Runs in Ninth and Win Overtime Tilt": 17.

8   "Red Sox Get Seven Runs in Ninth and Win Overtime Tilt": 17; John Thorn, "Pitching: Evolution and Revolution," *Our Game*, August 6, 2014. Retrieved April 18, 2020. ourgame.mlblogs.com/pitching-evolution-and-revolution-efd3a5ebaa83; Peter Morris, *A Game of Inches: The Story Behind the Innovations That Shaped Baseball* (Chicago: Ivan R. Dee, 2010), 277.

9   Herman Nickerson, "Red Sox Beat Tigers in 10-Inning Clash," *Boston Journal*, May 14, 1911: 8.

THE WILDEST, WOBBLIEST, WEIRDEST WINDUP

MAY 8, 1918: CINCINNATI REDS 9, ST. LOUIS CARDINALS 6, AT CARDINAL FIELD, ST. LOUIS

BY RICHARD RIIS

The outlook wasn't rosy for the Redland tribe that day;

The score was six to nothing with one inning left to play.

But in the final session they got busy with their sticks,

And when the smoke of battle cleared, the score was nine to six.[1]

In New York, the Giants were pulling away from the rest of the National League with a blistering 16-1 start, while in Boston a Red Sox pitcher and part-time first baseman named Babe Ruth was cause for awe by hitting a home run in a record-tying[2] third straight game, but the biggest news in the sports pages on May 8, 1918, came out of St. Louis. The Cardinals' rising star, Rogers Hornsby, had announced he would be retiring from baseball at the end of the season to care for his invalid mother. "No more baseball, no more jaunting round where I can't be home of nights," the 22-year-old shortstop told the press.[3] In 1917 Hornsby had finished second in batting in the NL at .327 while leading the league in triples and slugging percentage. Eventually he reconsidered and carried on with the profession that put him in the Hall of Fame, but for this day he was out of the lineup with a pulled groin muscle.[4] Filling in for the young star at shortstop was 44-year-old Bobby Wallace, playing in the 25th and final season of his own Hall of Fame career. Wallace had retired from the St. Louis Browns in 1915 to become an American League umpire for a season,

then managed Wichita in the Western League before joining the Cardinals as a free agent in July 1917.

The fourth-place Cardinals couldn't afford to lose a promising batsman like Hornsby. Mired in a collective hitting slump since the start of the season,[5] the team had been held hitless for seven innings the day before by the Cincinnati Reds' Rube Bressler until they broke through in the eighth and rallied to win the game. Except for first baseman Gene Paulette, off to a hot start at .375, no other Cardinals batter had a batting average approaching .300; second-best to Paulette was Hornsby's meager .273. By contrast, the Reds were socking the ball for a good average, second in the league behind the heavy-hitting Giants, but poor pitching had the team behind the Cardinals in seventh place. Center fielder Edd Roush, the defending NL batting champion, was off to a slow start at .282, but third baseman Heinie Groh was hitting .324, and second baseman Lee Magee was close behind at .319. First baseman Hal Chase and his .314 average was out of the lineup for the third of what would be 10 games with a sore shoulder, necessitating a shift to first by Sherry Magee (no relation to Lee). The veteran left fielder would take over as the team's regular first baseman in August when Chase was suspended for "indifferent play."[6] The notoriously troublesome Chase was dropped by the Reds after the season, charged with offering bribes to teammates and opponents to influence the outcome of games on which he had bets.

For this day's matchup before 1,200 fans, Cardinals manager Jack Hendricks handed the ball to left-hander Jakie May. The rookie May had pitched almost exclusively in relief since joining St. Louis during the 1917 season, but earned a place in this season's starting rotation by pitching seven innings of two-hit, scoreless ball in relief against the Pirates on April 23. With a won-lost record of 2-0 and an earned-run average of 1.27, "May's work since the team came north from Texas has bordered on the sensational."[7] Starting for Christy Mathewson's Reds was right-hander Pete Schneider. Since tossing a one-hit shutout against the Pirates on Opening Day, Schneider had pitched in poor luck and, despite a 1.57 ERA, took the mound with a record of one win in four decisions.

In attendance at the game was the baseball legend of a previous generation, Adrian "Cap" Anson, in St. Louis to appear in a theatrical engagement with his daughters, Dorothy and Adele. Members of both the Cardinals and the Reds were invited to be Anson's guests for the evening's performance at the Forest Park Highlands amusement park.

The Cardinals scored a run in both the second and third innings against the "wild and ineffective"[8] Schneider before driving him from the mound with a three-run rally in the fifth, helped along by a base hit and stolen base by Wallace. Snipe Conley replaced Schneider and successfully put the Cards away, although they scored once more in the sixth. The spitballing Conley had joined the Reds during the offseason after pitching in the Federal League in 1914-15 and winning 27 games, including 19 in a row, in 1917 for the Dallas Giants of the Texas League; he pitched only once more for the Reds before returning to pitch for Dallas.

For their part, the Reds did little at the plate through the first eight innings, knocking out only four singles and never threatening to score. With Cincinnati down by six runs in the bottom of the eighth, Mathewson sent in right-hander Mike Regan, 0-2 with an ERA of 22.85, to mop up for the Reds. Regan retired the Cardinals in order.

Taking the hill for the final frame, May, who had been wild all day, seemed to lose any semblance of control. He walked Roush leading off, then after a single by Sherry Magee, walked right fielder Tommy Griffith to load the bases.

"What's comin' off here?" shouted Mathewson from the first-base coach's box,[9] upon which May nicked left fielder Greasy Neale in the back with a pitch, forcing in Roush with the Reds' first run of the game. May then fell behind 3-and-1 to light-hitting shortstop Lena Blackburne. "It looked like bad baseball"[10] when, rather than take the next pitch,

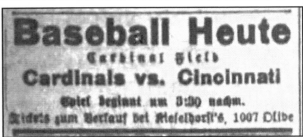

On May 8, English- and German-language St. Louis newspapers ran advertisements for the game. See the *St. Louis Post-Dispatch* and *Westliche Post* advertisements.

Blackburne swung and lined out to center field. With the bases still full and one out, May still couldn't find the plate, issuing a pass to catcher Harry Smith that forced home Sherry Magee with the Reds' second run.

Skipper Hendricks pulled May and sent in right-hander Lee Meadows to face Ivey Wingo, batting for Regan. Nicknamed Specs for being the first big-league ballplayer to wear eyeglasses since Will White in 1886, the side-armer Meadows got two quick strikes on Wingo before the batter lifted an easy fly ball to right-center. Converging beneath the ball were center fielder Red Smyth and right fielder Jack Smith, each thinking the other had it, allowing the ball to fall between them with Griffith trotting home. Meadows, appearing "unstable"[11] and perhaps rattled, then hit Groh with a pitch. Neale crossed the plate, and suddenly the Cardinals found their lead cut to two runs. With catcher Frank Snyder calling to the bench, "Get him out of there!"[12] Hendricks opted to stick with Meadows.

"There were entirely too many 'ifs,' 'ands,' and 'buts' connected with the horrible finish to state in detail what might have happened had Hendricks played his Cards differently," commented an anonymous St. Louis sportswriter.[13] The next batter, Lee Magee, tapped a pitch back to the mound and Meadows fumbled the ball, blowing the chance at a double play. Meadows recovered to toss to first to retire Magee, but Harry Smith scored on the play to cut the Cardinals' lead to a single run. Roush was walked for the second time in the inning and fourth time in the game, and, with the bases again loaded, a walk to Sherry Magee forced Wingo home to knot the score, 6-6.

The improbable rally continued with Griffith driving a pitch into right field for a single, scoring Groh and Roush and putting Cincinnati ahead. Neale then poked another single to right, bringing home Magee. Blackburne finally "brought the agony to a close"[14] by grounding to Wallace, who forced Neale at second.

Five walks, four singles, and two hit batsmen had pushed nine Reds across the plate and turned the tables on the Cardinals. Right-hander Hod Eller was brought in to face the stunned Redbirds in the bottom of the ninth, and set them down in order. Despite it being May's wildness that ignited the Reds' incredible comeback, it was the rattled Meadows, unable to put the fire out, who was tagged with the loss; Regan, for his single inning of work, got the win.

"It was the wildest, wobbliest, weirdest windup to a ball game that has been staged on a local lot in years," wrote one St. Louis sportswriter.[15] Cracked another, "They ought to have saved that explosion for the Fourth of July."[16]

Sources

In addition to the sources listed in the Notes, the author also consulted *The Sporting News* and a number of local newspapers, including the *Dayton Herald,* the *New York Herald,* the *New York Times,* and the *Paterson* (New Jersey) *News.*

Notes

1   L.C. Davis, "Sport Salad," *St. Louis Post-Dispatch*, May 9, 1918: 24.

2   Len Wooster, "Sport Topics," *Brooklyn Times Union*, May 8, 1918: 12.

3   "Hornsby to Quit Diamond," *Pittsburgh Press*, May 7, 1918: 20.

4   "Hornsby Injured; Bobby Wallace May Play Short Today," *St. Louis Post-Dispatch*, May 8, 1918: 22.

5   Clarence F. Lloyd, "Cardinals Home for Series of 22 Games; Reds to Call Today," *St. Louis Star and Times*, May 6, 1918: 13.

6   Jack Ryder, "Heat!" *Cincinnati Enquirer*, August 8, 1918: 8.

7   Clarence F. Lloyd, "Cardinals Home for Series of 22 Games."

8   "Cardinals Pull Great Rally in Favor of Reds," *Dayton Daily News*, May 9, 1918: 16.

9   "Reds Set Record for Season with 9 Runs in Ninth," *St. Louis Post-Dispatch*, May 9, 1918: 24.

10   Clarence F. Lloyd, "Thank Mr. Blackburn That Reds Brought Their Rally to End," *St. Louis Star and Times*, May 9, 1918: 15.

11   "Reds Set Record for Season with 9 Runs in Ninth."

12   "Reds Set Record for Season with 9 Runs in Ninth."

13   "Reds Set Record for Season with 9 Runs in Ninth."

14   Clarence F. Lloyd, "Thank Mr. Blackburn That Reds Brought Their Rally to End."

15   Clarence F. Lloyd, "Thank Mr. Blackburn That Reds Brought Their Rally to End."

16   Davis.

TIGERS RALLY FOR 6 IN NINTH, BEAT JOHNSON AND THE SENATORS IN 16 INNINGS

AUGUST 16, 1918:
DETROIT TIGERS 8,
WASHINGTON SENATORS 7,
AT GRIFFITH STADIUM, WASHINGTON

BY PAUL HOFMANN

This Friday afternoon game was the final meeting of the year between the Washington Senators and Detroit Tigers. The Senators entered the game with a record of 61-49, locked in a three-team race for the American League pennant. At the start of play, they were 3½ games behind the league-leading Boston Red Sox and two games behind the second-place Cleveland Indians. Although they were still in the running for the pennant, the Senators had given away a number of games during the weeks before their series with the Tigers, causing one sportswriter to refer to them as the champions of "baseball philanthropists."[1] The ninth-place Tigers were 48-60, 15½ games off the pace. Nearly a decade removed from their three consecutive American League pennants, the Bengals were playing out the string.

The weather was ideal for baseball. The afternoon high in reached 86 degrees in the nation's capital with unseasonably low humidity for the mid-Atlantic region in August. Rookie Rudy Kallio drew the starting assignment for the Tigers. The 25-year-old right-hander was 7-11 with a 3.45 ERA. He was opposed by left-hander Harry Harper. In his sixth major-league season, the 23-year-old "veteran" was 10-7 with a 1.86 ERA.

After keeping the Tigers off the scoreboard in the top of the first inning, the Senators scored five runs off Kallio in the bottom half of the inning. Left fielder Burt Shotton led off with a double to left. After Eddie Foster and Joe Judge were retired on fly balls to Ty Cobb in center field, Clyde Milan hit a single that advanced Shotton to third. Milan stole second ahead of

Frank Schulte's double that plated the game's first two runs. Second baseman Howie Shanks followed with a single to center that scored Schulte. Shanks took second on Cobb's throw to the plate. Shortstop Doc Lavan followed with an RBI single and moved up to second when Tigers catcher Tubby Spencer failed to corral Cobb's attempt to nail Shanks at the plate. Lavan scored when catcher Eddie Ainsmith tripled. Harper, the ninth batter of the inning, ended it by striking out.

Down 5-0, Tigers manager Hughie Jennings turned to right-hander Deacon Jones in the bottom of the second to keep the game close. For the next five innings, Jones, who entered the game with a record of 3-1 and a 4.39 ERA, "was the rock upon which the

Donie Bush's 16th-inning grounder to third base was mishandled and two runs scored, giving the Tigers the edge they needed.

Nationals split," setting them down "almost as fast as Griff's men came to the plate."[2]

The Senators broke through against Jones for what appeared to be an unnecessary insurance run in the seventh inning. Foster led off with a double. After Judge grounded out, Milan singled to score Foster. Jones retired Schulte and Shanks to end the inning. In the end, Jones did exactly what was asked of him as he scattered seven hits over seven innings and gave up only one run.

Behind 6-0, the Tigers looked destined to go down in defeat as the game entered the top of the ninth inning. However, "[T]he Griffs did enough unproductive and non-essential work in the ninth inning … to be sentenced to the rock pile for life."[3]

Jennings sent pitcher George Cunningham up to pinch-hit for Deacon Jones, who was to lead off the inning. Cunningham delivered a single and proceeded to steal second "with no one making an effort to cut him down."[4] After Harper struck out Donie Bush for the first out, Bob Jones singled Cunningham to third. Cobb followed with a groundout to second and the Senators were content with trading an out for a run as the Tigers scored their first run and Jones moved to second. The Tigers were now down to their last out.

Bobby Veach tripled to the right-field scoreboard to score Jones who had stolen third, again without a throw. Art Griggs followed with a single to center that scored Veach, narrowing the Senators' lead to 6-3. George Harper singled to right and second baseman Ralph Young drew a walk to load the bases before Spencer singled to center to drive in Griggs and Harper and trim the deficit to a single run. At this point, Senators manager Clark Griffith had "reached the same conclusion as every fan in the park – that Harper would never be able to get the side out."[5]

With the Tigers already having batted around, Griffith called on veteran Jim Shaw to preserve the victory. Griffith's decision to bring in the right-hander was widely questioned, especially given the fact that Shaw had experienced a ninth-inning meltdown against the Tigers only two days earlier and that Walter Johnson was also available to pitch.[6] Shaw entered the game with a record of 11-12 and a 2.82 ERA.

Handicapped by chronic control problems throughout his career,[7] Shaw walked Cunningham to load the bases and then walked Bush to force in Young with the tying run. The inning came to an end when Bob Jones grounded out to second. The Tigers had come back from five down with two outs in the ninth inning.

After starting the Tigers comeback rally in the ninth, Cunningham remained in the game to pitch. The right-hander, who was 4-4 with a 3.42 ERA, was nothing short of fabulous. He retired the Senators in order in his first four innings and gave up only two hits over his eight innings of work. His performance was even more impressive given the fact that he had tossed a complete game, albeit in a losing effort, against the Senators the day before.[8]

Walter Johnson came on to pitch for the Senators in the top of the 10th inning. The right-handed Johnson had already won 20 games that year – the ninth year in a row he had won 20 or more games – against 12 defeats. "Walter had the Tigers eating out of his hand all the way" until the 16th inning when he was victimized by poor defense.

George Harper led off the inning with a groundball to Foster at third. Foster's throw to first base ended up in the Washington dugout and Harper took second. Harper went to third when Young reached on a "lucky swinging bunt."[9] Spencer followed with a fly ball to center that advanced Young to second as Milan's throw held Harper at third. Cunningham struck out for the second out of the inning. It appeared that Johnson and the Senators were out of trouble when Bush hit another grounder to Foster at third. However, the Washington third baseman "got tangle footed and threw wide to Ainsmith, Harper and Young scoring."[10] Bob Jones flied out to Shotton in left to end the inning.

The Senators did not go quietly in the bottom of the 16th. After Schulte grounded out to second to start the inning, Shanks reached on an error by Tigers second baseman Young. Lavan singled, advancing Shanks to third. Ainsmith hit a fly ball to left to drive Shanks home and trim the deficit in half. That brought Johnson to the plate. Johnson was a good hitter, but this time he sent a fly ball to Cobb in center to end the game.

Cunningham earned the victory and improved his record to 5-4. Johnson, who allowed only two scratch hits in seven innings, deserved a better fate. With the loss he dropped to 20-13. The time of the game was 3 hours and 22 minutes.

The loss was another major blow to the Senators' pennant hopes, dropping them 4½ games off the pace. Despite winning 11 of their final 15 decisions, the Senators settled for a third-place finish. It was not until 1924 that the Senators would again contend for the pennant. That year they won their first American League pennant and went on to win the World Series.

Sources

In addition to the sources cited in the Notes, the author consulted Baseball-Reference.com and Retrosheet.org.

Notes

1   J.V. Fitz Gerald, "Griffs Loaf Away Another Game to Tigers by 8-7," *Washington Post*, August 17, 1918: 6.

2   "Tigers Beat Washington in Sixteenth," *Detroit Free Press*, August 17, 1918: 9.

3   Fitz Gerald.

4   Fitz Gerald.

5   Denman Thompson, "Griffmen Dissipate Chances by Losing Game to Detroit," *Washington Evening Star,* August 17, 1918: 10.

6   Shaw blew a 3-1 ninth-inning lead against the Tigers on August 14, 1918.

7   Bill Lamb, "Jim Shaw," SABR BioProject, sabr.org/bioproj/person/5f888acd.

8   Thompson.

9   Thompson.

10   Fitz Gerald.

CINCINNATI IS RED AS THE CUBS OVERCOME 6-0 DEFICIT IN THE NINTH

MAY 5, 1919:
CHICAGO CUBS 7,
CINCINNATI REDS 6
(12 INNINGS),
AT REDLAND FIELD, CINCINNATI

BY STEPHEN D. BOREN

Things looked bleak for the Chicago Cubs in the top of the ninth inning against the Cincinnati Reds on May 5, 1919. They had made two Keystone Kops plays and they were down 6-0 and had only four hits. Ironically, a third Keystone Kops play by the Cubs in the ninth actually helped them tie up the game which they won in the 12th inning.

The home team had scored single runs in the first two innings and four more in the fifth inning. Actually,

Max Flack singled twice in the ninth inning, then worked a walk and scored the go-ahead run in the 12th.

the first inning Cincinnati run was a pure Keystone Kops play. With two outs, Heinie Groh hit a routine fly to left field, where left fielder Turner Barber should have easily caught it. However, he did not shout "I've got it." Thus center fielder Dode Paskert did not think it was going to be caught and also ran for it. When Paskert arrived, each thought the other would catch it and this apparent routine out fell for a double. A single by Edd Roush then drove Groh home.

Entering the ninth inning, Cincinnati pitcher Hod Eller had given up only four hits and walked only one batter: That batter was then erased in a double play. Shufflin' Phil Douglas had given up six runs, but only three were earned; three of the runs in the fifth inning were unearned because of his error on a bunt. The Reds' half of the fifth inning had opened with a Larry Kopf single: actually, he bunted safely to Douglas. Bill Rariden singled him to third base. Eller then singled and drove in Kopf as Rariden advanced to second. Then Morrie Rath bunted toward third base. Douglas had an easy force play on Rariden, but he threw the ball over Charlie Deal's head at third base, and Rariden, Eller, and even Rath all scored.

Max Flack was first man up in the Cubs' ninth inning and singled to left field. Charlie Hollocher doubled down the left-field line, sending Flack to third base. Turner Barber hit a grounder to Jake Daubert at first base that hit a stone or a chunk of dirt. Instead of being an easy out, or perhaps cutting down Flack trying to score, the ball bounced over the first baseman's head.[1] Flack scored easily and Hollocher went to third base. A long fly ball by Dode Paskert to Edd

Roush in center field scored Hollocher, making the score 6-2. Fred Merkle then lined a double off the left-field wall, sending Barber to third base.

Charlie Pick singled to center, scoring Barber with the third run of the inning. Charlie Deal followed with a fly to short right-center field. Edd Roush dove for the ball but missed it. Instead of the ball being the second out of the inning, Merkle scored on the play to make it 6-4. Pick thought that Roush would catch the ball and delayed running to second base. Roush had lain there rolling on the center-field grass and it took several moments to determine that it had not been a catch. Greasy Neale in right field ran over, picked up the ball, and threw it to second, where Pick barely beat the throw. A physician who was in the stands was called to examine Roush.[2] He determined that Roush's shoulder was severely bruised and the center fielder had to leave the game, not to return to the lineup until May 14. He was replaced by Wally Rehg. This was only Rehg's second game played for Cincinnati, and after three more games, the last being May 10, he was gone from the major leagues.

Cubs manager Fred Mitchell replaced Deal with pinch-runner Bill McCabe. Bob O'Farrell batted for Bill Killefer. With McCabe on first base and Pick on second base, Mitchell ordered a double steal. Unfortunately, McCabe missed the sign, did not initially move, and finally ran to second.[3] Reds catcher Bill Rariden did not try to nab Pick trying to steal third. He reasoned that if McCabe stole second, there would be two runners in scoring position. His throw to second surprised McCabe, who did not even try to slide and was an easy out – the second out of the inning. Pick reached third base (no stolen base). However, this third Keystone Kops play actually helped the Cubs tie up the game. Greasy Neale in right field was playing very swallow to so that if a ball were hit past the infield, he could throw out Pick trying to score. Neale then moved further back to prevent O'Farrell from getting an extra base hit. Bob O'Farrell singled exactly where Neale had previously been standing and Pick's run made it a 6-5 game. It was noted that not only would O'Farrell's hit been caught, by Neale if he had not moved, but it might have resulted in a game ending double play. Les Mann batted for Douglas and singled to right, sending O'Farrell to second. Manager Mitchell inserted Fred Lear to run for O'Farrell, who represented the tying run. (O'Farrell had only 35 stolen bases in his 21 major-league seasons.) Jimmy Ring replaced Eller on the mound for Cincinnati. (Ring later became the answer to a baseball trivia question as the

Chicago Daily News headline, May 6, 1919.

man the New York Giants traded with Frankie Frisch to the St. Louis Cardinals for Rogers Hornsby after the 1926 season.)

Flack, batting for the second time in the inning, singled to left field. Sherry Magee's throw home was too late and too wide to catch Lear at home. This was the sixth run of the inning and now the score was tied, 6-6, and the Cubs had Mann on third and Flack on second, having advanced on the throw. Hollocher was hit by a pitch, and the bases were loaded. Rube Bressler replaced Ring on the mound and retired pinch-hitter Pete Kilduff on a fly to left. Chicago had made nine hits, scored six runs to tie the game, and had left the bases loaded.

In the bottom of the ninth inning, Cubs manager Mitchell had Mann, who had batted for pitcher Douglas, go to left field. Tom Daly, the Cubs' third-string catcher, replaced Lear, who had run for catcher O'Farrell after O'Farrell batted for catcher Killefer. Paul Carter went in to pitch. Kilduff, who batted for left fielder Barber, went to third base. Carter retired the Reds one-two-three; Magee grounded to second, Daubert grounded to third, and Larry Kopf flied to left.

The 10th and 11th innings were uneventful. But in the Cubs' half of the 12th, Reds pitcher Rube Bressler walked Flack and Hollocher sacrificed him to second. The next batter, Kilduff, singled to center and Flack scored to put the Cubs ahead for the first time in the game, 7-6. Bressler retired the next two batters on grounders to end Chicago's half. Chicago manager Mitchell did not want this game to be lost now. Thus he had Grover "Pete" Alexander go to the bullpen to warm up, in case Carter got into difficulty. In the bottom half of the inning, Magee flied to Paskert in center and Daubert fouled out to third baseman Kilduff. Cincinnati had some transient hope as Kopf reached first on an error by shortstop Hollocher. But Rariden flied out to Paskert, and the game was over. Pete was not needed.

Paul Carter was the winning pitcher and Rube Bressler the loser. The Cubs outhit the Reds 15 to 8. Since Eller went 19-9 that season, this game deprived him of a 20-win season. Cincinnati had won its first seven games of the season, lost one, and won two more for a 9-1 start. At the end of the day the Reds (9-2, .818) were in second place behind the Brooklyn Robins (7-1-1, .875) in percentage, but a half-game ahead of the Robins in the won-lost column. Chicago (6-4, .600) was in fourth place. With a roster almost identical to their 1918 pennant-winning team, they finished third, 21 games behind Cincinnati and 12 games behind the second-place New York Giants. In this season, the first after World War I, only 140 games were scheduled.

Ironically, the *Cincinnati Post* noted, "O'Farrell brought back the worry with a single and Mann's single, which followed, cast real gloom over all except some gamblers who had bet on the Cubs, getting 8 to 5 for their jack."[4] Was this Cincinnati Chicago game in 1919 a harbinger of the Cincinnati Chicago World series for 1919?

Sources

In addition to the sources cited in the Notes, the author also consulted Retrosheet and acknowledges its help.

Notes

1   James Crusinberry, "Cubs' Furious Attack in Ninth Ties Reds; Win in 12th, 7-6," *Chicago Tribune*, May 6, 1919: 19.

2   "Looks Like the Reds of Bygone Days," *Dayton Evening Herald*, May 6, 1919: 12.

3   Oscar Reichow, "Cubs Get the Breaks Win Exciting Ball Game," *Chicago Daily News*, May 6, 1919: 1.

4   "Cubs Murder Ball in Ninth Round," *Cincinnati Post*, May 6, 1919: 12.

PHILLIES RALLY FOR EIGHT RUNS IN NINTH INNING FOR COMEBACK VICTORY

SEPTEMBER 8, 1921: PHILADELPHIA PHILLIES 8, BOSTON BRAVES 6 (GAME ONE OF A DOUBLEHEADER), AT BRAVES FIELD, BOSTON

By Charlie Bevis

Joe Oeschger, the ace of the Braves pitching staff, cruised through the first eight innings of the opening game of a Thursday afternoon doubleheader. He gave up just three hits to the last-place Phillies, as he propelled the fourth-place Braves to a comfortable 6-0 lead going into the top of the ninth inning. However, Oeschger suddenly lost his mojo, as the Phillies unexpectedly rallied for eight runs to defeat the Braves, 8-6.

"The defeat came like a bolt of lightning out of a clear sky," James O'Leary of the *Boston Globe* described the unanticipated turn of events.[1] Instead of racking up his 21st pitching victory of the season, Oeschger was saddled with his 12th loss.

In the top of the ninth inning, Oeschger gave up three straight singles to Dots Miller, Bevo LeBourveau, and Cy Williams that produced the first Philadelphia run. Ed Konetchy then doubled to score two more runs and narrow the Boston lead to 6-3. After Lee King flied out, Oeschger walked Frank Parkinson and then yielded a run-scoring single to John Peters that cut the Boston lead to 6-4. The game should have ended with the next batter, Russ Wrightstone, who pinch-hit for pitcher Jesse Winters. Wrightstone grounded to second baseman Lloyd Christenbury, who initially fumbled the likely double-play ball and then threw wildly to first base to allow a fifth Philadelphia run to score.

Braves manager Fred Mitchell finally replaced Oeschger at this juncture, bringing Hugh McQuillan into the game to relieve him. McQuillan was no more effective than Oeschger, though, as John Monroe batted in the tying and go-ahead runs. Monroe made the second out of the inning when he was thrown out trying to steal second base. Miller, up for the second time in the inning, then walked and scored Philadelphia's eighth run on LeBourveau's triple to right-center field. The inning mercifully ended for the Braves when LeBourveau was thrown out at home plate trying to stretch his triple into an inside-the-park home run.

Sports page cartoon, *Philadelphia Inquirer,* September 9, 1921.

SENSATIONAL RALLY GIVES PHILLIES WIN

Score Eight in Ninth and Beat Braves, 8-6, but Lose Second Game.

Arkansas Gazette headline, September 9, 1921.

Huck Betts, in relief of Winters, shut down the Braves in the bottom of the ninth inning to preserve the Philadelphia victory.

Among the Boston sportswriters, there was some second-guessing of Mitchell's ninth-inning pitching decisions, in an era when relief pitchers were not yet the specialists of today and starting pitchers were expected to finish the game. Paul Shannon of the *Boston Post* called it "criminal negligence" that Mitchell left Oeschger in the game too long, writing that "after the first three men up hit safely and the fourth connected for a solid two-bagger, Oeschger should have been relieved."[2] However, O'Leary of the *Globe* excused Mitchell's tardiness in replacing Oeschger, writing that "Mitchell did not wish to humiliate him by sending in another pitcher after the wonderful work he had done in the previous eight innings and thought he might pull through."[3] O'Leary also noted that Oeschger, who had led off the bottom of the eighth inning with a base hit, "was loafing around on the bases with no sweater on and undoubtedly cooled off."[4]

There was little criticism of second baseman Christenbury, who botched the potential game-ending double-play ball, even though the 27-year-old journeyman was substituting for the Braves' regular second baseman, Hod Ford. "Mitchell benched Walter Barbare and put Ford at short and Christenbury at second," Gus Rooney wrote a week later in *The Sporting News*. "The new middle diamond combination was mostly responsible for the Braves' [recent] success."[5]

Christenbury was a good-hit, no-field utility player who had played just a handful of games at second base that season. Christenbury was the leading hitter for the Braves at the time (.446 batting average), but was next to last in defensive prowess (.898 fielding percentage).[6] True to form, Christenbury went 4-for-5 at bat in this game, but committed two of the team's three errors.

Boston won the second game of the doubleheader, which became the theme deployed not only in the *Boston Globe* headline ("Phils Land Opener in Ninth, Then Lose") but also in most wire-service accounts of the twin bill reported in newspapers across the country. The *New York Tribune* had one of the more colorful headlines: "Oeschger Collapses and Phils Overcome Six-Run Advantage."[7]

The ninth-inning rally nearly escaped communication to readers of the *Philadelphia Inquirer*, which in the trend of the era did not send a writer to cover road games and depended instead on "Special to the Inquirer" dispatches written by a local writer who covered the home team. The Boston writer ghosting the article for this game focused on Oeschger's "immaculate inning" in the fourth when he struck out three batters on just nine pitches.[8]

To supplement this story, the *Inquirer* sports editor commissioned a cartoon to better convey the ninth-inning rally to Philadelphia baseball fans who were interested in reading more than just the recap of the game at Shibe Park between the Athletics and the Yankees. Interestingly, the Athletics marshaled their own ninth-inning comeback, tallying two runs to overtake the Yankees, 6-5.

Sources

In addition to the sources cited in the Notes, the author consulted Baseball-Reference.com and Retsoheet.org.

Notes

1   James O'Leary, "Phils Land Opener in Ninth, Then Lose," *Boston Globe*, September 9, 1921: 15.

2   Paul Shannon, "Phils Handed Gift Then Get Walloped," *Boston Post*, September 9, 1921: 20.

3   O'Leary.

4   O'Leary.

5   Gus Rooney, "Hub Fairly Happy in Its Lower Altitude," *The Sporting News*, September 15, 1921: 3.

6   "Batting and Fielding of Red Sox and Braves," *Boston Globe*, September 5, 1921: 7. These statistics are through games played on September 4, not through September 7, the day preceding this comeback game.

7   "Oeschger Collapses and Phils Overcome Six-Run Advantage," *New York Tribune*, September 9, 1921: 12.

8   "Oeschger Fans Side on 9 Pitched Balls," *Philadelphia Inquirer*, September 9, 1921: 14.

YOU NEVER HAVE ENOUGH RUNS IN THE BAKER BOWL – ESPECIALLY IF YOU ARE THE PHILLIES

MAY 7, 1925:
NEW YORK GIANTS 11,
PHILADELPHIA PHILLIES 8,
AT BAKER BOWL, PHILADELPHIA

BY ALAN COHEN

"It was not a contest to contribute to the peace of mind and self-approval of pitchers."[1]

– W.B. Hanna

In a game featuring an absence of pitching talent by the home team in the ninth inning, the New York Giants came from behind, scoring nine runs on 11 hits, nine of them in a row, in their last at-bat to defeat the Phillies at the Baker Bowl, 11-8. The win on May 7, 1925, in front of 3,000 onlookers, gave the Giants two victories in the three-game series.

Jimmy Ring (0-2) started on the mound for Philadelphia and after allowing single runs in the first two innings shut the Giants down while his mates scored eight runs to take a commanding lead. This was a revelation for Ring, as his teammates had scored single runs in each of his two losses before this game.

The Giants broke out on top in the first inning on singles by Billy Southworth, Frankie Frisch, and Fred Lindstrom. The Giants' starting pitcher, Art Nehf, doubled in the second inning and came home on Southworth's second hit in as many innings.

Nehf's double proved to be the highlight of his day. He brought a 1-1 record and a 3.43 ERA into the game and by day's end, his ERA had jumped to 4.32.

The Phillies cut the lead in half in the second inning as Nelson "Chicken" Hawks, who had three hits in the game, doubled off the scoreboard in right-center and came home on the first of Jimmie Wilson's two RBI singles. A promising inning was disrupted by two Giants defensive gems. Hank Gowdy threw out Wilson trying to steal second base. After a single by Heinie Sand, Ross Youngs saved further immediate damage by charging to catch a line drive off the bat of Clarence Huber. Nehf struck out Ring to end the inning.

The Philadelphia scoring effort was aided by six errors by the visitors, three of which came in the fourth inning, when Philadelphia took the lead with four runs, only one of them earned. Hawks singled and Philadelphia had runners at the corners when Wilson followed with a single. Sand's single to center field tied the game, with Wilson advancing to third base. Nehf retired the next two batters, but the Phillies still had a pair of runners on base. The Phillies then at-

L to R: Frisch with Aaron Ward of Yankees, 1925.

tempted a double steal and Giants catcher Gowdy had Wilson caught between third and home. His throw to third baseman Fred Lindstrom surprised the cornerman. The third baseman muffed the throw, allowing Wilson to score. Sand took third on the play. George Burns hit a groundball to the right side. Frisch made a great play on the ball but threw errantly to first. Sand scored and Burns reached second. On the ensuing play, another fielding lapse by the Giants led to the Phillies' fourth run of the inning. Wally Kimmick bunted a slow roller that first baseman High Pockets Kelly fielded but his throw to first was wild, allowing Burns to score from second base. The Phillies took a 5-2 lead to the fifth inning.

Nehf was knocked out of the box in the fifth when the Phillies added two runs to their lead. A leadoff walk to Johnny Mokan and a homer by Hawks made the score 7-2 and earned Nehf some time off. He was relieved by Kent Greenfield. Greenfield pitched through the seventh inning and gave way to Walt Huntzinger, who pitched a scoreless bottom of the eighth.

Misplays by Greenfield and Southworth gave the Phillies their eighth run. In the sixth inning, Burns opened with a single and took second when center fielder Southworth mishandled the ball. Russ Wrightstone's grounder to first base resulted in an unearned run when Greenfield, late in covering first base, dropped the throw from first baseman Kelly.

In the top of the eighth inning, after a two-out single by Gowdy, Jack Bentley pinch-hit for Greenfield and was retired on a popup. Huntzinger took over on the mound and pitched a scoreless bottom of the eighth.

The Phillies, with Ring pitching in and out of trouble, took an 8-2 lead to the ninth inning. Although the Giants had managed to get a hit in every inning, Ring had managed the situation, leaving New York with seven stranded runners during the six scoreless innings.

Ring's luck ran out. After Southworth flied out to center field to open the ninth, Frisch doubled to right field. Singles by Youngs, Kelly, Lindstrom, and Irish Meusel scored two runs, chasing Ring from the mound. The Phillies brought in Art Decatur with the bases loaded.

The pitching change made no difference. Travis Jackson greeted Decatur with a run-scoring single. Due up for the Giants was Gowdy, but manager John McGraw sent up Bill Terry as a pinch-hitter. Terry kept the rally going with a hard single past second baseman Russ Wrightstone that scored two runs. Terry came out of the game for pinch-runner Mickey Devine. Hack Wilson batted for pitcher Huntzinger and cleared the bases with a three-run homer that gave the Giants a 10-8 lead. It also sent Decatur to the showers. The new Phillies pitcher, Johnny Couch, yielded a double to Southworth. The Giants' consecutive hit streak ended at nine as Couch got Frisch to fly out to Mokan in center field. Southworth took third base on the play, and a single by Youngs brought Billy with the ninth and final run of the inning. A single by Kelly knocked Couch out of the game and resulted in the Phillies using their fourth pitcher of the inning. Ray Pierce came in and retired Lindstrom for the final out.

Jack Scott retired the Phillies in the ninth inning to secure the win for New York, allowing a one-out double to Huber that proved harmless.

Huntzinger received credit for his first win of the season. He had yet to lose and his ERA was 0.00 after three appearances. For the season, he went 5-1 with a 3.50 ERA. The loss went to Decatur, who had crashed and burned with the bases loaded in the ninth inning. He was, at that point, 0-2 with a 12.86 ERA. After one disastrous appearance with Brooklyn on April 23, he had been traded to the Phillies and wound up having a rather forgettable season, going 4-13 with a 5.37 ERA.

With the win, the Giants, who were going for their fifth consecutive National League pennant, pushed their record to 12-5 and took a one-game lead over Cincinnati. For the season, they went 86-66 and finished second to the Pittsburgh Pirates. The Phillies' record stood at 9-10 and they went downhill to a 68-85 record, finishing in a sixth-place tie with Brooklyn.

Hack Wilson, who hit the decisive homer, was in the third year of his major-league career. In those first three years, all with the Giants, Wilson had a grand total of 16 homers and 87 RBIs. At the end of the 1925 season, he was traded to the Chicago Cubs and his career took off. In six of the next seven seasons, he had more than 20 homers and 100 RBIs. In 1930 he set National League records with 56 homers and 191 RBIs. The home-run record lasted until 1998. The RBI record still stood as of 2020.

After the 1925 season, Billy Southworth, who went 4-for-6 with a pair of doubles on May 7, was traded to the St. Louis Cardinals. He briefly managed during the 1929 season. He was brought back as manager in 1940 and took the Cardinals to three consecutive World Series, winning the title in 1942 and 1944. He also took the Boston Braves to the World Series in 1948. In 13 years as a manager, his record was a Hall of Fame-worthy 1,044-704. He went into the Hall of Fame in 2008.

Frankie Frisch, 2-for-6 with a double that launched the rally on May 7, was in the midst of his fifth consecutive season batting .300 or more. The streak would ultimately go to 11 seasons. He batted .316 during his 19-year career, won the MVP in 1931, led the league in hits (223) in 1923, and was a three-time stolen-base leader. He managed the Gas House Gang Cardinals to the 1934 World Series championship (batting .305 in the process) and entered the Hall of Fame in 1947.

Bill Terry was in the midst of his breakout year with the Giants. His ninth-inning hit brought his early season average to .313. He finished the season with a .319 average and his 254 hits in 1930 propelled him to a .401 average, making him the last National League player to reach the .400 threshold. He was a Hall of Fame inductee in 1954.

Sources

In addition to Baseball-Reference.com and the source cited in the Note, the author used:

Cross, Harry. "9 in 9th Win for Giants, 11-8," *New York Times*, May 8, 1925: 14.

Grauley, S.O. "Giants Score Nine Runs in Last Inning and Trounce Phillies, 11 to 8," *Philadelphia Inquirer*, May 8, 1925: 20.

Schumacher, Harry. "Giants in Great Victory," *New York Daily News*, May 8, 1925: 32.

Note

1   W.B. Hanna, "Giants Subdue Phils with Heavy Slugging in Ninth, 11-8," *New York Herald Tribune*, May 8, 1925: 17.

PHILLIES SNATCH DEFEAT FROM THE HANDS OF VICTORY

JULY 13, 1937:
NEW YORK GIANTS 11,
PHILADELPHIA PHILLIES 10
(10 INNINGS),
AT BAKER BOWL, PHILADELPHIA

BY ALAN COHEN

"Out of a clear blue sky, six runs came tumbling into (Bill Terry's) lap"[1]

– John Drebinger, New York Times,
July 14, 1937

"Of course, it was ghastly. But it's one in the old bankeroo – so wot tha heck."[2]

– John Ebinger, New York Daily News,
July 14, 1937

As the temperature soared on a sultry midsummer day, the fans in Philadelphia's Baker Bowl sat in their seats to watch the concluding inning of an apparent win against the New York Giants and a sweep of the two-game series. Their heroes had scored in each of the first four innings and had a 10-4 lead with only one inning left to play. However, the bats of the visitors got as hot as the temperature and the Giants came back with six ninth-inning runs to tie the game. An inning later, they punched across the game-winner, making their trip back home all the more pleasant. Those in attendance got to see 21 runs and 36 hits in 2 hours and 35 minutes.

New York had broken out on top in the first inning when Dick Bartell singled, advanced on a single by Jo-Jo Moore (who had five hits in the game), and came home on a single by Wally Berger. The Phillies countered in the bottom of the inning with a home run by Leo Norris off Giants starter Al Smith, a left-hander.

This Al Smith, as writer Gordon Mackay noted, was not to be confused with the former governor of New York. This Smith, Mackay said, "comes not from the sidewalks of New York, but the cowpaths of Kerry Patch in St. Louis." Mackay summarized Smith's effort by saying "he was ripped, riddled, and hazooed in two innings for five hits and three runs."[3]

Philadelphia scored a pair in the second inning. Dolph Camilli singled and took second on a bunt by Pinkey Whitney. Bill Atwood walked, and a single by George Scharein scored Camilli and moved Atwood to third. Smith struck out Claude Passeau, the Phillies' starting pitcher, but it was downhill from there. Norris singled Atwood home for his second RBI of the game. A single by Hersh Martin loaded the bases, but Smith avoided further damage by inducing Johnny Moore to hit into a force play. The score was 3-1, Phillies, and Smith was finished for the day.

Smith was replaced by Dick Coffman in the third inning, and Coffman did not fare much better than Smith. Indeed, he did worse.

The Phillies extended their lead to 4-1 with a third-inning rally that commenced with a hit batsman (Morrie Arnovich) and a walk to Camilli. After Whitney forced Camilli at second, advancing Arnovich to third, a fly ball by Atwood brought Arnovich home with the fourth Philadelphia run.

In the top of the fourth inning, the Giants had five singles, including the third hit of the game by Jo-Jo Moore, to score three runs and tie the game. Johnny McCarthy started the rally with a single and was forced at second by Burgess Whitehead. Singles by Gus Mancuso and Coffman loaded the bases. Lou Chiozza of the Giants was given a second life when Phillies right fielder Johnny Moore dropped a foul ball. Chiozza then singled in Whitehead and the bases remained loaded. After Bartell flied out for the second out of the inning, Jo-Jo Moore singled to center field. Mancuso and Coffman scored on the play, but when Chiozza tried to score, his path to the plate was blocked by catcher Atwood, who applied the tag. In the collision at the plate, Chiozza spiked Atwood, and the players exchanged words. Chiozza was about to throw a punch but was pulled away by Passeau. Cooler heads prevailed, and the game continued.

Philadelphia regained the lead with a five-run fourth inning, all runs charged to Coffman. With two out, Martin singled past first baseman McCarthy and came home on a homer by Johnny Moore. The Philadelphia scoring continued as Arnovich singled and Camilli doubled him home. Camilli came home ahead of Whitney's long home run to the bleachers in left field.

Tom Baker was the next Giants pitcher. He limited Philadelphia to one run over the next four innings, and that run, which came in the sixth inning, was somewhat tainted.

The Phillies in the fifth inning were frustrated in their attempt to extend their lead. Scharein singled and stole second base. But when he tried to steal third base, he was thrown out by Giants catcher Mancuso for the third out of the inning.

In the sixth inning with one out, Johnny Moore, who had homered two innings earlier, hit a ball to center field that eluded Berger and went for a triple. He came home on a single by Arnovich.

Moore's triple was the fifth extra-base hit of the game for the Phillies, who had 16 hits in all. After the sixth inning, they had only three hits and two of those runners were eliminated on double plays. Martin's third hit of the game, a double, came with two out in the eighth inning. He was left stranded.

Philadelphia's Passeau took a 10-4 lead into the ninth inning. He had been in and out of trouble early in the game as the Giants stranded five batters in the first four innings. He got his act together over the next four innings, retiring the side in order twice and not allowing a runner past first base.

The ninth inning was a different story. The Giants scored six runs in their half of the ninth inning to tie Philadelphia and force extra innings. In the 10th inning, they scored a run to win.

GIANTS COLLECT 20 BASE BLOWS TO WIN, 11 TO 10

Joe Moore, With Five Singles in as Many Tries, Batting Hero

Augusta Chronicle headline July 14, 1937.

"Jimmy Wilson has repeatedly said that his men are the greatest seven-inning ballclub in the National League, but the worst nine-inning aggregation."

– Stan Baumgartner [4]

The Giants began the ninth with five consecutive singles. Jimmy Ripple, pinch-hitting for Baker, got the first one. In quick succession came singles by Chiozza, Bartell, Moore, and Berger. Passeau's day was over and Philadelphia manager Jimmie Wilson went to his bullpen. Syl Johnson came in and the first batter he faced, Mel Ott, doubled. Out went Johnson and in came Hugh Mulcahy. Mulcahy got out of the inning, but not before allowing two inherited runners, including the tying run, to score. After retiring McCarthy on a fly ball to Johnny Moore, Mulcahy faced Sambo Leslie, pinch-hitting for Whitehead. Leslie singled across the fifth run of the inning. Then a fly ball by Harry Danning knotted the score at 10-10.

Cliff Melton pitched a scoreless bottom of the ninth for the Giants, and the game went into extra innings.

Mulcahy returned to the mound to pitch the 10th inning for Philadelphia, and Chiozza opened the inning with a double He moved to third on a bunt by Bartell. Jo-Jo Moore, with his fifth hit in six at-bats, drove in Chiozza with a single for his fourth RBI of the game. It was the last of the Giants' 20 hits in the game.

Melton wrapped things up with a scoreless 10th and was the winning pitcher. He allowed only one hit in his two innings on the mound and gained his sixth straight win, ninth overall, against four losses. Melton, in his first season, went on to record a 20-9 record with a 2.61 ERA. Although the statistic was not kept at the time, he led the league with seven saves. He finished 11th in the MVP balloting. He never came close to matching his first-year numbers in any of his seven subsequent big-league seasons, all with the Giants. Mulcahy (3-8) took the loss. Pitching for some awful teams, Mulcahy did not win nearly as many games as he lost. In 1937 he finished with an 8-18 record. He lost 20 or more games twice in his career (1938, 1940), and gained the nickname "Losing Pitcher."

A day after being ejected for the first time in his career after exchanging words in the ninth inning over balls and strikes with umpire Bill Klem, Giants manager Bill Terry was all smiles as his team escaped Philadelphia with a split in the two-game series. Their record was 46-29 and they had pulled to within a half-game of the league-leading Cubs, who did not play on July 13.

Terry was in his fifth full season as the Giants' manager. In each of those seasons, beginning in 1933, the Giants won at least 90 games. In 1933 Terry's Giants had won the World Series against Washington. In 1937 they went on to win the National League pennant but lost to the Yankees in the World Series for the second time in as many years.

The Phillies on the other hand had their escape from the cellar stalled. With a win, they could have been in a seventh-place tie with Cincinnati. They were 29-46 and on the way to their fifth consecutive season with a record below .500. They won enough games over the balance of the season to finish in seventh place with a 61-92 record, 5½ games ahead of Cincinnati.

Sources

In addition to Baseball-Reference.com, Retrosheet.org, and the sources cited in the Notes, the author used:

Baumgartner, Stan. "Giants Score Six in Ninth and Tie as Passeau Fades," *Philadelphia Inquirer*, July 14, 1937: 21, 23.

Rennie, Rud. "Giants Defeat Phillies in Tenth, 11 to 10, and Again Move Within Half Game of Idle Cubs," *New York Herald Tribune*, July 14, 1937: 22.

Notes

1   John Drebinger, "Giants Tally Six in Ninth and Beat Phils in Tenth; Dodgers Also Triumph," *New York Times*, July 14, 1937: 25.

2   John Ebinger, "Giants Rally in 10th, Defeat Phillies, 11-10," *New York Daily News*, July 14, 1937: 52.

3   Gordon Mackay, "Giants Rally to Beat Phils, 11-10," *Camden* (New Jersey) *Courier-Post,* July 14, 1937: 14.

4   Stan Baumgartner, "Giants Score Six in Ninth and Tie as Passeau Fades," *Philadelphia Inquirer*, July 14, 1937: 21.

BLAST BY BURGESS CAPS EIGHT-RUN NINTH

MAY 8, 1958:
CINCINNATI REDLEGS 10,
CHICAGO CUBS 8,
AT WRIGLEY FIELD, CHICAGO

BY RUSS LAKE

On a clear and cool day, the Cincinnati Redlegs and Chicago Cubs prepared for an early May finale of a five-game series at Wrigley Field. A Cubs vice president estimated that the team lost at least 100,000 fans to unstable Chicagoland weather during this 10-game homestand.[1] Another small crowd (5,936) entered the turnstiles at Clark and Addison with a forecast high of 53 degrees.

Cubs manager Bob Scheffing was pleased that his 13-7 squad had won six of eight. Chicago was in sole possession of first place in the National League by a half-game over the defending World Series champion Milwaukee Braves. It was their best start since 1947, and that was five "field bosses" ago.[2] Scheffing tabbed right-hander Dick Drott, who was 15-11 in 1957, and finished third in Rookie of the Year voting. The 21-year-old Drott was 1-0 with a 5.47 ERA in four starts and a short relief outing. A nagging groin injury had bothered his mound stability this season.

Cincinnati skipper Birdie Tebbetts opined that Chicago should continue to do well if shortstop Ernie Banks and center fielder Bobby Thomson stayed sound. Tebbetts labeled the nucleus of Drott, Moe Drabowsky, and Don Elston as three of the best pitchers in the eight-team league. "What scares me about the Cubs is that they beat us three out of four without throwing Drott or Drabowsky at us," said Tebbetts.[3]

The Redlegs at 8-8 were in fifth place a game out of the first division. Right-hander Tom Acker took the hill. The 28-year-old spot starter had no decisions with a 3.00 ERA in three appearances. Cincinnati's current roster listed nine players who had once been under contract with the Cubs: Steve Bilko, Smoky Burgess, Dee Fondy, Don Hoak, Hal Jeffcoat, Johnny Klippstein, Turk Lown,[4] Bob Thurman,[5] and Pete Whisenant.

Drott was not sharp: He walked leadoff hitter Johnny Temple and hit Frank Robinson with one out. After a double steal, George Crowe doubled both runners home for a 2-0 Cincinnati lead.

Smoky Burgess pinch-hit in the ninth inning and hit a three-run homer to put the Reds over the top.

Tony Taylor and Lee Walls singled off Acker to open Chicago's offense. Banks reached on a force that moved Taylor to third, and he eventually scored on Walt Moryn's sacrifice fly. Dale Long belted a drive high off the receding portion of the right-field wall. Banks sprinted around the bases to tally standing up, but confusion reigned at the conclusion of this play.[6]

Second-base umpire Jocko Conlan appeared to signal that Long's shot was a two-run homer, but he was actually pointing to where the sphere was touched by a fan after it had bounced off the top of the barrier. Accordingly, the safety was a ground-rule double and Banks was sent back to third.[7] Both runners were stranded as Thomson took a called third strike.

An easy second inning materialized for Drott as he retired the Redlegs in order. Tempers flared before the teams exchanged sides when plate arbiter Hal Dixon ejected Temple for throwing his bat in the air after a called strike three. Tebbetts marched out to confront Dixon, and he also received the heave-ho.[8]

Alex Grammas replaced Temple in the lineup at second base, and third-base coach Jimmy Dykes took over the Cincinnati reins. Acker was in trouble immediately when consecutive hits by Johnny Goryl and Sammy Taylor were followed by Drott's bunt single to load the bases. Goryl tagged and scored on Tony Taylor's fly ball to knot the contest, 2-2.

Vada Pinson was plunked to start the third, and Scheffing visited with Drott. It was determined that the hurler needed to be removed.[9] Drott dejectedly trudged off as Ed Mayer entered. The 26-year-old rookie southpaw got out of the frame unscathed. Mayer had thrown 5⅔ hitless innings in the second game of a doubleheader four days before.

Acker and Mayer matched zeroes until the bottom of the fifth, when Walt Moryn opened with a home run to give the Cubs the lead. His fifth homer was a tremendous blast to right that sailed over the back screen and landed on Sheffield Avenue.[10] Acker's day ended when Long followed with another double. Right-hander Willard Schmidt was summoned to quiet Chicago's bats. Schmidt managed to secure two outs, but his ERA jumped from 1.50 to 5.40 within a six-batter spread.

Goryl doubled Long home for a 4-2 advantage. Mayer singled in Goryl for his first (and only) major-league RBI. A hit by pitch and a walk loaded the bases, so Dykes summoned Bill Wight to relieve. Banks greeted the lefty veteran with a two-run single to keep the "yellow-colored numbers" changing on

the scoreboard. The Cubs were up 7-2 when the inning ended.

The curveballing Mayer permitted a pair of sixth-inning hits, but Cincinnati did not score off him.[11] Long started the Cubs' sixth by tagging a deep drive to the right-center bleachers for an 8-2 mark.[12] It was the left-handed slugger's third home run of the year and his third extra-base knock of the day.

Mayer's two-out bases-loaded situation in the seventh caused Scheffing concern as Robinson batted. Scheffing realized that Robinson, who was struggling to drive in runs, could break out at any time. The right-handed Elston entered to stifle the threat, and he secured an inning-ending fly out. Left-hander Joe Nuxhall relieved for Cincinnati in the bottom half and put Chicago down in order in this and the following frame. Elston, who entered with an ERA of 0.82 avoided eighth-inning trouble and stranded two more runners.

Elston attempted to finish his fifth game of the season; however, his luck turned. Whisenant walked, and left-handed pinch-hitter Dee Fondy pulled a sharp double-play grounder that Tony Taylor fumbled[13] for the rookie second baseman's fifth error of the season. Lefty swinging Jerry Lynch delivered a pinch single to plate the first Cincinnati tally since the opening frame.

Robinson singled home Fondy to close the spread to 8-4. Rookie right-hander Dolan Nichols replaced Elston, and George Crowe grounded to the right side. Taylor gloved this one and fired to second for the force. Banks did not get off a relay; the ball became stuck in his glove's webbing.[14] Hoak blistered a groundball to third, and Goryl crouched to scoop it and begin an around-the-horn game-ending double play. However, the ball glanced off a pebble and bounded over Goryl's head for another run-scoring hit.[15] The Redlegs now trailed 8-5.

Ed Bailey continued the surge with a single to right to make it 8-6. Pitcher Harvey Haddix (who was the tying run) came in to run for Bailey. Gus Bell fashioned a similar run-scoring hit, and it was 8-7. Haddix advanced to second, and Scheffing went to right-hander Freddy Rodriguez. Fred Hatfield was scheduled to get his first at-bat with Cincinnati, but the reserve infielder was lifted for Burgess. The pudgy, lefty-swinging catcher smacked the first pitch, a screwball from Rodriguez, deep into the right-center-field bleachers for a three-run homer.[16] It was his first round-tripper of the season, and the Redlegs had a 10-8 lead. Two batters later, right-hander Dave Hillman entered and mercifully secured the third out while stranding a runner.

Cincinnati parlayed eight runs from an error, two walks, five singles, and a home run as 12 batters faced four Chicago pitchers. A trio of prospective double-play grounders generated one putout. Ironically, Tebbetts had been questioned before the game about momentum turns. He stated prophetically, "A team gets careless and makes a mistake. That's all there is to it."[17]

Cincinnati had used 22 players by this time. Dykes's ninth-inning substitution assignments looked like a laundry list to the home-plate umpire.[18] Jeffcoat was on the mound, Burgess was catching, Whisenant moved from right field to second base, Robinson relocated from left to third, Hoak switched from third to shortstop, Fondy went to left, and Lynch to right. These changes had several Redlegs playing out of position, but that proved to be a nonfactor as Chicago was thoroughly shell-shocked. The Cubs, who had a sure victory snatched away, were retired quickly and quietly in their final at-bat.

Left-on-base numbers were 10 for the Redlegs and nine for the Cubs. The line score displayed Cincinnati with 10 runs, 11 hits, and no errors. Nuxhall (1-0) picked up the win while Jeffcoat achieved his fourth save. Chicago had 8 runs on 13 hits with one very costly error. Nichols (0-2) was charged with the loss, and the contest lasted 3:04.

After this stunning defeat, the Cubs lost 11 of their next 13 games to bid adieu to first place. Scheffing did not panic with wholesale changes, but his team's solid defense had naturally acquired the jitters.[19] Chicago ended up fifth, tied with St. Louis, at 72-82.

The Redlegs did not channel the comeback into a lengthy winning streak as they fell victim in 9 of their following 11 contests. Tebbetts eventually resigned for health issues in early August,[20] with Dykes taking over as fourth-place Cincinnati ended 76-78.

Sources

In addition to the sources cited in the Notes, the author accessed Retrosheet.org, Baseball-Reference.com, Newspapers.com, SABR.org/bioproj, and *The Sporting News* archive via Paper of Record.

Notes

1   Lou Smith, "Deal Prompts No Celebration," *Cincinnati Enquirer*, May 9, 1958: 39.

2   Despite being 14-7 and in first place on May 11, 1947, the Cubs ended up sixth under the direction of Charlie Grimm. He was followed by Frankie Frisch, Phil Cavarretta, and Stan Hack.

3   Edward Prell, "Tebbetts Sees Cubs in Race All the Way," *Chicago Tribune*, May 9, 1958: 46.

4   Smith, "Deal Prompts No Celebration." Lown was traded to Cincinnati for pitcher Hersh Freeman the morning of this game.

5   Rick Swaine, "Bob Thurman," SABR Baseball Biography Project, sabr.org/bioproj/person/23f9d960. Although Thurman never suited up for the Cubs, he had a contract to play for the organization. Cincinnati bought Thurman's pact from the Cubs in 1955.

6   Edward Prell, "Redleg 8 Run 9th Jolts Cubs from 1st," *Chicago Tribune*, May 9, 1958: 45.

7   Prell, "Redleg 8 Run 9th Jolts Cubs from 1st."

8   Smith, "Deal Prompts No Celebration."

9   Prell, "Redleg 8 Run 9th Jolts Cubs from 1st." Drott was admitted to Wesley Memorial Hospital for observation. His injury was diagnosed as a ruptured blood vessel on the inner side of his right thigh.

10 Lou Smith, "Reds Score Eight in Ninth to Cool Torrid Cubs, 10-8," *Cincinnati Enquirer*, May 9, 1958: 39.

11 Smith, "Reds Score Eight in Ninth to Cool Torrid Cubs, 10-8."

12 Smith, "Reds Score Eight in Ninth to Cool Torrid Cubs, 10-8."

13 Smith, "Reds Score Eight in Ninth to Cool Torrid Cubs, 10-8."

14 Edgar Munzel, "Jitters Turn Bold Bruins to Cold Cubs," *The Sporting News*, May 21, 1958: 25.

15 Munzel.

16 Prell, "Redleg 8 Run 9th Jolts Cubs from 1st," *Chicago Tribune*, May 9, 1958: 46.

17 Prell, "Birdie Tells Just How It Can Happen," *Chicago Tribune*, May 9, 1958: 46.

18 Smith, "Reds Score Eight in Ninth to Cool Torrid Cubs, 10-8."

19 Munzel.

20 Tom Simon, "Birdie Tebbetts," SABR Baseball Biography Project, sabr.org/bioproj/person/bacfc0e7.

METS SCORE SEVEN RUNS IN NINTH INNING TO BEAT BRAVES, 8-7

JULY 17, 1973:
NEW YORK METS 8,
ATLANTA BRAVES 7,
AT ATLANTA STADIUM, ATLANTA

BY THOMAS J. BROWN JR.

The Mets were playing poorly in July 1973. They arrived in Atlanta with a 6-10 record and their struggles continued when they lost the first game of the series, 8-6. The loss had led to speculation that Mets management might make some changes. Guido Cribari wrote in the *White Plains Journal News*, "One thing is certain, where the down-trodden Mets are concerned, manager [Yogi] Berra or someone will have to be

'73 WORLD SERIES Game #2

Courtesy The Topps Company.

Pinch-hitter Willie Mays singled and drove in the tying and go-ahead runs in the Mets' seven-run rally.

made the goat for the unexpected collapse of the once proud occupants of Shea."[1]

The Braves were having a terrific July when the Mets arrived in town. They had won 11 of 17 games before the series with the Mets. After beating New York on July 16, they entered the second game of the series with a four-game winning streak.

Braves manager Eddie Mathews started Carl Morton. The right-hander had won two of his three July starts, including going seven innings in his last start, a 15-6 Braves win on July 13. Morton looked strong out of the gate. He allowed just three base-runners through the first four innings. Wayne Garrett walked to lead off the game, Ron Hodges reached first on an error in the second and Rusty Staub got the first Mets hit in the fourth, a single.

Harry Parker had been slated to start for the Mets but at the last minute Berra made a pitching change and sent reliever Tug McGraw to the mound in hopes that he would pull out of a slump. It was McGraw's first start since September 15, 1971. Berra's move fooled everyone but the Braves.

Ralph Garr led off and homered on McGraw's first pitch, his eighth home run of the season. The Braves struck again in the second after Paul Casanova singled and ended up on third when right fielder Rusty Staub booted the ball. He scored the Braves' second run when McGraw threw wild to the next batter, pitcher Morton.

The Braves continued to hit McGraw in the third. After he walked the first two batters, Dusty Baker hit a one-out RBI single. Davey Johnson's sacrifice fly brought in another run to give the Braves a 4-0 lead.

The Mets got on the scoreboard in the fifth, on singles by John Milner and Hodges and Don Hahn's sacrifice fly. But Morton shut down the next two batters, leaving the Mets trailing by three runs.

The Braves added to their lead in the sixth. Marty Perez hit his fourth home run of the season with a runner on board. Two batters later, Hank Aaron hit a solo blast into the left-field seats. It was his 25th home run of the season and the 698th of his career, leaving him 16 home runs behind Babe Ruth. "I felt like when I hit it that it was the icing on the cake, that it was just another run," Aaron said later.[2]

With the Mets in a six-run hole, McGraw was not sent back out in the seventh. It was clear that his struggles were not yet over; his ERA had risen from 5.85 to 6.17. Berra said, "He had a good screwball tonight. It was his fastball that they hit." He added that the Mets needed McGraw to turn things around, saying, "We're gonna have to have him. If you don't have relief pitching, you ain't gonna win."[3]

John Strohmayer and Buzz Capra got the Braves out in order in the sevngh and eighth innings to send the game to the ninth with the Mets down 7-1. Morton had handcuffed the Mets through eight innings, allowing just five hits. But Garrett led off the ninth with a single. After Felix Millan lined out, Staub stepped to the plate. He had grounded into a double play on his last at-bat. This time he hoisted the ball over the fence for a two-run homer.

The Braves still led, 7-3. But Cleon Jones singled and Milner sent the ball over the fence for another Mets homer. Suddenly things looked shaky. Manager Mathews called in Adrian Devine from the bullpen.

Devine got the second out when Hodges grounded out to second base. But a single by Hahn and a walk to pinch-hitter Ed Kranepool put another runner in scoring position. Berra substituted Ted Martinez for the slow-footed Kranepool. Jim Beauchamp pinch-hit for pitcher Capra and singled. Hahn crossed the plate, leaving the Mets trailing by just one run at 7-6, while Martinez ended up on third.

Mathews went back to his bullpen and called on left-hander Tom House to save the game. Berra went to his bench and sent Willie Mays to pinch-hit for Garrett. Mays hadn't started due to a sore back after crashing into the outfield wall the day before. His sore back didn't seem to bother him this afternoon. With the count 3-and-2, Mays singled, driving home two runs, to give the Mets the lead, 8-7.

"I was just lucky to hit it," said Mays. "The pitch was up and out. I was just trying to make contact."[4]

It was the second time Mays had upstaged Aaron. On April 27, 1971, Aaron hit the 600th home run of his career, only to see it go for naught when Mays singled in the 10th inning to give the San Francisco Giants a 6-5 victory.

Harry Parker, who was supposed to start the game, now got a chance to save it, and he pitched a perfect ninth, getting two strikeouts and a foul pop fly to end the game.

Aaron said he thought his home run had cemented the Braves victory, "but that's baseball for you, I guess." He defended the Braves relief pitchers saying, "[T]hose guys have good stuff, but they're young and just in the process of learning. It takes time. This was a tough one to lose, the kind that will hurt your morale. But not this club. … It will bounce back."[5]

Staub, likely talking about the struggles the Braves relievers had in the last inning, said, "Obviously, until there are three out, the game is not over."[6]

The Mets had halted the Braves' four-game winning streak. Berra, perhaps hoping that the Mets would begin a streak of their own, said, "That just might turn something around. I hope it starts something good."[7]

Although the Mets remained in the National League East cellar and continued to struggle for the rest of July, they eventually turned things around to go 40-28 in the second half of the season and win the National League East Division championship, then beat the Cincinnati Reds for the pennant, before losing to the Oakland A's in the World Series. Berra's Mets did indeed "turn something around" and the speculation regarding his tenure eventually disappeared.

Sources

In addition to the sources cited in the Notes, the author used the Baseball-Reference.com and Retrosheet.org websites for box-score, player, team, and season pages, pitching and batting game logs, and other pertinent material.

Notes

1   Guido Cribari, "Yogi's First in Line if Mets Start Firing," *White Plains* (New York) *Journal News*, July 18, 1973: 45.

2   Wayne Minshew, "Mets 7 Run Rally Nips Braves in 9th," *Atlanta Constitution*, July 18, 1973: 57.

3   Ed Shearer, "Mets Overcome Aaron's 698th," *Bridgewater* (New Jersey) *Courier News*, July 18, 1973: 33.

4   Shearer.

5   Minshew.

6   Minshew.

7   Shearer.

YANKEES SCORE 12 RUNS IN EIGHTH FOR BIG COMEBACK WIN

MAY 27, 1933:
NEW YORK YANKEES 15,
CHICAGO WHITE SOX 11,
AT YANKEE STADIUM, BRONX, NEW YORK

BY ALAN RAYLESBERG

The Yankees of the 1920s won six American League pennants and three World Series. After failing to win the pennant from 1929 through 1931, the Yankees won the World Series in 1932, and looked to repeat in 1933. As they took the field on Saturday afternoon, May 27, they were in first place by one game over the Washington Senators and 1½ games over the visiting Chicago White Sox. The White Sox had won the opener on Friday, and a Saturday win could knock the Yankees out of undisputed possession of first place. A close game through six innings suddenly turned into a rout for the White Sox – that is, until the Yankees scored 12 runs in the bottom of the eighth to pull off one of the greatest comebacks in their history.

New York's star-studded lineup featured four of the core players – all future Hall of Famers – from the 1927 Yankees, perhaps the greatest team of all time. Earle Combs led off in center field, Babe Ruth (right field) and Lou Gehrig (first base) were batting in their usual third and fourth spot in the lineups, and Tony Lazzeri hit sixth at second base. At age 38, Ruth was coming to the end of his phenomenal career in what would be his next to last season with the Yankees. Still

Chicago Daily Times headline, May 28, 1933.

dangerous, however, Ruth hit .301 with 34 home runs and 104 RBIs in 1933. Gehrig, in his prime, at age 29, hit .334 with 32 home runs and 140 RBIs.[1]

In the seventh spot in the lineup was another future Hall of Famer, Bill Dickey, and batting eighth was the shortstop, 22-year-old Frank Crosetti, who went on to have a 37-year career with the Yankees, 17 as a player and 20 as a coach.[2]

The White Sox were a perennial second-division team.[3] After having finished seventh in 1932, they were not expected to do much better in the new season. To be challenging for first place in late May was an unexpectedly pleasant surprise. Chicago was not without talent, with future Hall of Famers Al Simmons in left field and Luke Appling at shortstop. Jimmy Dykes, a future major-league manager, was at third base.

On the mound for the White Sox was Ted Lyons, another future Hall of Famer, in the midst of a 21-year career, all with Chicago. The Yankees started a 29-year-old rookie named Don Brennan, pitching in what would be his only season in the Bronx.

It was an ordinary game through seven innings. The Yankees took an early lead when Gehrig hit a two-run homer in the first. Chicago came back with three in the third before New York tied it with a run in the fourth. The see-saw continued as the White Sox regained the lead with a run in the fifth, with Lyons helping his own cause with his second single of the game.

It was 4-3, Chicago, going to the top of the seventh and that's when the White Sox broke it open, scoring four times, including a two-run homer by Simmons. The rally sent Brennan to the showers, to be replaced by another former member of the 1927 Yankees, Wilcy

Moore.[4] After Lyons retired the Yankees in the bottom of the seventh, the White Sox had a commanding 8-3 lead going to the eighth. Things got worse for the Yankees in a hurry. With Walter "Jumbo" Brown now on the mound, the White Sox struck for three more.[5] Now it was a laugher, 11-3, White Sox, in the middle of the eighth.

With Lyons on the mound, few could have expected what was about to occur in the Yankees eighth, especially after the leadoff hitter, Gehrig, flied out. Then Ben Chapman singled.[6] Lazzeri and Dickey both walked. Crosetti singled to make it 11-4, leaving the bases still loaded. With the pitcher Brown up, Red Ruffing, a good hitting pitcher and another future Hall of Famer, was called on to pinch-hit.[7] Ruffing singled, and it was now 11-5 with the bases still loaded. Combs walked, forcing in another run to make it 11-6. Finally, Lyons was gone, replaced by J. Walter Miller.[8]

The onslaught continued as Joe Sewell singled in another run to make it 11-7, leaving the bases full yet again. Things were getting interesting in the Bronx, with Ruth up as the tying run at the plate! Ruth singled to score two as the Yankees had their fifth hit of the inning – all singles – to go with three walks. Six runs were now in and it was 11-9, with Gehrig coming up.

Ruth and Gehrig, if nothing else, were great in the clutch and now with six runs in and two men on, Gehrig had a chance to put the Yankees ahead. Gehrig doubled to right, scoring one to make it 11-10 and leaving runners at second and third. Manager Lew Fonseca removed Miller, who did not get a single out.[9] In came Eddie Durham with the game incredibly slipping away from the White Sox. After an intentional walk to Chapman loaded the bases again, the batter was Lazzeri. He came through with yet another single, with the runners again advancing only a single base. The Yankees had tied the game, 11-11.

Now it was Dickey's turn, as the seventh player of the inning to bat with the bases loaded. There would be no single this time: Dickey hit a "prodigious blast" into the right-field bleachers for a grand slam.[10] The Yankees had 12 runs in on eight hits (six singles) and three walks – they had gone ahead and now led by four runs – 15-11. The next two batters struck out, ending the inning.

Describing the eighth inning in the *New York Times,* John Drebinger wrote that "[it] shook both banks of the Harlem and confounded 20,000 spectators as the Yanks, in one of the most remarkable batting orgies ever staged by the world's champions, piled twelve runs across the plate."[11]

Taking no chances, Yankees skipper Joe McCarthy brought in yet another future Hall of Famer (and 1927 Yankee) to pitch the ninth. Herb Pennock, a left-hander, was then 39 years old in his 21st season in the majors. While Pennock gave up two hits, he kept the White Sox off the scoreboard and the game was over.

The White Sox had come so close to being within a half-game of the first-place Yankees. Instead, the elation of an apparent blowout victory had turned into a crushing defeat. Chicago never recovered; the White Sox went on to lose a doubleheader to the Yankees the next day, in the midst of losing six of seven games. In the blink of an eye, the White Sox had gone from challenging for first place on May 27 to 6½ games behind on June 2. They went on to finish sixth in the eight-team American League.

The Yankees won their next three games and 10 of their next 11 to take a six-game lead in the American League. They were in first place as late as July 23, before falling to second where they ended the season, seven games behind the Washington Senators.

Sources

In addition to the sources cited in the Notes, the author consulted Baseball-Reference.com and Retrosheet.org.

Notes

[1] Combs, 34 years old, hit .300 in what would be his last season as a regular. Lazzeri was still only 29 and hit .294 with 18 home runs.

[2] Crosetti wore the Yankees uniform from 1932 through 1964 and was a member of 17 world championship teams and 23 pennant winners, the most in both categories of anyone in baseball history.

[3] When the American and National Leagues each had eight teams, those that finished fifth or lower were said to be in the second division.

[4] The 36-year-old Moore pitched for the Yankees from 1927 to 1929 and then, after a stint with the Red Sox, returned to New York during the 1932 season. The 1933 season was his last.

[5] Brown's nickname derived from his 295 pounds on a 6-foot-4 frame. The 26-year-old was in his second season with the Yankees, part of a 12-year career playing for five teams.

[6] In 1947, as the manager of the Phillies, Chapman verbally assaulted Jackie Robinson in Robinson's debut season. The incident was portrayed in the biopic about Robinson, *42*.

[7] In 22 seasons and 1,937 at-bats, Ruffing had a career average of .269 with 36 home runs. As a pitcher, he won 273 games. After playing for the Red Sox beginning in 1924, Ruffing was traded to the Yankees early in the 1930 season and played the bulk of his career (through 1946) with New York.

[8] Baseball-Reference.com lists him as "Jake Miller" without any reference to his name being "J. Walter." Jake was his nickname but sportswriters in 1933 called him "J. Walter." {See Chris Rainey, "Jake Miller," sabr.org/bioproj/person/fef98ce5. Miller pitched eight seasons for Cleveland through 1931 but did not play in 1932, suffering from a "dead arm." At the age of 33, Cleveland did not want him back and he failed to catch on with another team until the White Sox decided to give him a chance. "Finds

Life in Dead Arm," *The Sporting News*, June 1, 1933: 1. Miller pitched in 26 games for Chicago in 1933, with a 5.62 ERA. It was his final season.

9   Fonseca, 34 years old, was a player-manager in his last season as a player. He managed the White Sox for two full seasons (1932 and 1933) and 15 games in 1934.

10 John Drebinger, "Yanks 12 in 8th Subdue White Sox," *New York Times,* May 28, 1933: 3, 1.

11 Drebinger. The 12 runs in an inning were two shy of the then modern day major-league record. As of May 2020, the modern-day record for most runs in an inning was 17 by the Boston Red Sox, against Detroit, on June 18, 1953.

PADRES OVERCOME EIGHTH-INNING 8-0 DEFICIT TO WIN

JUNE 10, 1974:
SAN DIEGO PADRES 9,
PITTSBURGH PIRATES 8,
AT SAN DIEGO STADIUM, SAN DIEGO

BY GREGORY FUNK

The year 1974 started as a season of optimism for San Diego as the Padres were rescued from their aborted move to Washington, DC, and ultimately purchased by Ray Kroc. During the offseason, even before Kroc's name came up, the Padres, in anticipation of better times, traded for Willie McCovey, Matty Alou, Glenn Beckert, and Bobby Tolan, players past their prime, but names nonetheless, something Padres fans were not used to. However, their sixth season's beginning resembled the previous five. Starting 0-6, they were at 23-39 when the Pirates came to town on June 10.

Lowell Palmer, purchased from the Yankees 10 days earlier, was making his second San Diego start, while Jim Rooker was on the mound for the Pirates. Pittsburgh had a terrific hitting lineup that year: first in batting and top three in most offensive categories. The first seven in that day's lineup were named Clines, Hebner, Zisk, Stargell, Oliver, Sanguillen, and Stennett.

Palmer got into trouble in every inning, while Rooker breezed. In the first, Palmer got out of a bases-loaded jam, but in the second he allowed a sacrifice fly by Gene Clines after Rennie Stennett and Mario Mendoza singled. A third inning two-run homer by Manny Sanguillen made it 3-0, and Palmer managed to strand a runner at second in the fourth. In the fifth, another two-run homer, this time by Willie Stargell, and a one-out single by Sanguillen finished Palmer.

In the seventh, off Dave Tomlin, Stargell tripled home Richie Zisk, and then scored on a single by Al Oliver to make it 7-0.

Meanwhile Rooker was sailing along with a five-hit shutout through seven innings. Other than a third-in-ning hiccup during which Enzo Hernandez walked and reached second, but was thrown out after hesitating when Tolan lined off the right-field wall, Rooker appeared to be in total command of the game.

In the eighth, Rooker himself upped the score to 8-0 when he doubled to left and scored on Richie Hebner's single.

Four runs in the eighth and four runs in the bottom of the ninth – and then Horace Clarke singled to drive in the winning run.

It looked like just another game in which the Padres were headed for their sixth consecutive last-place finish and fourth 100-loss season. One of the bright spots in this particular season was a young tuba player named Jim Eakle, a Marine who had begun showing up at games near the end of the dismal 1973 season, playing hand-clapping tunes and familiar songs on a green-painted tuba. By 1974, a Pied Piper-like following had formed, marching down the stadium aisles generating enthusiasm throughout, playing flutes, drums, and other assorted instruments. Calling themselves McNamara's Band, after newly hired manager John McNamara, they marched around virtually every game.

But on this particular day, with many of the 7,309 spectators already on their way home by the middle of the eighth inning, even the Tuba Man wasn't getting much response during this one-sided affair.

Bobby Tolan led off the bottom of the eighth, and, before the inning started, was engaged in some sort of squabble with home-plate umpire Andy Olsen. Tolan, standing in the batter's box, but facing away from the mound, with his bat in only one hand, arms dropped at their sides, continued to bark at Olsen. The umpire, appearing to have heard enough, signaled to Rooker to begin pitching. Rooker wound up and only after the pitch was on its way did Tolan turn around and drop a perfect drag bunt past the mound toward second base for an infield hit. Whether or not this was any kind of catalyst could be open for debate, but it's a matter of record that the next five batters all reached base.

Dave Winfield doubled to center, scoring Tolan, Nate Colbert walked, and even though it was still only 8-1, manager Danny Murtaugh replaced Rooker with Bruce Kison. Cito Gaston greeted Kison with a three-run home run to make it 8-4. Fred Kendall walked, and Dave Roberts reached base on an error by Stennett. But a strikeout and two flyballs ended the eighth.

Vicente Romo pitched a perfect ninth for the Padres.

Ramon Hernandez, who had come in to get all three outs in the previous inning, retired Tolan to start the ninth. But Winfield shot a home run over the center-field fence to make it 8-5. At that point, Murtaugh elected to go to his ace reliever, Dave Giusti, who, after throwing a strike, issued consecutive walks on eight straight balls to Colbert and Gaston. Murtaugh quickly yanked Giusti, and brought in a young rookie pitcher named Kent Tekulve. Called up from Triple-A

Charleston in May, Tekulve was making his eighth appearance for the Pirates. Kendall singled to right, loading the bases. Roberts then grounded the ball back to Tekulve who threw home for the second out.

Tekulve got two strikes on pinch-hitter Derrell Thomas, who then lined a base hit into left-center to make it 8-6. Bob Barton, also pinch-hitting, and also with two strikes, hit a routine grounder into the 5.5 hole[1] that barely eluded shortstop Mendoza. Two runs came in and the game was tied.

Horace Clarke was next. Tekulve again got two strikes on the batter, but Clarke hit a soft liner over second base, scoring Thomas, for the unexpected victory.

An hour before the game, Pirates general manager Joe L. Brown had said, "This club is built on two things – our hitting and our bullpen."[2]

After the game, an enraged Rooker said, "The job isn't being done by the bullpen and that's the truth. No matter how well I pitch, they figure out a way to put men on and to let them in." It was the fourth time in 10 starts that Rooker reached at least the seventh inning with a lead that the bullpen failed to protect. He was also upset after being pulled with a seven-run lead.[3]

For Padres fans, though, it wasn't the usual victory celebration. Many walked away stunned at what they had just witnessed: the greatest Padres comeback ever, accomplished in the last two innings. No San Diego team (as of 2018) has ever been behind by more runs at any stage in a game and won.[4]

Sources

In addition to the sources cited in the Notes, the author consulted Baseball-Reference.com and Retrosheet.org, and relied on his personal memory of the game, which he attended. The following two articles were also helpful:

Collier, Phil. "Padres' Five-Run Ninth Startles Pittsburgh, 9-8," *San Diego Union*, June 11, 1974.

Feeney, Charles, "Padres Explode to Whip Bucs," *Pittsburgh Post-Gazette*, June 11, 1974.

Notes

1   The term "5.5 hole" is one that is very familiar to Padres fans. It was invented by Tony Gwynn to describe his favorite target: hitting a line drive between third base and shortstop.

2   Bob Smizik, "Bullpen Leaves Pirates for Dead," *Pittsburgh Press*, June 11, 1974.

3   Smizik.

4   On May 23, 1970, San Diego fell behind 8-0 to San Francisco, but closed the gap to 8-7 by the fourth inning, and won 17-16 in 15 innings.

TRIBE RALLIES FROM EIGHT DOWN IN BOTTOM OF EIGHTH

AUGUST 31, 1999:
CLEVELAND INDIANS 14,
ANAHEIM ANGELS 12,
AT JACOBS FIELD, CLEVELAND

BY WILLIAM GRMEK

Two teams going in opposite directions met on a beautiful summer evening in Cleveland. This was the second of a four-game series. The Angels, who had playoff aspirations at the beginning of the season after acquiring Mo Vaughn in free agency in the offseason, limped into the game with a 51-79 record, riding a six-

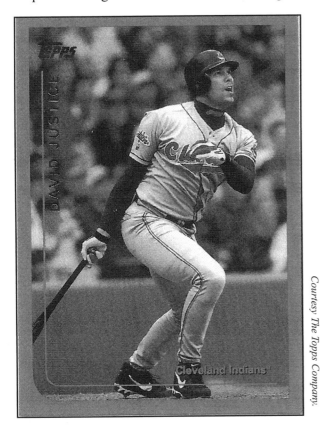

David Justice was the first batter up after Richie Sexson's three-run homer gave the Indians 10 runs in the eighth inning. For some reason, he was hit by a pitch and charged the mound.

Courtesy The Topps Company.

game losing streak. Manager Terry Collins was in his third season at the helm, and finished both of the first two seasons above .500. A spate of injuries starting in spring training derailed a once promising season for the Angels. The Indians, in the middle of their string of 455 consecutive sellout crowds, started the night 80-50, 19 games ahead of the second-place White Sox in the American League Central Division.

Chuck Finley, a player the Indians were trying to trade for at the trade deadline a month earlier, took the mound for Anaheim against Doc Gooden. After six innings, the Angels were ahead, 5-4. Gooden had lasted only five. Third baseman Troy Glaus was looking like a hero; he'd already hit a pair of two-run home runs, in the fourth and the sixth.

Mo Vaughn scored on Tim Salmon's home run in the top of the seventh to push the Angels' lead to 7-4. The eighth inning would be unforgettable for both clubs.

In the top of the eighth, right-hander Sean DePaula made his major-league debut. He'd just come up from Buffalo the day before. He was not treated kindly. He walked the first two Angels he faced, and then watched Gary Disarcina execute a sacrifice bunt. It was the only out DePaula got. Orlando Palmeiro singled to drive in both baserunners, and DePaula walked the next batter, before Indians manager Mike Hargrove pulled him in favor of Jim Poole, who allowed a single and a double before getting out of the inning on a double play. The Angels had sent nine men to the plate. Three hits and four walks later, they took the field for the bottom of the eighth inning leading 12-4. Finley's night was done after the long inning, and it looked as if the Angels' losing streak would be snapped.

Mark Petkovsek relieved Finley to start the inning. Hargrove sent Alex Ramirez up to pinch-hit for Manny Ramirez to start the frame. (Hargrove probably did not realize at the time that he would pinch-hit for Alex Ramirez later in the same inning, and subsequently pinch-run for that pinch-hitter.) Alex Ramirez singled up the middle. After Jim Thome doubled to put runners on second and third, Richie Sexson's single made the score 12-6. David Justice and Enrique Wilson both singled to load the bases. Petkovsek's night was over; he faced five batters and gave up five consecutive hits. Shigetoshi Hasegawa walked to the mound with nobody out, the bases loaded, and his team leading by six runs. Einar Diaz popped up Hasegawa's second pitch for the first out of the inning. Dave Roberts popped out to second base on the next pitch. Omar Vizquel singled in a run, and Hasegawa's night was over. Troy Percival came in to close out the inning with two outs and the bases still loaded. At this point the Angels were ahead 12-7.

Roberto Alomar sent Percival's first pitch to him into right field for a two-run single, Vizquel moving from first to third. It was 12-9. Hargrove called on Harold Baines to pinch-hit for Alex Ramirez, the man who started the inning. Alomar stole second on the first pitch to Baines. With an 0-and-2 count, Baines singled to right, scoring Vizquel and Alomar. The score was now 12-11 with Jim Thome coming to bat. Percival walked Thome, and Carlos Baerga ran for Baines at second base. It was Richie Sexson's turn in the order again. With an 0-and-2 count, Percival threw a wild pitch; Baerga advanced to third base and Thome to second. Percival's next pitch was rocketed over the wall to deep left-center and the comeback/collapse was complete. The score was Indians 14, Angels 12. Sexson had five RBIs in the inning. Percival was one strike away from getting out of the jam twice but on this night he could not get that third strike.

Percival took offense at Sexson's showboating and the over-the-top way his teammates celebrated with him at the plate. "It looked like Game 7 of the World Series," he griped. "I'm not going to be their whipping boy. ... I'm going to move their feet away from the plate."[1]

David Justice stepped into the batter's box and was hit in the ribs by Percival's second pitch, a 95-MPH fastball. Justice charged the mound and threw his batting helmet at Percival. "I have never charged the mound," said Justice later. "I have never been a player like that. You're not going to punk me, though. ... I didn't see us throwing at Glaus after he hit his two home runs."[2]

Percival, Justice, and manager Collins were thrown out of the game by home-plate umpire Eric Cooper.[3] When play resumed, pitcher Charles Nagy ran for Justice. Enrique Wilson grounded out to end the inning. In the top of the ninth, after Paul Shuey struck out two batters, the Angels got back-to-back singles from Jim Edmonds and Orlando Palmeiro to bring the go-ahead run to the plate. But Todd Greene's ground-out to third ended the game.

The win went to left-handed reliever Jim Poole, who had been recalled from the Akron Aeros earlier in the day. He faced four batters, retiring two while seeing three runs score, but he was in the right place at the right time. The ejected Percival was charged with both a blown save and the loss. His career record against Cleveland became 0-6 with an 8.41 ERA.

"We've played worse. Maybe not pitched worse," said Angels manager Collins after the game.[4]

The win put the Indians at 81-50, tied with the New York Yankees for the best record in the league.

The Associated Press noted that the Indians' win was the third time in 1999 that the team had overcome an eight-run deficit.[5] The two previous games had been on May 7, a 20-11 win over Tampa Bay, and the first game of a July 3 doubleheader, a 9-8 win over Kansas City, both at Jacobs Field. They were the first major-league team to rally three times in one season from being down eight runs.[6]

The Angels lost the last two games of the series on Wednesday and Thursday. Angels manager Collins resigned on Friday with the team at 51-82, the worst record in baseball. Joe Maddon became the interim manager and the team snapped its losing streak with a home win against the Yankees. The Angels finished the season 19-10 under Maddon's leadership. In the offseason, new Angels general manager Bill Stoneman hired Mike Scioscia as the team's manager for the 2000 season. Scioscia led the Angels to their first World Series title in 2002.

Sources

In addition to the sources cited in the Notes, the author consulted Baseball-Reference.com and Retrosheet.org. Thanks to Joe Wancho for supplying the *Cleveland Plain Dealer.*

Notes

1   Cheryl Rosenberg, "Punched Out," *Santa Ana Orange County Register*, September 1, 1999: Sports 1.

2   Burt Graeff, "Justice Doesn't Regret Charging Mound After
    Percival Shot," *Cleveland Plain Dealer,* September 1, 1999: 5D.

3   Percival took note that a number of his teammates had
    not come out to defend him. See Rosenberg.

4   Associated Press, "No Lead Is Safe," *Sandusky*
    (Ohio) *Register*, September 1, 1999: B1.

5   Associated Press, "Cleveland Rallies Past Anaheim,"
    Milwaukee Journal Sentinel, September 1, 1999: 35.

6   Paul Hoynes, "Tribe Stuns Angels in 8th," *Cleveland
    Plain Dealer*, September 1, 1999: 1D.

AILING TIGERS RALLY TO TOP INDIANS

JULY 3, 1923:
DETROIT TIGERS 12,
CLEVELAND INDIANS 8 (10 INNINGS),
AT DUNN FIELD, CLEVELAND

BY BRIAN M. FRANK

The Tigers limped into Cleveland as a battered and bruised ballclub. They'd recently learned that first baseman Lu Blue, who had a broken rib, and third baseman Bobby Jones, who had a broken finger, would join their long list of walking wounded. The Tigers' injury list was growing so long that Harry Bullion wrote in the *Detroit Free Press*: "One would jump to the conclusion after perusing the list of injured that the

Del Pratt drove in the first run of an eighth-inning Tigers rally, then doubled to drive in the final two runs in the top of the 10th.

Bengals had been caught in a collision of trains or an explosion of a boiler somewhere."[1] In large part due to their many injuries, the team was 31-34 and wallowing in sixth place, 12½ games behind the league-leading Yankees but just 2½ games out of second place. "It is my firm belief we would be first or second in the race if we would have kept our team intact," lamented player-manager Ty Cobb. "No club in the league has had the misfortunes we have had this year. We had won 11 out of our first 16 games when the accidents began to happen. Since then, we have had Jones, (Topper) Rigney, Blue, (Bobby) Veach, (Ken) Holloway, (Bob) Fothergill, and (Harry) Heilmann out anywhere from five days for Heilmann to a month for Blue and six weeks for Jones."[2] Even Cobb was playing with a left hip that "creaks when he walks and the knee on the same side has a knot on it like the bulge on a tree branch."[3] As Bullion wrote in the *Free Press*: "[T]he team is just about staggering along with an ambulance in its wake, ready to pounce on the victims as they fall out of line."[4]

To add to the Tigers' woes, they would have to face Cleveland's veteran right-hander Stan Coveleski, who had only an 8-8 record, but owned an impressive 2.45 ERA. Cobb and the Tigers countered with right-hander Herman Pillette, who was 4-7 with a 3.87 ERA.

Pillette had a rough day. In the second inning, Joe Sewell reached when a "bounder got away from (George) Cutshaw."[5] Riggs Stephenson followed with a single and Rube Lutzke lined a fly to center to put the Indians on the scoreboard. Frank Brower then smashed a ball over the right-field wall, and Cleveland had an early 3-0 lead.

Cleveland continued to pile up runs off Pillette in the third. Homer Summa tripled to left-center

Indians Pile Up Lead of Eight Runs, but Lose to Tigers in Tenth, 12 to 8

Newspaper headline from *Cleveland's Plain Dealer.*

field with one down and scored on player-manager Tris Speaker's single. After Sewell grounded out, Stephenson singled home Speaker with his second hit of the day. Trailing 5-0, Cobb decided Pillette's day was done and replaced him with Ole Olson, who escaped the inning without any further damage.

However, in the fourth inning, Olsen was unable to slow the Indians' offense. After Steve O'Neill walked and Coveleski and Charlie Jamieson singled, Speaker stepped to the plate with two down and the bases full. Cleveland's player-manager delivered a triple "clearing the bases of all inhabitants" and gave the Tribe a commanding 8-0 lead. The offensive outburst prompted Francis J. Powers to write in the *Cleveland Plain Dealer,* "Seldom have the Indians done more effective hitting than in three innings yesterday."[6]

Everything seemed to be going Cleveland's way. Coveleski was in total control on the mound, having scattered six hits through six shutout innings. Meanwhile, rookie Ed Wells came in to restore order for the Tigers, setting the Indians "on their separate and collective heads."[7] Wells came in to start the fifth inning and allowed just one hit and two walks over three shutout frames.

Trailing 8-0 entering the seventh inning, the Tigers finally broke through on the scoreboard. Topper Rigney started the inning by belting a triple to center field. Coveleski retired the next two batters but Fred Haney singled home the first run of the day for Detroit. George Cutshaw brought home another run when he doubled to center. Cobb grounded back to the mound to end the inning and "the lonesome pair accumulated by the Bengals" had cut their deficit to a still substantial six runs.[8]

The Tigers' bats exploded in the eighth. Heinie Manush started the rally with a double, followed by Heilmann's single up the middle to put runners at the corners. Del Pratt singled through the box off Coveleski's glove, to bring home the first run of the inning. Rigney followed with another run-scoring single to cut the lead to 8-4. Johnny Bassler hit a groundball to first, but in his effort to turn a double play, Frank Brower threw low to second and all hands were safe. Cobb elected to send Bob Fothergill to the plate to pinch-hit for Wells with the bases loaded and nobody out, but he hit a tapper to third baseman Rube Lutzke, who was able to get the force at home.

With the bases still loaded, Haney hit a groundball back to Coveleski that looked as if it might be a double play. Harry Bullion wrote in the *Detroit Free Press* that "Stanley elected first to try and make the putout himself, and then seeing that he couldn't make it tossed the ball to O'Neill (to get the force at home). But he lost so much time in the parlay that Haney was safe at first base, where had Covey hurried his throw, he would have been retired."[9] The inning-ending double play averted, the Tigers continued to bat. Cutshaw singled home Bassler and Fothergill to cut the once seemingly insurmountable deficit to just two runs. Cobb "completed the wrecking of Coveleski" with a two-run double to right to tie the game.[10] After allowing eight runs in two innings, Speaker finally pulled Coveleski from the game. Bullion wrote, "What possessed Speaker to leave Stanley in there for so long nobody could figure correctly."[11] Reliever Phil Bedgood walked Manush before striking out Heilmann to end the inning. But 11 Tigers had come to the plate, collecting six runs on six hits, a walk, and an error, to tie the game at 8-8.

The game went to extra innings and the Tigers had another big rally in the 10th to win the game. Haney started the rally when he was hit by a Bedgood pitch. Cutshaw sacrificed him to second and Cobb drew a walk. After Manush flied out, Heilmann gave Detroit its first lead of the day with an RBI single to right. That brought Del Pratt to the plate with runners on second and third and he "cut a double inside third base" to bring home Cobb and Heilmann.[12] Rigney finished the scoring with an RBI single to center to give the Tigers a 12-8 lead.

Ray Francis and Ken Holloway split the final three innings on the mound for the Tigers and neither "allowed the Indians to even double up their fists or make a threatening move toward the plate."[13] The game ended when Holloway induced Glenn Myatt to ground out harmlessly to first, and the Tigers had an improbable 12-8 win.

As with any 12-run game, Detroit had many offensive stars in its comeback win. Rigney went 4-for-5 with a triple, walk, and two RBIs. Cutshaw finished 2-for-5 with a double and three RBIs. Heilmann had three hits in six at-bats, while driving home a run, and Cobb went 2-for-5 with a walk and two RBIs.

The victory was all the more satisfying because Detroit had overcome an eight-run deficit without the injured Blue and Jones in the lineup. Also, they were able to come back against Coveleski, who'd dominated them over the first six innings. As Bullion wrote in the *Detroit Free Press*, the Tigers' effort "ought to be positive proof that a ball game never should be counted as over until the last man is out."[14]

Sources

In addition to the sources cited in the Notes, the author consulted Baseball-Reference.com and Retrosheet.org.

Notes

1   Harry Bullion, "Injuries Will Keep Out Jones and Blue," *Detroit Free Press*, July 3, 1923: 15.

2   "Cobb Frowns When Doctor Issues Edict," *Cleveland Plain Dealer*, July 3, 1923: 21

3   Bullion, "Injuries Will Keep Out Jones and Blue."

4   Bullion, "Injuries Will Keep Out Jones and Blue."

5   "Game in Detail," *Cleveland Plain Dealer*, July 4, 1923: 20.

6   Francis J. Powers, "Redskins, Leading by Eight Runs, Collapse," *Cleveland Plain Dealer*, July 4, 1923: 1.

7   Harry Bullion, "Coveleskie Falls Despite Early Lead," *Detroit Free Press*, July 4, 1923: 8.

8   Bullion, "Coveleskie Falls Despite Early Lead."

9   Harry Bullion, "Tiger Tales," *Detroit Free Press*, July 4, 1923: 9.

10   Bullion, "Coveleskie Falls Despite Early Lead."

11   Bullion, "Coveleskie Falls Despite Early Lead."

12   Bullion, "Coveleskie Falls Despite Early Lead."

13   Powers.

14   Bullion, "Coveleskie Falls Despite Early Lead."

YANKEES RALLY FROM NINE DOWN TO BLOW OUT RED SOX

APRIL 21, 2012:
NEW YORK YANKEES 15,
BOSTON RED SOX 9,
AT FENWAY PARK, BOSTON

BY PETER SEIDEL

While fans lament the Red Sox collapse of 1978, their 2011 collapse was actually worse. The Sox entered September with a nine-game lead only to lose not only the division, but a wild-card berth as well in what was an epic final day of the 2011 season. There were reports that the Red Sox pitchers had been drinking beer and eating fried chicken in the clubhouse and dugout during games. It had appeared that skipper Terry Francona, who led the Red Sox to two World Series titles and helped break the "Curse of the Bambino," had lost control of his players. The chicken and beer scandal led to the end of Francona's tenure in Boston. The front office decided that the new Red Sox manager would need to restore order in the clubhouse, and that Bobby Valentine was the man to do just that.

The Red Sox began the 2012 season on the road, where they lost five of their first six games. It seemed that the friendly confines of Fenway Park could be the remedy as they won the first three of four games in their home opening series against the Tampa Bay Rays. After dropping the last game against the Rays, the Red Sox were then swept by the Texas Rangers and their hated rival Yankees came to town for a two-game series. The first game was the 100th anniversary of the opening of Fenway Park and resulted in another Red Sox loss. Red Sox fans could only hope for a different result in the second game.

After the the Yankees went down in the top of the first, the Red Sox' bats heated up quickly against Freddy Garcia, starting with Ryan Sweeney reaching out across the plate to bloop a one-out double down the left-field line. After Garcia got Dustin Pedroia to hit a pop foul for the second out, Adrian Gonzalez just missed a home run; the ball bounced over the short fence in right field, scoring Sweeney and putting the Red Sox on the board. David Ortiz's double to left scored Gonzalez, giving the Red Sox a 2-0 lead.

The Red Sox continued to hammer Garcia in the second, starting with a one-out single by Cody Ross,

Nick Swisher and Mark Teixiera each drove in six runs as the Yankees scored seven runs in the seventh and seven more in the eighth.

who took third on a double by Darnell McDonald off the left-field wall. Mike Aviles's single scored Ross and sent McDonald to third. He scored on Sweeney's sacrifice fly to right. After swiping second base, Aviles scored on an opposite-field single by Pedroia that ended Garcia's afternoon. Gonzalez's flyout to deep center field off reliever Clay Rapada ended the Boston threat with the home team leading 5-0.

Boston tacked on two more in the third. Ortiz led off with a single to right field. David Phelps replaced Rapada and hit Kevin Youkilis in the hip with his second pitch. Jarrod Saltalamacchia's single to right loaded the bases with no outs. McDonald's sacrifice fly scored Ortiz and Aviles's single plated Youkilis, extending the Red Sox lead to 7-0.

Saltalamacchia led off the bottom of the fifth with a 420-foot double to the deepest part of Fenway Park in center field. Ross's blast to center cleared the fence and made it 9-0, Red Sox.

Red Sox starter Felix Doubront kept the Yankees off the scoreboard for the first five innings and struck out Robinson Cano and Alex Rodriguez to start the sixth. Switch-hitting Mark Teixeira, looking for a fastball from Doubront, deposited a 2-and-1 offering into the seats above the left-field wall, putting the Yankees on the board, 9-1.

Valentine replaced an effective Doubront with reliever Vicente Padilla to start the top of the seventh. Andruw Jones struck out looking to lead off the seventh. Russell Martin hit an opposite-field bloop single to right. Eduardo Nuñez reached safely on a weak grounder to third. After Derek Jeter walked, Nick Swisher stepped to the plate with the bases loaded and none out. Swisher entered the 2012 season trying to shake off another poor postseason performance, and was off to a great 2012, which was the final year of his contract after the Yankees exercised their team option. "Last year was a super stressful season for me, man," Swisher said. "I am not going to be stressed out like that this year. I'm going to have as much fun as I can and just enjoy it. This is such a great place to play. I'm just enjoying every minute of it."[1]

Swisher continued with his hot start by smacking an opposite-field grand slam over the left-field wall, inching the Yankees closer at 9-5. Cano followed up with a double off the wall, ending Padilla's afternoon. Off Matt Albers, Rodriguez hit a groundball to short that Aviles bobbled, giving the Yankees runners at the corners with none out and Teixeira stepping to the plate. Teixeira, who had homered from the right side of the plate off lefty Doubront in the previous inning,

batted from the left side against the righty Albers. With a 2-and-2 count, Teixeira reached out and smacked an outside pitch over the wall for an opposite-field three-run homer, bringing the Yankees within one: 9-8.

After scoring seven in the seventh inning, the Yankees weren't done beating up the Red Sox bullpen. In the eighth lefty Franklin Morales, who retired the Yankees in the seventh in relief of Albers, surrendered a leadoff single to Nuñez, putting the tying run on first. Valentine called on closer Alfredo Aceves for a six-out save. After walking Jeter, Aceves surrendered a sky-high double to Swisher that bounced off the center-field wall, scoring Nunez and Jeter, giving the Yankees a 10-9 lead and Swisher six RBIs for the game. After walking Cano intentionally and then walking Rodriguez to load the bases with none out, Aceves surrendered a line-drive double to Teixeira that bounced over the short wall in the right-field corner. Swisher and Cano scored, Rodriguez went to third, and the Yankees now led 12-9. Like Swisher, Teixeira also had six RBIs. After intentionally walking Curtis Granderson to load the bases again, Aceves was replaced by Justin Thomas. Valentine was met with a chorus of boos when he marched onto the field to lift Aceves; he responded by tipping his cap to the fans. He later said, "I've been booed in a couple of countries; a few different stadiums. I don't want to be booed."[2]

It took only two pitches to get two outs as Raul Ibañez hit into an unassisted double play at first base. But Martin sent the first pitch he saw from Thomas to the center-field wall for a double, scoring Rodriguez and Teixeira and extending the Yankees' lead to 14-9. Jeter's single off Junichi Tazawa plated Martin, giving the Yankees a 15-9 lead that would stand as the final score.

"You're down 9-0 and Tex hits what looks like an innocent home run. Then we come back with back-to-back seven-run innings," Yankees manager Joe Girardi said after the game "I don't think I've ever been a part of that."[3]

"I don't like to lose. I don't know anybody who does," Aviles said. "This wasn't fun at all. I don't want to see it if it gets any worse."[4]

While it might not have gotten any worse than this particular game, the Red Sox did do plenty of losing in 2012, 93 games to be exact, and finished in last place. Valentine was fired after the last game of the season. The bad times would end quickly in Boston as they rebounded amazingly and won the 2013 World Series.

The Yankees won 95 games in 2012 and took first place in the AL East. They were swept by the Tigers in the ALCS.

Sources

In addition to the sources cited in the Notes, the author relied on Baseball-Reference.com and the MLB Video Channel on YouTube.

Notes

1   [1] Ken Davidoff, "Swisher, Teixeira Help Yankees Rally from 9 Runs Down to Blow Out Red Sox," *New York Post*, April 22, 2012.

2   Associated Press, "Yankees Blast Back Against Red Sox – New York Scores 7 Runs in Back-to-Back Innings," *Albany Times Union*, April 22, 2012.

3   Associated Press.

4   Associated Press.

BUCS SCORE 10 IN NINTH TO BEAT THE REDBIRDS

JUNE 11, 1933:
PITTSBURGH PIRATES 11,
ST. LOUIS CARDINALS 7 (FIRST GAME OF
DOUBLEHEADER),
AT SPORTSMAN'S PARK, ST. LOUIS

BY GREGORY H. WOLF

The Pittsburgh Pirates were slumping when they arrived in the Gateway City for a four-game series with the St. Louis Cardinals in June 1933. Skipper George Gibson's Bucs (27-21) had lost eight of their last 11

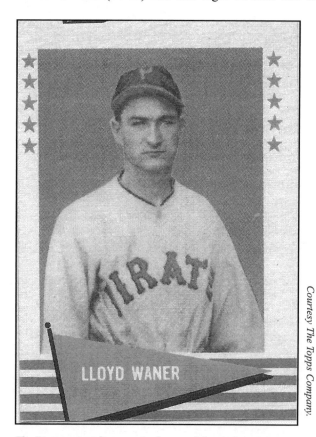

The Pirates scored 10 runs in the top of the ninth inning. Lloyd Waner singled, driving in two, then came up again later in the inning and singled again, driving in two more.

games to fall from first to third place, three games behind the New York Giants. The Redbirds, however, were on a roll and playing their best ball since they won the World Series in 1931. Manager Gabby Street's squad (30-19) had won 16 of its last 20 games to move to within a half-game of the NL's top spot.

Sportsman's Park, located at the intersection of Grand Avenue and Dodier Street on the north side of the city, was packed with the largest crowd of the season, according to the *St. Louis Post-Dispatch*, 21,000-strong for a Sunday afternoon doubleheader.[1] It was a typical June day in St. Louis: hot and humid with temperatures in the mid-90s.

The first game featured hurlers who had tied for the NL lead with 19 victories two years earlier. The Bucs called on 37-year-old right-hander Heinie Meine, who sported a 5-3 slate (and 49-39 in his career). He faced Bill Hallahan, whose 7-2 record (1.90 ERA) improved his career numbers to 59-35. The two-time NL strikeout leader was acknowledged to be one of the hardest throwers in the big leagues; however, Wild Bill often struggled with control and was en route to leading the circuit in walks for the third time in four seasons.

Hallahan and the Cardinals looked like champions through the first eight innings. After Wild Bill breezed through the first two frames, allowing only a leadoff single to Lloyd Waner, Cardinals hitters went to work. In the second, Ripper Collins led off with a single and moved to third on Joe Medwick's single. Third sacker Pie Traynor fielded Jimmie Wilson's grounder and caught Collins between third and home, but catcher Tom Padden's errant throw, his second error of the inning (the first came on a dropped foul ball), enabled Collins to return to third. With the bags loaded, Leo Durocher singled, driving in two. Meine was hit hard in the third. With one out, Ernie Orsatti and Collins lined singles, but right fielder Paul Waner's throw cut down Orsatti trying to reach third. After George Watkins doubled, Medwick doubled to right to drive both home for a 4-0 Cardinals lead.

The Pirates had two runners in each inning from the fifth inning through the eighth, yet managed just one run. In the fifth, Gus Suhr and Tommy Thevenow led off with singles, but were left stranded when Adam Comorosky, pinch-hitting for Meine, grounded into a 6-4-3 twin killing. The Bucs tallied a run in the sixth on Traynor's double driving in Arky Vaughn, who had singled. The seventh and eighth innings both ended with runners on first and third.

It seemed like the Pirates "traded their cutlasses and pistolas for powder puffs and nosegays," quipped St. Louis sportswriter J. Roy Stockton.[2] The Cardinals blasted Ray Kremer, the third Bucs pitcher, in the eighth. Watkins led off with a single and moved to third on Medwick's double off the right-field wall. Durocher's fly ball and Hallahan's single accounted for two more runs. After Pepper Martin walked, Frankie Frisch's blast "hit the projecting roof of the right field stand," reported sportswriter Edward F. Ballinger.[3] Hallahan scored the Cardinals' seventh and final run on play, but Martin was caught in a rundown at third.

The Pirates appeared "hopelessly beaten" to start the ninth inning, wrote the *Pittsburgh Press*.[4] The Bucs, however, were a good-hitting team, which led the NL with a .285 batting average in '33 and scored more runs than any NL team except the Cardinals. Their lineup featured four starters who batted at least .300 that season: Vaughn (.314), Freddie Lindstrom (.310), Paul Waner (.309), and Traynor (.304).

The ninth inning unfolded as a "maze of sensational developments," gushed the *Pittsburgh Sun-Telegraph* and left Cardinals fans second-guessing their skipper's decisions.[5] All told, the Bucs sent 14 batters to the plate, collected seven hits, drew three walks, profited from an error, a passed ball, and a wild pitch, and executed a squeeze to score 10 runs, all of which came against the Cardinals' three best hurlers.

The Pirates quickly loaded the bases with no outs. Thevenow walked and moved up on a passed ball. Tony Piet, pinch-hitting for Padden, reached on third baseman Pepper Martin's fumble. Hal Finney, hitting for Kremer, singled, but coach Grover Hartley held

Thevenow at third even though it appeared he could have scored, reported the *Post-Dispatch*.[6] Manager Street went to the mound and conferred with Hallahan and his infielders. Sportswriter Martin J. Haley of the *St. Louis Globe-Democrat* reported that Street "signaled in" Tex Carleton, who had been warming up in the bullpen, but acquiesced to Hallahan's request to remain in the game.[7] Lloyd "Little Poison" Waner singled to left to drive in two runs. After "Big Poison" Paul Waner flied out for the first out, Vaughn drew a free pass to send Hallahan to the showers.

In came Carleton, who like all of Street's primary starting pitchers, was slated for relief duty in high-leverage situations. It was a disaster. Traynor singled to drive in two runs, followed by Lindstrom's run-scoring single to pull the Pirates to within one, 7-6, and force Carleton's exit.

With runners on first and second and one out, Street called on Dizzy Dean, his wildly popular 23-year-old right-hander, to save the game. Suhr greeted him with a single to tie the game. After Dean's wild pitch put both runners in scoring position, Thevenow singled to right to give the Pirates the lead, 8-7. The Cardinals' dramatic collapse, quipped Gateway City sportswriter Ray J. Gillespie, resembled a comedic routine by Leon Erroll, a film star at the time known for wobbly walk, unsteady legs, and goofy falls.[8] But the Cardinals' tumble was far from over. After Dean walked Piet to load the bases, Hal Finney's squeeze sacrifice bunt worked perfectly to plate another run. Lloyd Waner collected his second single of the inning, driving in the Bucs' final two runs to increase their lead to 11-7.

The Redbirds seemed demoralized after the Pirates unexpected offensive outburst. Reliever Bill Harris worked around Collins's one-out triple and fanned Medwick to put an emphatic exclamation point on one of the Pirates' most dramatic comebacks in franchise history.

The Pirates were outhit 17 to 16 and collected just one extra-base hit, but went 7-for-8 with men in scoring position in the ninth. Lloyd Waner led the attack with four hits and four runs batted in; Traynor had three hits and three RBIs.

In the second game, the Pirates demonstrated they could pitch. Larry French spun an eight-hit shutout, defeating Bill Walker to complete the doubleheader sweep. The Pirates remained in third place, but just 1½ games separated the Giants, Cardinals, and Bucs atop the NL.

The following day was an offday for the two teams before they resumed the series on Tuesday. While many of the Pirates traveled to Springfield, Missouri, for an exhibition game, the Cardinals players had time to read local newspapers' musings about the collapse. One from the *St. Louis Star and Times* aptly captured the mood and the zeitgeist of 1930s Depression-era America. "In the rathskellers and delicatessens today, and even in the beer gardens tonight, you'll hear grief-stricken baseball addicts calling our Red Birds scalawags, rapscallions and perhaps ragamuffins."[9]

Sources

In addition to the sources cited in the Notes, the author accessed Retrosheet.org, Baseball-Reference.com, SABR.org, and *The Sporting News* archive via Paper of Record.

Notes

1. J. Roy Stockton, "Cards Have Open Date After Double Defeat at Hands of Pirates," *St. Louis Post-Dispatch*, June 12, 1933: 13.

2. Stockton.

3. Edward F. Balinger, "Pirates Capture Twin Bill from Cards," *Pittsburgh Post-Gazette*, June 12, 1933: 16.

4. "Pirates Zoom Back into the Thick of Pennant Race," *Pittsburgh Press*, June 12, 1933: 23.

5. "Buccos Take Double Bill from Cards," *Pittsburgh Sun-Telegraph*, June 12, 1933: 24.

6. Stockton.

7. Martin J. Haley, "Pirates Thump Cardinals Twice; 11-7 and 3-0," *St. Louis Globe-Democrat*, June 12, 1933: 6.

8. Ray J. Gillespie, "Weird Ten-Run Rally in 9th Helps Pirates Take Double-Header," *St. Louis Star and Times*, June 12, 1933: 20.

9. Gillespie.

MOOSE BECOMES GOAT AFTER INDIANS GIVE UP SIX-RUN NINTH-INNING LEAD TO RED SOX

JUNE 8, 1937:
BOSTON RED SOX 10,
CLEVELAND INDIANS 8,
AT LEAGUE PARK, CLEVELAND

BY VINCE GUERRIERI

As the Boston Red Sox came to the plate in the top of ninth inning at League Park on June 8, 1937, first place was within sight for the Indians.

Since the team's World Series win in 1920, the Indians had been largely mediocre, but there was cause for optimism in 1937. The pitching staff was guided by the steady hand of veteran Mel Harder, and Bob Feller, though still a teen, had developed veteran poise to go with his fastball. Talented but mercurial pitcher Johnny Allen, who faced the Red Sox in this game, was on the mend from an attack of appendicitis early in the season, and was starting to round back into form.[1]

In eight innings, Allen had scattered nine hits and led, 8-2. He had been staked to an early lead thanks to Earl Averill's home run in the bottom of the first. A four-run fusillade in the sixth gave Allen even more insurance. The scoreboard showed that the Yankees had lost to the White Sox – the 10th straight win for Chicago – and a win would put the Indians a game ahead of both teams in the loss column. "That glittering gold top rung of the American League ladder," as the next day's *Plain Dealer* put it, awaited.[2]

To start the ninth inning, Allen walked rookie Bobby Doerr, pinch-hitting for pitcher Jack Wilson. He then surrendered three successive singles, to Buster Mills, Mel Almada, and Joe Cronin, Almada's and Cronin's hits each driving in a run. After Cronin's hit, Indians manager Steve O'Neill lifted Allen for relief pitcher Joe Heving. The Indians were still leading 8-4, but Heving had his work cut out for him, facing

the always dangerous Jimmie Foxx with Almada at second, Cronin at first, and nobody out. But Indians fans cheered Heving, believing the win was still within reach.[3]

Foxx launched a fly ball to left field that should have been easy pickings for Moose Solters.[4] But Solters, according to the *Cleveland Press*, let the ball fall without molestation. "Maybe Judge Landis should investigate this," the *Press* intoned, noting that Solters had previously played for the Red Sox.[5] Both Cronin

Headline from the June 9, 1937 *Dallas Morning News.*

141

and Almada came home to score, cutting the Indians' lead to two runs, at 8-6.

Up stepped Eric McNair for the Red Sox, hitless in the game. He too hit a fly ball to left field, giving Solters a chance to redeem himself. Instead, Solters staged a "Statue of Liberty" play – and not the football type. He stood motionless as the ball dropped behind him for another double, with Foxx taking third.

Pinky Higgins then singled, scoring Foxx and sending McNair to third. It was now 8-7, with the tying run 90 feet from home – and there were still no outs! O'Neill made another pitching change, this time bringing in Whitlow Wyatt to face Fabian Gaffke. Gaffke put a charge into one, sending it to left-center field – the deepest part of League Park for a double that scored Higgins and McNair as the Red Sox took their first lead of the game.

Gene Desautels dropped a sacrifice bunt to advance Gaffke to third, and the pitcher's spot came up next. The Red Sox had batted around, but Doerr was lifted for pitcher Wes Ferrell, who was as much a threat at the plate as he was on the mound. Ferrell flied out to right field, but Gaffke tagged up and scored. Mills grounded out to shortstop Lyn Lary to end the inning, but the damage had been done.

The 2,500 fans in attendance, stunned to silence by the Red Sox' rally, regained their voices in the bottom of the ninth as the Indians went meekly in order to Red Sox pitcher Johnny Marcum. Hal Trosky lined out to right field. Solters, who had become the game's goat, was booed heartily as he fouled out to catcher

Desautels for the second out, and Odell Hale ended the game with a fly ball to center field.

"It was the rally of rallies for the year, and when it all was over, the Boston dressing room was a mad house," said the *Boston Globe*.

Things were just as mad at the *Plain Dealer* offices, as "scores of fans phoned … with denunciations of the Tribe's play."[6] But O'Neill planned to keep Solters in the lineup, saying, "You can't take a man out of the line-up just because he looked bad on two fly balls. He deserves some consideration and I am going to see that he gets it. The morals of many players have been ruined by taking them out after they have been guilty of fielding lapses and I do not think that Solters deserves such treatment."[7]

Solters ended up playing 149 games for the Indians that year – all of them in left field.

Notes

1   Scott Longert, *Bad Boys, Bad Times* (Athens, Ohio: Ohio University Press, 2019), 26.

2   Sam Otis, "Boston's 8 in 9th Keep Indians Out of First Place," *Cleveland Plain Dealer,* June 9, 1937: 18.

3   Eugene Whitney, "Fans Wire, Call in Bewilderment," *Cleveland Plain Dealer,* June 9, 1937: 18.

4   Melville E. Webb Jr., "Red Sox Cut Loose for 8 Runs in Ninth," *Boston Globe,* June 9, 1937: 22.

5   Stuart Bell, "Tribe Falters, Blowing Six-Run Lead in Ninth," *Cleveland Press,* June 9, 1937: 22.

6   Whitney.

7   Whitney.

CUBS' NINTH-INNING COMEBACK SPOILS CHURCH'S OUTING

JUNE 29, 1952:
CHICAGO CUBS 9,
CINCINNATI REDS 8
(FIRST GAME OF DOUBLEHEADER),
AT CROSLEY FIELD, CINCINNATI

BY RICHARD CUICCHI

After having been traded from the Philadelphia Phillies to the Cincinnati Reds in late May 1952 and making nine appearances in June with disappointing results, Bubba Church was looking for a positive turnaround in his season. He needed a good outing to boost his confidence. With two fine seasons with the Philadelphia Phillies under his belt, he wasn't used to the struggle he was experiencing. For 8⅔ innings in the first game of a home doubleheader against the Chicago Cubs on June 29, it appeared Church was finally going to realize his much-needed breakthrough. But the bottom fell out on his effort before he could complete the game, and the Cubs wound up scoring seven runs to defeat the Reds.

Church had been an important cog in the dramatic 1950 pennant-winning season by the Phillies' Whiz Kids. The 25-year-old rookie worked his way into the starting rotation by mid-July, and he finished the season with an 8-6 record and a 2.73 ERA while completing eight of his 18 starts. He finished fourth in the voting for National League Rookie of the Year.

In 1951 Church emerged as the number-two starter for the Phillies, behind Robin Roberts. He won 15 games while posting a 3.53 ERA and four shutouts among his 15 complete games.

During spring training in 1952, Church had pitched ineffectively after hurting his arm. He clashed with Phillies manager Eddie Sawyer and was used sparingly during the first four weeks of the season.[1] In late May he was traded to Cincinnati for pitcher Kent Peterson and outfielder Johnny Wyrostek.

After a no-decision in his first outing for the Reds on May 27, Church made nine appearances in June that included four starts and five relief efforts. During that stretch he struggled to get back on track, as he compiled a 7.56 ERA and two losses.

BUBBA CHURCH
pitcher CINCINNATI REDS

Courtesy The Topps Company.

Bubba Church was the hard-luck loser, working 8 2/3 innings and only giving up three earned runs, but was victim to a two-out error on a play that would have given him an 8-3 win.

In the first game of a doubleheader at Crosley Field, in scorching 97-degree weather, right-hander Church drew the starting assignment from manager Luke Sewell in his 10th game of the month. The Reds were in sixth place, already well out of contention for the league lead.

The Cubs countered with 24-year-old Johnny Klippstein, who was 4-5 coming into the game. Under manager Phil Cavarretta, they were in third place, 11 games behind league leader Brooklyn. Chicago had suffered a nine-game losing streak that ended five days earlier.

First baseman Dee Fondy got the Cubs on the scoreboard first with a solo home run in the top of the first. The Reds bounced back in the bottom of the frame with two runs coming on singles by Grady Hatton and Joe Adcock. Altogether the Reds had four hits and a walk off Klippstein.

In the bottom of the second, the Reds scored another run on a quirky play that involved back-to-back singles. Cal Abrams singled with two outs. When Bobby Adams singled, Abrams initially made an attempt to reach third base. Then he changed his mind and retreated to second only to find Adams headed there. In the Cubs' attempt to get Adams out as he ran back toward first base, Abrams wound up scoring.[2]

Fondy led off the top of the fourth inning with a double and scored on Toby Atwell's single to score the Cubs' second run.

Klippstein started the fifth inning with the Cubs behind, 3-2. He gave up singles to Bob Borkowski and Adams, then retired Hatton on a pop fly. Ted Kluszewski singled to score Borkowski. Cavarretta brought in Willie Ramsdell to replace Klippstein. Willard Marshall's grounder to second scored Adams, while Wally Westlake, running for Kluszewski, went to second. Adcock's single scored Westlake, and it was 6-2, Cubs.

With Bob Schultz in the game for Ramsdell in the bottom of the seventh, Marshall's single drove in Adams.

After Andy Seminick and Roy McMillan singled to lead off the bottom of the eighth, Church aided his own cause by singling and driving in Seminick.

Through the eighth inning, Church had largely been in control of the game, having allowed only two runs on eight hits with no walks. With a comfortable 8-2 lead, he started the ninth by retiring the first two Cubs batters, and it appeared he was on the brink of a complete game for his first win of the year.

However, a collapse by Reds pitchers ensued. Church gave up a double to Bill Serena and issued his first walk, to Roy Smalley. Gene Hermanski batted for pitcher Joe Hatten, and hit a broken-bat single to score Serena. Eddie Miksis's bunt to third was fielded by Eddie Kazak, whose throw home was wild. Smalley scored on the play.

Frank Smith took over for Church and hit his first batter, Hal Jeffcoat, loading the bases. Fondy followed with his third hit of the game, driving in Hermanski and Miksis. Hank Sauer missed a home run by inches and had to settle for a double that scored Jeffcoat and pulled the Cubs within one run of the Reds.

Ken Raffensberger, who was normally a starter, replaced Smith. He loaded the bases when he intentionally walked Bruce Edwards, pinch-hitting for Atwell. Sewell used his third pinch-hitter of the inning, Johnny Pramesa, a former Red batting for Bob Addis. Pramesa hit a single that scored the Cubs' final two runs and put them ahead 9-8. Altogether, six of the seven runs scored by the Cubs were unearned.

Dutch Leonard pitched the ninth for the Cubs and secured the win. Hatten, who relieved Schultz in the eighth inning, got his fourth win of the season. Smith took his sixth loss. The heat likely contributed to a total of eight pitchers being used, five by the Cubs.

Fondy was the Cubs' offensive star of the day, going 3-for-5 with three RBIs. Adams got three hits and scored three runs for the Reds.

Church got a complete-game win in his next start, against Pittsburgh, and followed that with four straight losses, then four straight wins. He finished the season with a 5-9 record. For the rest of his career, he was unable to rebound to the form he demonstrated during his first two seasons.

In the second game of the doubleheader, the Reds again built an overwhelming lead, but didn't allow the Cubs to mount another comeback. The Reds won, 9-1, behind Harry Perkowski's four-hitter.

Sources

In addition to the sources cited in the Notes, the author consulted Baseball-Reference.com and Retrosheet.org.

Smith, Lou. "Reds Blow Big Lead, Trim Cubs in Final, 9-1," *Cincinnati Enquirer*, June 30, 1952: 24.

Notes

1   C. Paul Rogers III, "Bubba Church," SABR BioProject, sabr.org/bioproj/person/d59a11d0.

2   Irving Vaughan. "Cubs Win 9-8; Lose 2d, 9-1, to Cincinnati," *Chicago Tribune*, June 30, 1952: 4,1.

BUMBRY BREAKS 0-FOR-23 WITH RARE HOMER TO TIE GAME IN ORIOLES COMEBACK

JULY 27, 1975: BALTIMORE ORIOLES 11, MILWAUKEE BREWERS 6 (10 INNINGS) (SECOND GAME OF DOUBLEHEADER), AT COUNTY STADIUM, MILWAUKEE

BY LAURA H. PEEBLES

The visiting Baltimore Orioles had taken three of the first four games of the unusual five-game series from the host Milwaukee Brewers. The 26,705 fans attending this Sunday doubleheader had already witnessed their home team lose 7-4, although they did see a piece of baseball history: Oriole Tommy Davis whacked his 2,000th hit.[1] Milwaukee had held a piece of first place in the AL East earlier in July but they had slipped to fourth, nine games back of Boston before beginning play on the 27th. Baltimore was just ahead of the Brewers, eight games back of Boston.

Rookie Tom Hausman (3-2, 3.99 ERA) was making only the third start of his major-league career (although he had made 20 relief appearances in 1975). He had little trouble with the top of the Brewers lineup: Ken Singleton flied out, Al Bumbry fouled out to the catcher, and Davis grounded to first.

Paul Mitchell (1-0, 3.38 ERA) matched Hausman's performance in the home half of the first with a strikeout of Don Money, a lineout by Charlie Moore, and a fly out by George Scott. Mitchell was also a rookie, also making his third start. He had only pitched 18⅔ innings but that included a complete game in his most recent outing, on July 19.

Hausman allowed his first baserunner in the second when he walked Lee May and balked him to second. But he still didn't allow a hit: Jim Northrup flied out, Bobby Grich and Elrod Hendricks struck out.

The bottom of the second and the top of the third were equally uneventful.

The Brewers got on the board in the bottom of the third. Paul Mitchell walked Bobby Mitchell in front of Robin Yount. Yount's homer put the Brewers up by two. Money's one-out solo homer gave the Brewers' fans more to cheer. Mitchell recovered to get a fly out and a strikeout but the Brewers led, 3-0.

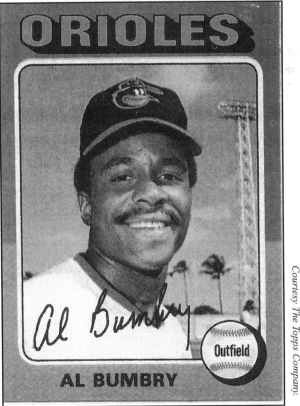

Al Bumbry's three-run homer brought Baltimore to a 6-6 tie.

The Orioles threatened but did not score in the fourth. Hausman got two quick outs then allowed back-to-back singles to May and Northrup. He walked Grich to load the bases. The Orioles failed to capitalize: Hendricks flied out to right to end the frame.

Each pitcher allowed just one walk in the bottom of the fourth and the top of the fifth.

The Brewers padded their lead in the bottom of the fifth. Kurt Bevacqua hit a one-out double. After Money struck out, Moore's single scored Bevacqua. Scott flied out to end the inning with the score 4-0, Brewers.

Each team had only one baserunner in the sixth. Northrup reached on an error but was left on base, Millwaukee's Gorman Thomas walked but was erased on a double play.

Doug DeCinces hit a one-out double in the top of the seventh, but neither Mark Belanger nor Singleton was able to knock him in.

The Brewers looked as if they might add to their lead in their half of the seventh. Bill Sharp singled and Yount sacrificed him to second. Bevacqua singled but Sharp had to hold at second. That led to a pitching change: Dyar Miller replaced Mitchell to face Money. Money flied to left but shallow enough that the Orioles caught the runner off second for a double play.

All Hausman allowed in the top of the eighth was a single to May. That was only the fourth hit allowed by Hausman although he did allow three walks.

The Brewers added to their lead in the home half of the eighth. Miller walked Moore, so Scott's home run put the Brewers up 6-0. Miller allowed two more singles but neither scored.

Going into the top of the ninth Baltimore's win expectancy (per Baseball Reference) was zero.[2] Hausman, apparently tiring,[3] walked Grich and allowed a single to Hendricks. To a chorus of boos from the crowd, manager Del Crandall made a pitching change to the usually dependable relief pitcher Tom Murphy (1.96 ERA, 14 saves, only two blown saves). Murphy failed to record an out (and raised his ERA to 2.74). The first batter he faced, DeCinces, tripled, scoring two. Pinch-hitter Tony Muser singled, scoring another. Singleton singled, putting two on for Bumbry. Bumbry, whose .284 BA as a designated hitter had led the league at the All-Star break,[4] hadn't had a hit since before the break. He broke out of his 0-for-23 slump in a big way, hitting only his second homer of the year to tie the game, 6-6.[5]

Crandall pulled Murphy, calling on Rick Austin, who had been closing games while Murphy had been

out for a month with a sore arm.[6] Murphy had been solid in his first game back on July 23, allowing only one hit in two innings. But from this game to the end of the season, he was not the same pitcher as he had been before: He earned only six saves, had seven blown saves, and an 8.89 ERA. For his part, Austin had pitched an inning in the first game of the doubleheader, facing only four batters. Relieving Murphy, Austin got the necessary three outs.

Of course the Brewers had the opportunity for a walk-off in the bottom of the ninth. Unlike in the eighth inning, they were unable to do anything against Miller: Bevacqua, Money, and Moore were out one-two-three thanks in part to a fine defensive play by third baseman DeCinces.[7]

Austin stayed in to pitch the top of the 10th. A multiple-inning appearance wasn't unusual for him. However, this one was disastrous for him – and his team. He started by walking Grich. Paul Blair popped out to the catcher.[8] Austin walked DeCinces and struck out Tim Nordbrook.[9] The third out proved elusive: Singleton singled, scoring Grich. Austin issued his third walk of the inning to pinch-hitter Don Baylor to load the bases. Davis unloaded them with a 400-foot grand slam into the center-field seats.[10] That wasn't all: May doubled before pinch-hitter Dave Duncan finally struck out. May had quite the day: he was 3-for-4 with an HBP in the first game and 3-for-5 with a walk in the second.

Given the 11-6 score, the chances of a Brewers comeback in the bottom of the 10th were small. Sixto Lezcano[11] hit a one-out single and Mike Hegan walked to put two on. Grant Jackson took the mound to face the next batter: pinch-hitter Hank Aaron. He looked at strike three to end the game.

After the game Crandall was asked about his decision to pull Hausman. Both Hausman and Orioles manager Earl Weaver defended the decision. Weaver said, "Crandall made all the right moves. It looks like he made the wrong ones, but I've seen it before." Certainly Crandall hadn't seen anything like it before, saying it was the hardest defeat of his career.[12]

Baltimore finished second in the AL East, 4½ games back of Boston. Milwaukee, though tied for first briefly earlier in July, gradually sank through the season to finish fifth in the AL East, 28 games behind Boston. Crandall was fired before the last game of the season. He said one of the reasons for the Brewers' poor performance was lack of pitching depth, something that was certainly on display in this game.[13]

Sources

In addition to the sources cited in the Notes, the author consulted Retrosheet.org.

Notes

1   "Davis Not Too Excited About Getting 2,000th hit," *Baltimore Sun*, July 28, 1975: C3.

2   See the Win Probability Chart, top of the ninth inning, on the baseball-reference.com page for this game, at baseball-reference.com/boxes/MIL/MIL197507272.shtml.

3   Mike O'Brien, "Crandall Shaken After Twinbill Loss," *Fond du Lac* (Wisconsin) *Reporter*, July 28, 1975: 23.

4   "Orioles' Bumbry Leads DH's," *Naples* (Florida) *Daily News*, July 17, 1975: 2C. The press release gave him credit for a .291 average as a DH, but the current calculations from Baseball-Reference show .284.

5   That was also Bumbry's last homer of the year. In his 14-year career, he never reached double-digits in home runs.

6   O'Brien.

7   Lou Hatter, "2d-Game Rallies Help Birds Take 2 from Brewers," *Baltimore Sun*, July 28, 1975: C3.

8   Blair had been substituted in as the center fielder in the top of the ninth.

9   Nordbrook had been substituted in as the shortstop in the top of the ninth.

10 Hatter.

11 Lezcano had been substituted in as the right fielder in the top of the seventh.

12 O'Brien.

13 Mike O'Brien, "Many Factors Led to Crandall's Demise," *Fond du Lac Reporter*, September 29, 1975: 19.

MARLINS SHOCK CARDINALS WITH FOUR NINTH-INNING HOME RUNS

AUGUST 26, 1998:
FLORIDA MARLINS 7,
ST. LOUIS CARDINALS 6
(10 INNINGS),
AT BUSCH STADIUM, ST. LOUIS

BY RUSS LAKE

A transformation of baseball's fandom in St. Louis was undeniably apparent in 1998. Crowds pouring into Busch Stadium had shifted their fans-in-the stands appreciation moments from stolen bases, pitching skill, and defensive gems of the 1980s to batting practice, the booth announcer, and home-run derby.

Despite the fact that a disappointing season in the standings was taking shape for the Cardinals, "McGwire-Mania" had overwhelmed the Mound City.[1] The ballpark opened an hour earlier than normal for thousands to view batting practice.[2] During most contests the voice of public-address booth announcer John Ulett was drowned out due to energetic standing-ovation cheers when he informed the multitudes, "Batting third, number 25, first baseman, Mark McGwire."

Chicago Cubs outfielder Sammy Sosa and McGwire had morphed into sensational gate attractions as the friendly competitors chased the season home-run record of 61 set by Roger Maris in 1961. Fans flocked to home and road venues in which these sluggers performed to see them hit. Even the final scores of games had become secondary at times.

This night's contest pitted the Cardinals versus the Florida Marlins in the finale of a two-game set. Though the Marlins were defending World Series champions, their roster was quite a deviation from 1997. A dismal record of 46-86 was indicative of an after-championship salary dump orchestrated by team owner Wayne Huizenga.[3] The 62-69 Cardinals were progressing toward a losing record for the fourth consecutive month, and were 20 games behind in the NL Central Division.

Left-hander Darren Oliver (1-2, 4.63 ERA) was given his fifth start for St. Louis while southpaw knuckleballer Kirt Ojala (1-3, 3.90) got the nod for Florida. Oliver had been acquired on July 31 from the Texas Rangers. Darren's father was Bob Oliver, who had played for five major-league clubs during an eight-year career. The game-time temperature was 87 degrees with an 8 MPH wind in from left. McGwire came in with 53 home runs, and Sosa had already nailed number 52 at Cincinnati's Cinergy Field before McGwire's initial plate appearance.[4]

In the opening frame, the first ball put in play caused a slight interruption. Switch-hitter John Cangelosi was retired at first base by Delino DeShields, but the Cardinals second baseman injured his left shoulder with a diving stop.[5] Pat Kelly came in to replace DeShields. Ojala pitched around a walk to Kelly, who stole second and went to third on a passed ball before the side was retired.

Both starters thwarted trouble to keep the contest scoreless through six frames. In the top of the seventh, Oliver escaped a bases-filled situation when Ojala grounded into an unassisted force for the third out. Ojala gave up his third hit when Ron Gant doubled to right-center to open the bottom half. John Mabry bunted and Ojala threw wildly past third. The error allowed Gant to score the first run while Mabry advanced to second. Placido Polanco hit a comebacker to Ojala, and Mabry was retired at third. Oliver, who had allowed three hits and three walks while striking out six in seven innings, was lifted for switch-hitter Willie McGee. Ojala fanned McGee, and then allowed an infield single to Eli Marrero. Marlins manager Jim Leyland brought in right-hander Justin Speier to register the third out.

Right-hander John Frascatore took over the St. Louis mound duties and retired the side in order in the eighth. During the break, stadium organist Ernie Hays revved up the crowd with his fan-favorite hand-clapping rendition of "Here Comes the King."[6] The 24-year-old Speier, who was the son of longtime major-league infielder Chris Speier, continued his relief duty for Florida. The Redbirds teed off on him for the cycle (and beyond). First, Fernando Tatis tripled to right-center. McGwire, after going 0-for-3 with two fly balls and a strikeout, connected on an 0-and-1 fastball for his 54th home run.[7] It was a 509-foot drive to straightaway center that caromed off the top of the 35-foot batter's eye and fell to the grass berm. Two men scurried from their bleacher seats and wrestled for the sphere.[8]

Naturally, the crowd of 30,004 went from being restless to wild as their hero trotted around the bases. McGwire was greeted at the plate by his 10-year-old son, Matt,[9] and then acknowledged a rousing dugout curtain call.[10] Speier sailed the next pitch close to the head of Brian Jordan. The former NFL defensive back removed his helmet, stepped forward, and pointed his bat toward the mound.[11] Gant walked away from the on-deck circle, and started to move in the same direction.[12]

Plate umpire Harry Wendelstedt intervened and warned Speier. This action prompted Leyland to argue with Wendelstedt, and a nose-to-nose confrontation ensued. The veteran arbiter did not take kindly to Leyland's quarrel, and ejected the Florida skipper.[13] Leyland later explained, "I snapped because it was a 75 MPH split-finger in the wrong location. We're not throwing at anybody." Hitting coach Milt May took over as the Marlins manager.[14]

Jordan dropped a single into short left, and he scored when Gant doubled. Mabry hit his ninth homer to up the lead to 6-0. Speier's ERA after one-third of an inning increased from 7.94 to 11.57. Right-hander Donn Pall came on and eventually halted the St. Louis onslaught. Pall actually permitted three singles, but a double play staved off additional tallies. The Cardinals sent 10 batters to the plate while scoring five runs on eight hits.

With the Cardinals ahead, 6-0, after eight innings, only three outs stood in the way of a win.

Frascatore, in his 61st appearance, had finished 15 games this season. However, the first three Marlins

Down 6-0, the first three Marlins hit solo home runs in the ninth inning, then pinch-hitter Mark Kotsay homered for three more.

Courtesy The Topps Company.

batters in the ninth – Derrek Lee, Cliff Floyd, and Kevin Orie – powered back-to-back-to-back homers to cut the lead in half, 6-3. It was Lee's 15th, Floyd's 18th, and Orie's fifth home run. This marked the first time in franchise history that Florida hit three consecutive home runs.[15] It was also the first (and only) time that Frascatore allowed a trio of homers in a major-league game.

Left-hander Lance Painter relieved and retired his first hitter, but then walked Luis Castillo and allowed a single to Dave Berg. Manager Tony La Russa came out to the mound, and in came veteran right-handed reliever Jeff Brantley. Lefty-swinging rookie Mark Kotsay whacked a pinch-hit three-run home run to right. It was his eighth of the year, and knotted the game, 6-6. Kotsay yelled at the top of his lungs as he returned to the dugout.[16] Brantley then struck out the next two Marlins. Nine Florida hitters batted and they made good for six runs on five hits.

Right-hander Antonio Alfonseca made his 48th relief appearance, and the crowd rose to their feet as McGwire approached the plate. McGwire singled to center, but was forced at second. Later, with two runners on and two away, pinch-hitter Ray Lankford flied out to send the contest into extra innings.

Juan Acevedo came on to face Florida for the 10th. The right-hander fanned Lee, but Floyd managed an infield hit for his fourth safety. Floyd moved to second as Orie reached first when his potential double-play grounder was muffed by shortstop Luis Ordaz.[17] Randy Knorr, who had just been called up from Triple-A Charlotte the day before, bounced a double past third to plate Floyd and hand the Marlins their first lead, 7-6.[18] Acevedo retired the next two batters.

Left-handed pinch-hitter Tom Lampkin pulled an infield hit to the right side to begin the bottom of the 10th. A strikeout followed by a 6-4-3 twin-killing grounder earned Florida an astonishing comeback victory in a game lasting 3:33. Line scores totaled 7 runs, 10 hits, and 3 errors for the Marlins while the Cardinals accumulated 6 runs, 14 hits, and 2 errors. The winning pitcher was Alfonseca (3-6) with Acevedo (6-3) taking the loss.

Leyland was waiting in the tunnel and celebrating with high-fives for his squad on their way to the locker room. The no-nonsense mentor was giddy about the comeback. Leyland exclaimed, "This was one of the greatest wins I've had in all my years of baseball." Knorr, who produced the game-winning hit, commented, "If this doesn't pump us up for the rest of the year, I don't know what will."[19]

But the 1998 Marlins lost 22 of their final 29 games and finished with the major-leagues' worst record at 54-108. They ended up a whopping 52 games out of first place. After Florida grabbed the victory away from the Cardinals, the team dropped two of its next three and fell into last place at 63-72. The Redbirds surged and won 20 of 27 to close at 83-79 for third place in the NL Central.

The drama of the home-run chase continued throughout the end of the regular season as McGwire led the majors with 70 and Sosa was runner-up with 66.

Sources

In addition to the sources cited in the Notes, the author accessed Retrosheet.org, Baseball-Reference.com, Newspapers.com, and SABR.org/research.

Notes

1   Mike Berardino, "McGwire Sends Current Through His River Town," *South Florida Sun Sentinel* (Fort Lauderdale), August 27, 1998: 28, 30.

2   Mike Eisenbath, "McGwire's Flex Appeal," *St. Louis Post Dispatch*, June 20, 1998: 72.

3   Stephen R. Keeney, sabr.org/research; sabr.org/research/miami-marlins-team-ownership-history; Accessed December 25, 2019.

4   Associated Press, "Sosa Gets No. 52, Bouquets in Cincy," *St. Louis Post Dispatch*, August 27, 1998: 24, 26.

5   Rick Hummel, "McGwire Hits One; Marlins Hit Four," *St. Louis Post Dispatch*, August 27, 1998: 24, 26.

6   YouTube file, youtube.com/watch?v=suVHmNusPfc; accessed 12/29/2019.

7   Mike Berardino, "Marlins' 4 HRs in 9th Upstage Slugger's 54th," *South Florida Sun Sentinel*, August 27, 1998: 28, 30.

8   Cheryl Rosenberg, "Mac Hits 509-foot HR; Marlins Pound 4 in 9th," *Palm Beach Post* (West Palm Beach, Florida), August 27, 1998: 27, 32.

9   Hummel, "McGwire Hits One; Marlins Hit Four,"

10 Rosenberg, "Mac Hits 509-foot HR; Marlins Pound 4 in 9th."

11 Berardino, "Marlins' 4 HRs in 9th Upstage Slugger's 54th."

12 Rosenberg.

13 Berardino, "Marlins' 4 HRs."

14 Rosenberg.

15 Rosenberg.

16 Rosenberg.

17 Hummel.

18 Rosenberg.

19 Rosenberg.

CARDINALS SCORE SEVEN IN NINTH FOR LARGEST COMEBACK

MAY 2, 2005:
ST. LOUIS CARDINALS 10,
CINCINNATI REDS 9,
AT GREAT AMERICAN BALL PARK, CINCINNATI

BY JUSTIN MATTINGLY

In the first month of the 2005 season, the St. Louis Cardinals had again established themselves as the force of the National League. The Cincinnati Reds, meanwhile, faced a nine-year playoff drought and had returned to near the cellar of the Central Division.

On a 49-degree night in early May, the Reds and an official attendance of 15,961 hosted the Cardinals at the Great American Ball Park (early in its third year) for the teams' second series of the year. The home team appeared to have the game in hand through eight innings, potentially handing the Cardinals their fourth loss in five games.

The fans who remained witnessed the largest ninth-inning comeback in Cardinals history.

Eric Milton, who had signed a three-year contract in the offseason, started the game for Cincinnati, while Chris Carpenter, the Cardinals ace who was on his way to the Cy Young Award, took the mound for the visitors.

After a scoreless first two innings, the Cardinals' So Taguchi, filling in for a resting Larry Walker in right field, lined a fastball into the left-field seats for the game's first run – the 11th home run allowed by Milton in the young season after allowing a NL-leading 43 the year before. Carpenter, meanwhile, breezed through the first four innings, striking out six while allowing three hits.

The Reds got on the scoreboard in the fifth inning on a home run by Rich Aurilia, the team's new shortstop after franchise cornerstone Barry Larkin retired in the offseason.

The Cardinals struck back in the sixth inning to take a 2-1 lead. First baseman Albert Pujols led off

with a double and scored on an error after first baseman Sean Casey was unable to scoop third baseman Joe Randa's throw – a precursor to the fielding woes set to plague the Reds in later innings.

Ken Griffey Jr., the center field superstar who had his best season in Cincinnati in 2005, led off the home half of the inning stuck in a power slump, having hom-

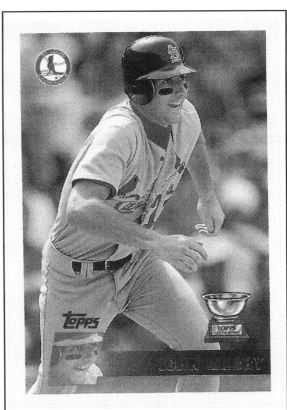

John Mabry's two-run ninth-inning homered carried the Cardinals to a 10-9 win over Cincinnati.

ered just once in April. Opposite him was Carpenter, against whom, among active pitchers, Griffey had gone the most at-bats (22) without a home run.

He hit a pitch from Carpenter to center field, off what was initially considered to be the outfield wall and back into play. Griffey ran into second base with an apparent leadoff double, but crew chief Ed Montague brought the umpiring crew together and broke a 2-2 tie in favor of giving Griffey a leadoff home run and his second homer of the year.[1] He ended up hitting 35 home runs in 2005, something he did eight times and just twice with the Reds.

The Reds then loaded the bases on a single by Casey, a walk, and first baseman Pujols' throwing error. Aurilia drove in Casey with a sacrifice fly to give the Reds their first lead of the game.

Catcher Jason LaRue hit the next pitch down the right-field line for a two-run double, and the Reds led 5-2. Carpenter recorded the next out to complete the inning and his outing, finishing with a line of six innings pitched, five runs (two earned), and eight strikeouts.

The Reds also went to their bullpen in the seventh with Ryan Wagner relieving Milton, who also pitched six innings while allowing two runs (one earned) and recording five strikeouts.

Cardinals catcher Yadier Molina, in his first season as the team's primary backstop, led off the seventh with a double. He scored two batters later on a David Eckstein sacrifice fly, bringing the Cardinals within two runs.

Carmen Cali remained in the game to start the home half of the eighth after holding the Reds scoreless in the seventh. Left fielder Adam Dunn deposited his first pitch of the inning into the right-field stands to make it a 6-3 game and Randa followed by doubling down the left-field line, sending Cali to the showers and setting up more Reds insurance.

Randa scored on Aurilia's double off new reliever Jimmy Journell, who struck out the next two batters to potentially hold the score at 7-3. A single and two walks brought another run around to score and pinch-hitter Felipe Lopez singled home another to make it 9-3, Reds.

Heading into the ninth inning, the Cardinals had a 1 percent chance at winning, according to Baseball-Reference.com's Win Probability Chart, and were set to lose their third straight game, something they hadn't yet done in 2005.

Molina, the light-hitting catcher with an on-base percentage of only .197 entering the game, led off

facing reliever David Weathers, who came into the game after two-time All-Star closer Danny Graves stopped warming up with the home team extending its lead in the eighth inning.

The Cardinals backstop drew a walk, and Abraham Nunez followed with another. Eckstein poked a single to right field to load the bases. Pinch-hitter Roger Cedeno struck out on three pitches, stalling the visitors' momentum.

Up came Pujols, who entered the game hitting .417 with runners in scoring position.[2] The eventual National League MVP hit a groundball to Aurilia for what appeared to be a game-ending double play. The Reds got the force out at second base, but Casey, the first baseman, was unable to make the pick, allowing Molina to score and the rally to continue.

Reggie Sanders, the veteran outfielder signed by the Cardinals in 2003, brought Nunez home with a single to left field, making it 9-5.

Reds manager Dave Miley turned to his bullpen, bringing in Graves, who had completed his first eight save opportunities in 2005 after a career-high 41 in 2004. He had yet to give up a home run in his first 11 appearances of the year and Edmonds, who along with Pujols and third baseman Scott Rolen made up the club's three-headed "MV3" moniker for their middle-of-the-order potency, had gotten just three hits off him in 16 tries to date.

Graves hung a curveball and Edmonds, homerless since April 19, hit it into the right-center-field stands for a three-run home run. The Cardinals were within a run of tying the game, but still an out away from losing.

Mark Grudzielanek, the beneficiary of a misplay by Casey in the sixth inning, again found himself on the receiving end of one after hitting a hard groundball to the first baseman that he was unable to corral.

John Mabry, who had started the game at third base in place of an ailing Rolen, came to the plate homerless so far in the season. He sent Graves' first pitch over the center-field wall – not far from where Griffey's controversial sixth-inning home run hit – for a two-out, two-run go-ahead home run. The Cardinals had scored seven runs in the frame, including six with two outs, to take the lead.

"We kept building on mistakes," Sanders said.[3]

Boos rained down from the Cincinnati fans, but the game wasn't over yet.[4]

Closer Jason Isringhausen was on the disabled list, leaving Julian Tavarez, who had just one save in the season, to close out the comeback.[5]

Randa hit a leadoff single to left field, putting the tying run on base. Aurilia tried to sacrifice him to second, but Molina pounced on the bunt and recorded the force out at second base. LaRue was hit by a pitch, but a groundball to shortstop by right fielder Austin Kearns turned into a game-ending double play – the twin killing the Reds weren't able to turn in the Cardinals' half of the inning.

"It's not easy to give a big-league game away, but we did," Miley said.[6]

The comeback was the biggest for the Cardinals since they came from eight down against the Reds on May 12, 2002, and the biggest ninth-inning comeback ever for the team.[7]

For the Reds, it was the first time they blew a six-run lead in the ninth inning since 1952. The Reds released Graves, the only Vietnamese-born player in major-league history, later in May.[8]

The Reds finished in fifth place in the Central Division, 27 games behind the Cardinals, who came within two games of repeating as National League champions after winning 100 games in the regular season – none more improbable than this one.

Sources

In addition to the sources mentioned in the Notes, the author consulted the Baseball-Reference.com box-score and game logs.

Notes

1   Joe Strauss, "Cards Stun Reds with 7 in 9th," *St. Louis Post-Dispatch*, May 3, 2005.

2   Strauss.

3   Strauss.

4   Associated Press, "Edmonds, Mabry Cap Biggest 9th-Inning Rally in Cards History," ESPN, May 3, 2005.

5   Isringhausen had been an All-Star with Oakland in 2000. He was named to the All-Star team in 2005 as well.

6   "Edmonds, Mabry Cap Biggest 9th-Inning Rally in Cards History."

7   Strauss.

8   Bob Nightengale, "'I Was OK with Not Living': What Happens When an All-Star Pitcher Suffers From Depression," *USA Today*, September. 29, 2019.

BUCS' SIX-RUN NINTH COMPLETES COMEBACK AND MAKES BURLEIGH GRIMES WINNER IN FIRST BIG-LEAGUE APPEARANCE

SEPTEMBER 10, 1916: PITTSBURGH PIRATES 8, CHICAGO CUBS 7, AT WEEGHMAN PARK, CHICAGO

BY GREGORY H. WOLF

"The Buccaneers turned impending defeat into a glorious victory snatched from the very jaws of disaster" gushed the *Pittsburgh Press* about the Pirates' six-run ninth inning to beat the Chicago Cubs, 8-7, in the

Catcher Walter Schmidt drove in the final run for the Pirates.

Windy City.[1] The *Pittsburgh Post* called the Deadball Era offensive explosion a "sensational slugfest,"[2] while sportswriter J.J. Alcock of *Chicago Tribune* considered it "one of the gamest rallies" ever witnessed in the metropolis on Lake Michigan.[3]

The Pirates and Cubs had little to play for as the 1916 season came to a close except for an outside chance to move into the first division. Baseball schedule makers, however, had done them no favors in September. A day after suffering consecutive shutout losses in a Sunday afternoon doubleheader sweep by the Cubs at Forbes Field, Jimmy Callahan's fifth-place Pirates (61-69) faced the sixth-place Cubs (61-72) again, but some 460 miles away in Chicago. It marked the Pirates' first game of a grueling road swing during which they played 23 games in 18 days, including eight twin bills. The Cubs barely had time to unpack. After just one game in front of their partisan fans, manager Joe Tinker's squad commenced an 18-game road trip.

It was a gorgeous late summer day in Chicago with clear skies and temperatures in the low 70s as the two teams met at Weeghman Park.[4] The Cubs were finishing their first season playing in the three-year-old ballpark, which had originally been built for the Chi-Feds/Whalers of the upstart Federal League. When that circuit disbanded after the 1915 season, club owner Charles Weeghman bought the Cubs and relocated them from their wooden park on the west side of the city.

Prior to the game the Cubs received some bad news. Their second baseman, former MVP Larry Doyle, whom they had acquired two weeks earlier in a blockbuster trade with the New York Giants, would miss the rest of the season. He had broken his ankle in the first game of the doubleheader the day before.[5]

On the mound for the Cubs was left-handed swingman Gene Packard (9-6), who had starred in the Federal League in its two-year existence, winning 20 games twice for the Kansas City Packers. Through the first five innings, Packard "southpawed with pleasing effect," cooed Alcock, mowing down the Pirates on three scattered singles.[6] It must have been a strange sensation for Packard when the crowd erupted in a "spontaneous ovation" after a Pirates batter dug in at the plate in the second inning.[7] That player was Frank "Wildfire" Schulte, a star from the Cubs' dynasty that captured four pennants and won two World Series titles in a five-year stretch (1906-1910). Making his first appearance in Chicago since his trade to the Pirates on July 29, he smacked a "vicious liner," noted the *Post*, but right to center fielder Les Mann for an out.[8]

The Cubs took the lead in the first inning against right-handed rookie Frank Miller. A surprise find for the Pirates, Miller (7-9, 2.09) had tossed a four-hit shutout in his last start, but lacked that sharpness in this outing. With two men on (via a single and walk), rookie Earl Smith, making his major-league debut, stroked a two-out triple to left to put the Cubs on the board. The Cubs tacked on three more in the fourth. Vic Saier led off with a double, moved to third on Smith's single, and scored on Jimmy Archer's sacrifice. Singles by three of the next four hitters brought in two more runs. Chuck Wortman and Rollie Zeider, the latter on a two-out hit-and-run, picked up an RBI to build the Cubs' seemingly commanding 5-0 lead.

In the bottom of the fifth, Callahan sent in a rookie hurler who had just joined the team that morning: Burleigh Grimes. A 22-year-old right-hander who had won 20 games for the Birmingham Barons in the Southern Association, Grimes retired the Cubs in order. The Pirates gave the recruit two runs to work with in the sixth. Max Carey led off with a single and came home on Bill Hinchman's blast to left field that "took a mighty bound and landed in the seats," reported the *Post*, for a two-run home run.[9]

Save for the Pirates' ninth-inning heroics, Grimes would have been the team's bright spot of the day and "seen his name in large type" in the newspaper, opined

Courtesy The Topps Company.

This comeback win gave righty Burleigh Grimes a surprising but quite welcome win in his major-league debut.

the *Tribune*.[10] Thrust into an emergency appearance, Grimes pitched four innings and yielded just three hits, though he struggled with his control, walking four. Sportswriter Charles J. Doyle of the *Pittsburgh Gazette-Times* noted his "fine delivery and plenty of speed" to go along with a spitball.[11] He yielded two runs in the seventh, but also exhibited coolness under pressure. Max Flack walked to start that frame and raced to third when Mann beat out a bunt and Grimes' throw to first sailed into right field for an error. Saier knocked Flack in and Mann scored on Smith's sacrifice to give the Cubs a 7-2 lead. The *Pittsburgh Press* reported on Grimes' "peculiar experience" at Weeghman Park.[12]

"[A]ccustomed to pitching from a strictly level box," said the paper, Grimes felt that Weeghman Park's nine-inch-high pitching mound was like "on a hill."

A weak offensive team ranking last in the NL in runs scored with just 3.08 per game, the Pirates exploded in the ninth and "started to hammer the ball to all parts of the field," wrote Doyle.[13] Walter Schmidt led off with a single and moved to third on third baseman Charlie Pechous's throwing error. After

PIRATES' FLASHY SPLURGE IN NINTH BEATS CUBS 8-7

Callahan's Crew Registers Six Runs in Closing

Headline from Cleveland's *Plain Dealer* of September 11, 1916.

Grimes fanned, Packard fell apart. Frank Smykal's single scored Schmidt and Carson Bigbee also singled. With three balls to Carey, Packard was pulled in favor of Mike Prendergast, a former Whalers hurler. He completed the walk to load the bases, then dodged a bullet when Hinchman popped up to second base. And then the wheels fell off. With Honus Wagner at the plate, Prendergast uncorked a wild pitch that brought in a run. Still a threat at age 42, Wagner singled, driving in two more, to pull the Bucs to within one run. Hometown hero Schulte, who had blasted a double off the right-field wall in the previous inning, collected his third hit of the game, a deep line drive that looked like a triple, opined Doyle, but Mann made a good play to hold Schulte to a single and keep Wagner at third.[14] Doug Baird rapped a bullet that "almost crippled" shortstop Chuck Wortman, wrote the *Gazette-Times*, while Wagner crossed the plate to tie the game.[15] Schmidt collected his second single of the inning, driving in Schulte to give the Pirates an 8-7 lead and complete the comeback with "high class" battling, lauded the *Press*.[16]

The Pirates weren't out of trouble yet. After flying out to end the top of the ninth, Grimes was back on the mound and issued a leadoff walk to Flack. Callahan yanked Grimes and called on Al Mamaux, the club's best starter, who had won 21 games in 1915 and would finish with the same number in 1916. Flack moved up a

station on a passed ball and Mann's sacrifice. Needing just a deep fly ball to tie the score, Saier popped up to the catcher. Mamaux then denied rookie Earl Smith a chance for a fairy-tale ending to his debut by striking him out and ending the game in 1 hour and 50 minutes.[17]

The Pirates' stunning comeback made Grimes a winner in his big-league debut. After a rough first full season with the Pirates in 1917, he was traded to the Brooklyn Robins (Dodgers), with whom he became a star and built his Hall of Fame bona fides.

Just hours after the game, the Pirates boarded a train bound to Buffalo, New York, en route to play an exhibition game the following day in Binghamton. Their road trip proved disastrous. They won only four of 23 games (and also tied two) and finished the season in sixth place (65-89). The Cubs didn't fare much better, winning just four of 18 games with one tie, and finished in fifth place (67-86).

Sources

In addition to the sources cited in the Notes, the author accessed Retrosheet.org, Baseball-Reference.com, SABR.org, and *The Sporting News* archive via Paper of Record.

Notes

1   "Pitcher Grimes Looks Like Find," *Pittsburgh Press*, September 11, 1916: 20.

2   "Buccos Surprise Bruins," *Pittsburgh Post*, September 11, 1916: 8.

3   J.J. Alcock, "Pirates Defeat Cub Team, 8 to 7, by Six in Ninth," *Chicago Tribune*, September 12, 1916: 13.

4   "The Weather," *Chicago Tribune*, September 11, 1916: 1.

5   "Doyle Out for the Year," *Chicago Tribune*, September 11, 1916: 13.

6   Alcock.

7   Charles J. Doyle, "Pirates Rally in Ninth and Beat Cubs, 8-7," *Pittsburgh Gazette-Times*, September 11, 1916: 6.

8   "Buccos Surprise Bruins."

9   "Buccos Surprise Bruins."

10   Alcock

11   Doyle.

12   "Pitcher Grimes Looks Like Find," *Pittsburgh Press*.

13   Doyle.

14   Doyle.

15   Doyle.

16   "Pitcher Grimes Looks Like Find," *Pittsburgh Press*.

17   The *Chicago Tribune* gave the game time as 1 hour and 50 minutes. Pittsburgh papers had 2 hours.

ROBINS STUN GIANTS WITH FIVE NINTH-INNING RUNS TO TIE BALLGAME, THEN WIN IN 10TH

JUNE 25, 1929:
BROOKLYN ROBINS 12,
NEW YORK GIANTS 10
(10 INNINGS),
AT POLO GROUNDS V, NEW YORK

BY GORDON GATTIE

The Brooklyn Robins and New York Giants were seemingly participating in different leagues though the teams were adjacent in the standings in late June of 1929. The fifth-place, 26-34 Robins were 11½ games behind the NL-leading Pittsburgh Pirates, and a half-game ahead of the Boston Braves. The fourth-place, 34-26 Giants fared better, 3½ games from first place and one game behind the third-place St. Louis Cardinals. The teams were nearly meeting expectations; during spring training, 103 writers from the Baseball Writers' Association of America picked New York to finish second and Brooklyn sixth.[1] The cross-town rivals already met 13 times in 1929; somewhat surprisingly, Brooklyn had won eight times.

The Dodgers were managed by Wilbert Robinson, who had guided Brooklyn since 1914. The team was attempting to break its four-year streak of finishing sixth; Brooklyn hadn't contended for the pennant since its 1924 second-place finish. The Robins' leaders included veteran pitcher Dazzy Vance and young hurler Watty Clark, complemented with outfielders Babe Herman and Johnny Frederick. The team struggled during spring training, lacking offense, with a 3-10 record against major-league and Double-A teams. *The Sporting News* said, "They had no punch last season, and no hope is in sight unless it should be provided by shortstop Glenn Wright and Heinie Nicholas Cullop."[2]

The Giants enjoyed more recent successes, winning four pennants and two World Series from 1921 to 1924, but had finished two games from first place

in 1927 and '28. Manager John McGraw was leading New York for his 30th campaign, and the Giants had brimmed with confidence since spring training.[3] Twenty-year-old outfielder Mel Ott was enjoying a breakout season. The an infield was anchored by shortstop Travis Jackson and first baseman Bill Terry. The pitching staff featured two 20-game winners, Larry Benton and Freddie Fitzsimmons. The Giants won six straight games at Philadelphia,[4] scoring double-digit runs in each game, before losing back-to-back con-

ROBINS COME FROM BEHIND TO TAKE GAME

Larry Benton Chased From Mound in 9th; Ott Hits His 21st Homer

Headline from the June 26, 1928 *San Francisco Chronicle.*

tests to Brooklyn entering the afternoon matchup on the 25th.

Doug McWeeny started for Brooklyn. The lanky right-hander struggled through mid-June after a solid 1928 campaign when he posted career highs in wins (14) and innings (244) while leading the NL with four shutouts and 114 walks issued. McWeeny expected to significantly contribute in 1929,[5] but had just a 3-7 record and a 5.16 ERA through 89 innings entering the game. McWeeny had allowed at least three runs in each of his previous nine starts dating to May 8, though he had recently displayed a return to his 1928 form.[6] In his last start, a no-decision, McWeeny allowed three runs on 10 hits in 11⅓ innings. He struggled with controlling his primary pitch, a fastball. He also threw "a fair screw ball and only a mediocre curve."[7]

Larry Benton started for New York. In 1928 he won 25 games and pitched 28 complete games, tied for the NL league lead with Burleigh Grimes in both categories. Entering this game, the veteran right-hander was 6-7 with a 4.03 ERA in 102⅔ innings. Benton had won his last decision, pitching 4⅓ relief innings three days earlier. In a start against Brooklyn a week earlier, he allowed five runs on five hits without recording an out in the first game of a Robins doubleheader sweep.[8] Benton's primary pitch during the first half of his career was his fastball.[9] After pitching over 300 innings for the first time in his career during the 1928 season, his fastball slowed and he developed a wide sweeping curveball during the 1929 season.[10]

Brooklyn's offense started quickly against Benton once again; Frederick and Wally Gilbert led off the game with singles. Frederick then scored when second baseman Billy Rhiel threw wild on Harvey Hendrick's grounder. With one out, Rube Bressler doubled home Gilbert and Hendrick. Benton prevented further damage on a strikeout and fly out though Brooklyn built an early 3-0 lead.

New York also started quickly. Edd Roush and Freddy Leach singled, then Freddie Lindstrom walked to load the bases with no outs. Ott grounded into a fielder's choice and Roush scored. Leach scored next on Terry's fly ball. Andy Cohen singled to place runners at the corners, but Jackson grounded out to end the inning with the Giants trailing by one run.

Benton pitched better during the second inning, giving up just a walk. McWeeny struggled again; Shanty Hogan started New York's half with a single, then took second base on a wild pitch. Benton flied out and Roush singled as New York again threatened.

Wasting no time, Robinson replaced McWeeny with Ray Moss. Moss was greeted with run-scoring singles by Leach and Lindstrom, followed by a two-run blast by Ott, his 21st of the season. New York led 6-3.

Both teams then cooled off. The Robins had one baserunner per inning from the third through the sixth; the Giants loaded the bases in the fifth inning on a walk, single, and intentional walk, but didn't score.

The Giants pressed again in the sixth. After a leadoff groundout, Leach and Lindstrom singled; Ott reached on an error to load the bases. Terry singled home two runs, and Cohen followed with another run-scoring single. Brooklyn's Lou Koupal relieved Moss and Jackson hit into a fielder's choice. But Hogan continued the merry-go-round by singling Terry home. Hogan was caught stealing but the Giants now led 10-3.

Brooklyn scored a pair of runs in the seventh. Frederick singled, took second on a groundout, and scored on Bissonette's single. Bissonette scored on Bressler's single. New York now led 10-5. In the Giants' seventh, Koupal settled down, retiring the Giants in order. The Robins couldn't carry their momentum into the eighth and went down one-two-three. In the bottom half Terry singled and Cohen walked with two outs, but Jackson popped out.

The Giants' Benton returned to the mound for the ninth. Frederick reached first base for the third time as the leadoff hitter of an inning. He scored his third run after Herman and Hendrick singled. Bissonette singled to load the bases with no outs and Brooklyn was within striking distance of tying the game. Bressler grounded out but all runners moved up 90 feet, including Watty Clark, who pinch-ran for Herman and scored Brooklyn's seventh run. Dave Bancroft lined out to right field, but Hendrick scored and Bissonette advanced. Brooklyn's veteran catcher Val Picinich then launched a Benton fastball into the left-field seats. The Robins had come back from a seven-run deficit to tie the score, 10-10. A pop fly ended the rally.

Johnny Morrison relieved Koupal in the bottom of the ninth. Hogan and Crawford walked, and a groundout moved Hogan to third, but he was stranded on a popout.

New York reliever Dutch Henry relieved Benton for the 10th. With one out, Frederick beat out a slow roller for an infield hit.[11] Eddie Moore singled Frederick home with the go-ahead run and reached second on the throw home. Hendrick tripled, plating Moore with an insurance run, but was thrown out trying for an inside-the-park home run. Bissonette grounded out but the Robins led for the first time since the first inning.

Morrison returned for a second inning, and Ott greeted him with a left-field double as New York brought the tying run to the plate. Terry flied out to center field and Ott advanced. Then Cohen and Jackson both grounded out, giving Brooklyn a 12-10 victory with nine unanswered runs that "ruined Mr. McGraw's afternoon,"[12] although one could "imagine the joy of the Brooklyn fans and 8,000 schoolboys who had been guests at the game."[13]

Morrison improved to 4-0 with two scoreless innings, his fourth win in 11 Brooklyn appearances, tying him with McWeeny,[14] while Henry absorbed the loss. Brooklyn's Frederick, Bissonette, and Bressler had three hits apiece with Frederick scoring four runs and Bressler driving in four. Each team banged out 17 hits and was charged with two errors.

As in to the previous four seasons, the Robins finished in sixth place. With a 70-83 record, the Robins were 28½ games behind the pennant-winning Cubs. Though they scored 90 more runs than in the prior season, their pitching staff allowed 248 more runs, the NL's second-highest total. Johnny Frederick hit .328 and led Brooklyn with 127 runs. The Giants finished third, 13½ games behind Chicago, with an 84-67 record. Their 3.97 team ERA paced NL staffs. One key pitching component was leading the NL with the fewest walks. But Benton was 12-17 with a 4.14 ERA. The teams continued their intra-city rivalry, playing several close games, with Brooklyn winning 14 of 21 contests.

Sources

Besides the sources cited in the Notes, the author consulted Baseball-Almanac.com, Baseball-Reference.com, Retrosheet.org, and the following:

Golenbock, Peter. *Bums: An Oral History of the Brooklyn Dodgers* (New York: Putnam Books, 1984).

James, Bill. *The New Bill James Historical Abstract* (New York: The Free Press, 2001).

Thorn, John, and Pete Palmer, et al. *Total Baseball: The Official Encyclopedia of Major League Baseball* (New York: Viking Press, 2004).

Notes

1   Dick Farrington, "Major League Writers Pick Yankees and Cubs to Win Pennants," *The Sporting News*, April 11, 1929: 3.

2   "Robins Lead Fans to No False Hopes," *The Sporting News*, April 11, 1929: 2.

3   Bob Franklin, "McGrawites Take Selves Seriously," *The Sporting News*, March 28, 1929: 2.

4   "Mel Ott's Three Home Runs Help Giants Take Two," *Brooklyn Daily Eagle*, June 23, 1929: 35.

5   Wilbert Robinson, "Four Players Developed by Robins This Season," *Brooklyn Standard Union*, September 29, 1928: 13.

6   Henry Richards, "Fifth Position Is the Best Robins Can Hope for at Present," *Brooklyn Standard Union*, June 24, 1929: 36.

7   Thomas Holmes, "Brooklyn Team's Batting Punch May Be Down, but It's Never Out," *Brooklyn Daily Eagle*, June 26, 1929: 27.

8   Pat Robinson, "Robins Grab 2; Yanks Split Even," *New York Daily News*, June 19, 1929: 45.

9   Bill James and Rob Neyer, *The Neyer/James Guide to Pitchers: An Historical Compendium of Pitching, Pitchers, and Pitches* (New York: Fireside Books, 2004), 132.

10   Holmes.

11   Frank Wallace, "Giants Blow, Robins Cop in 10th," *New York Daily News*, June 26, 1929: 36.

12   Holmes.

13   Wallace.

14   Holmes.

RED SOX COME BACK TO WIN, "CRONIN FOR PRESIDENT"

AUGUST 5, 1938:
BOSTON RED SOX 9,
DETROIT TIGERS 8
(10 INNINGS),
AT BRIGGS STADIUM, DETROIT

BY MATTHEW PERRY

Lefty Grove hadn't pitched in a game since July 14 after his arm went "dead."[1] He was scheduled to go against the Cleveland Indians on August 4, but the game was rained out, and Lefty would have to wait for another day and a trip to Detroit to return to the

Courtesy of the Boston Red Sox.

Red Sox shortstop (and manager) Joe Cronin hit a grand slam in the top of the ninth, and drive in seven of the eight runs the Red Sox needed to come back and tie the Tigers.

Red Sox rotation. Player-manager Joe Cronin was disappointed that Grove was unable to come back in Cleveland. "It's a big place, that stadium ballyard. A pitcher does not have to be quite so careful of the exactness of his control in such a large park," the manager said.[2]

The return for Boston's ace went okay. His arm did not go numb again, and he allowed four runs over six innings. Unfortunately for the Red Sox, the relief pitchers who came in to pitch were not able to slow down the Tigers, and going into the ninth inning, the Red Sox found themselves down 8-3.

The Red Sox started off the scoring in the top of the first after doubles by left fielder Joe Vosmik and shortstop Cronin. In the second the Tigers scored three runs on a bunt single by Chet Morgan, two ground-outs, a run-scoring wild pitch by Grove, and a two-run double by Billy Rogell. The Red Sox tied it, 3-3, in the fifth inning on a two-run single by Cronin, but the Tigers took the lead again in the bottom half, scoring an unearned run after Cronin booted a grounder.

Fritz Ostermueller replaced Grove in the seventh and the Tigers pounced on him. With two outs, second baseman Charlie Gehringer singled and moved to second on a wild pitch. Slugger Hank Greenberg was intentionally walked for the second time in the game, and catcher Rudy York walked to load the bases. Center fielder Morgan took advantage and drove in two runs with a single, forcing Ostermueller out of the game. Joe Heving replaced him and gave up a two-run double to right fielder Pete Fox before striking out pitcher Elden Auker to end the inning.

This game featured many of the contemporary stars of the game. Red Sox first baseman Jimmie Foxx was on his way to being named the American League Most Valuable Player, posting a league-best .349 batting average and 175 RBIs; Grove led the American League in ERA with a 3.08 mark; and Hank Greenberg led the major leagues with 58 home runs. However, it was the 31-year-old manager and shortstop Cronin's day to shine.

The score stood Tigers 8, Red Sox 3 after the first eight innings. The 7,200 in attendance had every reason to anticipate a win. Johnny Peacock batted for Gene Desautels in the Red Sox ninth and worked a walk. Leo Nonnenkamp hit for the pitcher, Heving, and singled to left field. Center fielder Doc Cramer singled to left, loading the bases. Vosmik drove in a run with a fly ball to deep center field. Jimmie Foxx's grounder was mishandled by shortstop Rogell and the bases were loaded again.

Boston had lowered the deficit to four runs. Joe Cronin stepped up to the plate and with one swing, he tied the game. "Cronin's grand-slam homer was his 11th round-tripper of the year," said the *Boston Herald*. "It came on the two-two pitch by the starting pitcher Elden Auker and sailed majestically into the lower right-centerfield stands, up 15 or 20 rows."[3] Tommy Bridges relieved Auker. Ben Chapman doubled and Jim Tabor singled but the Red Sox scoring was done. The game was tied.

The Red Sox had a new battery, Peacock behind the plate and Jim Bagby on the mound. The Tigers went down one-two-three.

Bagby led off in the top of the 10th and struck out. But Doc Cramer and Vosmik both doubled, and it was 9-8, Red Sox. Once again the Tigers went down in order in the bottom of the 10th.

The box score in the following day's *Herald* was topped with the title "Cronin for President." The win brought the Sox to 53-37 for the season, keeping them within striking distance of the first-place New York Yankees, who were 60-31.

Reviews of Grove's comeback performance were mixed. The *Boston Globe* praised him: "Today's actually was a double celebration. Bob Grove felt in good trim to pitch. He delivered the ball to the Tigers 85 times in his five innings and was hit safely only five times. ... After the game, Bob said his arm felt great, the lower forearm warm. He added that he had felt a slight tenderness in the cords under his pitching wing but he was not at all bothered about that."[4]

Cronin's Bat Has Busy Day

Red Sox Win, 9-8; Joe Drives in 7 Runs

Headline from the *Omaha World Herald* of August 6, 1938.

The *Herald* was not so generous, with the headline "Lefty's Control Very Uncertain." Burt Whitman noted, "Morgan scored from third on a Grove wild pitch. That shows you how uncertain was the returning Grove's control. He gave further evidence of this as he walked Auker."[5]

The Red Sox beat the Tigers again the next night, 14-8, extending Detroit's losing streak to four games. Tigers manager Mickey Cochrane was fired after the game by club owner Walter Briggs. The *Herald* immediately began speculating that Red Sox owner Tom Yawkey was interested in hiring Cochrane, who was three years removed from a World Series championship with Detroit and was a native of Bridgewater Massachusetts. "The report was prevalent here tonight that Owner Tom Yawkey of the Red Sox would make a place for Mickey with the Boston club. ... Tom and Mike are close friends. They have hunted together. That gave rise to the story that the Red Sox would take on Mickey," wrote Burt Whitman.[6] This was all speculation, however, and the Red Sox made no such attempt. "Iron Mike is to be paid for the balance of season and undoubtedly will go into retirement for the balance of year."[7] Cochrane was replaced by Del Baker.

The Red Sox would stick with their grand-slam-hitting manager Cronin until 1947, when he became the team's general manager. In 1959 he was elected president of the American League, an office he held until 1973.

Both teams had respectable seasons, finishing in the first division with the Red Sox in second and the Tigers in fourth. The Tigers were two years away from an American League pennant in 1940, and the Red Sox in 1939 added a young left fielder named Ted Williams.

Sources

In addition to the sources cited in the Notes, the author consulted Baseball-Reference.com and Retrosheet.org.

Notes

1   Associated Press, "Red Sox Overcome Tigers in 10th, 9-8," *New York Times*, August 6, 1938: 8.

2   Burt Whitman, "Grove, Rained-Out Sox Tackle Tigers Today," *Boston Herald*, August 5, 1938: 12.

3   Burt Whitman, "Grove Satisfactory in Comeback as Sox Defeat Tigers in 10th, 9-8," *Boston Herald*, August 6, 1938: 1.

4   Melville E. Webb Jr., "Cronin 4-Run Slam Puts Hex on Tigers," *Boston Globe*, August 6, 1938: 7.

5   Burt Whitman, "Grove Satisfactory in Comeback as Sox Defeat Tigers in 10th, 9-8."

6   Burt Whitman, "Cochrane Fired as Detroit Manager; Yawkey May Place Him with Sox," *Boston Herald*, August 7, 1938: 19.

7   Burt Whitman, "Cochrane Fired as Detroit Manager."

WAR WORRIES OVERSHADOW NATS' HUGE NINTH INNING AGAINST A'S

SEPTEMBER 20, 1942:
WASHINGTON SENATORS 11,
PHILADELPHIA ATHLETICS 9,
AT SHIBE PARK, PHILADELPHIA

BY ANDREW SHARP

When the two worst teams in the American League met at Shibe Park for a September 20, 1942, doubleheader, Philadelphia's legendary owner-manager Connie Mack readily admitted that the results were not foremost on his mind.

His A's had clinched the basement for a third season in a row, but the team avoided 100 losses by winning the second game, 2-1, in 10 innings. Despite losing 12 players to the military, he told the *Philadelphia Inquirer,* he wasn't bitter the way his 42nd season had turned out.

"War is with us, and the most important thing is winning it," Mack said at a time when the outcome of World War II was uncertain. "If we should lose … there would be no such thing as baseball."[1]

Through a scheduling quirk, the Sunday doubleheader ended the Athletics' season a week earlier than those of some of the other clubs. The Senators had two more games to play, with the Yankees in New York, and would finish at 62-89.[2]

Between games, 100 mechanics were inducted into the Army Air Corps on the field, while military aircraft roared over the ballpark in salute.[3]

Mack's focus on the nation's struggle against the Axis powers kept his postgame comments away from the jaw-dropping result of the day's first game. In that one, the Senators snatched a seeming victory from the A's by scoring seven runs in the ninth, winning 11-9. That had been the same score as the previous day's second game when the Nats completed a sweep of Saturday's Shibe Park doubleheader.

The lowly A's had reason to be confident of their chances in Sunday's first game. The team's workhorse

starter, 17-game winner Phil Marchildon, was on the mound.[4] Philadelphia jumped out to a 7-2 lead with five runs in the second inning. Buddy Blair's three-run homer was the big blow. The A's led 9-3 after Pete Suder's two-run double in the seventh off Nats starter Alex Carrasquel, a Venezuelan right-hander.[5]

George Case, Washington's speedy left fielder, produced the bulk of the visitors' offense before the explosion in the ninth. Leading off the game, he singled and stole his 43rd base before scoring.[6] He homered leading off the seventh and singled in a run in the eighth.

By late afternoon, the temperature on a cool day had dipped. Those in the crowd of 6,112 who stayed until the end of the twin bill "shivered through the late innings of the second game as the biting winds swept through the stands."[7]

With a 9-4 lead, Marchildon immediately ran into trouble in the ninth. A walk to Bruce Campbell was followed by consecutive singles by Mickey Vernon, Bobby Estalella,[8] and John Sullivan, the third one bringing in Campbell. Marchildon briefly restored order by striking out Ellis Clary, but a walk to Jake Early brought in another run. Frank Croucher, pinch-hitting for the pitcher, singled to left, scoring Estalella.

Croucher's hit ended the day for Marchildon. Right-hander Fred Caligiuri came in with a two-run lead, but the bases were loaded with one out. In what would be his last appearance in the majors, Caligiuri tossed fuel on the fire by balking home a run with Case, his first batter, at the plate. Case then walked, loading the bases again. A wild pitch to Stan Spence scored Early, tying the game. Spence singled to center, scoring Croucher and putting Washington up 10-9. Campbell's fly ball to right scored Case with an insurance run. Vernon mercifully struck out, but the Nats had scored seven times to lead 11-9.

Bill Kennedy, a rookie lefty in just his eighth game, came in to earn his second save, inducing three groundball outs.

A fly ball that scored a run in the bottom of 10th salvaged the second game for the A's. Mack kept it all in perspective: "I am not crying over the men I lost" to the military. "I am sure the fans realize we, all of us, are in a much bigger game. … We are all playing this one for keeps."[9]

Sources:

In addition to the sources cited in the Notes, the author also consulted Baseball-Reference.com and Retrosheet.org.

Notes

1. Hank Simmons, "A's Split Bill with Senators," *Philadelphia Inquirer*, September 21, 1942: 23.

2. The Senators, surprisingly, would finish second the next season at 84-69. The '43 season would be worse for the A's, last again at 49-105.

3. Nats Defeat Athletics, 11-9, Then Lose, 2-1," *Washington Post*, September 21, 1942: 8.

4. Later in the war Marchildon joined the Royal Canadian Air Force. His plane was shot down by the Germans in August 1944 and he spent nine months in a prisoner-of-war camp.

5. Carrasquel, the first Venezuelan to pitch in the majors, worked more often out of the bullpen this season and throughout his career. He had a 2.49 earned-run average after the game on September 1, but after a couple of rough outings and giving up nine runs in this game, his ERA jumped to 3.43 for the year.

6. Case ended the season with 44 steals, leading the league for the fourth of five straight times (and six overall).

7. "Nats Defeat Athletics."

8. Estalella could have been considered the first black player in the twentieth Century. Some teammates thought of him as being black. He was a dark-skinned Cuban and routinely was subjected to racial taunts.

9. Simmons.

MILWAUKEE BRAVES MAKE DRAMATIC COMEBACK IN 9TH, WIN IN 11

APRIL 20, 1961:
MILWAUKEE BRAVES 7,
PHILADELPHIA PHILLIES 6,
AT CONNIE MACK STADIUM, PHILADELPHIA

BY NATE GILMAN

The Phillies home opener on April 20, 1961, was a cool spring day at Connie Mack Stadium. The afternoon was cloudy with temperatures in the low 50s. Philadelphia fans should have left happy with an Opening Day win. The Braves had done almost everything wrong heading into the top of the ninth inning. The Phillies were capitalizing on opportunities. They were coming up with hits with runners on and their pitching held the Braves to a lone run. In the top of the ninth inning, though, the Braves completed one of the greatest comebacks in franchise history, tying the score 6-6. The game was pushed into extra innings and the Braves won, defeating the Phillies 7-6 in 11 innings.

The Phillies had returned from the West Coast for their home opener against the Braves with a 2-4 record. They lost two and won one against the Dodgers before heading to San Francisco to walk away with the same record. The Braves came into Philadelphia with a 1-3 record after splitting a two-game series against St. Louis and getting swept in a two-game series in Chicago. Their two biggest sluggers, Hank Aaron and Eddie Mathews, had yet to get their bats going. Aaron came into Philadelphia hitting 3-for-16 with one home run for a .188 average. Mathews was batting slightly better, going 5-for-17 with one home run for a .294 average. The pitching had been competitive, but the Braves' offense had let them down.

Entering the top of the ninth inning in Philadelphia the Phillies were ready to cruise to a 6-1 win. The Braves' pitching performance had been lackluster at best. Lew Burdette took the mound to start for the Braves but could not make it out of the fourth inning.

In 4⅔ innings Burdette surrendered five runs, all earned, on 10 hits. In relief of Burdette, Seth Morehead came in for 2⅓ innings and gave up another earned run on two hits, leaving the Braves down five runs as they entered the ninth inning.

The Braves offense put together several scoring opportunities through the first eight innings but were able to get only one run across the plate. Hank

Courtesy The Topps Company.

Mel Roach, pinch-hitting in the top of the ninth, hit one into the upper deck and tied the game.

Aaron had two singles and a stolen base in three plate appearances. Del Crandall, Eddie Mathews, and Joe Adcock were each 1-for-3 with Adcock and Crandall hitting doubles. Burdette even tried to help himself by hitting a single in the top of the third inning, but the offense could not capitalize. Aaron's single in the fourth was the only hit to plate a run, scoring Crandall from second. Allen Lewis of the *Philadelphia Inquirer* wrote, "The Braves got a gift run in the fourth when Tony Curry misjudged Del Crandall's liner and let it sail over his head for a double, and Aaron singled to center."[1]

Philadelphia, on the other hand, capitalized on scoring plays. In the second inning they got two runners on but didn't score. However, in the third inning Johnny Callison hit a double, scoring Bob Sadowski and Tony Taylor. In the fifth inning, Taylor singled, stole second, and came home on Tony Gonzalez's single. Pancho Herrera singled, and with Gonzalez and Herrera on base, Clay Dalrymple hit Seth Morehead's second pitch over the wall in right field for a three-run homer. The score stayed 6-1 going into the top of the ninth.

Don Ferrarese, who relieved the Phillies' Dallas Green to start the fifth inning, returned to the mound in the ninth as the majority of the 9,531 fans headed to the exits. Mathews got a bunt single and Aaron and Frank Bolling hit back-to-back doubles to make the score 6-3. Phillies manager Gene Mauch yanked Ferrarese and brought in Turk Farrell. Farrell gave up a single to Adcock but got Wes Covington to foul out to third baseman Bobby Malkmus and struck out Roy McMillan. The Phillies were one out away from closing out the game when Mel Roach came to the plate as a pinch-hitter to bat for pitcher Ken MacKenzie. On a 1-and-2 count, Roach tied the game with a home run into the upper deck in left.[2]

After giving up the home run, Farrell hit John DeMerit with a pitch, and manager Chuck Dressen pulled Farrell for Ken Lehman. He walked Charlie Lau but struck out Mathews to end the inning. In the bottom of the ninth the Phillies loaded the bases with two outs but could not get a run across. The score stayed tied until the 11th.

In the top of the 11th, Phillies pitcher John Buzhardt hit McMillan, leading off. Braves pitcher Ron Piche bunted and reached first on third baseman Bobby Malkmus's wild throw, but was thrown out trying for second when the ball went into the outfield. McMillan reached third. Lee Maye, batting for John DeMerit, walked, and Lau's single sent McMillan home and gave the Braves a 7-6 lead. The inning ended when Mathews hit into a double play.

Piche quickly closed out the game in the bottom of the 11th. He got center fielder Tony Gonzalez on a comebacker. First baseman Herrera singled to left, but Dalrymple hit into a fielder's choice and Bobby Del Greco, batting for pitcher Buzhardt, struck out to end the game.

After the loss Mauch was not a happy man. Wrote Stan Hochman of the *Philadelphia Daily News,* "'We gave them too many outs,' he muttered. 'We gave them five outs in the ninth inning, and we gave them the first run they got too. … 'The kid (31-year-old Don Ferrarese) might have come up with Mathews bunt. It would have been a helluva play, but he might have made it. Farrell should have had the ground ball Adcock hit. The homer, well, there isn't a pitcher around who hasn't had a three-run homer hit off him one day.'"[3]

The Phillies' loss foreshadowed the remainder of their season, which they ended with a record of 47-107-1. While the Braves did not have a pennant-winning season, they ended their 1961 campaign with a winning record of 83-71-1.

Sources

In addition to the sources cited in the Notes, the author consulted Baseball-Reference.com and Retrosheet.org.

Notes

1   Allen Lewis, "Braves Tab 5 in 9th, Nip Phils in 11th, 7-6," *Philadelphia Inquirer,* April 21, 1961: 38 & 41.

2   Associated Press, "Braves Win In 11-Inning Marathon Game from Phils 7-6," *Janesville* (Wisconsin) *Daily Gazette,* April 21, 1961: 16.

3   Stan Hochman, "Bitter Loser Mauch: 'We Gave Them Too Many Outs,'" *Philadelphia Daily News,* April 21, 1961: 69.

YANKEES SCORE 5 RUNS IN 9TH TO TIE AND 5 IN 16TH TO WIN

MAY 18, 1976:
NEW YORK YANKEES 11,
CLEVELAND INDIANS 6,
AT CLEVELAND STADIUM, CLEVELAND

BY THOMAS J. BROWN JR.

The New York Yankees, arriving in Cleveland for a two-game series against the Indians, had just lost two of three games in Baltimore but remained three games ahead of the Orioles. Only 3,895 fans showed up on a chilly night at Cleveland Stadium hoping to see their team gain ground on the division leader. The Indians were 6-9 in May under second-year manager Frank Robinson but were just 4½ games out of first early in the season.

The Yankees had made a trade for Carlos May in order to improve their offense. The trade was completed at 4 A.M. May learned about the trade that morning but was unable to get to Cleveland in time for the game.

Fritz Peterson, a former Yankee, was making his seventh start for Cleveland. He entered the game with a 5.17 ERA and was still seeking his first win of the season. Peterson got in trouble in the first when Roy White doubled and reached third on a passed ball. But Peterson got the next two outs to keep the Yankees from scoring.

Catfish Hunter started for the Yankees. He entered the game with a 3-5 record. Hunter struggled early in the season. He had allowed his opponents to jump on him in the first inning in three of his eight prior starts. This game began in a similar fashion when the Indians scored three runs in the first.

Duane Kuiper and Buddy Bell led off with singles. Hunter walked Rick Manning to load the bases. Rico Carty singled to drive Kuiper and Bell home.

George Hendrick's sacrifice fly brought home the third run. Hunter struck out the next two batters to close out the inning. Phil Pepe of the *New York Daily*

News wrote: "Hunter had his usual first-inning trouble, and this time he didn't spend the morning making a television commercial."[1]

Hunter got through the second unscathed before the Indians struck again in the third. He got a break to start the inning when Bell singled but was thrown

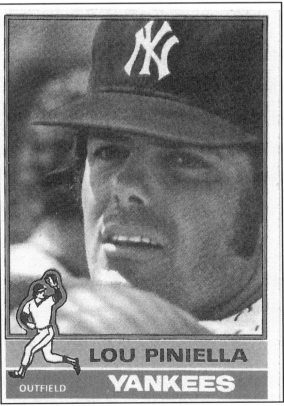

Lou Piniella's single in the Yankees' ninth started the rally that tied the game; his two-run single in the 16th inning proved to be the game-winner.

out trying to stretch his hit into a double. With two outs, Carty singled and Hendrick followed with his seventh home run of the season to put Cleveland ahead by five runs. It was the ninth home run Hunter had surrendered in his eight starts.

Peterson got in trouble in the next two innings but kept the Yankees from scoring each time. Singles by Otto Velez and Willie Randolph put a runner in scoring position in the second. But Fred Stanley bounced out to end the inning. Sandy Alomar beat out a bunt leading off the third and reached second on a fielder's choice. But Peterson got out of the jam when Chris Chambliss popped out to short.

The Yankees got on the scoreboard in the fourth when Lou Piniella doubled into the left-field corner and scored on Velez's second straight single. But Peterson retired the next two batters to limit the Yankees to the lone run.

It would be the only run they scored until the ninth, as Peterson retired the next 11 batters. Thurman Munson doubled in the eighth inning. But the Yankees were unable to capitalize on it when Chambliss hit an easy pop fly for the third out.

Hunter got through the middle innings unscathed but the Indians tagged him for another run in the seventh. After he walked Frank Duffy, Kuiper singled to leave runners at the corners. Duffy scored when Bell hit a grounder to Nettles that "kicked up, caromed and forced him to throw to first."[2]

Heading into the ninth, with the Indians leading 6-1, Hunter was still on the mound and "just three outs away from his sixth defeat, and with five runs to get, this seemed like Mission Impossible."[3] Peterson was on the verge of his first win of the season.

When Peterson gave up two singles to lead off the ninth, Robinson lifted him for Dave LaRoche. LaRoche struck out pinch-hitter Oscar Gamble but "in rapid succession gave up a single to Randolph, a walk to Rick Dempsey, a single to Alomar, and a walk to White, who fouled off eight pitches before getting his pass."[4]

With three runs scored, the Indians' lead was cut to just two runs. LaRoche was quickly replaced by Tom Buskey. But Munson singled over second base and drove in those two runs, tying the game.

Buskey got the next two outs quickly but the damage was done. Hunter got the Indians out on three fly balls in the bottom of the ninth to send the game into extra innings. Buskey pitched well for the next four innings, allowing only two hits during that stretch.

Sparky Lyle relieved Hunter in the 10th inning. He immediately got himself in trouble, giving up a single and a walk. But Nettles saved a loss when "Hendrick lashed a grounder over third base and Nettles dived to stop it. Then he dived again to reach the bag before the runner from second could reach there."[5]

"It was a do or die thing," Nettles said. "Once I was in the air, I saw I could get it. I got it right out in the web. I was about 25 feet back of the bag. A step and a half from the bag, when I dived again, I could see I beat him. I just hoped that I didn't drop the ball."[6]

After the 10th, Lyle settled down and produced five scoreless innings.

Jim Kern replaced Buskey in the 14th and pitched two scoreless innings before things fell apart for him in the 16th. He walked the leadoff batter, Alomar. White bunted and ended up on first when Kern threw the ball away.

Alomar was thrown out at home on Munson's grounder to short. Kern then walked Chambliss to load the bases. Piniella singled to bring home two runners. "I hit it so bad nobody could have caught it," he said afterward. "But I went up there feeling I was going to get a run in one way or the other."[7]

Second baseman Kuiper hurried a throw home to try to get White but it went wide and Piniella landed on second. (Manager Robinson said the Indians right fielder, Charlie Spikes, should have fielded the ball instead of Kuiper.)

Nettles, the next batter, lofted a sacrifice fly to right, scoring Chambliss. Kern walked Gamble intentionally to set up a double play. But Randolph doubled to score Piniella. Although Kern struck out Jim Mason, a passed ball allowed Mason to reach first and Gamble to score. After Alomar grounded out for the third out, the Yankees were up by five runs, 11-6.

After the Yankees' explosion, Dick Tidrow replaced Lyle to mop things up. He got the Indians out in order in front of the "few hundred fans left in the lakefront stadium, huddled under blankets in the 42-degree chill and lighting little fires to keep warm."[8]

As the extra innings dragged on, Bob Nold of the *Akron Beacon Journal* wrote, some of the sportswriters commented that "I bet Catfish and Peterson are out having a drink together right now, commiserating."[9] That would have been a marked contrast to the "wall-to-wall scowl" that Robinson wore when his team left the field with a disappointing loss.[10]

Yankees skipper Billy Martin "grew testy" when asked about Carlos May after the game. "I tell you what, I wish that he'd been here. I hope that he doesn't stay away much longer. I'd appreciate his presence."[11] But he went on to say, "Anything is better than a loss. Even this."[12]

Sources

In addition to the sources cited in the Notes, the author used the Baseball-Reference.com and Retrosheet.org websites for box-score, player, team, and season pages, pitching and batting game logs, and other pertinent material.

Notes

1   Phil Pepe, "Yanks Win 11-6 in 16 After Scoring 5 in 9th," *New York Daily News*, May 19, 1976: 74. Pepe was referring to the fact that Hunter had given up at least one run in the first or second inning of half his previous starts that season, the most recent being the May 14 game when the Orioles scored four runs in the first.

2   Bob Nold, "Cleveland Lets Catfish, Yankees Off the Hook," *Akron Beacon Journal*, May 19, 1976: E2.

3   Pepe.

4   Paul Montgomery, "Yanks Get 5 in 9th, Win in 16th, 11-6," *New York Times*, May 19, 1976: 62.

5   Montgomery.

6   Nold.

7   Montgomery.

8   Montgomery.

9   Nold.

10   Montgomery.

11   Montgomery.

12   Montgomery.

BRAVES TOMAHAWK DODGERS FOR SIX RUNS IN THE NINTH FOR EPIC 9-8 COMEBACK VICTORY

JULY 5, 1978:
ATLANTA BRAVES 9,
LOS ANGELES DODGERS 8,
AT DODGER STADIUM, LOS ANGELES

BY FREDERICK C. BUSH

As the 1978 Los Angeles Dodgers prepared to host the Atlanta Braves in the third game of a four-game series on July 5, the Dodgers were on their way to a third National League pennant in the decade while the Braves were struggling to avoid the fate of another 100-loss season as had befallen them the previous year. Tommy John, the Dodgers' southpaw standout, took the mound in quest of his 10th win of the season. John's supporting cast included both speed – in the form of Davey Lopes and Bill North – and power in the persons of Reggie Smith, Ron Cey, Steve Garvey, and Dusty Baker. As for the Braves, well, their best weapons entering the game appeared to be Bob Horner and a not yet MVP-level Dale Murphy.

Baseball is filled with clichés like "That's why they play the games" and "It's not over till it's over," and even the best of teams lose, on average, one-third or more of their games. However, some losses sting more than others, and the outcome of this day's game resulted in a classic rant by Dodgers skipper Tom Lasorda, who, "using a number of words frowned on by the Supreme Court, said: 'It's a (expletive) crime to lose a (expletive) game like that. A (expletive) eight-run lead. A (expletive) two-run lead with two (expletive) strikes on the hitter. (Expletive) no. I can't ever (expletive) remember losing a game like that. I can't ever remember a (expletive) tougher loss.' He then grabbed a piece of baloney and said: '(Expletive) the diet.'"[1] Although Lasorda would out-expletive himself on the topics of Dave Kingman and Kurt Bevaqua in the

future, on this day his ire was directed at his team's ninth-inning collapse against the Braves.

The game started out well enough for the Dodgers. John cruised through the Braves' lineup for the first five innings while allowing a mere four singles. The batters who reached base in the third and fourth innings were erased on inning-ending double-plays. In the meantime, Dodgers hitters were providing what appeared to be ample run support to back up their starting pitcher.

The Dodgers' scoring commenced in the first inning. Lopes drew a leadoff walk from Atlanta starter Adrian Devine and went to second on Bill Russell's grounder. After Smith also worked a walk, Cey, showing no ill effects after being beaned in the previous night's game, doubled to drive in both runners and took third base when Braves left fielder Cito Gaston threw to home to try to nail Smith; Gaston had replaced Jeff Burroughs in left after Burroughs fouled a ball off his knee while batting in the top of the inning.[2] Garvey then smacked a single that plated Cey and gave LA a quick 3-0 lead. Devine, whose command was nonexistent, issued his third walk of the inning to Baker but got Joe Ferguson to ground into a double play that stopped the bleeding for the moment.

As it turned out, Devine would face only one additional batter. After he allowed a leadoff single to North in the bottom of the second, Braves manager Bobby Cox pulled him from the game due to a strained right elbow and "an inflamed ERA."[3] Eddie Solomon took the mound for Atlanta and put himself in a jam. North stole second base and advanced to third on John's sacrifice. Solomon, exhibiting the same control as his predecessor, created double trouble by walking Lopes. Sure enough, Lopes stole second and North scored when Dale Murphy, the catcher, made an errant throw to second baseman Jerry Royster that rolled into the outfield. After this bit of excitement, Solomon retired Russell and Smith to keep the game at 4-0.

The Dodgers continued their onslaught in the bottom of the third inning. This time, Cey led off with a single and Garvey hit his 12th homer of the season, a two-RBI shot. After Baker walked, Ferguson drove him in with a double that increased the lead to 7-0. Solomon then issued his third walk of the day – and the Braves' sixth of the night – to put runners at first and second with no outs. Cox trotted out to the mound and inserted Jamie Easterly, the third Braves hurler of the night, into the game. Easterly managed to do what his mound mates could not accomplish: He set down the three batters he faced in order.

Things calmed down considerably in the fourth and fifth innings. The Dodgers struck only one more blow in the form of Ferguson's fifth-inning solo homer that made the score 8-0, at this point in the game a seemingly insurmountable lead. To invoke another cliché, "things aren't always as they seem."

John, who had been pitching efficiently, suddenly began to get knocked around in the top of the sixth inning. He walked Rod Gilbreath and Royster and Bob Beall followed with back-to-back singles to load the bases. Gary Matthews rapped the Braves' third consecutive hit, which drove in Gilbreath for the first Atlanta run. Consecutive fielder's-choice grounders by Gaston and Horner allowed Royster and Beall to score to make it an 8-3 game. After Murphy doubled, a hit on which Horner advanced to third, Lasorda had no choice but to remove John. Lance Rautzhan entered in relief and retired Barry Bonnell to preserve the five-run lead, which still was likely to be plenty against the Braves' anemic offense.

And so it was. At least, that is, until the final frame. 8-3 after eight. Then, "the boos of a Dodger Stadium crowd of 39,036 came down on the Dodgers as the Braves sent 11 men to the plate" and scored six runs to take an improbable 9-8 lead that would hold up for an Atlanta victory.[4]

Rautzhan, who had encountered little resistance from the Braves since taking the hill, opened the ninth by inducing a fly out from Bonnell. After that, he failed to retire another batter. He surrendered four consecutive singles, to Pat Rockett, Darrell Chaney

Courtesy The Topps Company.

BARRY BONNELL

Barry Bonnell flied out as leadoff batter in the Braves ninth. They scored five runs to come from behind and tie the Dodgers, 8-8, and Bonnell came up once more and singled in the go-ahead run.

(pinch-hitting for pitcher Dave Campbell), Royster, and Beall; Royster's hit drove in Rockett to make it 8-4. That was "four straight singles by men hitting .139, .207, .281, and .211," which was far more likely than too much lasagna to give Lasorda heartburn in the Dodgers' dugout.[5]

Indeed, Lasorda had seen enough and, likely spewing expletives on his way to the mound, replaced Rautzhan with knuckleballer Charlie Hough. Lasorda was probably apoplectic when Hough walked Matthews, the first batter he faced, to force in Chaney with another Braves run. Things got really rough for Hough when Garvey booted Gaston's grounder at first, allowing Gaston to reach base safely and Royster to score Atlanta's sixth run of the game. When Hough struck out Horner, it looked as though all might end well for the Dodgers after all. Murphy had other ideas, however, and he hit a two-run single that tied the game and ended Hough's mound stint.

Terry Forster became the Dodgers' third pitcher of the inning, and he fared no better than the first two. Bonnell greeted him with a single that drove in Gaston with the go-ahead run for the Braves. Rockett flied out to end the inning, but the collapse was complete. The Dodgers went down meekly in order against Gene Garber in the bottom of the inning, suffering the ignominy of having blown an eight-run lead and incurring their manager's profane wrath.

Although Lasorda could erupt at the drop of a hat, he had ample reason to be upset on this occasion. The 9-8 loss to the Braves marked the ninth time in the 1978 season that the Dodgers had lost a game in which they scored six or more runs. They also fell into third place in the NL West, three games behind the division-leading San Francisco Giants and a half-game behind the Cincinnati Reds who had both won their games this night.

While Lasorda was doing his best Rumpelstiltskin impression after the game, Bonnell – the Braves center fielder – was exulting in his team's unlikely triumph. Bonnell confessed, "I didn't really think we'd score six runs" before adding, "This is the most fun I've had all year."[6] By the end of the season, it was likely still Bonnell's fondest memory as the Braves finished with a record of 69-93 that put them in last place in the NL West, 26 games behind the division-champion Dodgers.

Sources

Baseball-reference.com was consulted for the game box score and play-by-play as well as for player and team statistics.

Retrosheet.org was also consulted for the game box score and play-by-play.

Notes

1   Ross Newhan, "Dodgers Let 8-0 Lead Vanish," *Los Angeles Times*, July 6, 1978: 38, 45.

2   Newhan: 45.

3   Newhan: 45.

4   Newhan: 38.

5   Newhan: 38.

6   "LA Blows 8-0 Lead, Drops to 3rd Place," *Kansas City Star*, July 6, 1978: 16.

BOBBY MURCER'S NINTH-INNING SLAM SHOCKS BRAVES

APRIL 29, 1979:
CHICAGO CUBS 6,
ATLANTA BRAVES 5,
AT ATLANTA-FULTON COUNTY STADIUM, ATLANTA

BY RICHARD CUICCHI

On a day when a sparse crowd was hoping to see its home team sweep its first series of the season, Atlanta Braves fans left the game with a shocking surprise. With a 5-0 lead in the ninth inning, a Braves victory seemed a sure thing. Even after their reliable closer gave up two singles that yielded three Cubs runs, a Braves win was still in sight. However, Cubs outfielder Bobby Murcer had other ideas, as he clouted a three-run home run with two outs to down the Braves, 6-5.

Braves left-hander Larry McWilliams had turned in a masterful two-hit shutout going into the ninth. He ran into trouble by loading the bases and relinquished the mound to Gene Garber, who couldn't shut down the Braves.

Neither the Cubs nor the Braves had gotten off to a good start of the season. Chicago had been a streaky team in April, having gone through periods of four consecutive losses, five consecutive wins, and three consecutive losses during the first three weeks of the season. They were 7-9, while Atlanta was 7-12.

The 33-year-old Murcer, an eight-year veteran of the New York Yankees who also put in two seasons with San Francisco, had hit only nine home runs for the Cubs the previous season, and his struggle continued at the beginning of the 1979 season; he had hit only one home run coming into the game. He was starting to fall into disfavor with the Cubs' front office, although his teammates had selected him as team captain, a role he had previously shunned. He didn't think he had the requisite personality to carry out its responsibilities.[1]

On the Braves' side, Dale Murphy, who was in his second full season with the team, led the team in home runs at the time. His slash line was .328/.410/.701 with 8 home runs and 17 RBIs in what would become his breakout season.

A small crowd of 5,041 attended the game at Atlanta-Fulton County Stadium. The *Chicago Tribune* surmised that most Atlanta fans had stayed home to

It was 5-0, Braves, after eight innings. The Cubs scored three times, and Bobby Murcer homered with two on to give them a sudden lead.

watch the basketball Hawks on TV in the NBA play-offs. However, the Braves' recent level of play probably had something to do with the crowd size, too.

McWilliams was getting his fifth start of the season for the Braves, but his 7.59 ERA coming into the game was not indicative of the performance he would turn in. Cubs manager Herman Franks went with right-hander Dennis Lamp, who had won his only two starts after beginning the season out of the bullpen.

The Braves pushed across a run in the first inning and added two more in the third, on back-to-back doubles by Gary Matthews and Jeff Burroughs.

McWilliams's control was a bit shaky; he issued six walks, but he managed to get out of innings without scores. He even helped himself at the plate by hitting a double off Lynn McGlothen in the sixth inning. He scored on Jerry Royster's single to give the Braves a 4-0 lead.

It appeared the Cubs had thrown in the towel, as Franks let McGlothen bat for himself leading off the top of the seventh. Murphy added another run in the seventh inning with a solo home run off McGlothen.

A tired McWilliams was sent out in the top of the ninth, because Braves manager Bobby Cox wanted to give him a chance to record a shutout. He had given up only two hits, but allowed a leadoff single to Dave Kingman, then walked Steve Ontiveros. After McWilliams retired the next two batters on fly balls, Ted Sizemore, a .250 hitter with no home runs, stood between him and his shutout. McWilliams walked Sizemore to load the bases.

Cox called on oft-used Garber to put out the fire. As the Braves' primary closer, he had made four multi-inning appearances in the six previous Braves games that resulted in a win, two losses, and a save. Perhaps Garber's best-known relief effort occurred the year before, when he struck out Pete Rose in the ninth inning to deny Rose's bid for a 45-game hitting streak.

Garber could have used a strikeout now, but instead gave up a two-run single to Tim Blackwell. Pinch-hitter Larry Biittner then delivered a run-scoring single to make the score 5-3.

With two runners on base, Murcer hit a fastball for a home run, clearing the right-field fence 10 feet inside the foul pole and putting the Cubs ahead, 6-5. Bruce Sutter closed out the bottom of the ninth to clinch the miraculous comeback victory, but only after allowing runners to reach second and third. Murcer said, "I've seen it happen a few times … in 16 years. You've just got to get lucky for something like that to happen." He added, "I just wanted to hit the ball hard someplace.

It was a sinker down and in. I wasn't really sure if it would be off the fence or what."[2]

Cox said in hindsight, "I probably should have brought Garber in to face Sizemore. Larry was very tired."[3] He added, "Nine times out of ten, the game is locked up in that situation and I'm headed home. Geno is our man in that situation. But it happens sometimes."[4]

Blackwell observed, "Most of our hitters have been off to a slow start, including Bobby. But we elected Bobby team captain because of his leadership and experience. He's the one we look to out on the field and the captain came through in the clutch today."[5]

The loss was consistent with Braves fortunes in April. They held the worst record in the National League. Royster reflected the team's disgust, saying, "Can we afford to blow games like that? If we are going to win any, we have to take games like that when we are completely in command. This is awful."[6]

Sutter got his fifth save of the season. Having emerged as one of the top relievers in the National League during his previous three major-league seasons, he wound up winning the Cy Young Award in 1979.

Murphy was on the verge of an All-Star career. He wound up hitting 21 home runs for the season, missing almost two months because of an injury. His breakout year occurred the next season (33 home runs, 89 RBIs), followed by two National League MVP seasons in 1982 and 1983.

The 38-year-old Cox was in his second season with Braves, who finished with the second-worst record in the National League (66-94). He served two dissimilar terms with the Braves. In his first four seasons with the Braves, his teams posted a 266-323 record. After a four-year stint as manager for Toronto and five years as the Braves GM, he returned to the Braves dugout in 1990. During the decade of the '90s, his teams won five pennants and one World Series. He managed the Braves through 2010 and was elected to the Baseball Hall of Fame in 2014.

Murcer's dramatic home run temporarily put him back into the Cubs' good graces; but they decided a couple of months later that they no longer wanted him. They shopped him around to other teams, despite his no-trade contract. When the Murcer agreed to go back to the Yankees (with whom he had played from 1965 to 1974), the Cubs traded him on June 26 for minor-leaguer Paul Semall.[7] He was with the Yankees when his best friend, Thurman Munson, was tragically killed in a private plane crash on August 2. Murcer finished out his career with the Yankees in 1983.

Sources

In addition to the sources cited in the Notes, the author consulted Baseball-Reference.com and Retrosheet.org.

Nightingale, Dave. "Cubs Late Lightning Shocks Braves," *Chicago Tribune*, April 30, 1979: 4,1.

Notes

1   Clifford Blau. "Bobby Murcer,: SABR BioProject, sabr.org/bioproj/person/9f758761.

2   Ken Picking. "Cubs Beat Braves with 6-Run Ninth," *Atlanta Constitution*, April 30, 1979: 7-D.

3   Picking, 1-D.

4   Picking: 1-D.

5   Picking, 7-D.

6   Picking, 1-D.

7   Blau.

ROYALS STAGE "A COMEBACK FOR ALL SEASONS" IN DEFEATING BREWERS

JUNE 15, 1979: KANSAS CITY ROYALS 14, MILWAUKEE BREWERS 11, AT COUNTY STADIUM, MILWAUKEE

BY MIKE HUBER

Yogi Berra is credited with saying the baseball truism "It ain't over till it's over."[1] Until the final out is made, don't count out any team. The *Garden City* (Kansas) *Telegram* aptly summed up the late-night heroics of the Kansas City Royals after they defeated the Milwaukee Brewers on June 15, 1979: "It was a comeback for all seasons – one nearly as swift as a Willie Wilson dash around the bases, as rare as a save by the gasoline splashers who inhabit the Milwaukee Brewers' bullpen."[2] Before a County Stadium crowd of 32,812, the Royals erased a nine-run deficit and stormed back in the ninth inning to shock the Brewers, 14-11. Wilson's inside-the-park home run with two aboard sealed Milwaukee's fate.

Left-hander Mike Caldwell, the Sporting News American League 1978 Comeback Player of the Year, got the starting nod for the Brewers. With an earned run average of 2.93, Caldwell was seeking his seventh win of the season. Opposite him for the Royals was southpaw Paul Splittorff (8-5, 3.66 ERA). The Royals had lost seven of their previous 10 games, while the Brewers had a mini-win streak of two games going for them. It appeared that the Brewers were on a roll.

Milwaukee jumped on Splittorff in the bottom of the first. Back-to-back singles by Paul Molitor and Cecil Cooper brought Sal Bando to the plate, and he wasted no time in propelling a ball over the fence for a three-run home run, his fifth of the year. The Brewers then started another rally, getting two more runners on base before Splittorff retired the inning's eighth batter, Dick Davis, on a groundout to third.

The Royals went quietly in the second; in fact, Caldwell cruised through the first three innings, allowing just two singles. In the bottom of the second, the Brewers started again. Molitor singled with one out. After Cooper flied out, Molitor stole second and then stole third. Bando walked and Gorman Thomas stroked a single to right, plating Molitor. In the third, Sixto Lezcano led off with a walk and was still aboard two outs later when Charlie Moore rocketed a home run, his second of the season. With the score 6-0, Royals skipper Whitey Herzog made the call to the bullpen. Eduardo Rodriguez, pitching in his final major-league season (even though he was just 27 years old), came on in relief and, after a single by Molitor, retired Cooper for the third out on a fly ball to center fielder Amos Otis.

The Kansas City bats finally came to life in the fourth. Darrell Porter's RBI single and a groundout RBI by designated hitter John Wathan brought in two runs. However, in the bottom half, the Brewers treated Rodriguez's pitching as if it were batting practice. Bando singled. An out later Ben Oglivie walked. Lezcano singled, driving in Bando. Robin Yount walked, loading the bases, and Davis crushed a grand slam. Suddenly, the score was 11-2 in favor of the home team. With the game seemingly out of reach, Herzog kept Rodriguez in the game.

The Royals scratched back a run in the fifth on consecutive singles by Wilson, George Brett, and Otis. In the sixth, Jerry Terrell (who had replaced Porter at third) and Frank White singled, and with two outs,

Wilson hit his third home run of the season, his first homer to leave a ballpark in two seasons.[3] The score was now 11-6 in favor of Milwaukee.

Rodriguez survived the fifth and sixth innings and gave way to Steve Mingori in the seventh. Mingori faced the minimum in the two innings he pitched. Caldwell did not pitch the seventh. Recently acquired righty Paul Mitchell[4] set the Royals down in order in the seventh and eighth innings.

In the final frame, with Kansas City still trailing by five runs, Wilson started things with a single to right. Jamie Quirk, who had entered defensively for Porter in the fifth, copied Wilson with another single to right. Otis smashed the ball, but he hit it right to center fielder Thomas for the first out. Al Cowens singled, loading the bases. George Scott then singled to left, with Wilson and Quirk crossing the plate and Cowens scampering to third. Brewers manager George Bamberger called for Reggie Cleveland to pitch to Terrell. Herzog countered by sending up Pete LaCock, whose sacrifice fly brought in Cowens. Wathan then hit a seeing-eye single up the middle and into center field. White followed with the sixth single of the inning, driving in Scott from second base. With runners again on first and second, Bill Castro strolled in from the Brewers bullpen to take over. U L Washington greeted Castro with a hard single to left, and Wathan raced home with the game-tying tally. The Royals had batted around and had knotted the score, 11-11. Switch-hitter Wilson, batting left-handed, then sent the ball into the right-field corner and was off to the races. By the time Lezcano came up with the ball and relayed it to second baseman Molitor, who fired it home to catcher Moore, Wilson was sliding across home plate with an inside-the-park three-run homer. Kansas City led 14-11. Quirk doubled to right but was stranded when Otis lined out to center for the second time in the inning. Marty Pattin came in to close the ninth for the Royals, retiring the three batters he faced, and Kansas City had completed one of the greatest comebacks in franchise history.

The Royals saved nine of their 21 hits for their final at-bat. The Brewers allowed eight runs "against a Kansas City lineup dotted with reserves."[5] Former Brewer Quirk, who had six at-bats all season, and Terrell, who had 11, both played several innings. Quirk went 3-for-3 and Terrell 1-for-2. Scott, recently acquired by Kansas City,[6] collected two hits. Herzog used every nonpitcher on his roster, and the reserves (Quirk, Terrell, and Washington) came through with five hits. He explained his rationale after the game: "I

WILLIE WILSON OF ROYALS

An eight-run inning overcame an 11-6 deficit. Royals left fielder Willie Wilson hit two three-run homers in the game, one in the sixth and one in the ninth.

took Brett and Porter out because they've been playing every day. And Caldwell's in there and it's 11-3."[7]

Six Kansas City batters had multi-hit performances, led by Wilson's 4-for-6 day at the plate. The Royals' leadoff hitter also scored four runs and knocked in six with his two three-run homers. The comeback left the "stunned fans booing and the principals groping for appropriate words to describe it."[8] The Brewers had banged out 14 hits of their own, led by three home runs (Bando, Moore, and Davis) and Molitor's 4-for-6 performance in the leadoff spot.

Wilson, the hero for the Royals, commented, "It was a weird game, that's for sure. I'm just glad it came out our way."[9] He added, "I popped one out – my first hit out of the park in two years. Then we started thinking we had a chance. But it was still 11-6 going into the ninth. It has to be a thrill."[10]

Milwaukee manager Bamberger had "exhausted his supply of spicy expletives on the bench while Wilson was streaking around the bases in the ninth." In the clubhouse, the somewhat composed, "noted nice guy"[11] Bamberger told reporters, "There's no sense in saying anything right now. What can I say? I did enough screaming on the bench. You can't print what

I said. I'll tell you, you could put (the Royals) out there right now and tell them, 'Here's a fastball,' and throw it right down the middle. They wouldn't hit it any better."[12]

He added, "That is the worst, worst game I ever [have] been associated with in 34 years of baseball. That was worse than getting beat 25-0. And to lose a game like that after you have been winning 11-2, that's terrible for morale."[13] The press agreed. Thos. A Hawley of the *Wisconsin State Journal* wrote, "What happened to the Milwaukee Brewers Friday night was either the worst game ever played in franchise history or something close to it."[14]

Herzog shared with reporters that he'd "seen about four or five (comebacks) like that. But I was playing with Washington then."[15] He added, "And the funny thing is the three outs we got in the ninth were all hard hit. What kept us alive was that little dribbler over the mound by Wathan."[16]

Sources

In addition to the sources mentioned in the notes, the author consulted baseball-reference.com and retrosheet.org.

Notes

1   According to the BBC (bbc.com/news/magazine-34324865), Berra first uttered the phrase when speaking about the 1973 National League pennant race, as his 82-79 New York Mets rallied to win the divisional title, defeated the heavily favored Cincinnati Reds in the League Championship Series and eventually played in the World Series. Accessed July 5, 2018.

2   "Royals Blast Brewers," *Garden City* (Kansas) *Telegram,* June 16, 1979: 8.

3   Wilson's first two home runs of the 1979 season were inside-the-park homers, against the Chicago White Sox on May 13 and the New York Yankees on June 9.

4   Mitchell had been traded by the Seattle Mariners to the Brewers on June 7 for Randy Stein.

5   Thos. A Hawley, "Wilson's Homer caps Brewers' Nightmare," *Wisconsin State Journal* (Madison), June 16, 1979: 13-14.

6   Scott had been traded by the Boston Red Sox to the Royals in exchange for Tom Poquette just two days earlier, on June 13, 1979.

7   Hawley.

8   "Royals Blast Brewers."

9   "Royals Blast Brewers."

10   "Royals Blast Brewers."

11   Hawley.

12   Hawley.

13   "Royals Blast Brewers."

14   Hawley.

15   Hawley.

16   Mike O'Brien, "Royal Rally Stuns Brewers," *Sheboygan* (Wisconsin) *Press,* June 16, 1979: 16.

SEVEN-RUN NINTH INNING LAUNCHES ASTROS TO 9-8 VICTORY OVER EXPOS

JULY 25, 1980:
HOUSTON ASTROS 9,
MONTREAL EXPOS 8,
AT STADE OLYMPIQUE, MONTREAL

BY GARY BELLEVILLE

Over the course of a 162-game season, there will invariably be games in which a team squanders a lead in the late innings and suffers a painful loss. When the season draws to a close and that team narrowly misses the playoffs, it's only natural to look back upon the games that slipped away and wonder, "What if?" The July 25, 1980, matchup between the Houston Astros and the Montreal Expos was a textbook example of one of those games.

The Astros and Expos had been on similar trajectories in the late 1970s. Neither of the two expansion teams had ever qualified for the postseason, although both came tantalizingly close in 1979.[1] The two squads had led their respective divisions in September before fading down the stretch and finishing in second place. Montreal wound up only two games behind Pittsburgh, the eventual World Series champions, while Houston ended its season a mere 1½ games back of Cincinnati.

Both teams continued their winning ways in 1980, with the Astros coming into their late-July series against Montreal with a 53-41 record and a 2½-game lead over the Dodgers in the NL West. The Expos had led the Eastern Division at the All-Star break for the second consecutive season, but they had gone 8-7 since the break, dropping them two games behind the Pirates with a 50-42 mark.

For this game, Houston sent 33-year-old Nolan Ryan to the hill. The Astros had signed him to a four-year, $4.5 million free-agent contract in the offseason, making him the first player to earn a million dollars per season in a team sport. Ryan, who had recorded his 3,000th strikeout exactly three weeks earlier, entered the game with a 5-7 record and a 3.14 ERA. The Expos

countered with their ace, 30-year-old right-hander Steve Rogers (11-6, 3.06 ERA).

Montreal second baseman Tim Raines was penciled into the starting lineup for the first time in his big-league career. Raines had just been called up from the Denver Bears after hitting .330 with 63 stolen bases in Triple A. The 20-year-old speedster had made his

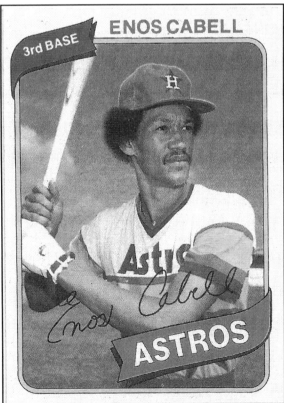

Courtesy The Topps Company.

Enos Cabell and Alan Ashby each drove in three runs, Cabell singling in two of them during a seven-run top of the ninth.

major-league debut in September of 1979, stealing two bases and scoring three runs as a pinch-runner in six games, all without the benefit of a single plate appearance.

Those among the 50,217 fans in attendance who were expecting a pitchers' duel were sorely disappointed, as neither starter was particularly effective on this day. Rogers allowed four hits and a walk over the first two innings, although he wiggled out of jams in both innings and was fortunate to fall behind by only 1-0. The Astros run came in the second inning on an RBI single by Alan Ashby that caromed off the glove of second baseman Raines and trickled into shallow center field.

After a one-two-three first inning, Ryan scattered five singles in the second and third innings without giving up a run. His luck ran out in the bottom of the fourth inning, however, as Larry Parrish brought in a run with an infield single, and then Ron LeFlore drove home two more runs with a two-out double to put Montreal ahead 3-1.

In the bottom of the fifth inning, Ellis Valentine extended the lead to 5-1 with a single to left field that scored a pair of Expos runners and knocked Ryan out of the game. It turned out to be Ryan's worst outing of the entire season.[2]

The Astros cut the lead to 5-2 in the top of the sixth on Enos Cabell's RBI double. Raines, who had reached base on a fielder's choice and an error earlier in the game and had stolen second base both times, came to the plate against reliever Bert Roberge with two out and nobody on in the bottom of the inning. After beating out an infield single for his first major-league hit, Raines stole his third base of the game, tying a team record.[3] Andre Dawson followed with a double to left field to bring home Raines, and when José Cruz booted the ball at the wall, Dawson circled the bases, putting the Expos out in front 7-2.

Rogers escaped a bases-loaded threat in the seventh inning without giving up any runs, and when the tiring right-hander took to the hill to start the ninth, the Expos still held a five-run lead. Canadian Terry Puhl, still holding a grudge against the Expos for not giving him a proper tryout when he was in high school, smacked a home run to lead off the inning.[4] After a walk to the light-hitting Craig Reynolds, Rogers surrendered a double to Danny Heep, advancing Reynolds to third base. It was Heep's first extra-base hit in 46 career at-bats. Mercifully, Expos manager Dick Williams pulled Rogers from the game after his 152nd pitch of the night.[5]

With the left-handed-hitting Cruz coming to the plate and the potential tying run in the on-deck circle, Williams chose to bypass his most effective reliever, 40-year-old lefty Woodie Fryman, and bring in his least effective one, southpaw Fred Norman.[6] Cruz singled off Norman to drive in Reynolds and Heep and cut the lead to 7-5, and then Williams summoned Montreal's prized free-agent acquisition, Elias Sosa, to face Jeffrey Leonard. After Leonard singled, Sosa walked 36-year-old Joe Morgan to load the bases. Cabell followed with a single to center field, which drove in Cruz and Leonard and tied the game at 7-7. The switch-hitting Ashby, hitting from the left side against the righty Sosa, stroked a double that scored Morgan and Cabell and put the Astros up 9-7. Now that eight consecutive batters had reached base, Williams finally went to his ace reliever, Fryman. The ageless wonder retired the next three hitters in order.

After Frank LaCorte retired the first two batters in the bottom of the ninth, Gary Carter closed the gap to 9-8 with a solo home run, his 20th round-tripper of the season. LaCorte then struck out Parrish to end the game, and frustrated Expos fans voiced their displeasure with a loud chorus of boos.

Williams was asked after the game about the slow hook of Rogers. "He was pretty well spent," the manager explained. "He threw a lot of pitches early and he threw a lot in the game. But if your bullpen can't do the job…"[7] Astros manager Bill Virdon took it all in stride. "It's unusual to win a game like that, but that's baseball," he reasoned.[8]

After a successful 1980 debut that featured his first major-league hit, two runs scored, and three stolen bases, Raines went 0-for-13 over his next three games and was hastily relegated to the bench. He didn't get another start – or even a hit – for the remainder of the season. Raines was sent back to Denver in August and returned to Montreal as a pinch-runner and pinch-hitter when the rosters expanded in September. The future Hall of Famer, named the 1980 Minor League Player of the Year by *The Sporting News*, would have to wait until the following season to make an impact at the big-league level.

The blown five-run lead turned out to be a costly loss for the Expos. With Montreal and Philadelphia tied for first place heading into the final weekend of the season, the Phillies took two out of three games from the Expos at Olympic Stadium to win the division by a single game.

The improbable come-from-behind victory also proved to be significant for the Astros. With three games remaining in the season, the Astros held a three-game lead over the Dodgers with the two teams finishing out the year with a series at Chavez Ravine. In a tense weekend of baseball, the Dodgers eked out three one-run victories to force a one-game playoff. The Astros, led by the stellar pitching of Joe Niekro, defeated the Dodgers 7-1 in game number 163 to earn their first playoff appearance in their 19-year history.[9]

Sources

In addition to the sources cited in the Notes, the author consulted Baseball-Reference.com and Retrosheet.org.

Notes

1   The Expos entered the National League in 1969, and their first winning season was in 1979, when they went 95-65. The Astros, who began play in 1962 as the Houston Colt .45s, had played .500 or better in six of their first 18 seasons, although 1979 was the first one in which they finished less than 11 games out of the playoffs.

2   Nolan Ryan registered a Game Score of only 26 in this outing, the lowest Game Score in all his 1980 starts. His lone strikeout was in the first inning, when the rookie Tim Raines was caught looking in his first major-league plate appearance.

3   The team record for most steals in a game by a player was broken two weeks later when Ron LeFlore stole four bases against the Cubs on August 8, 1980. As of the end of the 2018 season, the franchise record was still four stolen bases in a game, although it had been accomplished 11 times in 50 years. Raines was responsible for five of those 11 four-steal games.

4   David E. Skelton, "Terry Puhl," SABR BioProject, sabr.org/bioproj/person/d809c38f, accessed August 6, 2019.

5   Glenn Cole, "Expos Fall Apart in Loss to Astros," *Montreal Gazette*, July 26, 1980: 62.

6   The Expos were playing with a four-man bullpen for this game: Woodie Fryman (4-4, 2.26 ERA, 10 saves), Stan Bahnsen (6-4, 3.14 ERA, 2 saves), Elias Sosa (5-3, 3.34 ERA, 7 saves), and Fred Norman (0-1, 4.70 ERA, 4 saves). Bill Gullickson had been working out of the bullpen until an injury to David Palmer resulted in his return to the starting rotation. Reliever Dale Murray had been called up from Triple A to take Gullickson's place in the bullpen, but he had not yet arrived in Montreal. The Expos did not play the previous day, making all four remaining relievers available to pitch.

7   Cole.

8   United Press International, "Astros Roll a Seven Against Expos," *Pittsburgh Press*, July 26, 1980: A-6.

9   The Astros suffered a heartbreaking loss to the Phillies in the National League Championship Series. Houston held a two-games-to-one lead in the best-of-five series, only to lose the final two games at home in extra innings. Philadelphia went on to win the World Series in six games over the Kansas City Royals.

YANKEES AND RIVERA STUMBLE IN AN OTHERWISE WONDERFUL YEAR

AUGUST 18, 2000:
ANAHEIM ANGELS 9,
NEW YORK YANKEES 8
(11 INNINGS),
AT YANKEE STADIUM, NEW YORK

BY ALAN COHEN

"One of the toughest losses I've had to deal with in a while."

– Joe Torre, August 18, 2000[1]

"I haven't been around that long, but to me, that was the biggest comeback we've ever had."

– Darin Erstad, August 18, 2000[2]

Not too many fans in the announced crowd of 37,053 were still at Yankee Stadium 4 hours and 11 minutes after the first pitch, especially as the Yankees, with Roger Clemens going for his seventh consecutive win, had surged into a big lead thanks in large part to a pair of homers by Glenallen Hill. They were not around to see the Yankees victimized by a come-from-behind rally. The Anaheim Angels tied the score in the ninth inning and won the game on a homer by Darin Erstad in the top of the 11th. The final score was 9-8.

The Angels had broken on top in the first inning. Erstad, leading off, singled to center. Orlando Palmeiro's grounder in the hole between shortstop and third was not corralled by Derek Jeter, although he got his glove on the ball. Erstad went to third on the play and scored when Mo Vaughn grounded into a double play.

The Yankees wasted little time tying things up against Angels starter Ramon Ortiz, who had entered the game with a 4-3 record. Jeter walked, moved to second on a groundout, and scored on a single by Paul O'Neill. The Yankees took the lead an inning later. With Luis Sojo on second and Jose Vizcaino on first, Ortiz balked the runners to second and third. Jeter seized upon the opportunity and drove both runners home with a single, making the score 3-1.

Tim Salmon of the Angels homered in the fourth inning to make the score 3-2. The homer, the 223rd of Salmon's career, broke the Angels' franchise record, previously held by Brian Downing. But the Yankees countered in the bottom of the inning. The first of Hill's two homers made the score 4-2. The homer by Hill was followed by a single by Sojo. Vizcaino's sacrifice bunt became a single when Angels second baseman Adam Kennedy was slow in covering first base.

Jeter then sent a hard smash past first baseman Vaughn to right field, and the Angels took a page out of the 1962 Mets playbook. Sojo, not sure if Vaughn would field the ball, had stopped at third base and Vizcaino, by the time he realized third base was occupied, had rounded second a bit too far. He was caught in a rundown where seemingly every member of the Angels touched the ball. The ball went from third baseman Troy Glaus to three other players and back to Glaus again. As Glaus finally ran down Vizcaino, Sojo scored from third, making the score 5-2. Jeter wound up on second and advanced to third on a fly ball by Jorge Posada. O'Neill was called out on strikes by umpire Gary Cederstrom. O'Neill disputed the call but was restrained by manager Torre as the inning ended.

The Angels closed the gap an inning later. Kennedy singled and moved to third on a single by Kevin Stocker. Erstad, in another productive at-bat, forced Stocker at second as Kennedy scored.

"It's ridiculous. Every time he comes up, he's hitting something hard. It he is not hitting it out of the park, he is scaring some of the infielders."

– Derek Jeter, speaking of Glenallen Hill before the game[3]

The Yankees countered in the bottom of the fifth. With two out, Tino Martinez singled and came home on the second of Hill's two homers, making the score 7-3.

The Angels mounted a threat in the sixth inning but came up empty. A single by Vaughn and walks to Salmon and Glaus loaded the bases with one out. Bengie Molina's fly ball to left field was too short to advance the runners, and Kennedy lined out to short to end the threat.

The Yankees got a run in the bottom of the sixth when Posada singled with two out and Paul O'Neill doubled. It would be the end of the Yankee scoring for the game.

The Yankees led 8-3 going into the ninth inning with Clemens still on the mound. Clemens looked invincible at that point and was three outs away from his 258th career win. He had retired eighth straight Angels, getting the side in order in the seventh and eighth innings after his Houdini act in the sixth. After Clemens allowed groundball singles to Glaus and Molina, and his pitch count had risen to 122, manager Torre brought in Jeff Nelson to pitch. After retiring Adam Kennedy on a fly ball to center fielder Bernie Williams, Nelson walked Stocker to load the bases. That prompted Torre to bring in closer Mariano Rivera. The first batter he faced was Erstad. Erstad's grounder to third was fielded by Sojo, who touched third for the force play and threw to first for what was expected to be a game-ending double play.

However, Erstad beat the throw to first and Glaus scored for the Angels, who now had runners on first and second and trailed by four runs. Stocker scored on a double by Palmeiro, making the score 8-5. With Erstad on third, Palmeiro on second, and first base unoccupied, Rivera elected to pitch to the lefty-swinging Vaughn. Mo's three-run blast to right field, his 30th homer of the season, tied the game at 8-8. The Yankees had blown a five-run lead for only the second time

since they started playing at Yankee Stadium in 1923.[4] Rivera struck out Salmon to end the inning, but the damage was done.

"When he dove, you held your breath. You hoped you would see it bounce out, but it didn't."

– Joe Torre, reflecting on what he saw in the bottom of the 10th inning[5]

Shigetoshi Hasegawa, the fourth Angels pitcher, came on to pitch a scoreless bottom of the ninth and force extra innings. Rivera pitched a scoreless top of the 10th for the Yankees. New York mounted a rally in the bottom of the 10th inning. Hill had an infield single off Hasegawa and left the game for pinch-runner Luis Polonia. Sojo bunted the runner to second base. A fly-ball out by Jose Canseco, pinch-hitting for Jose Vizcaino, advanced Polonia to third base, and Jeter was walked intentionally. When it appeared the Yankees were poised to win the game. Erstad dashed into left-center field and went airborne to make an over-the-shoulder circus catch on a ball hit by Posada. The threat died.

In the top of the 11th, Darin Erstad's third RBI of the game was the one that made the difference in the end, a home run and the game-winner.

183

Mike Stanton came on to pitch the 11th inning for the Yankees and Erstad, batting second and feeling the effects of being pounded by his teammates after his great catch, delivered the game-winning homer, his 21st home run of the season. Stanton hung a curveball and paid the price, as the ball went into the right-field stands.

Hasegawa, in his third inning of relief, shut down the Yankees in the bottom of the 11th, retiring O'Neill, Williams, and David Justice. The three shutout innings against the Yankees extended Hasegawa's scoreless streak to 22 innings over a 14-game stretch. (The steak reached 27⅓ innings on August 29.) With the win, his record went to 8-2. Stanton was charged with the loss, bringing his record to 2-2.

The Yankees, despite the loss, which cut their lead over the Red Sox to three games, remained atop the AL East with a 66-52 record, thanks in part to the contributions of players like the 35-year-old Hill. Hill's two homers made it nine homers with the Yankees in 43 at-bats since he joined them on July 21 in a trade with the Cubs. He hit seven more homers before the season ended. His total homer count for the season, 27, was the highest of his career, which ended the next season.

The win brought the Angels' record to 63-59, which put them in third place in the AL West, six games behind the division-leading Seattle Mariners. They would essentially play .500 ball for the remainder of the season and remained in third place. The hero of the April 18 game, Erstad, who had his career game on August 18, had his career season in 2000, leading the American League in hits with 240, and batting .355, second to Boston's Nomar Garciaparra (.372). He won the Gold Glove and Silver Slugger Awards, was named to the All-Star team, and finished eighth in the MVP balloting.

Rivera's blown save was his fifth of the season, but he had by that point saved 26 games and had a 3.15 ERA. Over the remaining weeks of the season, Rivera was virtually untouchable. He saved 10 games. His ERA down the stretch was 2.11.

The Yankees won the AL East by 2½ games over the Red Sox, went on to win the pennant, and defeated the Mets in the World Series for their 26th World Series championship.

Sources

In addition to Baseball-Reference.com and the sources cited in the notes, the author used:

Abraham, Peter. "Angels Fight to the Finish," *Journal News* (White Plains, New York), August 19, 2000: C1.

Associated Press. "Erstad Steals One from the Yanks," *Daily Advocate* (Stamford, Connecticut), August 19, 2000: B1, B2.

Haakenson, Joe. "Erstad Provides Late-Night Thrills: Game Saving Catch, Home Run Lift Angels – Angels 9, New York 8," *Los Angeles Daily News,* August 19, 2000: S1.

Hill, Thomas. "Vaughn, Angels Rock Rivera," *New York Daily News*, August 19, 2000: 49.

Kernan, Kevin. "Say It Ain't Mo – Thanks to Rivera, Yanks Blow 5-Run Lead in Ninth," *New York Post*, August 19, 2000: 48.

Lennon, David. "One That Got Away: Erstad's Homer in 11th Wins It After Rivera Blows Lead," *Newsday*, August 19, 2000: A36.

Notes

1   Mike DiGiovanna, "Erstad Heroics Just Super for Angels," *Los Angeles Times*, August 19, 2000: D6.

2   DiGiovanna.

3   Ohm Youngmisuk, "With Two More Homers, Hill Thrills Bombers," *New York Daily News*, August 19, 2000: 49.

4   Buster Olney, "Erstad Steals One from the Yankees," *New York Times*, August 19, 2000: D1.

5   Matt Eagan, "Dive Drive, Sting Yanks: Erstad's Stab, Grab Do It for Angels," *Hartford Courant*, August 19, 2000: C6.

PHILLIES LEAVE BREWERS FLAT WITH PAYBACK COMEBACK

AUGUST 5, 2007:
PHILADELPHIA PHILLIES 8,
MILWAUKEE BREWERS 6
(11 INNINGS),
AT MILLER PARK, MILWAUKEE

BY JIM SWEETMAN

Phillies fans would be forgiven if they had turned off the broadcast of the Sunday afternoon game at Milwaukee on August 5, 2007, in the late innings. The Brewers held a 6-1 lead going into the ninth. They had won the weekend's previous two games, including a stunning comeback win from a 5-1 deficit the night before. The Brewers were also riding a seven-game win streak against Philadelphia at Miller Park.[1]

As for the sellout home crowd, they were likely preparing to celebrate another strong win by their division-leading team against a third-place team. Instead, they went home in shock.[2]

Milwaukee built an early lead, getting to Phillies starter Adam Eaton in the bottom of the first. Leadoff hitter Corey Hart singled to center. After recording an outfield fly and an infield popup, Eaton walked Prince Fielder, Milwaukee's cleanup hitter. Three straight doubles then gave the home team a solid lead. First, right fielder Kevin Mench doubled to right, scoring Hart. Geoff Jenkins was next with a two-bagger to center that brought in Fielder and Mench. Catcher Damian Miller plated Jenkins with his own double. Eaton intentionally walked the Brewers' number-eight hitter, Craig Counsell, to get to opposing pitcher Jeff Suppan, who ended the inning with a groundout.

Neither team was able to score again until the bottom of the fifth. Ryan Braun, the Brewers' rookie third baseman, greeted Eaton with a leadoff home run. It was his 20th since joining the club 64 games earlier – a new team record.[3] After retiring Fielder on a groundout, Eaton gave up a second double to Mench. Jenkins singled him home, prompting Phillies

manager Charlie Manuel to replace Eaton with Clay Condrey, who stopped the bleeding. The day's performance left Eaton with an NL-worst 6.09 ERA. He had had trouble in the first two innings of the games he pitched, with a 7.63 ERA over the first two but

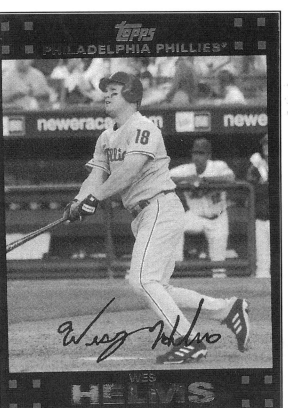

Wes Helms entered the game early as a pinch-hitter. His fourth at-bat won it, with a two-run double to right field in the 11th inning.

then a 5.25 ERA from the third inning on.[4] Responding to reporters' questions about how he could improve, Eaton replied, "Maybe just go after it in the first inning then settle in," before admitting he didn't really have an answer.[5]

After managing only two singles and a walk through five innings, the Phillies finally got on the board in the sixth, thanks in part to Suppan. With one out, singles by Tadahito Iguchi and Pat Burrell put two on. Suppan then uncorked a wild pitch that put them on second and third. After Ryan Howard popped up, center fielder Aaron Rowand hit a single to deep short, bringing home Iguchi. Milwaukee skipper Ned Yost then pulled Suppan, replacing him with Brian Shouse, who retired pinch-hitter Wes Helms to end the threat.

The Philadelphia bullpen held Milwaukee to a couple of isolated hits, and the Phillies' offense was poised to strike again in the top of the eighth. Jimmy Rollins, who had challenged his team at the start of the season by calling them "the team to beat in the NL East," drew a leadoff walk from Carlos Villanueva.[6] Iguchi doubled to left, putting runners on second and third with no outs. Yost went to Scott Linebrink, who shut the door on the threat, striking out the next three Phillies.

The visitors fared better in the ninth. After pinch-hitting for Linebrink in the eighth, Yost handed the five-run lead to Matt Wise. Wise had struggled some since hitting Cincinnati's Pedro Lopez in the face with a pitch on July 25, including walking the only two batters he faced in his previous outing. He induced a comebacker from Wes Helms (who had stayed in the game to play third base), but was unable to make the play, allowing Helms to reach safely. The next batter, center fielder Jayson Werth, took him deep to left for a two-run home run. Wise admitted that hitting Lopez was still affecting him, but said he had no choice but to get past it.[7]

Yost decided to bring in closer Francisco Cordero, who earned saves in the first two games of the series. He retired the next two batters but walked Rollins on four pitches. Rollins went to second uncontested, and Iguchi followed with an infield single. Cordero then walked Burrell and hit Howard with a pitch, sending Rollins home with the Phillies' fourth run. Rowand then came up big. After falling behind, he worked a full count before powering a shot down the third-base line that got past Braun. Two runs scored for the Phillies, tying the game. Helms popped out in his second at-bat of the inning, but the damage was done. Braun said after the game that it was a play he should have made.[8]

Phillies relievers J.C. Romero and Brett Myers (the team's main closer) combined to strike out the side in the bottom of the ninth, sending the game to extra innings. Derrick Turnbow similarly shut down the Phillies in the 10th, with two strikeouts and a ground-out. Myers came back for the 10th, giving up a single among three groundouts.

Manny Parra took the mound for Milwaukee in the 11th. He got two quick outs but Howard was able to work a four-pitch walk. Rowand singled to center, Howard taking second. Helms was next. He hit Parra's first pitch deep into the right-field corner, bringing in both Howard and Rowand and giving the Phillies an 8-6 lead. A walk to Werth and Chris Coste's popup ended the inning.

The Phillies sent Jose Mesa in for the bottom of the 11th. Mesa was the Phillies' primary closer from 2001 to 2003, but he bounced around to three teams before being released by Detroit and returning to the Phillies in June. Braun, his first batter, led off the inning with a hit to deep center that looked as though it would go for extra bases but was corralled by Rowand. After Mesa retired Fielder and walked Mench, Jenkins doubled to deep right, sending Mench to third. Yost sent former Phillie Johnny Estrada to pinch-hit for Miller. With first base open, Mesa put him on intentionally. Craig Counsell had the chance to turn the game around again, but he lined Mesa's first pitch to Iguchi, sealing the win for the Phillies.

Mesa made light of the outcome, saying, "Sometimes it's better to be lucky than good."[9] Regardless, Mesa earned his only save of the year, which was also his 112th as a Phillie – a franchise record.

Braun summed up the home team's perspective, saying, "It's a game we should have won. ... We let them back in the game."[10] Asked if the Phillies' win was poetic justice for the night before, Yost replied, "I don't like poetry."[11] Manuel partly agreed with Mesa. "I figure it's real lucky," he said, adding, "We come back on you."[12] Helms agreed, saying, "You never give up. ... That's just the nature of this ballclub."[13]

Sources

In addition to the sources listed in the Notes and Retrosheet's game record, the author used ESPN's pitch-by-pitch record (espn.com/mlb/boxscore?gameId=270805108) to reconstruct this game.

Notes

1   Marcus Hayes, "Phils Leave 'em Crying in Their Beer," *Philadelphia Daily News*, August 6, 2007.

2   Tom Haudricourt, "A Slap in the Face; Phillies Pay Back Brewers with Own Dramatic Rally," *Milwaukee Journal Sentinel*, August 6, 2007.

3   Tom Haudricourt, "Game Report," *Milwaukee Journal Sentinel*, August 6, 2007.

4   Todd Zolecki, "Phillies Notes," *Philadelphia Inquirer*, August 6, 2007.

5   Zolecki, "Phillies Notes."

6   Associated Press, "Rollins, Phillies Confident About Chances in '07," January 23, 2007, retrieved from espn.com/mlb/news/story?id=2740529, November 20, 2020.

7   Tom Haudricourt, Notes," *Milwaukee Journal Sentinel*, August 6, 2007.

8   Haudricourt, "A Slap in the Face."

9   Todd Zolecki, "This Time, Phils Rally to Win," *Philadelphia Inquirer*, August 6, 2007.

10   Haudricourt, "A Slap in the Face."

11   Zolecki, "This Time, Phils Rally to Win."

12   Hayes.

13   Hayes.

TWINS CAUSE A ROYAL RUCKUS WITH LARGE COMEBACK WIN

MAY 28, 2008:
MINNESOTA TWINS 9,
KANSAS CITY ROYALS 8
(10 INNINGS),
AT KAUFFMAN STADIUM, KANSAS CITY, MISSOURI

BY ANDREW STOCKMANN

Allowing five runs in the top of the ninth inning, the Kansas City Royals wasted a quality start from Zack Greinke and blew an 8-3 lead in front of 13,621 fans at Kauffman Stadium. Veteran right-hander Liván Hernández, pitching his lone season in the American

CRAIG MONROE

Craig Monroe's pinch-hit three-run ninth-inning home run completed the comeback and set up the Twins' ultimate win.

League, opposed Greinke and threw six innings, allowing 13 hits and six earned runs.

Zack Greinke's 2008 campaign set the stage for his Cy Young Award season in 2009. He surpassed 200 innings for the first time in his career, notched 13 wins and posted a 3.47 ERA over 32 starts. His 117 pitches in this start were his most in any start during the 2008 season. Lasting eight innings, he allowed five hits and three runs, while walking two batters and striking out eight.

As is usually the case in a game featuring a large comeback, one team jumped out to a large lead. The Royals led 3-2 after three innings, after a run-scoring double play from José Guillén in the first inning and a two-out rally in the third. Two errors by left fielder Delmon Young contributed to three more runs in the fourth, making the Twins' deficit 6-2 after four frames. When Miguel Olivo led off the Royals' fifth against Hernández, the Royals' win expectancy was 93 per cent.[1]

This game was the second home game for the Royals since they returned from an 11-game road trip that saw them fall from 1½ games back to seven games back in the American League Central Division. The Royals had also been no-hit by Jon Lester nine days before this matchup with the Twins, who were firmly in second place in the Central Division. They finished 12-6 against the Royals in 2008 and began their comeback when Mike Lamb singled in Twins outfielder Jason Kubel with one out in the seventh inning.

Twins manager Ron Gardenhire finally yanked Hernández out of the game after a Joey Gathright single and stolen base, followed by Alex Gordon's ground-rule double. Juan Rincón, who pitched in more games for the Twins than either Brad Radke or Bert Blyleven, allowed a single by Olivo to make the score 8-3.

Greinke breezed through the top of the eighth and Twins reliever Bobby Korecky worked around a lead-off single by Alberto Callaspo to set down the Royals in their half of the inning. Going into the top of the ninth, the Royals' win expectancy was 99 percent. Ramón Ramírez, pitching on two days' rest, entered the game and wrapped two strikeouts around a single by Jason Kubel. For the second time in the game, Mike Lamb singled Kubel home and took second when Brendan Harris singled to right field. After rookie outfielder Carlos Gómez singled in Lamb, the score was 8-5 with runners on first and second.

Both managers made lineup changes after Gomez's single. Gardenhire pinch-hit Craig Monroe for Alexi Casilla and Royals manager Trey Hillman countered with Joel Peralta relieving Ramirez. On a full-count fastball, Monroe hit a three-run homer, tying the game at 8-8 and completing the Twins' comeback. After the game, Peralta quietly reflected, saying, "I've faced [Monroe] before, I just made a mistake. Fell behind in the count and had to throw a strike and – home run."[2] Monroe retired in 2009 with two home runs and a 1.200 OPS against Peralta in 10 plate appearances. Before Kennys Vargas hit a home run in 2017, this homer by Monroe was the last tying/winning pinch-hit home run by a Twin in the ninth inning.[3]

After the Royals were unable to score in the bottom of the ninth inning against a trio of Twins pitchers, Justin Morneau led off extra innings. Morneau won the 2006 American League MVP award and finished second to Dustin Pedroia this season. He hit a leadoff homer to give the Twins a 9-8 lead, raising their win expectancy from 50 percent to 83 percent. Peralta retired the next three hitters, but the damage was done. The Twins had quickly erased a five-run deficit and possessed the lead with one of the game's most dominant closers on the mound. Joe Nathan had a fantas-

tic season in 2008, posting the highest ERA+ of his career at 316. He made quick work of the Royals in the bottom of the 10th to secure the win for the Twins.

After just the 53rd game of Trey Hillman's managerial tenure, tensions boiled over in the Royals clubhouse. José Guillén, frustrated at the supposed lack of effort of his teammates, went on an obscenity-laced rant, saying in part, "Too many babies here. ... Now I know why this organization's been losing for a while. Now I know."[4]

Upon further analysis, this game was ripe for a Twins comeback. The Royals were scuffling after a difficult road trip and their bullpen was depleted after a 12-inning loss to the Twins the night before. Hillman admitted as such after the game, saying, "From the extra innings last night, we didn't have anyone else available."[5]

The Twins' comeback showcased their bullpen strength and ability to use home runs to punish teams offensively. For the Royals, their 10th straight loss meant additional clubhouse tension during another lost season.

Sources

The author consulted Baseball-Reference.com for the game's box score and other details such as splits and play-by-play information, as well as Retrosheet.org.

Notes

(1   Win expectancy is a complex mathematical formula which helps to explain the chance an average team has of winning the game using variables such as inning, score and number of outs. Each play has an effect on the win expectancy for each team. Baseball-Reference.com has a detailed explanation of its win probability/expectancy stats and includes a win probability chart for each game on its site. Tom Tango also has a detailed explanation here.

2   Associated Press, "Royals Ripped by Guillen after 5-Run Lead in Ninth Turns to 10th Straight Loss," May 28, 2008. espn.com.au/mlb/recap?gameId=280528107. Date accessed: July 13, 2019.

3   Phil Miller, "Kennys Vargas Delivers in Pinch Before Twins Beat Royals in 10 Innings," *Minneapolis Star Tribune*, May 20, 2017. startribune.com/kennys-vargas-delivers-in-pinch-before-twins-beat-royals-in-10-innings/423268013/.

4   "Royals Ripped by Guillen."

5   "Royals Ripped by Guillen."

TWINS BENCH TWICE AS NICE

JUNE 19, 2010:
MINNESOTA TWINS 13,
PHILADELPHIA PHILLIES 10
(11 INNINGS),
AT CITIZENS BANK PARK, PHILADELPHIA

BY BRIAN WILLIAMS

On the cusp of the summer equinox, the Minnesota Twins made a rare interleague appearance at Citizens Bank Park for a weekend series. Saturday's 4:11 P.M. start time accommodated national TV coverage as "The Bank" enjoyed its 73rd consecutive sellout. Temperatures hovered in the 80s under a mostly sunny sky following an early-afternoon peak of 90 degrees.

The Philadelphia Phillies were enjoying a mini-run this week, going 4-1 (averaging six runs per game) and were 35-31 overall. Over the past three-plus weeks, they had sputtered offensively (only 2.4 runs per game). Philadelphia was battling uphill after two consecutive World Series appearances.

Southpaw Cole Hamels warmed up with Brian Schneider in the home bullpen. Starting catcher and fan favorite Carlos Ruiz was plunked by a broken bat during the eighth frame the previous evening. Although he didn't have a concussion, he wouldn't be available until midweek at the earliest.

Minnesota came in at a strong 39-29. The Twins countered Hamels with Kevin Slowey, who graduated from Upper St. Clair High School in western Pennsylvania. Slowey was in his fourth season in the Twins rotation and was coming off a 10-3 record in 2009.

The Twins wasted no time by batting around in the first inning. Hamels walked leadoff hitter Denard Span on a full-count pitch. Orlando Hudson singled and a passed ball advanced both baserunners. Justin Morneau singled to left and drove them both in. Michael Cuddyer reached on a throwing error by Hamels. Delmon Young doubled home an unearned run.

Slowey went on to achieve his career high in wins in 2010; however, this day wasn't his day. Down 3-0 early, Philadelphia battled to tie in the bottom of the first. Highlighted by Chase Utley's two-run triple to right and Jayson Werth's foul sacrifice fly, the Phillies' offense continued to operate in high gear.

The home team tacked on four more in the second. Home runs by Wilson Valdez and Ryan Howard chased Slowey. Valdez's round tripper just inside the left-field foul pole represented one-sixth of his major-league total. Valdez had circled the bases only once before this game, six years earlier while playing for the White Sox. Meanwhile, Howard connected 45 times in 2009; this game's blast was his 14th of the season.

Raul Ibanez homered off Jeff Manship to begin the third with the Phillies riding high, 8-3. Each team scored once more, so Jose Contreras inherited a 9-4 advantage as he struck out Cuddyer to finish the eighth frame. Three more outs and the game would be over.

Young singled off Contreras to open the ninth, which brought Jim Thome to the plate to a standing ovation. Knowledgeable Phillies fans appreciated Thome's effort and enthusiasm while donning the red pinstripes from 2003 to 2005 when he reunited with manager Charlie Manuel. Collecting 96 home runs and 266 RBIs for the Phils tended to positively reinforce fans' memories; and those totals include an injury-riddled 2005 season of fewer than 200 at-bats.

Most seasoned baseball fans know of Thome's long-term relationship with Manuel, his former hitting coach and manager in the Cleveland organization. When they combined their talents, both developed into baseball legends, having first crossed paths in the Gulf Coast League when Thome was 19 years old.

Now, closing in on his 40th birthday, Thome accepted his Twins role. With Morneau manning first base, Ron Gardenhire penciled in Thome exclusively as a DH and pinch-hitter in 2010. He had picked up a bat to hit for Danny Valencia.

Contreras and Thome stalemated to a full count. The next pitch was belted high and far, sailing beyond the center-field fence. Thome's two-run blast was the 570th home run of his Hall of Fame career, which passed Rafael Palmeiro on the all-time list. With this dramatic round-tripper, Thome had homered against all 30 major-league teams.

With the score now 9-6, Contreras nibbled and walked former Phillie Nick Punto on another full-count pitch. That forced Manuel to call on Phillies closer Brad Lidge for what had become an unlikely save situation.

Lidge had been a perfect 4-4 in save situations, just as he was perfect (41-for-41) during the Phillies 2008 World Series championship season. In this game, Lidge struggled with command, uncorking a wild pitch before Span singled home Minnesota's seventh run.

Span then swiped second base. Lidge whiffed Orlando Hudson. The Twins were down to their final out trailing 9-7.

Joe Mauer dug in and took strike one. On Lidge's next delivery, the reigning AL MVP launched a game-tying two-run shot to center. After depositing 28 home runs the season before, this was just Mauer's third of 2010, but his only hit of the day (1-for-5) couldn't prove more clutch.

The game went to the bottom of the ninth deadlocked at 9-9. The Phillies threatened with two baserunners, but came up empty against Matt Guerrier. Chad Durbin took over for Lidge to start the 10th and surrendered pinch-hitter Drew Butera's first career home run. The significance of this blast by a .154 hitter (6-for-39) harked back to May 16, 1983, the last time the Twins achieved two pinch-hit home runs (Dave Engle and Mickey Hatcher) in a game.

With the Twins enjoying their first lead since the top of the first inning, 6-foot-11 Jon Rauch recorded two weak outs before Ross Gload stepped in for Valdez and connected for a homer to right to tie the game at 10-10. Each team had been down to its final out (Twins in the ninth and Phillies in the 10th) before smoking a dramatic game-tying home run. Gload also enjoyed smacking the third pinch-hit home run of the game.

Danys Baez walked Mauer with one out in the 11th. Manuel had Baez walk Morneau intentionally to push

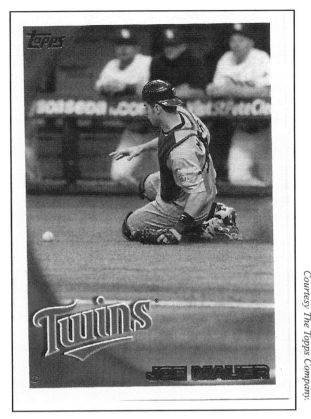

Courtesy The Topps Company.

His two-out, two-run homer tied the game, 9-9. Joe Mauer's drive put the Twins/Phillies game into extra innings.

the go-ahead run into scoring position with the pitcher on deck.

Rauch successfully bunted an 0-and-2 pitch to move the runners to second and third. Young dribbled a weak groundball toward new shortstop Juan Castro, for a run-scoring infield single to score Mauer. Morneau scooted to third base.

Matt Tolbert came to the plate and ripped a 1-and-1 pitch down the left-field line to score two more. The relay throw from Ben Francisco and Utley nailed Tolbert trying to stretch his hit into a two-out triple; however, the Twins took a 13-10 lead. Utley kept the game alive by stroking a two-out double off Rauch, who struck out Howard on a 3-and-2 pitch to bring down the curtain on this wild 11-inning affair.

Rauch (2 innings pitched, 2 hits, 1 earned run, 1 strikeout) picked up a well-earned victory (2-1), even helping his team with the bat. In his only plate appearance of the season, the towering right-hander laid down a sacrifice bunt on an 0-and-2 pitch to set up the game-winning infield hit.

The Twins outscored the Phillies 9-1 in the ninth and later to snap a tiny two-game losing streak. Both teams combined to entertain 45,254 fans with 23 runs on 29 hits. Nine of those safeties left the ballpark, and pinch-hitters launched three of them.

After slugging his first career home run to give Minnesota its short-lived 10th-inning lead, Butera said, "When I hit it, I started running and then I thought, 'Whoa, it has a chance.'"[12]

"We're known not to quit and we didn't quit," Twins manager Gardenhire said. "A lot of great things happened out there."

The home clubhouse was more subdued, but hardly devastated. "This is a tough one," said Phillies skipper Manuel, "But we've been there before and we've always come back."

Even Lidge looked forward after his ninth-inning blown save. "We've been feeling real good about the way we've been pitching, but tonight we were just bad," he said. "We didn't do our job collectively, individually. We have to rebound from it."

Lidge's rebound would need to wait a little longer. The Twins' Carl Pavano outdueled Roy Halladay, 4-1, on Sunday afternoon. Pavano's complete-game four-hitter earned Minnesota the improbable series win, even after they lost Game One and trailed 9-4 in the ninth in this game.

Sources

In addition to the sources cited in the Notes, the author relied on Baseball-Reference.com for boxscores and play-by-play information.

See also:

Baseball Almanac: baseball-almanac.com/box-scores/boxscore.php?box-id=201006190PHI. Accessed April 13, 2020.

The Good Phight: thegoodphight.com/2018/7/30/17629510/jim-thome-and-charlie-manuel-formed-a-relationship-that-changed-phillies-baseball. Accessed April 13, 2020.

Note

1   Associated Press, "Mauer Caps Rally with Homer in 9th, Scores Twins' Winning Run in 11th," ESPN.com, June 20, 2010. espn.com/mlb/recap?gameId=300619122. Accessed April 13, 2020. All quotes come from this article.

A'S STAGE HISTORIC WORLD SERIES COMEBACK WITH 10-RUN INNING

OCTOBER 12, 1929:
PHILADELPHIA ATHLETICS 10,
CHICAGO CUBS 8,
(GAME FOUR OF THE 1929 WORLD SERIES)
AT SHIBE PARK, PHILADELPHIA

BY SCOTT FERKOVICH

The Chicago Cubs' Hack Wilson jogged out to his position in center field to start the home half of the seventh inning. Turning toward the diamond, he again took note of the late afternoon sun, which had descended to a point almost directly above Shibe Park's double-decked grandstand behind home plate. The dazzling orb's slanting rays were now aimed straight into his eyes. It had already made trouble for Wilson. Two innings earlier, in this fourth game of the 1929 World Series against the Philadelphia Athletics, he had dropped a fly ball after losing it in the October brightness. But he made a spectacular running, leaping grab of a deep fly off the bat of Joe Boley, the next batter. To many observers, it was one of the finest catches they'd ever seen in a World Series. Then, in the sixth, he had trouble with another ball because of the sun, but was able to corral it.

Luckily for the Cubs, Wilson's struggles had not resulted in any damage. Their starting pitcher, Charlie Root, winner of 19 games in 1929, was cruising, having allowed only three hits. Chicago's vaunted offense, meanwhile, had taken an 8-0 lead. It simply was not the Athletics' day.

Nine more outs was all Root needed. Nine more outs, and the Series would be tied at two games apiece. Just two days ago, the Series had seemed all but over, the Athletics having won the first two contests at Wrigley Field, including a 13-strikeout gem by seldom-used journeyman Howard Ehmke. Chicago took Game Three, however, in a hostile Shibe Park, behind Guy Bush's tough pitching. Now, the momentum seemingly had shifted back to manager

Joe McCarthy's Cubs. They had 22-game-winner Pat Malone ready for Game Five, and the final two would be back at Wrigley, where Chicago had been nearly

Down 8-0 in Game Four of the 1929 World Series, the Athletics scored 10 times in the bottom of the seventh. Jimmy Dykes singled in the second run of the rally and doubled in the ninth and 10th.

HISTORY MADE IN WILD GAME

Athletics Go Into Frenzy And Score Ten Runs In Seventh.

Headline from *Denver Post,* October 13, 1929.

unbeatable that summer, at 52-25. Only the Athletics, at 57-16, had had a better home record in the majors in 1929.

Al Simmons, Philadelphia's slugging left fielder, led off the seventh. On Root's third offering, "Bucketfoot Al" hit a home run to left that cleared the roof. The shutout was lost, and the home crowd finally had something to cheer about. Root took a new ball from home plate umpire Roy Van Graflan.

Jimmie Foxx singled, and Bing Miller hit a fly ball to center. The staggering Wilson lost it in the sun, and it fell in for a single, with Foxx taking second. Singles by Jimmy Dykes and Boley scored Foxx and Miller to make it 8-3.

With runners on first and third and nobody out, George Burns pinch hit for pitcher Eddie Rommel. He was quickly dispatched on a pop fly to shortstop Woody English, the runners holding.

Max Bishop, who had hit only .232 during the regular season but had also led the league with 128 walks, singled to left, scoring Dykes, sending Boley to third. Suddenly, the Cubs lead had been cut in half. McCarthy headed to the mound, took the ball from a frustrated Root, and waved in lefty Art Nehf from the bullpen to face the left-handed-hitting Mule Haas.

In center field, Wilson adjusted his cap and dark sunglasses, the better to peer in against the blinding beams of the sun. At 29, Wilson had led the National League in home runs three of the previous four seasons. Born in the steel mill town of Ellwood City,

Pennsylvania, he was the illegitimate son of an alcoholic steelworker and a teenage mother who died when he was seven.

Wilson didn't appear athletic at 5 feet 6 inches tall, 190 pounds, with an 18-inch neck, spindly lower legs, and size 5 1/2 feet that only a ballerina could love. Yet he could hit a baseball a mile. He began his big-league career with the New York Giants. But manager John McGraw, the dinosaur disciple of small ball, wasn't won over by the top-heavy Wilson, despite his .295 average in a limited role in his rookie year of 1924. The Giants traded him to the Toledo Mud Hens in August of 1925. Following that season, the Cubs, in an unnoticed transaction, acquired Wilson in the Rule 5 draft.

Wilson and Jazz-Age Chicago were partners in perfect pitch. In awe of his clouts onto Waveland Avenue, Wrigley Field's denizens cheered him in the afternoon, and then toasted him late into the night as he made the rounds of the Windy City's numerous speakeasies. In 1930, his *annus mirabilis,* Wilson whacked 56 home runs, and established a major-league single-season record with 191 RBIs, one of baseball's most enduring numbers. 1931 was Wilson's *annus horribilis,* with only 13 home runs and 61 RBIs; within three years his career was finished, the fall precipitated by alcohol and riotous living. He gained induction into Cooperstown in 1979, 31 years after his death. But on the late afternoon of October 2, 1929, at the corner of 21st and Lehigh in the City of Brotherly Love, Hack Wilson was about to engage in combat one too many times with Hyperion the sun-god, and end up getting burned.

One out, runners on first and third, 8-4 in favor of Chicago. Mule Haas, who had hit 16 home runs in 1929, sent Nehf's first fastball on a line toward center field. Wilson drifted back. Despite his sunglasses, he again lost the ball in the glare. It soared over his head and rolled to the fence. The desperate outfielder ran the ball down, Boley and Bishop scoring. Haas, defying his nickname, sprinted like lightning around the bases. Wilson heaved a late throw in, and Haas slid into the home dish in a cloud of dust. Safe, declared Van Graflan.

The Cubs had blinked, and the score was suddenly Chicago 8, Philadelphia 7, with only one out.

The 36-year-old Nehf, winner of 184 games over 15 seasons, walked Mickey Cochrane. McCarthy, for the second time in the inning, marched out to the mound, and Nehf, for the final time in his big-league career, marched off of it.

Enter pitcher John Frederick "Sheriff" Blake, who failed to lay down the law. Al Simmons, back in the saddle for the second time that inning, singled to left. Foxx did the same, scoring Cochrane to tie it. McCarthy yanked the badge off Blake and tried his luck with Pat Malone, who plunked Bing Miller with his first pitch. Jimmy Dykes doubled, driving in two more to put the Athletics up by a deuce.

The Shibe Park crowd was delirious with delight. Strikeouts by Boley and Burns brought the frame to an end, but the book had already been written.

Athletics manager Connie Mack brought in Lefty Grove, winner of 20 in 1929, to start the eighth. He fanned four of the six batters he faced. At 3:42 pm, Rogers Hornsby flied to left for the final out of the game. Wilson was left on one knee in the on-deck circle.

What had looked like a 2-2 Series tie had suddenly become a three-games-to-one Athletics lead. Chicago never recovered. They lost the Series the following day in equally heartbreaking fashion, when Philadelphia scored three runs in the bottom of the ninth to wipe out a 2-0 Cubs lead.

Declared Mack to his men after Game Four, "I'd just like to be able to express to you the things I feel. But I can't. I'll have to let it go at that." To reporters he gushed, "I've never seen anything like that rally. There is nothing in baseball history to compare it with. It was the greatest display of punch and fighting ability I've ever seen on a field."[1]

In the dejected Cubs clubhouse, McCarthy mumbled, "You can't beat the sun, can you?"[2] Then, in an effort to deflect blame from his star center fielder, he pointed out, "The poor kid simply lost the ball in the sun, and he didn't put the sun there."[3]

Ed Burns of the *Chicago Tribune* wrote, "The greatest debacle, the most terrific flop in the history of the World Series. We've been looking at our score book for an hour now, thinking there must have been some horrible mistake, but ten she is folks."[4]

"Couldn't see the balls," Wilson clarified.[5] "I'm a big chump, and nobody's going to tell me different."[6]

Wilson and his four-year-old son Bobby departed the park together in a taxi. "The devil with them, Daddy," he remarked. "We'll get them next year."[7]

Sources

In addition to the sources cited in the Notes, the author also consulted Baseball-Reference.com and the following:

Chastain, Bill. *Hack's 191: Hack Wilson and His Incredible 1930 Season* (Guilford, Connecticut: Lyons Press), 2012.

Kashatus, Bill. *Connie Mack's '29 Triumph* (Jefferson, North Carolina: McFarland), 1999.

Notes

1   Roberts Ehrgott, *Mr. Wrigley's Ball Club: Chicago and the Cubs During the Jazz Age* (Lincoln: University of Nebraska Press, 2013), 200.

2   Ehrgott, 201.

3   Clifton Blue Parker, *Fouled Away: The Baseball Tragedy of Hack Wilson* (Jefferson, North Carolina: McFarland, 2000), 85.

4   Ehrgott, 201.

5   Ehrgott, 201.

6   Parker, 85.

7   Parker, 85.

ALOMAR, BLUE JAYS EMERGE OUT OF SHADOWS IN ALCS GAME FOUR

OCTOBER 11, 1992:
TORONTO BLUE JAYS 7,
OAKLAND A'S 6
(11 INNINGS),
GAME FOUR OF THE AMERICAN LEAGUE
CHAMPIONSHIP SERIES
AT OAKLAND-ALAMEDA COLISEUM, OAKLAND

BY ADRIAN FUNG

When Blue Jays second baseman Roberto Alomar stepped into the late-afternoon shadows at home plate in the top of the ninth inning, a figurative darkness overshadowed Toronto as well. Needing two runs to tie the game, time was running out for the Blue Jays to rally. Toronto trailed 6-4 in Game Four of the 1992 American League Championship Series and was three outs away from a loss that would even their series against the Athletics at two games apiece.

Alomar dug in against Dennis Eckersley.

All-Star vs. All-Star.

Best vs. best.

It was the apical moment of the Toronto-Oakland rivalry that had simmered over the past few years. Since 1985, both clubs had won their respective division four times. Yet in the postseason, the Blue Jays always fizzled while Oakland sizzled. The Athletics added three pennants and the 1989 World Series title after easily pushing aside the Blue Jays in a five-game ALCS that ended tersely. In the ninth inning of the final game, Toronto manager Cito Gaston asked the umpires to check if Eckersley was scuffing baseballs. An insulted Eckersley shouted profanities at an irate Gaston who fired right back at the Oakland closer after the game.[1]

In Game Four of the 1992 ALCS Oakland jumped out to a 6-1 lead, and the Toronto bats looked lifeless entering the eighth inning. However, Alomar led off with a double, chasing Oakland starter Bob Welch and ushering in reliever Jeff Parrett. Alomar promptly stole third and scored on a Joe Carter single. After Dave Winfield singled Carter to third, Oakland manager Tony LaRussa had seen enough. With the potential tying run on deck, he signaled for Eckersley from the bullpen.

The Oakland-born Eckersley, 37, was a six-time All-Star, widely acknowledged as the best closer in the game. He started 1992 with 36 straight saves en route to a major league-leading 51.[2] Since 1988, Eckersley was simply dominant. No reliever in either league recorded more saves (220), had a lower WHIP (walks plus hits per innings pitched) ratio (0.792), or had a strikeout-to-walk ratio (9.95) that was even half as good as his mark.[3] His 10 career LCS saves were already a record that would not be broken until 2009.[4]

But on this afternoon, Toronto was not interested in history, only in stringing together hits to climb back into the game. The next two Toronto hitters – John Olerud and Candy Maldonado – attacked early, each jumping on Eckersley's first pitch for run-scoring singles, cutting the Athletics lead to 6–4, putting the tying runs on first and second. However, Eckersley coolly retired the next three batters, ending the inning with a strikeout of pinch-hitter Ed Sprague. Following the strikeout, Eckersley pumped his fist, and then yelled and pointed at the Toronto dugout. Immediately, the Blue Jays bench rose up indignantly. "It was a little gesture and the guys responded. We got very, uh, vocal. It's a good thing the TV cameras weren't in the dugout," said Winfield.[5] "He should know to let sleeping dogs lie. You don't wake 'em up. It's a cardinal sin in baseball," added Toronto starter Jack Morris.[6]

Eckersley later downplayed his actions. "Aw hell, I was just excited. I mean, things were starting to slip away and I thought that strikeout of Sprague was the ballgame. Sometimes I do crazy stuff, but I didn't mean to show those guys up. It was just a reaction to the moment."[7]

In the ninth, as darkness enveloped the home-plate dirt, leadoff hitter Devon White lined a single to left field, then raced all the way to third when Rickey Henderson misplayed the ball. Up stepped Alomar, representing the tying run.

Alomar, 24, was already a three-time All-Star and two-time Gold Glove Award winner. The Toronto second baseman was considered one of the best young all-around, five-tool players in baseball. Alomar had already generated 23.3 wins above replacement (WAR) in his first five seasons. Only four other second basemen before him had accumulated more than 23.3 WAR over the first five seasons of their respective careers, and he was the first to do so since Jackie Robinson 41 years ago.[8]

Carter had given Alomar some simple advice moments before in the on-deck circle: "Look for a strike … hit the ball hard and try to keep the inning going."[9] With the count 2-2, Eckersley fired. Alomar swung, immediately dropped his bat and thrust both arms upward in triumph as he slowly trotted up the first-base line, out of the darkness at home plate and into the sunshine of the basepath, knowing his line drive would clear the right-field wall. When the ball landed, just to the left of a policeman standing on a stairway beyond the fence, Alomar continued to slowly circle the bases. The entire Toronto bench rose up, shouting, gesturing, and staring out at the stunned Eckersley.

"Eck stuck it in our faces and we kicked his ass," a fired-up Morris thundered, after the game. "We're happy as hell about it. I used to do a lot of gesturing and stuff like Eck does … and I realized I had to change. You just don't go around trying to show teams up – it may finally have come back to hurt him today."[10]

For the tying run, Alomar emphatically jumped on home plate with both feet. It was his fourth hit and fifth consecutive time reaching base on the day. The Blue Jays had finally broken through. On one swing of Alomar's bat, the constant disappointment of postseasons past seemed to melt away. His game-tying home run was not only the biggest clutch hit in Blue Jays history, but it lifted the franchise to uncharted territory: Never before had a Toronto player come through under intense playoff pressure as Alomar had, rejuvenating his team when all hope looked lost.

"This was the greatest game of my career, and that home run was the best thing that ever happened in my life," gushed Alomar. "As soon as I made contact, I knew it was out of there. As I was rounding the bases, I was thinking, 'Yeah, that ball is gone, gone, GONE!'" Analyzing the at-bat, Alomar continued, "That's not the Eckersley I've come to know. He wasn't throwing the good slider he usually does – it was flat and his fastball wasn't moving that much. On the home run, I was hoping he'd come inside and he did."[11]

A somber Eckersley was matter-of-fact about what transpired. "Hey, it's Toronto's day. They hit the f--- out of me . . . I just couldn't stop the bleeding. That's as hard as I've gotten hit since I can remember. Failure of this magnitude is tough to handle. I wanted to throw it down and away but I threw it high and he hit the s--- out of it. What can I say? It's going to be tough to sleep tonight."[12]

The remainder of the game was similarly pressure-packed. Toronto nearly took the lead after Alomar's home run by loading the bases, but reliever Jim Corsi retired Pat Borders on a groundout to end the inning. For Eckersley, it was his final postseason appearance in an Oakland uniform.

In the last of the ninth, the Athletics were 90 feet from winning the game, but with one out, fireballer Duane Ward got Terry Steinbach to hit a grounder to second. Alomar came up throwing to the plate to gun down pinch-runner Eric Fox, and one pitch later, Carney Lansford grounded into a fielder's choice to send the game to extra innings.

Finally, in the top of the 11th, Toronto took the lead. Derek Bell worked a nine-pitch leadoff walk, and moved to third on the next pitch when Maldonado, again attacking early, punched a single to right field. With one out, Borders lined to left, deep enough so that Bell could tag and score. In the bottom of the inning, Toronto closer Tom Henke threw just 13 pitches to lock down the most improbable victory in Blue Jays history, and ending the longest game in ALCS history at that time (4 hours and 25 minutes).[13]

The Blue Jays became the first team in postseason history to come back and win after trailing by at least five runs after seven innings.[14]

Somehow, Toronto had the 7-6 victory, a 3-1 ALCS lead, and the psychological edge of knowing it could beat the best, Eckersley, the winner of both the 1992 Cy Young and Most Valuable Player Awards. The game was a gilded building block in Toronto's path to eventually winning its first World Series two weeks later in Atlanta. It would not have been possible, however, had Alomar not struck the biggest blow, helping Toronto emerge from the shadows of another possible ALCS defeat and ultimately triumph.

Sources

Besides the sources listed in the Notes, the author consulted the following:

https://www.baseball-reference.com/boxes/OAK/OAK199210110.shtml

https://www.retrosheet.org/boxesetc/1992/B10110OAK1992.htm

Notes

1   Dave Perkins, "'I Don't Cheat,' Eck Rasps at Cito," *Toronto Star*, October 9, 1989: D1.

2   Craig Barbarino, "1992 Year in Review," *Official Major League Baseball Program – World Series* (1992): 29.

3   http://bbref.com/pi/shareit/sX3xf

4   http://www.baseball-reference.com/postseason/LCS_pitching.shtml

5   Rosie DiManno, *Glory Jays: Canada's World Series Champions* (Champaign, Illinois: Sagamore Publishing, 1993), 252–253.

6   DiManno.

7   Tom Cheek and Howard Berger, *Road to Glory: An Insider's Look at 16 Years of Blue Jay Baseball* (Toronto: Warwick Publishing, 1993), 299.

8   http://bbref.com/pi/shareit/P4eOo

9   Dave Perkins, "Alomar's Heroic Homer A Shot Heard Around Blue Jays' World," *Toronto Star*, October 12, 1992: D2.

10   Cheek and Berger, 299-300.

11   Cheek and Berger, 300.

12   Cheek and Berger, 300.

13   "Extra-Inning Affair Marks Longest Game in AL Playoff History," *Toronto Star*, October 12, 1992: D5.

14   Jack Curry, "The Playoffs: Who's Sorry Now? The A's, Not Jays," *New York Times*, October 12, 1992: C4.

BLUE JAYS BATTLE BACK
TO WIN HIGHEST-SCORING GAME
IN WORLD SERIES HISTORY

OCTOBER 20, 1993:
TORONTO BLUE JAYS 15,
PHILADELPHIA PHILLIES 14,
AT VETERANS STADIUM, PHILADELPHIA

BY BRIAN M. FRANK

"I think this might go down as one of the great games in the annals of World Series history," proclaimed Philadelphia Phillies manager Jim Fregosi after his team fell to the Toronto Blue Jays in a wild, high-scoring affair.[1] Declaring a game as one of the all-time greatest is not something you'd expect from the losing manager. However, it's not that shocking considering the incredible events Fregosi had just witnessed.

Toronto sent Todd Stottlemyre, 11-12 with a 4.84 ERA during the regular season, to the mound in Game Four in an attempt to take a three-games-to-one lead in the 1993 World Series. Stottlemyre had been in the news during the week for a public verbal spat with the mayor of Philadelphia, Ed Rendell, who'd mockingly said he'd like to hit off the Blue Jays right-hander.[2] He was opposed by Tommy Greene, who went 16-4 during the regular season with a 3.42 ERA. Greene was coming off a clutch performance in a series-clinching Game Six of the NLCS over Greg Maddux and the Atlanta Braves.

Frank Fitzpatrick of the *Philadelphia Inquirer* described the scene at Veterans Stadium, writing that there was "a deep grey mist hanging over the jammed stadium, moistening the turf to a treacherous sheen, muddying the mound and leaving baseballs difficult to grasp."[3] The eerie weather was fitting for some of the bizarre events that were about to take place.

Rickey Henderson started the game by lining Greene's third pitch into left-center field for a double. Greene then walked Devon White on four pitches. After Roberto Alomar was retired, Joe Carter hit a

groundball to third that Dave Hollins made a diving stop on, but his throw to second was too late to get the speedy White, and the bases were loaded. It looked as if Greene might be able to get out of the jam unscathed

It was a high-scoring game, 14-0 through seven, but a six-run eighth put the Jays on top, the final two coming on Devon White's triple to center field.

when he retired American League batting champion John Olerud on a foul popup for the second out. However, Paul Molitor drew a four-pitch walk and Tony Fernandez hit a two-run single to give the Blue Jays a 3-0 lead.

The lead didn't last long. Stottlemyre struggled with his control in the early going. He walked leadoff man Lenny Dykstra and, after retiring the next two batters, walked Dave Hollins, Darren Daulton, and Jim Eisenreich to bring home the Phillies' first run. Milt Thompson then lined a ball off the wall in center field just over the glove of a leaping Devon White for a three-run triple, and the Phillies led 4-3.

Stottlemyre walked to lead off the second inning, and when Roberto Alomar singled on a chopper up the middle with two outs, the Toronto hurler attempted to go from first to third. Unaccustomed as an American League pitcher to running the bases, he made a less than graceful slide into third and was called out on a close play. During his head-first slide, his helmet flew off as his face slammed into the dirt. "I don't know if I would call it a slide or what," Stottlemyre said. "When I hit the ground, I went black. I don't know what happened really. I blacked out for a while and when I got up, I went out to the mound and just tried to throw the ball down the middle of the plate."[4]

Stottlemyre returned to the mound with his chin bloodied but unbandaged. The first batter he faced, Tommy Greene, lined a single up the middle. The next batter, Lenny Dykstra, blasted a two-run home run just inside the right-field foul pole, and Philadelphia had a 6-3 lead.

The Blue Jays battled back in the third. Run-scoring singles by Fernandez and Pat Borders off Greene and a two-run single by White off reliever Roger Mason put Toronto back on top, 7-6. But Mariano Duncan's looping single in the fourth inning off Blue Jays reliever Al Leiter tied the score.

Earlier in the day, Toronto manager Cito Gaston had decided to play Paul Molitor, normally Toronto's designated hitter, at third base in place of Ed Sprague in order to keep his hot bat in the lineup.[5] Entering the game, Molitor was 6-for-11 in the Series with a home run and a triple. Dave Hollins, who'd been struggling at the plate, took advantage of the fact that Molitor hadn't played third since 1990, beating out a bunt down the third-base line to lead off the fifth. Darren Daulton followed by blasting a two-run homer deep to right field to give the Phillies a 9-7 lead. Eisenreich reached on a bunt toward second base, and Thompson brought him home on a double to increase the Phillies'

lead. Two outs later, as rain fell hard, Dykstra belted his second home run of the game, a two-run shot that gave the Phillies a 12-7 lead.

The next batter, Mariano Duncan, singled. Then one of the more bizarre incidents of the game took place. Gaston came to the mound and signaled for a left-hander to come in from the bullpen. As right-hander Mark Eichhorn came in and tossed a couple of warmup pitches, Gaston explained to the umpires that he'd actually wanted left-hander Tony Castillo. However, the phone from Toronto's dugout to the bullpen wasn't working and Castillo was unaware he was supposed to be warming. "The bullpen phone wasn't working at all," Toronto closer Duane Ward said. "The dugout just gave us hand signals: left-hander, right-hander, big guy, short guy. It didn't matter."[6] The umpires allowed Castillo to come into the game and take as many warmup pitches as he needed. For the rest of the game, both teams used walkie-talkies to communicate with their bullpens.

David West, who allowed all six batters he faced in the 1991 World Series to reach base, entered the game for Philadelphia in the sixth inning with a World Series ERA of infinity. He gave up a double to White and an RBI single to Alomar before getting Carter to fly out for his first World Series out, lowering his ERA to 162.00. Alomar scored on Fernandez's groundout to cut the Phillies' lead to 12-9. Philadelphia got the run back when Hollins scored on a single by Thompson in the sixth.

Some observers thought Toronto might be waving the white flag when Gaston didn't pinch-hit for his pitcher, Castillo, to lead off the seventh inning trailing 13-9. "Our bullpen is a little short right now," Gaston later explained.[7]

Castillo remained in the game for the seventh and loaded the bases on a single and a pair of walks. He then hit Daulton on the hand to force in a run and increase the Phillies' lead to 14-9.

But the night wasn't over yet. In the top of the eighth with two on and one out, Molitor hit a hard groundball that Hollins was unable to handle at third. It wound up being an RBI double to cut the Phillies' lead to 14-10.

Fregosi opted to bring in closer Mitch "Wild Thing" Williams. Williams had a well-earned reputation for flirting with disaster, to the point that Phillies ace Curt Schilling covered his head with a towel so he wouldn't have to watch when his team's closer was on the mound.

Fernandez greeted Williams with an RBI single to make it 14-11. Borders walked to bring the tying run to the plate. Pinch-hitter Ed Sprague struck out for the second out, but Henderson kept the rally going when he singled to center to bring home Molitor and Fernandez and cut Toronto's deficit to a single run. Devon White brought the Blue Jays all the way back with a two-run triple. Borders crossed the plate followed by a jubilant Henderson. Toronto was ahead 15-14, its first lead since the fourth inning.

On a night that it seemed no pitcher could be effective, the Blue Jays' Mike Timlin and Duane Ward came in to prove otherwise. The two combined to strike out the side in the bottom of the eighth, and Ward retired the Phillies one-two-three in the ninth. The final out was recorded at 12:28 A.M.

The marathon contest set many World Series records, notably: most runs scored by both teams (29); most runs scored by a losing team (14); and longest game (4:14).[8]

"We've played in a lot of funny, crazy games this year," Dave Hollins said. "And this may have been the craziest of all."[9] Blue Jays players agreed that the game was one for the ages. "I don't think I've ever been in a game that was quite that competitive," said Rickey Henderson, a veteran of 17 major-league seasons.[10] Paul Molitor, in his 16th season, said, "That was the most exciting win I've ever been a part of."[11]

Phillies second baseman Mickey Morandini may have summed up the game best: "You score 14 runs and lose. You can't do that. We've got to win this one. … It's hard to believe. Sure it is. But after the way the game went, it's not hard to believe at all."[12]

Sources

In addition to the sources cited in the Notes, the author consulted Baseball-Reference.com and Retrosheet.org.

Notes

1   Paul Hagen, "Blue Jays Win on Late TD," *Philadelphia Daily News*, October 21, 1993: 94.

2   Stottlemyre got the last laugh in the verbal tit-for-tat, when he exclaimed in his speech at the Blue Jays' World Series victory celebration, "I've got one message for the mayor of Philly, and I hope you're out there looking. You can kiss my ass!" youtube.com/watch?v=tefMJNIjzDE.

3   Frank Fitzpatrick, "Toronto Takes a 3-1 Lead on Phils," *Philadelphia Inquirer*, October 21, 1993: C6.

4   Sam Donnellon, "Stottlemyre: A Wild Two Innings," *Philadelphia Daily News*, October 21, 1993: 86.

5   The day before, in GameThree, the the first game without a designated hitter, Molitor played first base in place of the left-handed-hitting John Olerud against left-handed starter Danny Jackson.

6   Rich Hofmann, "As Strange as It Gets," *Philadelphia Daily News*, October 21, 1993: 95.

7   Michael Sokolove, "A Strategic Battle of the Middle Relief Versus the Closers," *Philadelphia Inquirer*, October 21, 1993: C10.

8   Game Three of the 2018 World Series between the Red Sox and Dodgers is as of 2020 the longest World Series game timewise. It went 18 innings and lasted 7 hours and 20 minutes. But Game Six of the 1993 World Series is still the longest nine-inning game.

9   Hagen.

10 Ted Silary, "We Feel Great," *Philadelphia Daily News*, October 21, 1993: 87.

11 Allan Ryan, "'I Wasn't Bad' at Third Base, Molitor Says," *Toronto Star*, October 21, 1993: C3.

12 Jayson Stark, "Sudden Twist Turns Must Win into Fight for Series Survival," *Philadelphia Inquirer*, October 21, 1993: C12.

DREW WALK-OFF CAPS COMEBACK, KEEPS DEFENDING SERIES CHAMPION RED SOX' REPEAT HOPES ALIVE

OCTOBER 16, 2008:
BOSTON RED SOX 8,
TAMPA BAY RAYS 7,
AT FENWAY PARK, BOSTON

BY MARK S. STERNMAN

After a scoreless American League Championship Series opener, the Tampa Bay offense exploded for a total of 31 runs to lead the Rays to victories in each of the next three games and put the franchise on the precipice of its first World Series appearance. With a

J. D. Drew homered for two runs in the eighth and then, in the bottom of the ninth, won the game for the Red Sox with a walk-off single.

Courtesy of the Boston Red Sox.

7-0 lead heading into the bottom of the seventh, a deficit so deep that only one team had overcome it in postseason history,[1] Tampa looked primed to advance.

The pitching matchup featured two of the wilder pitchers in the American League.

Daisuke Matsuzaka (5.0 walks per nine innings) had hurled seven innings of four-hit ball in Game One and had an extra day of rest going into Game Five. After allowing a single to countryman Akinori Iwamura, Matsuzaka faced the scalding-hot B.J. Upton, who had homered three times in the first four games. Upton went deep again, and the Rays had a 2-0 lead two batters into Game Five.

Matsuzaka retired the next three batters in order. Game Two starter Scott Kazmir (4.1 walks per nine), a controversial selection to pitch,[2] took the mound for Tampa Bay and worked around two walks in the bottom of the frame to preserve the lead.

Matsuzaka walked Gabe Gross with two outs in the top of the second. Gross stole second but failed to score. Kazmir again put two on in the bottom of the inning, this time via a single and a hit batter, but again stranded both runners.

The top of the order of the Rays struck again in the third. With one out, Upton singled. Carlos Peña, who attended Northeastern University about a half-mile from Fenway Park, homered to put Tampa up 4-0. Evan Longoria did the same, and the Rays held a seemingly commanding 5-0 lead. Boston had scored just five runs over its last 18 innings.

Matsuzaka got the next five batters in order. Kazmir's effective wildness continued. He gave up a single in the third and a walk and a wild pitch in the fourth, but the Red Sox still could not score.

Boston manager Terry Francona would not let Matsuzaka face Upton again after he walked Iwamura to start the fifth. Instead, Francona brought in lefty specialist Hideki Okajima, who had pitched two innings in a game only three times in the regular season before doing so in Game Two. Okajima proceeded to match that feat with two scoreless frames.[3] After fanning Upton, Okajima gave up an infield hit to Peña. Iwamura stole third, putting runners on the corners with one out. The Rays had the ideal batter at the plate, but the right-handed cleanup hitter Longoria struck out against the southpaw. Carl Crawford grounded out, and Okajima kept the score at 5-0.

"It had been a lifeless game for the Red Sox, a lifeless game for their fans, the 38,437 out of a game that seemed out of the Sox' reach from the start," said the *Boston Globe*. "Some began heading for the exits before the top of the seventh inning. And those who did missed the magic."[4]

Both pitchers cruised into the seventh, when Boston native Manny Delcarmen relieved Okajima and immediately put his hometown team into a deeper hole. Delcarmen walked Jason Bartlett, the light-hitting shortstop who batted last for the Rays, and compounded his sin by passing Iwamura as well. With the season fast slipping away and the terrifying Upton due, Francona brought in his closer. Undoubtedly unaccustomed to coming into a game in such a predicament, Jonathan Papelbon seemed to close out the hopes of the Red Sox. With Upton at the plate, the Tampa runners pulled a double steal. Upton promptly doubled them both home, and the Rays went up 7-0. Papelbon intentionally passed Peña to get the platoon advantage and set up the double play. Longoria complied, Crawford grounded out, too, but Boston faced a deep 7-0 deficit going into the bottom of the seventh.

Joe Maddon, the Rays' manager, removed Kazmir after he had thrown 111 pitches over six innings. Grant Balfour gave up a double to Jed Lowrie, the inning's first batter, but he remained at second with two outs. *Boston Globe* columnist Dan Shaughnessy wrote that at this point in the game the local nine "appeared to be rolling over like obedient canines."[5] Then Coco Crisp singled Lowrie to third, bringing Dustin Pedroia to the plate.

After the end of the season, Pedroia would win the AL Most Valuable Player Award for his regular-season performance. He delivered in the postseason clutch here, too, with a single that got the Red Sox on the scoreboard and brought up David Ortiz.

According to the sagacious Thomas Boswell of the *Washington Post*, "the situation called for a left-hander with power stuff, especially a tough curveball to overpower Ortiz. ... In other words, it called for [J.P.] Howell, who in fact did face Ortiz later in the game and struck him out easily."[6]

In a plate appearance that typified his glorious postseason career, Ortiz delivered "a dramatic, majestic three-run homer"[7] that got Boston within three runs at 7-4. Dan Wheeler replaced Balfour and retired Kevin Youkilis to end a seventh inning that saw both teams combine to score six runs.

Papelbon set Tampa Bay down in order in the eighth before Wheeler returned to the mound. He walked Jason Bay and then gave up a homer to J.D. Drew, a question mark for postseason play because of a herniated disk,[8] to shrink the lead to a single run. Wheeler got the next two batters, but "[w]hen Mark Kotsay's double sailed over B.J. Upton in center field, the Red Sox believed even more. Upton had seemingly caught every ball the Sox hit near center. ... Crisp fought through a 10-pitch at-bat and singled to right to drive in Kotsay with the tying run. In the space of 10 batters, the Red Sox had scored seven runs."[9]

Papelbon had thrown 38 pitches, a lot for a closer even in an elimination game, so Francona turned to Justin Masterson. Bartlett singled to start the ninth, and Upton walked after an out to put two Rays on base. Masterson had a masterful sinker, and his groundball stuff resulted in a Peña double play to keep the contest tied.

Howell came on for Tampa for the bottom of the ninth. The Rays could have understandably thought about extra innings after Howell got Pedroia on a grounder and struck out Ortiz. But Youkilis got a hit on a groundball to third and went to second on Longoria's throwing error. Howell walked Bay intentionally. Drew sent the crowd home in a delirium with a single, "a line-drive winner over the head of [right fielder] Gabe Gross, who appeared to be paralyzed by a screamer hit directly over his head[,]"[10] to score Youkilis. The defending champions had rallied from a near-death experience and lived to fight another day.

Boston took Game Six but fell in Game Seven. Rays fans would recall Game Five as a meaningless stumble on the franchise's way to the only World Series in its history (through 2019). Red Sox fans have forgotten about Game Five and instead rue what might have been had not future Red Sox David Price earned the save by striking out J.D. Drew with the bases loaded and two outs in the eighth inning of Game Seven to preserve a 3-1 lead and an ultimate 4-3 ALCS win for the Rays.

Notes

1   The 1929 Philadelphia Athletics trailed 8-0 against the Chicago Cubs going into the bottom of the seventh inning of Game Four of the World Series. The A's scored 10 in the seventh and went on to win the game, 10-8.

2   Michael Vega, "Their Magical Journey Came Out of Nowhere," *Boston Globe*, October 17, 2008: E7. Conventional wisdom suggests starting right-handed pitchers at Fenway Park as they will have the platoon advantage against right-handed hitters looking to take advantage of the proximity of the left-field wall. In two career postseason starts prior to this one, Kazmir also had an ERA in excess of 6.50.

3   Okajima would do the same in Game Six. He had an outstanding ACLS, facing 24 batters and retiring 22. Okajima gave up an infield single and a walk while striking out five.

4   Amalie Benjamin, "Sox Are Alive after Improbable Comeback," *Boston Globe*, October 17, 2008: E9.

5   Dan Shaughnessy, "Red Sox Stay Alive with Comeback Win vs. Rays," *Boston Globe*, October 17, 2008: A6.

6   Thomas Boswell, "Rays Manage to Lose," *Washington Post*, October 17, 2008.

7   Dave Sheinin, "Red Sox Back from the Dead," *Washington Post*, October 17, 2008.

8   Adam Kilgore, "Familiar Refrain: Drew Came Through," *Boston Globe*, October 17, 2008: E5. "Wheeler threw Crisp nothing bust fastballs" according to Chris Forsberg, "Crisp Went to Higher Power for Strength," *Boston Globe*, October 17, 2008: E6.

9   Jack Curry, "Down by 7-0, Red Sox Force a Game 6," *New York Times*, October 17, 2008.

10   Bob Ryan, "Champions Won't Go Quietly," *Boston Globe*, October 17, 2008: E7.

BEFORE DAVID ORTIZ, DAVE HENDERSON SPARKED RED SOX WITH POSTSEASON HEROICS

OCTOBER 12, 1986:
BOSTON RED SOX 7,
CALIFORNIA ANGELS 6
(11 INNINGS),
1986 AMERICAN LEAGUE CHAMPIONSHIP SERIES
GAME FIVE
AT ANAHEIM STADIUM, ANAHEIM

BY ALLAN WOOD

Before there was David Ortiz, there was Dave Henderson. Before Big Papi thrilled Red Sox fans with his October heroics, the man they called Hendu brought Boston back from the dead in Game Five of the 1986 ALCS.

With the Angels one strike away from winning the pennant, Henderson – a backup outfielder obtained from the Seattle Mariners in mid-August – crushed a home run that gave Boston a 6-5 lead. Then, after the Angels tied the game in their half of the ninth, Henderson knocked in the game-winning run with a sacrifice fly in the 11th. The Red Sox' 7-6 victory sent the ALCS back to Fenway Park for Game Six (and, possibly, Game Seven). (Henderson also homered in the 10th inning of Game Six of the 1986 World Series; it would have been the Red Sox' World Series-winning run if not for the Mets' comeback.)

The California Angels led this series three games to one and fully expected to clinch the pennant in front of their own fans. Before the game, Red Sox players cited the Kansas City Royals, who came from being down 1-3 in both the ALCS (against Toronto) and World Series (against St. Louis) to capture a world championship.

With his team's backs to the wall, manager John McNamara gave the ball to Bruce Hurst, who had pitched a complete-game victory in Game Two. Like Roger Clemens in Game Four, Hurst would be starting on three days' rest. The Red Sox faced Mike Witt, who had gone the distance in California's Game One win.

Boston drew first blood in the second inning, when Jim Rice led off with a single and Rich Gedman lined a two-run homer into the right-field seats.

Hurst ended up pitching six innings, and left the game trailing 3-2. Bob Boone led off the third inning with a solo home run down by the left-field corner. With two outs in the sixth, Doug DeCinces ripped a double into the gap in right-center. Bobby Grich, who had struck out in his two earlier at-bats, drove a 1-and-2 pitch to deep left-center. Dave Henderson, who had taken over for Tony Armas in center field in the previous inning, raced toward the wall. Henderson timed his leap perfectly and the ball landed squarely in his glove. But his momentum carried him into the wall and his wrist struck the top of the fence. The collision jarred the ball loose and it fell over the fence. It was a two-run homer for Grich – and the Angels led 3-2.

"I thought I had it all the way," Henderson said. "But when my wrist hit the top of the fence it shook the ball loose and it was out of there. I was really disappointed, because I thought I should have caught it."[1]

California added two runs off reliever Bob Stanley in the seventh, and led 5-2.

Meanwhile, Witt was (again) having little trouble with the Boston hitters. After Gedman's blast in the second, Witt retired the next eight batters and 10 of the next 11. Gedman broke up Witt's string with a one-out double in the fifth, but Armas flied to left and Spike Owen grounded to second. Boston had men on base in the sixth, seventh, and eighth innings, but could not get anyone past first base.

The Anaheim Stadium crowd was roaring as Witt faced the heart of the Red Sox order in the ninth inning. Three more outs – and the Angels would clinch their first-ever pennant. Bill Buckner grounded a single up the middle, and was replaced by pinch-runner Dave Stapleton. Jim Rice fouled off two pitches, then looked at strike three on the outside edge.

Don Baylor worked the count to 2-and-2 and took a very close pitch that was inside and called a ball. Witt's full-count pitch was outside, but Baylor reached out and hooked it, pulling it to deep left. The ball carried and carried, sailing over the fence for a two-run homer. The crowd was quieter, but they knew their Angels still held a 5-4 lead – and when Dwight Evans fouled to third for the second out, they began loudly cheering again.

One out away – and Gene Mauch came out of the dugout to make a pitching change. He wanted left-hander Gary Lucas to face Gedman, who had singled, doubled, and homered against Witt. Gedman had faced Lucas only twice before – July 27, 1986, and in Game Four of this ALCS – and he had struck out both times.

Witt, who had thrown 123 pitches, said he was not tired. "I felt like I was pitching from the seventh inning on, on adrenaline mostly. But I was getting people out. … I called Boone out. We were going to discuss how we were going to handle [Gedman]. But … we never got to discuss it."[2]

Lucas threw only one pitch – and it sailed up and in and hit Gedman on the right hand. As the Boston catcher trotted to first base, Mauch made another change, bringing in closer Donnie Moore to face Dave Henderson. Henderson took a ball low, then a strike that was a little higher. When he swung and missed on a pitch low and away, Moore and the Angels were one strike away.

Dave Stapleton: "I looked across the field and I could see everyone in the Angels dugout getting ready

to celebrate. … They had those nice little smiles that you get before you start hugging everyone."[3]

Moore threw ball two in the dirt, and Henderson fouled off two pitches. Moore's 2-and-2 pitch – the seventh pitch of the at-bat – came in a little low. Henderson swung and as soon as he hit it, he knew. The ball sailed far over the fence in left for a two-run home run – a shot that gave the Red Sox a 6-5 lead. Henderson took three steps out of the batter's box, watching the flight of the ball. As it cleared the fence, he jumped and spun around. And then he began a fast trot around the bases.[4]

Henderson: "The pitch I fouled off was a fastball I should have hit. I had to step out of the batter's box and gather myself, think about what I had to do. With two strikes I had to protect the plate. I really just wanted to reach down and make sure I at least put the ball in play."[5]

Moore: "I'd been throwing him fastballs, and he was fouling them off, fouling them off. Then I threw him an offspeed pitch and I shouldn't have thrown it. I should have stayed with the hard stuff. The kind of

The Anaheim Angels were one strike away from winning the American League pennant, Dave Henderson hit a ninth-inning homer that kept the Red Sox in contention, then an 11th-inning sacrifice fly for the win.

bat speed he has is offspeed. That pitch was right in his swing."[6]

Stanley began the bottom of the ninth – his third inning of work – by giving up a single to Boone. Ruppert Jones pinch-ran, and Gary Pettis bunted him to second. Lefty Joe Sambito came out of the bullpen. Rob Wilfong knocked Sambito's first pitch into right field. Dwight Evans charged the ball and made an accurate throw home, but Jones was too speedy and he slid in ahead of the tag. The game was tied: 6-6.

McNamara vowed before the game to stay away from Calvin Schiraldi, who had pitched in Games Three and Four, so he went with Steve Crawford, essentially the last man on the staff. Dick Schofield lined a single to right, sending Wilfong (carrying the AL pennant in his back pocket) to third base. The Red Sox intentionally walked Brian Downing, setting up a force at any base. With both the infield and outfield playing in, DeCinces flied out to short right field, too shallow for Wilfong to tag up. Bobby Grich then lined a pitch right back to the mound, which Crawford speared easily in his follow-through. Game Five went to extra innings.

The Angels nearly won the game in the bottom of the 10th, when Gary Pettis hit a drive to deep left field. Rice, with his back to the wall, caught the ball over his head for the third out.

Moore hit Don Baylor to begin the Red Sox 11th. Evans singled to center. Gedman popped up a bunt attempt to third. DeCinces barehanded the ball on a bounce, but his throw was off target, and the bases were loaded. Henderson swung at Moore's first pitch and flied to center – scoring Baylor and giving Boston a 7-6 lead.

Schiraldi ended up pitching in the game after all, coming in to face the top of the California order in the bottom of the 11th. He struck out Wilfong and Schofield, and ended the game when Downing fouled to first. "I was awake all night wondering if I'd ever get a chance to redeem myself," Schiraldi said, referring to his poor performance in Game Four. "This has to be the biggest game of my life."[7]

Notes

1 George Kimball, "Henderson's Unlikely Hero," *Boston Herald*, October 13, 1986: 96.

2 Ian Thomsen, "Angels' Party Gets Crashed," *Boston Globe*, October 13, 1986: 46.

3 Leigh Montville, "It Ain't Over Till It's Over," *Boston Globe*, October 13, 1986: 1.

4 In the major leagues' first 648 postseason games, no team had ever taken a lead of two or more runs into the ninth inning and lost. And then it happened *twice* within 24 hours. In ALCS Game Four, on October 11, Boston held a 3-0 lead before the Angels tied it and won in 11 innings. The following day the Red Sox scored four times in the top of the ninth in Game Five, and eventually won in 11 innings. It happened *a third time*, on October 15, when the Astros blew a 3-0 lead in Game Six of the National League Championship Series, as the Mets came back to win the game (and the pennant), 7-6 in 16 innings.

5 George Kimball.

6 Ian Thomsen.

7 Joe Giuliotti, "Schiraldi Gets Redemption," *Boston Herald*, October 13, 1986: 74.

METS SURVIVE 16-INNING BATTLE, WIN NL PENNANT

OCTOBER 15, 1986:
NEW YORK 7, HOUSTON 6
(16 INNINGS),
GAME SIX OF THE 1986 NLCS
AT THE ASTRODOME, HOUSTON

BY RORY COSTELLO

Time and again during their run to the world championship in 1986, the Mets clawed back in desperate situations. Later this October, they were all but eliminated in Game Six of the World Series, when the Red Sox were one strike away from winning it all for the first time since 1918. Yet in Game Six of the NLCS that year – an excruciating 16-inning battle – the Mets also climbed out of a deep hole. The incredibly suspenseful game had sportswriters from around the nation at their best. Mike Downey of the *Los Angeles Times* wrote, "(The Astros) made the Mets sweat and suffer, made them charge from behind and gasp to stay in front. … They were enervated, drained, battle-fatigued."[1] In his chronicle of the '86 Mets, *The Bad Guys Won*, author Jeff Pearlman also vividly portrayed the mental and physical exhaustion that the players felt. *Newark Star-Ledger* columnist Jerry Izenberg devoted an entire book to this single contest entitled *The Greatest Game Ever Played*.

Unlike Game Six of the '86 World Series, New York's season would not have ended with a loss to Houston. The Mets had won three of the first five games, including a 12-inning 2-1 victory the day before at Shea Stadium. Had the Astros won Game Six, though, they would have sent Mike Scott to the mound the next day. Scott had thrown a five-hit shutout in Game One, making a single second-inning run stand up. He went all the way again to win Game Four, 3-1. He was on a lethal roll with his split-finger fastball.

The Mets continued to believe that something else was helping Scott's splitter to "drop off the table."

Davey Johnson showed a group of reporters eight balls that were scuffed in exactly the same spot – a mark about the size of a 50-cent piece. Johnson said, "It [sandpaper] is in his palm. He doesn't rotate the ball, he just makes a grinding motion. It's blatant to me." However, NL President Chub Feeney called Scott "innocent until proven guilty" – though he added, "We will be watching closely the next time he pitches."[2]

Had the series gone to Game Seven, Scott would have faced Ron Darling. Darling had pitched well during the regular season (15-6, 2.81) but had given up four runs in five innings in Game Three, which the Mets came back to win on Len Dykstra's two-run homer in the bottom of the ninth. In 2006 Darling said, "I felt I couldn't give up any runs because Mike Scott wasn't going to."[3]

The adverb "desperately" has often been used to depict how much the Mets wanted to win Game Six. In their own words, this supremely confident team – viewed as arrogant in many quarters – didn't evince desperation. It is fair to say, however, that the lingering threat of Scott was a strong psychological undercurrent as the series shifted back to the Astrodome. Plus, the Mets' poor long-term record there led Hal Bock of Associated Press to dub it "their personal house of horrors" after Game Five.[4]

Another aside on that venue is in order, too. The Astrodome – once known as the Eighth Wonder of the World – hosted its last big-league game in 1999. It then fell into disuse and disrepair. In 1986, however, the Dome was also home to the Houston Oilers of the

NFL. The Oilers had hosted the Chicago Bears just three days before Game Six – yard lines were still visible on the Astroturf.

The starters in Game Six were both lefties: Bob Knepper for Houston and Bob Ojeda for the Mets. The reliable Ojeda had gone the route as the Mets won Game Two, 5-1. But the Astros got to him for three runs in the first inning, and it might have been more except that Kevin Bass was tagged at home on a missed suicide squeeze attempt. Ojeda settled down after that and did not allow another run before coming out for Rick Aguilera in the sixth inning. Aguilera pitched three shutout innings, giving up just one hit.

Meanwhile, Knepper – 17-12, 3.14 in the regular season, with a no-decision in Game Three – was cruising. He'd given up just two hits and a walk as he took a shutout into the ninth inning. Yet the Mets broke through for the tying runs; pinch-hitter Dykstra ignited the rally. As he had in Game Three, Johnson again made the unorthodox choice to send the lefty swinger up to lead off against Knepper. Bass in right field and José Cruz in left were playing deep, but center fielder Billy Hatcher remained shallow. He could not get back to make the play on Dykstra's fly ball, which became a triple.

Mookie Wilson singled off the tip of Bill Doran's glove to score Dykstra. One out later, Keith Hernandez doubled, Wilson scored, and Houston closer Dave Smith entered. Smith, who'd given up Dykstra's homer in Game Three, was ineffective again. He walked the first two men he faced. With the count 1-and-2 to Ray Knight, home plate umpire Fred Brocklander – whose controversial call at first base took a vital run away from Houston in Game Five – had the Astros screaming again when he called a ball. Two pitches later, Knight brought in the tying run with a sacrifice fly.

Roger McDowell entered in the bottom of the ninth for the Mets and went on to pitch five superb innings. He faced the minimum 15 batters; the only baserunner he allowed, Bass, was caught stealing second base. It was McDowell's longest relief stint ever in the majors; his only longer outing came in one of his two big-league starts as a rookie in 1985. Smith pitched a scoreless 10th for Houston, and Larry Andersen blanked the Mets from the 11th through the 13th.

In the 14th the Mets got a run against veteran reliever Aurelio López. The portly Mexican was no longer "Señor Smoke" at this stage of his career, allowing a single and a walk to lead off before Wally Backman's one-out RBI single. However, López contained the damage with runners on second and third. Jesse

Orosco came on to try to get the save for the Mets, but with one out Hatcher pulled a drive high and deep. Would it stay fair? It hit the screen on the left-field foul pole, and the game was tied again.

After a scoreless 15th, New York put up three runs in the top of the 16th. López gave up one on a double and a single, then gave way to Jeff Calhoun, who fueled the rally with two wild pitches. One question about this game is why Hal Lanier chose not to use lefty Jim Deshaies – twice passed over for starting assignments and thus well rested – at any point. Lanier said that Deshaies had not faced that kind of pressure before. But bullpen coach Gene Tenace apparently told Lanier that Deshaies didn't have good stuff while warming up.[5]

Yet the tension was far from over – the Astros chipped away for two. They had the tying run on second base and the winning run on first with two out and Bass at the plate. Hernandez warned the weary Orosco (accounts vary as to the choice of words) not to throw a single fastball. The count ran full, and Mets announcer Bob Murphy said, "Pulsating baseball. … Nobody has sat down for the last four or five innings. … Incredible." Finally – on the sixth straight break-

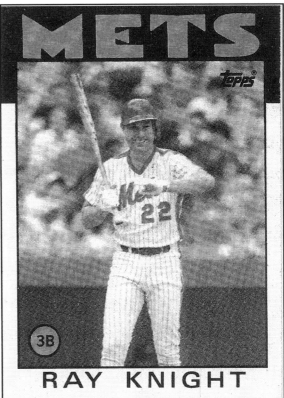

Ray Knight hit a sac fly in the ninth that kept Mets hopes alive, then singled in the first run of the 16th which helped spur them to victory.

ing ball – Bass fanned.[6] The Mets had won the NL pennant, and Orosco leaped in exultation. It had been the longest game in terms of innings in postseason history.[7]

Even if Houston had extended the series, at least some of the combative Mets still liked their chances against Scott. After Game Four, Ray Knight said, "You have to get that [the talk of scuffing] out of your mind and start thinking, 'What approach is best suited to hit this pitch?' and then you have to make adjustments at the plate."[8] The scrappy Backman said, "We're ticked and we're not going to take this lying down. I don't care if he scuffs 400 balls. I don't care if they're scuffed before the game. I don't think any pitcher can beat us three times in a row."[9]

On the flip side, however, Backman admitted, "If we had lost and had to face Scott tomorrow, I wouldn't have slept at all." Gary Carter said, "Mike Scott was our incentive to win."[10] Davey Johnson added, "Amen. I feel like I'm on parole, like I've just been given a pardon."[11] Perhaps a better choice of words would have been "reprieve" – the 1986 Mets just went from one grueling drama to the next.

Notes

1   Mike Downey, "All That Houston Has Ahead of It Now Is a Winter of Wondering," *Los Angeles Times*, October 16, 1986.

2   Bob Harig, "Mets accuse Houston's Mike Scott of scuffing baseball," *St. Petersburg Evening Independent*, October 14, 1986, C1. "Feeney clears Scott – for now," Associated Press, October 15, 1986.

3   Richard Sandomir, "Mets' Announcers Slide into New Roles," *New York Times*, October 14, 2006.

4   Hal Bock, "New York uses hits wisely to escape grip of [Nolan] Ryan," Associated Press, October 15, 1986.In the 22 seasons from 1965, when the Astrodome opened, through 1986, the Mets had a regular-season record there of 54-90 (.375). Over that period, their overall winning percentage was .472 and their winning percentage in road games was .450. They had a winning record at the Astrodome in just three seasons, though two of them were in 1984 and 1985.

5   Gordon Edes, "Mets Admit They're Glad to Get Off Scott-Free," *Los Angeles Times*, October 16, 1986.

6   Mike Downey described Bass as "overanxious" and Bass later confirmed this in a December 2010 meeting with SABR's Larry Dierker (Houston) chapter. See Bill McCurdy, "1986 NLCS Game 6: A Sacher Masoch Revisitation" (bill37mccurdy.wordpress.com /2010/12/15/1986-nlcs-game-6-a-sacher-masoch-revisitation/).

7   On October 9, 2005, the Astros and Atlanta Braves played 18 innings in Game Four of the National League Division Series.

8   Harig, "Mets accuse Houston's Mike Scott of scuffing baseball."

9   Terry Taylor, "Mets complain Mike Scott is 'scuffing' their attack," Associated Press, October 14, 1986.

10   Wire service reports, October 17, 1986.

11   Associated Press, October 16, 1986.

CUBS PULL OUT WEST COAST COMEBACK TO ADVANCE IN NLDS

OCTOBER 11, 2016:
CHICAGO CUBS 6,
SAN FRANCISCO GIANTS 5,
AT AT&T PARK, SAN FRANCISCO

By Nathan Bierma

After the Cubs won 103 games in the regular season, with their young stars and gritty veterans matching manager Joe Maddon's easygoing and playful vibe in the clubhouse, the only question was how the team would handle the shift to the postseason, when the stakes suddenly got so serious. Maddon had a heart-to-heart talk with his team before the National League Division Series, as the Cubs began their chase for the most elusive of championships.

"I said, 'Something bad is going to happen, and we have to stay in the moment and maintain our composure,'" Maddon told the *Chicago Tribune*. "That was the exact message."[1]

It didn't take long for Maddon's prediction to come true, and for his team to be tested. After beating the Giants in the series' first two games at Wrigley Field, the Cubs were defeated and deflated in a 13-inning Game Three, 6-5. Game Four would follow in a matter of hours.

"Another loss would not only have created a do-or-cry situation at Wrigley Field in Game 5 on Thursday, it would have fed into the narrative of the misery industrial complex," wrote Paul Sullivan in the *Chicago Tribune*. "After the Game 3 setback, the Cubs entered Game 4 on Tuesday ready to bury all those reminders of the past – the ghosts of 1984 and 2003 that continue to pop up every time they make it to October."[2]

For most of Game Four, it looked as though the Cubs had yet to hit bottom. Matt Moore was on the mound for Giants manager Bruce Bochy. Acquired in August, Moore showed what he could contribute to a postseason chase by taking a no-hitter into the ninth inning against the Dodgers on August 25. Now

he was just as dominant. He started out by striking out Dexter Fowler and Kris Bryant, and then, after walking Anthony Rizzo, getting a groundout from Ben Zobrist.

Taking the hill for the visitors was John Lackey, signed by the Cubs in the offseason to give them

Courtesy The Topps Company.

With the Cubs facing elimination, Javier Baez singled, driving in the final run in a 6-5 win that propelled the team to the NLCS and later to a world championship.

veteran composure in October. He stumbled out of the gate, giving up a leadoff double by Denard Span, who tagged up on two straight fly balls by Brandon Belt and Buster Posey to give the Giants a 1-0 lead.

David Ross, another veteran on the roster for leadership in the postseason, capitalized on what would be Moore's only major mistake of the night, leading off the third inning by driving a pitch over the left-field fence to tie the game. But Moore helped his own cause in the bottom of the fourth inning, hitting a one-out single with the bases loaded to score Conor Gillaspie and give the Giants the lead again. Span followed by grounding out to Rizzo, allowing Joe Panik to score from third. After four innings, the Giants led 3-1.

In the fifth inning, the Giants' infield gave the Cubs a rare opportunity, when shortstop Brandon Crawford's throw on a grounder by Javier Baez skipped past first baseman Belt into the bullpen, and Baez raced to third. Up next was Ross, who struck again for Chicago, launching a ball into shallow right field, where Pence made a diving catch but had no chance to catch a tagging Baez, and the score was 3-2.

With Justin Grimm taking over for the Cubs in the sixth, Pence singled up the middle and Crawford sent one soaring to Triples Alley in right. The ball bounced off the top of the wall, inches from leaving the ballpark, leaving Crawford on second and Pence on third. Maddon brought in Travis Wood to stop the bleeding, but he gave up one of Gillaspie's four singles in the game, this one scoring Pence, followed by a sacrifice fly by Panik to extend the lead to 5-2.

"While the Cubs looked like they were tired after their late-night loss in Game 3, the Giants appeared rejuvenated by the home crowd," wrote the *Chicago Tribune*.[3]

Neither team had another hit through the eighth inning. Moore's masterpiece included 10 strikeouts and just two hits, two walks, and one unearned run. But his pitch count stood at 120 after eight innings, and Bochy had to call on his bullpen.

"Starter Matt Moore was masterful and the hitters had severely outplayed their counterparts up until that point," wrote the *San Francisco Examiner*. "Yet, nothing matters if you can get those last three outs."[4]

That had proved a tall order for the Giants during the season. Their bullpen had blown a league-leading and franchise-record 32 eighth-inning leads,[5] and that was a big reason the Giants surrendered their division lead to the Dodgers and had to play their way into this series via a wild-card game.

Bryant led off the Cubs ninth against Derek Law and slapped a single to left. Taking no chances, Bochy brought in Javier Lopez, but Lopez walked Rizzo. With the tying run coming to bat, Bochy called for Sergio Romo, his closer from the 2012 title team who had recently reclaimed the role.

Zobrist worked a 3-and-1 count against Romo and rammed the next pitch into the right-field corner. Bryant scored, Rizzo reached third, and Zobrist had a double.

The lead was down to two, and the Giants had yet to record an out. The San Francisco crowd grew quiet, unaccustomed to postseason pain under Bochy; in a strange stretch over the last six seasons, the Giants alternated three championships with three idle Octobers.

Maddon sent pinch-hitter Chris Coghlan to the plate, prompting Bochy to call for a lefty from the bullpen, Will Smith. Maddon countered with the right-handed bat of Willson Contreras. Less than four months removed from his major-league debut, the fearless youngster already had three hits in the postseason, and now faced the opportunity to change the course of the series.

Contreras seized his chance. He chopped a ball past the mound, beyond the swatting hand of Smith and the lunging Panik. Rizzo scored, Zobrist followed, and the game was tied.

The next batter, Jason Heyward, laid down a bunt, but the ball shot directly back to the mound, giving Smith time to turn and throw to second to retire Contreras and Crawford a chance to relay to first. Crawford's throw, though, was wide of Belt, and Heyward went to second. Against the Giants' fifth reliever of the inning, Hunter Strickland, Baez laced an 0-and-2 pitch into center field, scoring Heyward without a throw.

"These young players for the Cubs are fearless, and don't give up any inch to their competitors," said analyst John Smoltz on the Fox Sports One telecast as Baez slammed his hands together in celebration at first base.

Taking an unexpected lead into the bottom of the ninth, the Cubs turned to flamethrowing closer Aroldis Chapman. Touching triple digits repeatedly, Chapman struck out the side.

The comeback Cubs were going back to the NLCS. Their ninth-inning rally matched the biggest postseason ninth-inning rally in major-league history, last achieved by the Mets in Game Six of the 1986 NLCS.[6]

"We grind," explained pitcher Jon Lester after the game. "We have some flashy guys, some guys who are

MVPs and Cy Youngs and stuff like that. But when it comes down to it, we're kind of like the 9-to-5 Chicago person that goes to work every day and grinds it out. That's what we do. And it showed tonight."[7]

"The biggest thing is it demonstrates that even if you get behind," said Maddon, "if you play nine innings hard the entire way anything can happen."[8]

"With the way the ball bounced that last inning, I hate to use the word 'destiny,' but they've had a great year," Bochy said of the Cubs. "That's quite a comeback they mounted."[9]

"Just when you concluded the Cubs were done, they reminded everyone how they won 103 regular-season games," wrote David Haugh in the *Chicago Tribune*. "Just when you thought their bats had died, they came back to life. Just when Chicago doubted the Cubs the most, they gave everyone reason to believe again. Just when you started to wonder if this really was the year, the Cubs left the impression the 108-year-wait might be ending soon."[10]

Sources

In addition to the sources cited in the Notes, the author consulted Retrosheet.org and Baseball-Reference.com.

Notes

1   Paul Sullivan, "Cubs Ain't Afraid of No Goats," *Chicago Tribune*, October 12, 2016: 2.

2   Sullivan, "Cubs Ain't Afraid."

3   David Haugh, "Doubt This Team? Comeback for the Ages Restores Faith," *Chicago Tribune*, October 12, 2016: 1.

4   Jacob C. Palmer, "The 2016 Giants: When Torture Goes Too Far," *San Francisco Examiner*, October 12, 2016: 8.

5   Palmer, "The 2016 Giants."

6   This fact was displayed on a graphic on the Fox Sports One telecast at the beginning of the ninth inning. Thirty years later, the October 11, 2016, Game Four of the NLCS produced an equally unlikely comeback.

7   Sullivan, "Cubs Ain't Afraid."

8   Sullivan, "Cubs Ain't Afraid."

9   John Shea, "Bullpen Fails in Giants' Season Finale," *San Francisco Chronicle*, October 12, 2016. Accessed at sfgate.com/giants/shea/article/Bullpen-fails-in-Giants-season-finale-9965700.php.

10   Haugh.

ALTITUDE DECIDES ANOTHER ONE

JULY 6, 2010:
COLORADO 12,
ST. LOUIS 9,
AT COORS FIELD, DENVER

BY JIM WOHLENHAUS

July 6, 2010, was a warm rainy evening in Mile High Denver when the first pitch by Jeff Francis was thrown to leadoff batter Felipe Lopez of the St. Louis Cardinals at 7:10 P.M.[1] Home-plate umpire Bill Hohn called the first pitch a ball and the game was underway. At the start of the game, the Rockies' record was 44 wins and 38 losses, and they were five games behind the San Diego Padres. St. Louis's record was similar at 45 wins and 37 losses, two games behind the Cincinnati Reds. At the end of this game both teams would have the same record. For the Rockies, this game was the second of a six-game winning streak before going on the road. Neither team made the play-offs in 2010.

In the first two innings, the Cardinals were three up, three down. The Rockies also went three up and three down in the first. In the second, Colorado got three runners on against Blake Hawksworth with two singles and a walk, but two strikeouts amid the baserun-

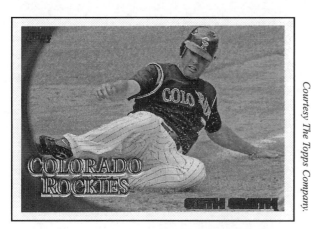

The greatest comeback in Rockies history was capped by Seth Smith's three-run homer in the bottom of the ninth, for a 12-9 win.

ners brought up pitcher Francis with the bases loaded. He grounded out to second to end the half-inning.

Saint Louis scored three runs in the third inning on a single by Aaron Miles, a home run by Lopez, another single by Colby Rasmus, and a double by Albert Pujols. Matt Holliday was walked intentionally but nothing happened with that as Nick Stavinoha batting fifth, flied out to right field. It is interesting to note that during the game, six other players would be in the fifth position of the Cardinals lineup, including the closer, Ryan Franklin.

The Rockies' third started with a walk to Dexter Fowler followed two batters later with a home run by Carlos González. The Rockies extended the rally, but with no further scoring. Jason Giambi singled to second, Miguel Olivo hit a ball back to Hawksworth, who tried for a double play by throwing to second, but Giambi was safe and Olivo was out at first. Seth Smith walked and he and Giambi were balked to second and third, a good opportunity to overcome the Cardinals' lead. Ian Stewart walked, bringing Clint Barmes up with the bases loaded, but like Francis in the second inning, he grounded out to second. By now the Rockies had scored twice and left six men on base. They would eventually leave 13 runners on base.

The Cardinals scored two more runs in the fourth on a walk to Yadier Molina, a single by Tyler Greene, a sacrifice by Hawksworth, a sacrifice fly by Miles for the first run, and a single by Lopez scoring Greene to complete the scoring.

The Cardinals scored again in the fifth on singles by Pujols, pinch-hitter Jon Jay, and Molina. The sixth inning brought St. Louis its last three runs on a three-run home run by Holliday after Miles had singled and Pujols walked.

In the meantime, the Rockies did not score in the fourth, fifth, or sixth innings, but left two men on base in each inning, making it a total of 12 for the game to this point.

Hawksworth lasted five innings, throwing 98 pitches. The *St. Louis Post-Dispatch* summed up his five innings: "Hawksworth ducked, dodged, evaded and otherwise shimmied free of trouble throughout his five innings of work – and though it took him a maximum amount of pitches, he did it with minimal damage from the Rockies."[2]

In the seventh inning, Colorado scored its third run on a single by Smith, a wild pitch by Trever Miller, a single by Stewart, and a force out of Stewart at second base by pinch-hitter Chris Iannetta.

St. Louis went three up and three down in the seventh, eighth, and ninth, grounding out in seven of the nine plate appearances. The Rockies also went three up and three down in the eighth. Nothing happened in the top of the ninth and the Cardinals had a seemingly safe lead of 9-3.

Olivo led off the bottom of the ninth and singled to center. Smith was out on a line drive to first base. One out. Melvin Mora pinch-hit for pitcher Manny Corpas.[3] Mora singled to right field and Olivo ran to third. Barmes walked on four pitches; on the fourth, the ball got away from Molina for a passed ball and Olivo scored while Mora took second. The score was now 9-4, Cardinals.

Franklin came in to relieve pitcher Dennys Reyes with runners on first and second and Iannetta due up. Franklin was the Cardinals' closer for 2010. At this point he had 16 saves and would end the year with 27 of the Cardinals' 32. After a called ball, a swinging strike, a foul, and two more called balls, Iannetta homered to left field, scoring Mora and Barmes ahead of him. The score was now 9-7, the Cardinals having had their six-run lead more than halved and still only one out.

Fowler, the next batter hit a line-drive double to right field. By this time the wind was absolutely howling, giving any elevated ball a chance to become a souvenir.[4] Pinch-hitter Brad Hawpe grounded out to shortstop, Fowler taking third. Only one more out and St. Louis would win this game. It never happened.

Next, González singled to right field. Randy Winn was playing on the warning track as González's drive landed at his feet, scoring Fowler with the eighth run and making it a one-run game.[5] Giambi followed with another single toward Winn. Winn got caught between hops, mishandled the bounce and struggled to pick up

the ball. That allowed González to score from first and tie the game.[6] Giambi did not advance to second on the error, which was Winn's first in 253 games.[7]

The Rockies were not through. Aaron Cook ran for Giambi. Olivo came up again and singled through the infield into right field, sending Cook to third with the potential winning run. After the game Giambi said, "That's when I knew we were winning."[8] Seth Smith came to bat. After watching two called balls go by, he fouled off a pitch. The fourth pitch was a called strike and on the next pitch Smith hit a fly-ball home run to right field to drive in three more runs for a 12-9 Colorado win. As of 2019 this was the greatest comeback win in the Rockies' history.

Afterward, Smith said, "I know people come up in that situation and want to hit one. But I swear I wasn't. I just didn't want to make my second out in the inning. I was analyzing it as I ran to first and thought, 'Why not just go out?' "Baseball is crazy."[9]

In this game with runners in scoring position, the Rockies were 3-for-13 in the first eight innings, then 3-for-4 in the ninth inning, for a game total of 6-for-17. They couldn't get a key hit when it was needed early.

A quick glance at the scorecard could lead the reader to believe that two of the runs in the ninth were unearned. But reconstructing the inning without the error and passed ball shows that those runners would have scored regardless, so all 12 Rockies runs were earned. It also appears that Franklin was brought into the game in a nonsave situation. But the score was 9-4, with two runners on base. Adding in the next batter, the batter on deck, and the batter in "the hold," it was barely a save situation.

After the game, Cardinals manager Tony La Russa said, "That loss wasn't on Ryan Franklin. It was on everybody who wore the gray, including the manager."[10] Rockies manager Jim Tracy said, "It's the best comeback I have ever been associated with. The lesson learned is that you never give away an at-bat and play until there is 27 outs."[11]

Sources

In addition to the sources cited in the Notes, the author relied upon Retrosheet.org, Baseball-Reference.com, MLB.com, and his own scorecard.

Notes

1   *Denver Post*, July 7, 2010: C1.

2   Derrick Goold, "Cardinals Collapse Against Rockies," *St. Louis Post-Dispatch*, July 7, 2010: C1.

3   Corpas entered the game in a double-switch after Iannetta pinch-hit and stayed in the game in the eighth inning to play third base. That

was only the second time he played third base in the major leagues. In his career through 2019, Iannetta has played third base only four times, none as a starter. He had no fielding chances in this game.

4   Troy Renck, "Nine-Run Ninth? Wow!", *Denver Post,* July 7, 2010: C5.

5   Renck.

6   Renck.

7   Goold.

8   Goold.

9   Goold.

10   Goold: C2.

11   Renck.

DODGERS LOSE TO GIANTS 14-10 AFTER LEADING 8-0

SEPTEMBER 23, 1970:
SAN FRANCISCO GIANTS 14,
LOS ANGELES DODGERS 10
(10 INNINGS),
AT DODGER STADIUM, LOS ANGELES

BY JOHN J. BURBRIDGE JR.

The San Francisco Giants journeyed to Los Angeles for a late-season three-game series with the Dodgers beginning on September 21, 1970. As the series began, the Dodgers, were in second place in the National League West but 12 games behind the Cincinnati Reds. The Giants, in third place, were just one game behind Los Angeles. The Dodgers were managed by Walter Alston and Charlie Fox was at the helm of the Giants. In the first game of the series, Juan Marichal of the Giants shut out the Dodgers, putting the two teams in a tie for second place. The Dodgers rebounded the next night, beating the Giants 1-0 and setting up a rubber match for Wednesday night.

For this final game, the Giants had future Hall of Famers Willie Mays and Willie McCovey in their lineup. The Dodgers were led by Maury Wills and Willie Davis. Gaylord Perry, another future Hall of Famer, was starting for the Giants, and rookie Sandy Vance was taking the ball for Los Angeles. Before the game, it was announced that Alston would be rehired for the 1971 season.[1] Alston had managed the Dodgers since 1954, all on one-year contracts.

Both teams went out in order in the first inning as did the Giants in the top of the second. In the bottom of the second, Wes Parker led off with a double and took third as Tom Haller grounded out to Perry. Bill Sudakis singled, scoring Parker. Sudakis stole second and went to third on a wild pitch. After Bill Buckner grounded out to second, Billy Grabarkewitz, the Dodgers second baseman, doubled to right, scoring Sudakis. Vance hit a grounder to McCovey, who flipped to Perry covering first but Perry couldn't handle the throw. Grabarkewitz

scored, making the score 3-0. Wills then flied out to shortstop, ending the inning.

The Giants again went out in order in the third. Vance retired the first nine Giants. In the bottom of the

Courtesy The Topps Company.

Dick Dietz's grand slam in the seventh inning helped overcome an 8-0 deficit at the time and kept them in a game that ran to the 10th.

third, Manny Mota reached first base on an error by Giants shortstop Hal Lanier. Mota went to second on a wild pitch and to third on a groundout, and scored on a sacrifice fly off the bat of Parker. At the end of three innings the Dodgers led 4-0.

Bobby Bonds led off the top of the fourth with a walk, the first Giants baserunner. Tito Fuentes followed with a single, moving Bonds to second. Willie Mays hit a liner to center. Willie Davis snagged the ball and who doubled Bonds off at second. Willie McCovey singled to right, moving Fuentes to third and McCovey took second on the throw to third. But Ken Henderson ended the threat by flying out to center field.

In the bottom of the fourth, the Dodgers added another run to their lead as Wills's single scored Buckner with an unearned run set up by McCovey's error. The Giants threatened again in the top of the fifth; they had runners on first and third with no outs but the next three batters, including Bernie Williams pinch-hitting for pitcher Perry, made outs.

The Giants had a new pitcher, Skip Pitlock, to begin the fifth, and Frank Johnson replaced McCovey at first base. Pitlock walked Willie Davis, who scored on a double by Wes Parker. Left fielder Ken Henderson booted Parker's hit and he went to third; he scored on a single by Bill Russell, pinch-hitting for Buckner. As the inning ended, the Dodgers had increased their lead to 7-0.

The Giants went out in order in the top of the sixth. The Dodgers added to their lead when Vance doubled to lead off the bottom of the inning, went to third on Mota's single, and scored when Davis hit a force-play grounder against John Cumberland, the Giants' third pitcher.

As the top of the seventh began, the Dodgers had a comfortable 8-0 lead but the Giants were not done. After Henderson grounded out, Dick Dietz singled to center and Jim Ray Hart homered. Ed Goodson batted for Hal Lanier and singled. Bob Taylor pinch-hit for Cumberland and flied to left field for the second out. Bonds singled to center. With runners on first and second, Alston called upon Pete Mikkelsen to relieve Vance, who had pitched well. Mikkelsen was greeted by run-scoring singles from Fuentes and Mays, whose hit made the score 8-4. Jim Brewer replaced Mikkelsen with the bases loaded and walked Henderson, scoring Fuentes. The Giants trailed 8-5. But Dietz hit a grand slam, giving the Giants a 9-8 lead. After giving up a single to Hart, Brewer finally got out of the inning. For the Dodgers, it was 33 nightmarish minutes.[2]

Jerry Johnson began the bottom of the seventh on the mound for the Giants and retired the Dodgers in order. The Giants went out in order in the top half of the eighth. In the bottom of the eighth, the Dodgers' Von Joshua, pinch-hitting for Brewer, singled but was thrown out at second trying to stretch his hit. Wills got an infield single, stole second, and went to third on a groundout. He scored on an infield single by Davis. After Parker walked, Don McMahon replaced Johnson and retired pinch-hitter Jim Lefebvre. The game was tied, 9-9, going into the ninth.

Ray Lamb began the ninth on the mound for the Dodgers. With one out, Frank Johnson singled and Ken Henderson walked. Dietz flied deep to right and Johnson took third. The Dodgers walked Jim Ray Hart intentionally. Art Gallagher pinch-hit for pitcher McMahon. He singled to center, scoring Johnson but Henderson was thrown out at home trying to score from second. The Giants led 10-9 going into the bottom of the ninth.

Rich Robertson was called upon by the Giants to finish off the Dodgers but he was unable to do so. Sudakis singled to lead off, was sacrificed to second by Russell, and went to third on a wild pitch. With two outs, pinch-hitter Len Gabrielson singled, tying the score and sending the game into extra innings.

In the top of the 10th with one out, Bobby Bonds got a second life as Dodgers catcher Joe Ferguson lost his foul pop behind home plate.[3] Bonds then singled to right and stole second. Fuentes followed with a walk. The Dodgers replaced Lamb with Mike Strahler, who walked Mays, loading the bases. Johnson hit a grounder that Wills bobbled for a second, negating what would have been an inning-ending double play.[4] Bonds scored while the other runners moved up. Ken Henderson then homered, and the Giants led, 14-10. In the bottom of the inning, Mota led off with a walk but Robinson retired the next three Dodgers, giving the Giants the victory. The two teams now had identical 84-71 records with six games to play in the season.

The hitting heroes for the Giants were Dietz, Ken Henderson, and Jim Ray Hart, who all homered. Dietz and Henderson each had four RBIs. Dietz's grand slam brought the Giants from three down to a one-run lead. Frank Johnson, who replaced McCovey, also had a big role in the win. Wes Parker and Willie Davis each had two RBIs for the Dodgers. Rich Robertson was the winning pitcher and Ray Lamb was the loser.

While the teams were now tied, the Dodgers were able to edge out the Giants for second place when the Giants lost their last four games of the season.

Both teams finished far behind the Cincinnati Reds in the National League West. McCovey was the Giants' season offensive leader with 39 home runs, 126 RBIs, and an OBP of .444. Wes Parker was the Dodgers' leader; he led the league in doubles and had an OBP of .392. Gaylord Perry, although ineffective in this start, had a remarkable season for the Giants, starting 41 games, pitching 328⅔ innings, and winning 23 games.

Sources

In addition to the sources mentioned in the Notes, the author consulted Baseball-Reference.com.

Notes

1   John Wiebasch, "Alston Rehired; Giants Win Wild Battle in 10th," *Los Angeles Times*, September 24, 1970: 53.

2   Wiebasch.

3   Wiebasch.

4   Wiebasch.

RAYS COME BACK TO BEAT THE BLUE JAYS IN 12TH INNING

JULY 25, 2009:
TAMPA BAY RAYS 10,
TORONTO BLUE JAYS 9,
AT ROGERS CENTRE, TORONTO

BY THOMAS J. BROWN JR.

The Tampa Bay Rays, 6½ games behind the New York Yankees, were trying to stay in contention for the playoffs against the tough competition of the American League East. The Toronto Blue Jays meanwhile struggled after the opening month of the 2009 season and were looking to trade their pitching ace, Roy Halladay, after he announced that he would consider free agency at the end of the season.[1]

Halladay pitched nine innings the previous night and but failed to get a win. Rays starter Matt Garza was his equal, also going nine innings. The Rays eventually won the game when they scored two runs in the top of the 10th off reliever Scott Downs.

Amid the trade talk, the Rays were not one of the teams that were likely to land Halladay. Rays President Andrew Friedman told reporters, "[A]t the end of the day it's going to take the guys that we have playing really good baseball for two months. We have a lot of confidence in the guys that we have and their ability to do that."[2]

Toronto started Brian Tallet, who was 5-6 and had last won more than a month earlier, when he pitched six innings in a 7-5 Blue Jays victory. Tallet cruised through the first two innings, getting the Rays out in order.

Meanwhile his teammates were building an eight-run lead for him against Rays rookie starter David Price. Price hoped to rebound from his last start, a six-inning no-decision in which he surrendered four earned runs in a loss to the Chicago White Sox.

But Toronto jumped on Price immediately, scoring two runs in the first. Marco Scutaro led off with a single and scored on Adam Lind's one-out double.

Scott Rolen's single left baserunners at the corners. Lind scored when Kevin Millar hit a weak groundball to short.

The Blue Jays added to their lead in the second. Jose Bautista led off with a home run. Three batters later, Aaron Hill hit another home run to give Toronto a four-run lead. One inning later, Alex Rios tagged Price for yet another round-tripper to put Toronto ahead by six runs.

Although Price didn't return for the fourth inning, the Blue Jays tagged his replacement, Lance Cormier, for two more runs when Hill hit his second homer of the game. It was Hill's 24th home run of the season and the second time in the season that he hit multiple round-trippers in a game. After scoring a pair of runs in each of the first four innings, Toronto led, 8-0.

Tallet kept Tampa Bay in check through the first five innings, allowing just two Rays to get on base. Tampa Bay finally got on the scoreboard in the sixth when Dioner Navarro doubled and scored on Melvin Upton's single to left field.

Cormier got the Blue Jays out in order in the fifth but they added their ninth run in the sixth. Raul Chavez led off with a single and took third when Hill singled, his third hit of the game. A weak grounder up the middle led to an error by Rays shortstop Ben Zobrist that allowed Chavez to score.

Tampa Bay cut further into Toronto's lead in the top of the seventh. A leadoff single by Evan Longoria and a double by Zobrist put two runners in scoring position. After Tallet walked Pat Burrell, Carlos Peña cleared the bases with a triple off the right-field wall. Brandon League replaced Tallet. Willy Aybar's one-out grounder brought Peña home and suddenly the Rays were down by only four runs, at 9-5.

Rays manager Joe Maddon had moved Peña to sixth in the batting order for the game in an attempt to help him come out of a slump. The move seemed to work. Maddon said before the game, "This guy, he is so helpful to everybody in the clubhouse and sometimes somebody needs to be helpful to him."[3] Maddon told him he could help the team win with his words of encouragement or by his fielding, that it was not just about his bat.

Dale Thayer took the mound for the Rays in the bottom of the sixth to get the final two outs but before he could face a batter in the seventh, Maddon decided to make a pitching change. As he waited for Grant Balfour to jog in from the bullpen, he told his players gathered at the mound, "Don't worry about it. We're going to win this game."[4]

Several days earlier, hitting coach Steve Henderson told the players that they needed to focus on quality at-bats. The Rays showed that they had heard him when they began their comeback in the seventh. "When we made it 9-5 it was like, 'Hey, we're within striking distance. We're definitely not quitting,'" Zobrist said.[5]

The Rays continued to gain ground in the eighth. Jeremy Accardo was on the mound for Toronto. After giving up a leadoff single to Upton, he got the first two outs when Upton was caught stealing and Carl Crawford grounded out.

But the third out proved elusive. Longoria hit a groundball single up the middle. Accardo walked Zobrist and a passed ball put both runners in scoring position. Burrell worked the count full before hitting a single down the left-field line and suddenly the Rays were down by only two runs, at 9-7.

For the second night, Toronto sent Downs to the mound with the game on the line. The first batter he faced, Peña, sent the ball over the left-field fence to bring the Rays just one run away from a tie. After Downs struck out Gabe Kapler, Aybar stepped to the plate and pummeled the first pitch over the center-field wall to tie the game, 9-9.

It was the second time in as many nights that Tampa Bay had gotten to Downs, who was charged with a blown save. "For me, it's embarrassing," Downs said later. "Bottom line, it's not executing. Yesterday I just beat myself and today it was bad location."[6]

The Rays bullpen shut down the Blue Jays the rest of the game. After Balfour gave up a leadoff double to Scutaro in the eighth and retired Aaron Hill, Maddon replaced him with Randy Choate. Choate got the next

Courtesy The Topps Company.

Tampa Bay's Carlos Pena drove in four runs, his biggest base hit a three-run triple in the seventh inning.

batter out and was replaced by Dan Wheeler, who struck out Rolen, leaving Scutaro stranded on third.

Wheeler picked up the mantle and pitched a one-two-three ninth. After he surrendered a leadoff single in the 10th and a sacrifice put the runner in scoring position, Maddon replaced him with J.P. Howell, who snuffed out another Blue Jays scoring opportunity, striking out Scutaro and getting Lind to foul out for the third out.

Neither team scored in the 11th. Former Ray Shawn Camp, who came out of the bullpen in the 11th, stayed in the game. Zobrist singled to lead off the 12th. Camp got the next two batters to fly out but walked Gabe Gross. Jason Bartlett, who had entered the game in the ninth, followed with a line-drive double that barely stayed fair to bring Zobrist home with the tiebreaking run.

"It had a hook on it and I didn't know what was going to happen. We've hit several balls recently just foul or somebody's catching it over the wall. It was nice to have one hit a line," Maddon said.[7]

All the Rays needed now were three outs to make their comeback complete. But they didn't come easily. Joe Nelson, the seventh reliever called on by Maddon, struggled to get the job done. He walked Rios to start the inning. After a sacrifice left Rios on second, Nelson became so concerned with Rios stealing that he walked the next two batters to load the bases.

Nelson knew that starter James Shields was waiting in the bullpen. "I would have had to walk 30 to get him in," Nelson said. He struck out Hill and then got Lind to ground out to second to end the game. "Never a doubt," he cracked in the clubhouse afterward. [8]

It was the biggest comeback in Tampa Bay's history so far. Their previous best had come two months earlier when they were down seven runs by the fourth inning against the Indians but came back to win 8-7. That game was not quite the nailbiter; the Rays had added runs in the final four innings of that game to overtake Cleveland.

"We just didn't quit today," Zobrist noted as the team celebrated. Peña, whose bat came alive when he was moved in the batting order, said, "That was a great game for us, an incredible boost for our confidence." But Nelson perhaps said it best: "Huge. Plain and simple, this could be one of those games you look back on."[9]

Unfortunately for the Rays, the inspiration lent by this game was fleeting. They were 30-34 the rest of the season and finished 19 games behind the division-winning Yankees.

Sources

In addition to the sources cited in the Notes, the author used the Baseball-Reference.com, and Retrosheet.org websites for box-score, player, team, and season pages, pitching and batting game logs, and other pertinent material.

Notes

1   Bob Elliott, "Trade Talks Surround Halladay in What May Be His Last Days as a Blue Jay," *London* (Ontario) *Free Press*, July 25, 2009: D1.

2   Marc Lancaster, "Rumors Are Just Part of the Game," *Tampa Bay Tribune*, July 25, 2009: C3.

3   Marc Lancaster, "Maddon Takes Pressure Off Pena," *Tampa Bay Tribune*, July 25, 2009: C3.

4   Marc Lancaster, "Rays Simply Refuse to Lose," *Tampa Bay Tribune*, July 25, 2009:C1.

5   "Rays Erase 8-0 Lead, Overtake Blue Jays in 12," *Ottawa Citizen*, July 26, 2009: 48.

6   "Rays Erase 8-0 Lead."

7   Marc Lancaster, "Rays Simply Refuse to Lose."

8   Marc Topkin, "Record Rally Is Rooted in Resolve," *Tampa Bay Tribune*, July 26, 2009: 15.

9   Marc Topkin, "Record Rally."

ATHLETICS ERASE EIGHT-RUN DEFICIT, BEAT RANGERS, 13-10

JULY 24, 2018: OAKLAND ATHLETICS 13, TEXAS RANGERS 10, AT GLOBE LIFE PARK, ARLINGTON

BY PAUL HOFMANN

The Tuesday evening game was a matchup between two teams headed in opposite directions. Third-place Oakland was the hottest team in baseball. Winners of 24 of their last 31, the A's came into the game with a record of 58-43, 7½ games behind the American League West-leading Houston Astros. In the other dugout, the Rangers had won only four games so far in July and were in last place in the AL West with a record of 42-59, a distant 23½ games off the lead. Even more telling were the 40 runs the Rangers' pitchers had given up in the four games since the All-Star break.

Frankie Montas, recalled from Triple-A Nashville earlier in the day, drew the starting assignment for the A's.[1] The 25-year-old right-hander from the Dominican Republic was making his ninth start of the season for the A's and brought a 5-2 record and a 3.35 ERA into the contest. The Rangers started 30-year-old Mike Minor. The 6-foot-4 left-hander was working his way back from surgery to repair a torn labrum that forced him to miss all of 2015 and 2016. He entered the game with a record of 6-6 and a 4.89 ERA.

It was a hot and humid evening, the type of night when leads were known to quickly evaporate in this ballpark. The temperature was a sticky 97 degrees when Minor delivered the first pitch at 7:05 P.M. Despite having to throw 20 pitches, Minor retired the A's in order in the top of the first. Montas was not as fortunate in the bottom of the inning.

Shin-Soo Choo drew a leadoff walk before being erased on a fielder's choice at second when Rougned Odor grounded to second. Shortstop Elvis Andrus followed with a groundball single through the hole

between first and second. Odor, racing around second, drew an errant throw from right fielder Stephen Piscotty that allowed him to score the game's first run and for Andrus to take third. Adrian Beltre sent a sacrifice fly to right to score Andrus. At the end of the first inning, the Rangers held a 2-0 lead.

Stephen Piscotty's leadoff home run in the ninth brought Oakland to a tie with the Rangers, coming back from being down 10-2.

The A's evened the score on a pair of one-out solo home runs in the third and fourth innings. In the top of the third, Mark Canha sent a home run deep into the seats down the left-field line. It was Canha's 13th home run of the season. In the top of the fourth, Jed Lowrie homered to center, his 17th of the year.

In the Rangers fifth, Willie Calhoun led off with his first home run of the season, a shot to deep right field. With one out, Choo singled to left-center and went to third on Odor's double. Andrus followed with a sacrifice fly to deep right-center that scored Choo to make the score 4-2.

With a two-run lead and Minor having already thrown 104 pitches, Rangers manager Jeff Banister went to his bullpen to preserve the lead. Right-hander Cory Gearrin, who was acquired from the Giants on July 8 and making his sixth appearance for the team, was the first in a parade of Rangers pitchers out of the weary bullpen. Gearrin, who had yet to yield a run in 5⅓ innings of work with the Rangers, pitched a scoreless sixth inning.[2]

The Rangers extended their lead in the bottom of the sixth. With left-hander Ryan Buchter on the mound for the A's, Rangers right fielder Joey Gallo led off with a home run to right field, his 25th of the season. With one out, Isiah Kiner-Falefa doubled down the left-field line. Two hitters later, with two away, center fielder Carlos Tocci singled to left to score Kiner-Faiefa. Tocci took second on the throw to the plate. Choo reached on an error by A's shortstop Marcus Semien and Tocci advanced to third. Odor walked on four pitches and the bases were loaded.

Attempting to keep the game close, A's manager Bob Melvin turned to right-handed rookie J.B. Wendelken to face the right-handed-hitting Andrus, who deposited Wendelken's seventh offering of the at-bat into the stands in left for a grand slam. It was Andrus's fourth home run of the season. After six innings, the Rangers appeared to have an insurmountable 10-2 lead and a 99 percent probability of winning the game.[3] In fact, history suggested the Rangers had an even higher probability of winning the game. According to the Elias Sports Bureau, the Rangers were 471-0 when leading by eight runs or more in the seventh inning or later in franchise history, and 429-0 since moving to Texas.[4]

Left-hander Brandon Mann, who had been recalled from Triple-A Round Rock after the Rangers' 15-3 loss to the A's the night before, started the seventh for the Rangers. Third baseman Matt Chapman drew a leadoff walk and took second on a wild pitch. Canha also walked. After Jonathan Lucroy flied out to center, Semien drove in Chapman and Canha with a double to left. Banister brought in right-hander Jose Leclerc to face the right-handed-hitting Chad Pinder. Melvin, the A's skipper, lifted Pinder for left-handed-hitting Nick Martini, who sliced a double to left to trim the Rangers' lead to 10-5.

Left-hander Jake Diekman came on to pitch for the Rangers in the eighth. With one out, Chapman, Canha, and Lucroy drew consecutive walks. Semien followed with a hard grounder to shortstop that Andrus booted. Chapman scored and everyone else was safe. Martini was hit by a pitch to push across a run and move everyone up another 90 feet. Sensing that the once insurmountable lead might be slipping away, Banister called on right-handed closer Keone Kela for a five-out save. Lowrie greeted Kela with a two-run single. Kela then threw a wild pitch that allowed Martini and Lowrie to advance. Kela struck out Khris Davis and retired Matt Olson on a fly ball to center to end the inning. Despite only one hit, the A's had scored four runs. At the end of eight innings the Rangers clung to a 10-9 lead.

Newly acquired right-hander Juerys Familia pitched a one-two-three eighth for the A's. Familia, who had come over from the New York Mets three days earlier, was making his second appearance for Oakland. (He was the winning pitcher in his A's debut, against the San Francisco Giants two days earlier.)

Any hope that Kela would shut down the A's in the ninth quickly dissipated when Piscotty hit his first offering of the inning for a home run to center field. It was Piscotty's 14th home run of the season and the first time Kela had blown a save all season. The Rangers had squandered an eight-run lead in the game's final three innings.

Familia pitched another perfect inning in the ninth to send the game into extra innings.

Right-hander Austin Bibens-Dirkx, the Rangers' seventh pitcher of the night, came in to pitch the 10th inning. He struck out Semien to start the inning. Martini single to short left and moved to second when Lowrie walked. Davis, who was 0-for-5 so far, followed with a three-run homer to left to give the A's their first lead of the game. The blast was Davis's 25th of the season.

Closer Blake Treinen came on to close things out for the A's in the bottom of the 10th. The 30-year-old right-hander, who was enjoying a career year with a record of 5-2, 24 saves, and a microscopic 1.08 ERA, wasted little time in retiring the Rangers in order to cap a stunning comeback.

Familia was credited with the victory, his second in as many appearances with the A's. Treinen earned the save, his 25th of the season. The loss went to Bibens-Dirkx, dropping his record to 2-3. The time of the game was 4 hours and 8 minutes.

The A's continued their fine play and captured the second AL wild-card spot with a record of 97-65. They lost the wild-card Game to the New York Yankees, 7-2. The Rangers began to turn over their roster soon after their improbable blown lead and finished the year at 67-95.

Sources

In addition to the sources cited in the Notes, the author consulted Baseball-Reference.com and Retrosheet.org

Notes

[1]   Dave Jackson, "Blown Lead: Davis' 3-Run Home Run in 10th Rallies Athletics Past Rangers," *McAllen* (Texas) *Monitor*, July 25, 2018: B2.

[2]   In 40 games with the Giants and Rangers, Gearrin was 1-1 with one save and a 3.57 ERA.

[3]   Baseball-Reference.com Win Probability - Oakland Athletics vs. Texas Rangers, July 24 2018. Retrieved from https://www.baseball-reference.com/boxes/TEX/TEX201807240.shtml

[4]   Dan Bernstein, "Frantic Comeback, Davis Homer Lift A's over Rangers," *San Francisco Examiner*, July 25, 2018: A10.

RANGERS, TIGERS COMBINE FOR 31 RUNS, INCLUDING 18 IN ONE INNING, AS TEXAS OVERCOMES A 10-RUN DEFICIT

MAY 8, 2004:
TEXAS RANGERS 16,
DETROIT TIGERS 15,
(10 INNINGS),
AT AMERIQUEST FIELD, ARLINGTON

BY PETER SEIDEL

Sometimes even a 10-run lead isn't enough. This was especially true in May 2004 when the Detroit Tigers, whose pitchers had the second-worst team ERA (4.93), traveled to Texas to face the Rangers, fourth in the American League in runs scored (5.31 runs per game).

The Rangers' starting pitcher was future Cy Young Award winner R.A. Dickey, who had not yet discovered his hard knuckleball. So far the Rangers' first-round pick in the 1996 amateur draft was proving to be a bust, thanks largely to a missing ulnar collateral ligament in his right elbow. In 2008 Dickey, commenting on his condition, said, "Doctors look at me and say I shouldn't be able to turn a doorknob without feeling pain."[1] As disappointing as Dickey's career had been, he was off to a solid start in 2004, winning four of his first five starts with a 3.48 ERA.

After breezing through a one-two-three top of the first and getting the first two Tigers out in the second, Dickey surrendered a line-drive single to left field by Carlos Guillen. Bobby Higginson followed with a blast to the right-field seats that gave the Tigers a 2-0 lead.

The Tigers' starting pitcher was third-year major leaguer Mike Maroth. Like Dickey, he had his challenges. In 2003 he led the American League in earned runs allowed (123) and surrendered a league-high 34 home runs. Like Dickey, Maroth was off to a promising start in 2004, going 3-1 with a 3.58 ERA in the

month of April. Also like Dickey, Maroth's fortunes would take a turn for the worse in May. Maroth's previous start was on May 3 against the Angels, when he gave up five earned runs in 5⅓ innings.

After being given the lead in the top of the second, Maroth gave it back In the bottom of the inning. Mark Teixeira led off and walked on four pitches. On a wild pitch while Brian Jordan was batting allowed Teixeira to take to second. Jordan flied out to left field and Eric Young grounded to third. Facing Kevin Mench, Maroth unleashed another wild pitch, and Teixeira went to third. Maroth walked Mench and Gerald Laird, loading the bases. Michael Young's grounder up the middle plated Teixeira and Mench, tying the game, 2-2. A walk to Hank Blalock loaded the bases again and sent Alfonso Soriano, recently acquired in a trade from the Yankees for Alex Rodriguez, to the plate. Soriano grounded to shortstop and when Guillen threw wild to first, Laird and Young scored, but Tigers right fielder Higginson threw out Blalock at the plate for the third out.

Alex Sanchez led off the top of the third with a line-drive double down the left-field line and scored on Fernando Vina's single, making the score 4-3. The Tigers touched up Dickey again in the fourth. Higginson walked, Craig Monroe singled, and Omar Infante's grounder up the middle scored Higginson, tying the game again, 4-4. Monroe came home in

Sanchez's squeeze play bunt, and Ivan Rodriguez's single drove in Infante and ended Dickey's night. Dickey's line: 3⅔ innings pitched, nine hits, six runs – all earned, which caused his ERA to balloon to 4.58. Doug Brocail relieved Dickey and got Rondell White on a comebacker for the final out of the inning with the Tigers ahead, 6-4. (White was the only Tiger not to get a hit in the game. He went 0-for-6.)

Brocail faced five Tigers in the fifth inning. He walked four of them and gave up a two-run single to Monroe, Ron Mahay relieved Brocail with the bases loaded and no outs and Sanchez smacked a line-drive up the middle, driving in two runs and giving the Tigers a 10-4 lead. Mahay hit Vina with a pitch, then surrendered an RBI single to Rodriguez. Mahay struck out White for the second out of the inning, but Carlos Peña lined a single to right for two more runs. Rodriguez scored on Guillen's force-play grounder to second. It was 14-4, Tigers.

Maroth took the mound in the bottom of the fifth with an extremely comfortable 10-run lead. It was not comfortable enough. After Michael Young's leadoff single, Blalock blasted a home run to deep center field. Soriano legged out a grounder down the third-base line into a double and scored on Herbert Perry's home run to right-center field. It was Perry's first home run since September 26, 2002. Maroth walked Teixeira and his night was finished. In his four-plus innings Maroth gave up nine runs (eight earned) on seven hits and six walks. "The other eight guys around me did their job," said Maroth, who had lost 21 games the previous season. "It's one thing to have a bad outing. But it hurts more since we scored 14 runs in five innings. I just couldn't find a way to get outs."[2]

Danny Patterson was replaced Maroth and walked two batters; that loaded the bases for the Rangers. Al Levine came in and gave up back-to-back singles that narrowed Detroit's lead to 14-11. Michael Young struck out in his second at-bat of the inning, but Soriano's single to center, his second hit of the inning and fourth hit of the game, drove in two more runs, making the score 14-13. Perry's RBI single, also his second hit and third RBI of the inning, tied the game, 14-14. Soriano said later about the Rangers' climb from 10 runs down, "I was thinking maybe we score two runs or three runs at a time. I never thought we could do anything like this."[3] Craig Dingman relieved Patterson and walked Teixeira to load the bases again for the Rangers, but Jordan grounded into a double play, bringing a remarkable inning to a close.

Courtesy The Topps Company.

Alfonso Soriano led the Rangers with runs batted in, with four RBIs.

The Tigers had scored eight runs in the top of the fifth and the Rangers countered with 10 runs. The 18 runs are the second most runs scored in one inning in a major league game, just missing the record of 19 runs scored by the Indians (13) and Red Sox (6) on April 10, 1977. It was the highest-scoring fifth inning in major-league history and lasted 1 hour and 8 minutes. There were 100 pitches thrown (54 by Texas, 46 by Detroit), 13 hits (8 by Texas, 5 by Detroit), 9 walks (5 by Texas, 4 by Detroit), and 28 batters (15 for Texas, 13 for Detroit).

The Tigers may have been stunned, but they quickly recovered and regained the lead in the top of the sixth. Infante led off with a walk, was sacrificed to second by Sanchez, and scored on a single by Rodriguez. Undeterred, the Rangers came back to tie the game, 15-15, in the bottom of the seventh on a leadoff triple by Blalock and a double by Soriano.

The Rangers got one-out back-to-back singles from Soriano and Perry in the bottom of the ninth. (It was Soriano's sixth hit of the game, a Rangers record, and raised his batting average from .302 to .336.) But Teixeira's strikeout and a groundout by Laynce Nix took the game into extra innings.

The Rangers' closer, Francisco Cordero, pitched the top of the 10th and breezed through a one-two-three inning with two strikeouts. In the bottom of the inning, the Tigers also sent in their closer, Ugueth Urbina, who gave up a leadoff walk to Eric Young. He was sacrificed to second, and scored on Michael Young's walk-off single. "It's not the way you draw up a big win," Young said in a jubilant Texas clubhouse. "But it's great for our club, and we proved something to ourselves."[4]

"In 27 or 28 years I've never seen anything like this," Texas manager Buck Showalter said. "Nothing these guys do surprise me anymore."[5]

The Tigers' reaction after the game was understandably more somber. "This shouldn't have happened, but it did," manager Alan Trammell said. "The fact we lost this game is very disturbing."[6]

Sources

In addition to the sources cited in the Notes, the author consulted Baseball-Reference.com, Retrosheet.org, and the following:

backtobaseball.com/playballregularseason.php?page=23&IDindex=TEX200405080.

Associated Press. "Rangers Come Back from 10-Run Deficit in 16-15 Win," *Los Angeles Times*, May 9, 2004.

Notes

1   Alan Schwarz, "New Twist Keeps Dickey's Career Afloat," *New York Times*, February 27, 2008.

2   Associated Press, "Rangers, Tigers Combine for 18-Run Inning," NBC Sports, May 9, 2004. web.archive.org/web/20121009181213/http://nbcsports.msnbc.com/id/4933772/.

3   "Rangers, Tigers Combine for 18-Run Inning."

4   "Rangers, Tigers Combine for 18-Run Inning."

5   "Rangers, Tigers Combine for 18-Run Inning."

6   "Rangers, Tigers Combine for 18-Run Inning."

MARINERS STORM BACK FROM 10-RUN DEFICIT TO DEFEAT HAPLESS PADRES

JUNE 2, 2016:
SEATTLE MARINERS 16,
SAN DIEGO PADRES 13,
AT PETCO PARK, SAN DIEGO

By Gary Belleville

The 2016 season could not have started in a more ominous fashion for the San Diego Padres. They opened at home with a three-game set against the mighty Dodgers, and it did not go well. San Diego was trounced by a combined score of 25-0, making the Padres the first team in baseball history to fail to score a run in a season-opening series.

The team stumbled through the first two months of the season, completely collapsing on a disastrous 1-7 road trip that culminated in a humiliating 16-4 loss in Seattle on May 31 that left them 12½ games out of first place. The next morning, Padres Executive Chairman Ron Fowler lambasted the team in an impassioned radio interview, calling them "miserable failures" and sharply criticizing an underachieving James Shields.[1] One could only imagine what he was thinking two days later when San Diego let a 12-2 lead slip away in a crushing loss to those same Mariners.

Unlike the floundering Padres, the Mariners were exceeding expectations early that season, with the veteran squad holding down first place for most of May. Seattle came into its June 2 game in San Diego a half-game behind the first-place Texas Rangers in the AL West standings. The Mariners sent Wade Miley (5-2, 4.95 ERA) to the mound to face Padres starter Colin Rea. The 25-year-old right-hander, making his 17th career appearance, came into the game with a 3-2 record and a 4.47 ERA.

Miley struggled through the first four innings, giving up five earned runs on nine hits and one walk, and he trailed 5-2 when he returned to the hill for the home half of the fifth. The Padres connected for three more hits against the lefty, including an RBI single by Alexei Ramírez. Miley appeared to have a way out of the inning when Rea came to the plate with two outs and runners on the corners, but he balked home a seventh run and committed the cardinal sin of walking the pitcher. Seattle manager Scott Servais called for the normally reliable Mike Montgomery to enter the game. Unfortunately for the Mariners, this was not Montgomery's day. He surrendered four singles, a walk, a hit-by-pitch, and a wild pitch before eventually getting the third out of the inning on Ramírez's strikeout. After sending 13 men to the plate in the inning, the Padres led 12-2.

The Mariners' chances of winning the game after falling behind by 10 runs obviously weren't good. When Norichika Aoki was retired on a popup to open the top of the sixth, Seattle's Win Expectancy dropped to a scant 0.11 percent.[2] Rea had been cruising up to that point, limiting Seattle to three hits over the first 5⅓ innings without walking a batter. And then suddenly he couldn't get anyone out. After loading the bases on a walk and two singles, he served up a double to Kyle Seager that brought home a pair of runs. With the left-handed-hitting Adam Lind due up next, Padres rookie manager Andy Green pulled Rea in favor of southpaw Brad Hand, which led to Servais countering with a right-handed pinch-hitter, 33-year-old South Korean "rookie" Dae-ho Lee. On a 2-and-2 pitch, Hand hung a curveball over the heart of the plate and Lee crushed it into the second balcony of the Western Metal Supply Co. building for a three-run home run, closing the gap to 12-7. "That (home run) gave us a little adrenaline, like, hey, we might have a shot here," Servais said after the game.[3]

Seattle continued to claw its way back into the game in the top of the seventh. Padres reliever Ryan Buchter loaded the bases on a single, a walk, and a hit-by-pitch before he struck out Nelson Cruz in an intense 11-pitch at-bat for the second out of the inning. Out number three proved elusive for the Padres, as the Mariners put together seven consecutive two-out singles against relievers Buchter, Brandon Maurer, and Matt Thornton. The key hits were an unlikely game-tying single by pinch-hitter Stefen Romero, who was batting .189 in 206 career at-bats, and a single into shallow center field by Shawn O'Malley to put the Mariners up 13-12. When the dust had settled and the inning finally ended, the Mariners had sent 13 hitters to the plate, faced 66 pitches, and scored nine runs to pull ahead 16-12. "That's just incredible the way we streamed those hits together in the seventh inning," recalled Seager. "That was crazy. I'll remember this one for a long time."[4]

Remarkably, the Mariners had turned a 12-2 deficit into a 16-12 lead in two innings. The first two of the seven consecutive two-out singles were from Seager and Lee, giving them four RBIs each during the 14-run outburst. Seager also drove in a run in the first inning to give him five RBIs in the game.

The Padres could only manage to push across an unearned run in the bottom of the seventh, and the Mariners hung on for a 16-13 victory. Cody Martin, called up earlier in the day from Triple-A, earned the victory by pitching a scoreless sixth inning. Seattle's miraculous comeback from a 10-run deficit represented both the largest come-from-behind victory in Mariners history and the biggest blown lead in Padres history. The game also set a record for the highest-scoring game at Petco Park (29 runs), and it tied the Padres' mark for the most hits by both teams in a nine-inning game (36).[5]

"I've been around baseball a long time and you don't see teams come back from 10 (runs down)," said Green. "It's just not something that happens very often."[6] Green was right. The last time a major-league team came back to win after falling behind by 10 runs was on July 20, 2009, when Oakland defeated Minnesota 14-13 after trailing 12-2 in the top of the third inning.

Lost in the shuffle was Jon Jay's 5-for-6 game for San Diego, which came on the heels of a 4-for-6 performance the night before. His nine hits in a two-game span put him into an exclusive club alongside Hall of Famer Tony Gwynn as the only two Padres to achieve the feat.

The improbable win pushed the Mariners into a first-place tie with the Rangers, with the two teams set to open a three-game series in Texas the following evening. Unfortunately for Seattle, it was the last time they would occupy even a share of the top spot in the Western Division that season. The Mariners were swept by the Rangers, which kicked off a disastrous string of 15 losses in 20 games that knocked them out of the race. Despite going 18-9 in September, Seattle still finished nine games back of the Rangers.

The Padres went into a major rebuild two days after their meltdown against the Mariners. Shields, who had signed a four-year, $75 million contract less than 16 months earlier, was traded to the White Sox in a deal that netted two players, including 17-year-old Fernando Tatis Jr. San Diego's best reliever, 39-year-old Fernando Rodney, was sent to the Marlins at the end of June in return for minor-league pitcher Chris Paddack, and their top starting pitcher, Drew Pomeranz, was traded to the Red Sox in mid-July. To top it all off, San Diego unloaded veteran Matt Kemp's hefty contract on the Atlanta Braves at the end of July in what was a cost-saving deal for the Padres.

Predictably, San Diego played uninspiring baseball for the remainder of the year, finishing in last place with a 68-94 record. It was the team's sixth consecutive losing season. As of the end of the 2019 campaign, that streak had been extended to nine in a row, which led to the dismissal of Green, the manager for four of those sub-.500 seasons. Fowler, upset about not seeing the desired results from the team's multiyear rebuild, blasted his team publicly, just as he had done three years earlier. He apologized to the fans in 2019 for an "embarrassing" season. "We sucked," he bluntly proclaimed, which sadly did not come as news to long-suffering Padres fans.[7]

Sources

In addition to the sources cited in the Notes, the author consulted Baseball-Reference.com and Retrosheet.org. Full video of the game is available on YouTube at youtube.com/watch?v=IgIv7idBZho.

Notes

1 Bill Shaikin, "Once the All-Star Game Is Gone, the Padres Go Back to Chanting, 'Beat L.A.' How Do They Plan to Do That?" *Los Angeles Times*, July 9, 2016, latimes.com/sports/mlb/la-sp-padres-shaikin-20160709-snap-story.html, accessed October 22, 2019.

2 Win Expectancy is the percentage chance a team will win based on the score, inning, outs, runners on base, and the run environment. These percentages are calculated using historical data, which means that if a team is losing and has a 0.11 percent Win Expectancy, only 0.11 percent (or 1 out of every 909) of teams in similar situations in the past have come back to win.

3 Bernie Wilson, "Mariners Stun Padres with 14 Runs in 2 Innings to Win 16-13," *San Diego Union-Tribune*, June 6, 2016, sandiegouniontribune.com/sdut-mariners-stun-padres-with-14-runs-in-2-innings-to-2016jun02-story.html, accessed October 22, 2019.

4 SportsPress NorthWest Staff, "An Epic Comeback: Mariners Trail 12-2, Win 16-13," *SportsPress NorthWest*, June 6, 2016, sportspressnw.com/2219412/2016/an-epic-comeback-mariners-trail-12-2-win-16-13, accessed October 22, 2019.

5 As of the end of the 2019 season, none of these records had been surpassed.

6 Wilson.

7 Kevin Acee, "Ron Fowler Apologizes to Padres Fans, Says 'Heads Will Roll' if 2020 Isn't Better," *San Diego Union-Tribune*, September 30, 2019, sandiegouniontribune.com/sports/padres/story/2019-09-30/padres-ron-fowler-apologizes-fans-heads-will-roll-myers-hedges, accessed October 22, 2019.

DIAMONDBACKS' LATE HEROICS TAP BREWERS

JULY 3, 2008:
ARIZONA DIAMONDBACKS 6,
MILWAUKEE BREWERS 5,
AT CHASE FIELD, PHOENIX

BY KEN CARRANO

The Milwaukee Brewers experienced a lot of ups and downs during their 2008 season, which ended with a wild-card berth. After a 6-2 start, the Brewers found themselves four games under .500 on May 25 (23-27), only to be six games over .500 by the end of June (44-38). The Brewers raised their record to 46-38 after winning the first two games of July, but

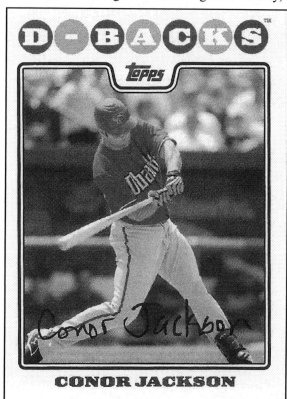

Courtesy The Topps Company.

CONOR JACKSON

It was 5-0 heading into the bottom of the ninth. The D'Backs scored four runs and had runners on second and third. Conor Jackson singled to center for two more runs and a walkoff win.

for the final game of the series against the Arizona Diamondbacks, they experienced all of the highs and lows of their season to date in nine innings on a warm Arizona afternoon.

The Diamondbacks for their part were simply trying to right their ship. Having taken over first place in the National League West Division on April 7, the Diamondbacks had as much as a 6½-game lead in the division, but hit a skid and were only 3-9 in their last 12 games heading into the July 3 game, and their lead had shrunk to 1½ games.

The Brewers started Manny Parra, who had been one of their best pitchers to that point, with an 8-2 record and wins in his last five starts. The Diamondbacks countered with Brandon Webb, who was trying to replicate his 2006 Cy Young Award season and was 12-4 but had lost two of his last four starts. Parra was the better pitcher on this day, but neither factored in the decision.

After stranding a runner at third in the top of the first, the Brewers took advantage of Webb's wildness and scored two runs in the second inning. Russell Branyan led off with a walk and took second on Gabe Kapler's single. Webb hit Mike Cameron to load the bases, then threw a wild pitch to Jason Kendall and Branyan scored. Kendall's weak grounder to third scored Kapler. Parra then grounded into a double play. The Brewers added a run in the third when J.J. Hardy got his second extra-base hit of the game, a bases-empty home run to left field.

The Diamondbacks got a runner on in every inning through the fifth but couldn't solve Parra. Their best chance came in the bottom of the fifth inning, when

Webb's single and a walk to Stephen Drew put two men on with no outs. But Parra retired the next three hitters with a fly out, a strikeout, and a fielder's-choice grounder. The mountain the Diamondbacks needed to climb got bigger in the sixth. Branyan singled to right-center to lead off the inning, and stole second with one out. Cameron then slugged his 13th home run of the season to give the Brewers a five-run advantage.

Brewers manager Ned Yost pulled Parra after a one-two-three sixth inning with his pitch count at an even 100. Yost may have been regretting his decision when reliever Mitch Stetter gave up a leadoff single to Chris Burke and walked Augie Ojeda, but for the third time in the game, the Diamondbacks failed to score after having two on with no one out; Stetter got Drew to pop out foul to first and struck out Justin Upton and Orlando Hudson. Yost brought in his former closer, Eric Gagne, for the eighth, and his one-two-three inning put the Brewers on the brink of their third straight victory. But just as with the Brewers' season to this point, the game took an unwanted turn. "We played possum for eight innings and then surprised them," Diamondbacks manager Bob Melvin later said.[1]

Yost's decision to start the ninth inning with reliever Guillermo Mota was one that left fans on both sides scratching their heads. Mota had started the season well, but the veteran had been ineffective of late. From June 6 through this game, he had struggled to an ERA of 7.56 with two losses and a blown save in nine appearances. But the Brewers had won six of those nine games, and a seventh in 10 Mota appearances seemed likely. "We had a five-run lead. Let's face the facts," said Yost.[2] The facts in this case are that Mota faced three hitters and didn't have a ball leave the infield, but he left the game with the bases loaded. Robby Hammock started the inning with a weak single to third that bounced off Branyan's glove. Burke followed with a walk, and Ojeda hit a grounder to the hole at second that Rickie Weeks knocked down but on which he couldn't make a play. "I made my pitches," insisted Mota. "What can I do? I just keep making my pitches."[3] Yost added, "He gave up two infield hits and a walk. They weren't balls that were hit hard. They were just well-placed balls."[4]

Yost replaced Mota with Brian Shouse to face pinch-hitter Chad Tracy. Tracy had faced Shouse twice before in his career with no success, but with the Brewers withering on the vine, this time was different. Tracy hit the first hard ball of the inning, to the right-center-field gap for a bases-clearing double,

and the Brewers' once-safe 5-0 lead was down to 5-3. "That hit gave us our pulse," Melvin said.[5] The game was still there to be won for the Brewers, who brought in their closer, Salomon Torres, who had been 14-14 in save opportunities after supplanting Gagne as closer. Torres had saved the Brewers' two wins against the Diamondbacks in each of the last two days and had successfully saved a game in May after pitching in the prior two games.

Torres faced Upton, and his single to shallow right moved Tracy to third. Hudson came up as the potential winning run and his double down the third-base line scored Tracy, making the score 5-4 Brewers, still with no one out. Torres now had to face the cleanup hitter Conor Jackson. Like Tracy, Jackson had had no success entering this game against Torres, having gone 0-for-7, including a fly out the day before. And again, like Tracy, this time he found success in the form of an agonizingly slow roller that avoided Hardy and scored Upton and Hudson to give the Diamondbacks their largest comeback win since they defeated the Tampa Bay Devil Rays 10-8 after trailing 7-1 in 2007. "It wasn't a pretty thing," Jackson said after the game, "but it will look like a line drive tomorrow."[6] Torres stated the obvious from a somber Brewers locker room: "With a 5-0 lead, it appeared the deal was sealed. Apparently it wasn't."[7] He added, "We can't let this game bother us. We have to shake it off and go back after it." Melvin's locker room was in a better place postgame. "That kind of game doesn't happen often," Melvin said. "I can't remember a game where a team has been shut out, rather meekly, and then goes out and puts up a six-spot."[8]

Sources

In addition to the sources listed in the notes, the author accessed Retorsheet.org, Baseball-Reference.com, SABR's BioProject via SABR.org, *The Sporting News* archive via Paper of Record, the *Arizona Republic* via newspapers.com, and the *Milwaukee Journal Sentinel* via NewsBank.

Notes

1   Don Ketchum, "Rousing Rally," *Arizona Republic,* July 4, 2008: 38.

2   Tom Haudricort, "Vulnerable to Collapse," *Milwaukee Journal Sentinel,* July 4, 2008: 1.

3   Haudricort.

4   Haudricort.

5   Ketchum.

6   Ketchum.

7   Haudricort.

8   Ketchum.

FOR WHOM THE BELL TOLES

AUGUST 31, 2016:
LOS ANGELES DODGERS 10,
ROCKIES 8, AT COORS FIELD, DENVER

BY TONY S. OLIVER

They just don't make doubleheaders like they used to do; in fact, they hardly make them anymore. Long a fixture of the national pastime, the twin bill has become a relic; forgotten, antiquated, like wool uniforms and train travel. In 2016 only 14 "doubleheaders" were played, all due to weather-related rescheduling of prior games.[1] None were true doubleheaders; all required separate admission to each game.

But on Wednesday night, August 31, this dinosaur roared, waking up a complacent club. While the Dodgers were far from struggling (they started the day with a .557 winning percentage), their NL West Division lead had shrunk to one game after they were shut out 7-0 in the day game against Colorado while the Giants beat the Diamondbacks. They still had another game to play: rain on Tuesday had pushed that night's game to Wednesday night.

The Dodgers and Rockies shared 23 years of undistinguished history together since Colorado joined the National League in 1993. Unlike LA's rivalry with the Giants, it did not start in New York City; unlike the Cubs and Cardinals, they were not bound by geographical proximity. Colorado entered the season 161-217 against the boys in blue; by the time the first game ended, they had split the season series. There was little reason to believe this makeup contest would be memorable. Official attendance was 22,683 though one would be hard pressed to find that many souls in the stands once the Rockies jumped to an 8-2 lead through seven innings.[2] With just two innings remaining, any bettors left in Coors Field would have begun making plans for the Broncos, Avalanche, and Nuggets seasons.

Jeff Hoffman felt good. Despite throwing on only four days' rest, he had kept Los Angeles to two runs in five innings, navigating through a powerful lineup relatively unscathed. He had been roughly welcomed by veteran Chase Utley, who swatted a home run to deep center field from the leadoff slot. Hoffman's club had backed him up with lumber, knocking out starter Bud Norris (three innings, six runs, five of them earned) before the Dodgers clotted the bleeding. Stephen Cardullo, celebrating his 29th birthday and himself a rookie playing in only his fifth big-league game, clobbered a grand slam in the first after an earlier run had scored; it was a storybook day for the first baseman, who had slugged a pinch-hit homer in the first game.[3] He had spent the last four years in the Independent League wilderness before the Colorado organization signed him to a Triple-A deal earlier in the year.

When Hoffman took the mound for the top of the second, he had a lead for the first time in his brief major-league career. Although the visitors added another run when Andrew Toles doubled in Yasmani Grandal, the Rockies riposted with an unearned run in the third to make it 6-2. Toles had been in the big leagues for less than two months, completing an unexpected progression by being promoted from Class A to Double A to Triple A and then the majors within the same year. "All I want to do is contribute," the soft-spoken outfielder said after the game.[4]

As he hit the showers, Hoffman could feel satisfied that no matter what happened, he could not lose the game. Then again, he wanted to win it. Jordan Lyles (one inning, two walks) and Jake McGee (one inning, one strikeout) kept it in cruise control. In the seventh, Nolan Arenado added a two-run blast, padding the lead to six runs.

Major-league teams were 1-448 thus far in 2016 when trailing by six or more runs in the eighth inning.[5] Perhaps no one told the Dodgers; maybe they did not want to hear it. Matt Carasiti began the eighth inning on the mound for the Rockies. Sporting an unsightly 10.61 ERA, he retired Justin Turner, then in his third year with the Dodgers. The tonsorially challenged third sacker battled to a full count but ended up meekly grounding to short. Veteran Adrián González, unfazed by an 0-and-2 hole, drilled a double to right field which was followed by another by Grandal, this one to center field, which scored González. A five-pitch walk to Josh Reddick ended Carasiti's evening and brought in Carlos Estevez. The tall Dominican had worked a perfect inning in the first game, but Dodgers outfielder Joc Pederson laced the first offering to right field, scoring Grandal. Toles then loaded the bases with a single, bringing Howie Kendrick to the plate. The veteran contact hitter poked a sacrifice fly to right field, scoring Reddick, before Utley grounded out to second base.

Though the Dodgers scored three runs in the eighth, their win probability added increased only from 1 percent to 4 percent, hardly the stuff of motivational posters.[6] But a comeback classic takes more than a highlight; it hinges on overconfident moves, poor positioning, or perhaps a blown call. It makes for a combustible mix, like Mentos and diet soda, agitated for explosion. In other words, it took the ninth inning.

Adam Ottavino faced eventual Rookie of the Year Corey Seager, who showed uncharacteristic plate discipline and took first base on five pitches. Turner struck out swinging and González lined out to short, putting the Rockies one defensive out from a doubleheader sweep. Seager moved to second on defensive indifference; he then daringly took third on Grandal's single to left field. Reddick singled to center out of the reach of middle infielders DJ LeMahieu and Cristhian Adames, scoring Seager. Pederson, himself a free-swinger, was granted a base on balls in a five-pitch appearance, loading the bases for Toles.

In the visitors bullpen, All-Star Kenley Jansen had quickly begun to loosen up. He had not seen action in the first game, and with the Rockies' six-run lead, he was not expecting to pitch. That all changed in a hurry. Ottavino's second pitch was too close to the middle of the plate and Toles hammered the baseball to deep left field for his first (and only) career grand slam. A shell-shocked crowd watched in silence as Ottavino retired Kendrick on two pitches to close the inning, but the damage had been done. The scoreboard now read 10-8, Los Angeles.

Toles's path to the majors had been both torturous and tortuous. His astonishing 2016 voyage was no overnight success. Selected by the Marlins in the 2010 draft, he chose to enroll at the University of Tennessee, though he transferred to Chipola College. Tampa

Courtesy The Topps Company.

Andrew Toles drove in five runs, the last four coming on a ninth-inning grand slam.

Bay selected him two years later, and he signed with the Rays. He performed well across the Rookie and Class-A leagues but took a year off baseball in 2015, struggling with anxiety. Major leaguers have long battled mental issues by euphemisms, from the "yips" when throwing to a base to a seemingly overnight inability to throw strikes. Khalil Greene, Dontrelle Willis, and Zach Greinke have taken time off in their careers to deal with the lingering issues of anxiety and depression, among other ailments.[7] The 24/7 coverage of social media has made their stories well-known, but others preceded them: Marty Bergen savagely assassinated his wife and children in 1900, but Jimmy Piersall beat the odds to enjoy an All-Star career.[8]

A converted catcher, Curaçao native Jensen wasted no time punching out Charlie Blackmon. LeMahieu gave him a tough, six-pitch at-bat but ultimately saw a third strike cross the plate. Arenado singled to left field but David Dahl struck out looking. In a scant 15 pitches, the game was over. Dodgers manager Dave Roberts was emphatic about Toles's strong contributions down the stretch: "To see where he's come from to now helping a contending team win games is remarkable. There's no reason why this ride can't stop for him. He's opened up a lot of eyes."[9]

Baseball, with seemingly unlimited scenarios, lends itself to "what ifs?" Would the game have ended differently had it been played on its original scheduled day? Perhaps. Maybe it would have been just as different had it been played a day later (September 1) when rosters expanded to 40 men. With more arms in the bullpen, Colorado could have mixed-and-matched lefties and righties and taken advantage of the match-ups against new faces. Then again, the Dodgers could have done the same.

Sources

In addition to the sources cited in the Notes, the author consulted game information on Baseball-Reference.com and Retrosheet.org

Notes

1   List of 2016 MLB Doubleheaders. espn.com/ mlb/stats/doubleheaders/_/year/2016.

2   Attendance for the day (first) game was 24,790.

3   Baseball-Reference Play Index, query term "2016 season, is birthday=yes, HR>=1." baseball-reference.com/tiny/D66BB.

4   Associated Press, "Andrew Toles' grand slam caps Dodgers' late comeback vs. Rockies," *USA Today*, August 31, 2016. usatoday.com/story/sports/mlb/2016/08/31/anderson-rockies-top-dodgers-to-open-doubleheader/89676380/

5   Michael Duarte, "Dodgers Avoid Sweep with Shocking 10-8 Comeback in Colorado Against Rockies," NBC Los Angeles, August 31, 2016. nbclosangeles.com/news/local/Dodgers-Avoid-Sweep-with-Shocking-Comeback-in-Colorado-391968581.html.

6   "Win probability" calculates the specific probability added or subtracted by each possible play. Baseball-Reference shows the data in the game summary. baseball-reference.com/boxes/COL/COL201608312.shtml.

7   Perry Schwartz, "Hong-Chih Kuo and 10 MLB Players Who've Hit the DL for Mental Health Reasons." *Bleacher Report,* May 26, 2011. bleacherreport.com/articles/711732-hong-chih-kuo-and-10-athletes-whove-hit-the-dl-for-mental-health-reasons.

8   Stacey Gotsulias, "Manicball: A History of Mental Illness in Baseball." Baseball Past and Present, retrieved August 31, 2019. baseballpastand-present.com/mlb/manicball-history-mental-illness-baseball-2/.

9   Duarte.

DAN UGGLA BEATS THE TEAM PAYING HIM

APRIL 28, 2015:
WASHINGTON NATIONALS 13,
ATLANTA BRAVES 12,
AT TURNER FIELD, ATLANTA

By Laura H. Peebles

A.J. Cole's major-league debut on this Tuesday night in Atlanta did not go well. The Washington Nationals right-hander was pulled at the end of the second inning, having given up nine hits and nine runs to Atlanta on seven singles, two doubles, and a sacrifice fly, although he did record his first major-league strikeout. Five of the runs were unearned,[1] as they scored after his own fielding error (he dropped the ball while covering first). With the score 9-1, Atlanta, when Cole departed, Matt Williams, the Nationals manager, brought in Tanner Roark to eat some innings: a reasonable choice, given that Roark had been a 15-game winner as a starter in 2014.[2]

Although the Nationals had scored in the first and third, the score at the end of the fourth inning was 10-2, and it was looking like a blowout victory for Atlanta and a seventh straight loss for the Nationals. But the Nationals chipped away at the deficit. They scored four runs in the fifth on a sacrifice fly and a three-run homer by José Lobaton. They followed that with a solo homer by Denard Span in the sixth, chasing Atlanta's starter, Julio Teheran, after 5⅔ innings. He had given up seven runs (three earned), leaving the score a much-less-lopsided 11-7 Atlanta at the end of the sixth. The homers by Lobaton and Span were the first of the year for each. Teheran was relieved by Michael Kohn, who earned a hold by getting the last out in the sixth.

Meanwhile, Roark had managed to limit the damage to one run in the fourth on a single by A.J. Pierzynski, but ran into trouble in the sixth. After Roark gave up a run on a single and a double, and then walked the next batter, Williams brought in Matt

Thornton. He did not allow either of his two inherited runners to score. Blake Trienen pitched the seventh and eighth, allowing only one run, Atlanta's 12th, on another single by Pierzynski in the Braves' seventh.

Atlanta had tapped Luis Avilán to pitch the seventh with the 11-7 lead. After getting two outs, he gave up a two-run triple to Dan Uggla. Reed Johnson followed

Dan Uggla drove in five of the Nats' 13 runs, with runs 11, 12, and 13 scoring on his ninth-inning home run.

with a ground-rule double, scoring Uggla. Uggla had been released by Atlanta the previous season; the Braves were paying him $12.69 million while the Nationals were paying only the major-league-minimum portion of his salary ($507,500). During the 2014-15 offseason, he had received treatment to correct an apparent problem with his vision, which had possibly been affected by being hit by pitches in 2012 and 2013.[3] His oculomotor dysfunction may have contributed to a steep decline in his playing abilities and his release by both the Braves and San Francisco Giants in 2014.[4] Given an opportunity with the Nationals at spring training as a nonroster invitee, he made the team in a spot-starting and pinch-hitting role.[5] This was the Nationals' first visit to Atlanta in 2015, and many among the 14,833 fans in attendance were not shy about booing him, especially after his triple and run scored reduced the Atlanta lead significantly.

Neither team scored in the eighth; Atlanta's Jim Johnson got a hold for his effort. The Braves called on closer Jason Grilli in the ninth with a 12-10 lead, looking for a save. Although Grilli started with a strikeout of Ryan Zimmerman, he followed that by allowing a single by Lobaton and a walk to Danny Espinosa. Uggla was up next. Grilli got ahead 0-and-2, but Uggla deposited his next offering well into the left-field stands. That made it 13-12 Nationals, with raucous cheering in the visitors' dugout and silence in the stands--with the exception of a few visiting Washington fans. It was Grilli's first blown save of the young season after seven successful outings.

The Nationals' Drew Storen earned his fifth save in the bottom of the ninth, surrendering a walk but no hits. Trienen, Washington's pitcher of record when they took the lead in the ninth inning, got the win.

The vicissitudes of baseball were in full display this night. In a game with 25 runs and 32 hits, Atlanta's Freddie Freeman went 4-for-6, but had no RBIs. The thirty-eight-year-old Pierzynski was the offensive star for Atlanta, going 4-for-4 with 4 RBIs.

Although Denard Span (5-for-6, 11 total bases) had a statistically better night at the plate than Uggla (3-for-5, 8 total bases), the game is remembered more for Uggla's performance against the team that released him the previous summer--which ended up paying him for a memorable performance against it. The Nationals' Max Scherzer apparently agreed, dousing Uggla with Hershey's chocolate sauce after the game in celebration.[6] Unfortunately for Uggla, this game was not the beginning of a big comeback: He hit only one more home run over the rest of the season, fin-

ished with a .183 average, and was out of baseball after the season at age 35.[7]

He did, though, enjoy the comeback and the chocolate sauce bath. "There are some crazy dudes in here. They get excited and they love to show it," Uggla enthused after the celebration.[8]

Span's five hits raised his early-season average from .207 to .314. With a single in the first, doubles in the third, fifth and ninth, and a solo homer in the sixth, he was missing only an elusive triple for the cycle. Unlike Uggla, perhaps this was the game that got his year kick-started; he finished 2015 at .301, in 61 games and 275 plate appearances.[9]

The big nights from Uggla and Span, with steady relief pitching from Thornton, Treinen, and Storen that slowed the Braves' attack over the final four innings, produced a comeback from an eight-run deficit--the biggest comeback in Nationals' history.[10]

Sources

In addition to the sources cited in the Notes, the author referred to the MLB.TV recording of the game at MLB.com, the call of the game on radio station 106.7 FM, Washington, D. C., and the game box scores at Baseball-Reference.com and Retrosheet.org.

Notes

1   The mlb.com box score shows all runs allowed by A.J. Cole and Julio Teheran as earned, but both sets of announcers' calls, the online record accompanying the recorded game, and the Baseball-Reference.com and Retrosheet.org box scores are consistent with this account. Cole allowed nine runs, four earned; Teheran allowed seven runs, three earned.

2   baseball-reference.com/players/r/roarkta01.shtml.

3   tomahawktake.com/2015/01/05/oculomotor-dysfunction-dan-uggla/.

4   Uggla had been released by Atlanta on July 18, 2014, then signed three days later by San Francisco. Released by San Francisco less than a month later (August 7), he was signed by Washington on December 26, 2014.

5   Chelsea Janes, "Career in the Balance: Dan Uggla, Cut by Braves, Hopes to Stick With Nats," *Washington Post,* February 27, 2015, washingtonpost. com/sports/nationals/career-in-the-balance-dan-uggla-cut-by-braves-hopes-to-stick-with-nats/2015/02/27/8faff33e-be8a-11e4-b274-e5209a3bc9a9_story. html?postshare=9681425115257256&utm_term=.83f5be4d9901.

6   This was the first time the chocolate sauce celebration occurred. It continued throughout the Nationals' 2015 season. . Scott Allen, "Max Scherzer Explains the Nats' Chocolate Syrup Celebration," *Washington Post,* May 14, 2015, washingtonpost.com/news/ dc-sports-bog/wp/2015/05/14/max-scherzer-explains-the-nats-choc-olate-syrup-celebration/?utm_term=.1bc36095af42#comments.

7   baseball-reference.com/players/u/uggla da01.shtml.

8   Chelsea Janes, "In a Flash, Nationals Spring to Life," *Washington Post,* April 28, 2017, washingtonpost.com, accessed November 2, 2017.

9   baseball-reference.com/players/s/spande01.shtml.

10   Bob Carpenter, Washington TV announcer, on game broadcast; Janes, "In a flash."

CONTRIBUTORS

Gary Belleville is a retired information technology consultant. He has written articles for the SABR Games Project and the *Baseball Research Journal*, and has contributed to several SABR books. Before working on SABR projects, Gary was the editor and lead writer for baseball blogs devoted to local independent league and college wood-bat teams. Gary grew up in Ottawa idolizing the Montreal Expos. He graduated from the University of Waterloo with a bachelor of mathematics (computer science) degree. He resides in Victoria, British Columbia, with his spouse, Shirley.

Charlie Bevis is the author of seven books on baseball history, most recently *Red Sox vs. Braves in Boston: The Battle for Fans' Hearts, 1901–1952*. A member of SABR since 1984, he has contributed more than five dozen biographies to the SABR BioProject as well as several to SABR books, including *The 1967 Impossible Dream Red Sox* and *The Glorious Beaneaters of the 1890s*. He writes baseball from his home in Chelmsford, Massachusetts.

Nathan Bierma is a SABR member and SABR Games Project contributor living in Grand Rapids, Michigan. His writing has appeared in the *Chicago Tribune, Chicago Sports Review*, and the *Detroit Free Press*, and in SABR's recent books on the greatest games at Wrigley Field and Comiskey Park. He is the author of *The Eclectic Encyclopedia of English: Language at Its Most Enigmatic, Ephemeral, and Egregious*. His website is nathanbierma.com.

David Black is a displaced Chicago Cubs fan who resides in Highlands Ranch, Colorado. While relatively new to baseball writing, having composed only one previous summary for the SABR Games Project, he has been a member of SABR since 2001, enjoying the fine research and writing of so many SABR members. He hopes this article serves to accelerate his own involvement in SABR publications. As of 2020, he is a 32-year veteran in education, currently teaching at Lutheran High School in Parker, Colorado, and as an adjunct college professor. David's baseball research interests include last games and events at ballparks, Denver baseball history, and anything else in the history of the game that attracts his attention.

Stephen D. Boren, MD, MBA, FACEP, is an emergency-medicine physician who graduated from the University of Illinois and did his emergency-medicine residency training at Milwaukee County Hospital. There he first heard about SABR and joined in 1979. His articles have appeared on multiple occasions in the *Baseball Research Journal, The National Pastime*, and *Baseball Digest*.

Thomas J. Brown Jr. is a lifelong Mets fan who became a Durham Bulls fan after moving to North Carolina in the early 1980s. He was a national board-certified high-school science teacher for 34 years before retiring in 2016. Tom still volunteers with the ELL students at his former high school, serving as a mentor to those students and the teachers who are now working with them. He also provides support and guidance for his former ELL students when they embark on different career paths after graduation. Tom has been a member of SABR since 1995 when he learned about the organization during a visit to Cooperstown on his honeymoon. He has become active in the organization since his retirement and has written numerous biographies and game stories, mostly about the New York Mets. Tom also enjoys traveling as much as possible with his wife and has visited major-league and minor-league baseball parks across the country on his many trips. He also loves to cook and makes all the meals for at his house while writing about those meals on his blog, Cooking and My Family.

Dr. John J. Burbridge Jr. is currently professor emeritus at Elon University, where he was both a dean and professor. He is also an adjunct at York College of Pennsylvania. While at Elon he introduced and taught *Baseball and Statistics*. He has authored several SABR publications and presented at SABR conventions, NINE, and the Seymour meetings. He is a lifelong New York Giants baseball fan. The greatest Giants-Dodgers game he attended was a 1-0 Giants victory in Jersey City in 1956. Yes, the Dodgers did play in Jersey City in 1956 and 1957. John can be reached at burbridg@elon.edu.

Frederick C. "Rick" Bush joined SABR in March 2014. Since that time he has written articles for numerous SABR books as well as the Biography and Games Project websites. Together with Bill Nowlin, he has co-edited three SABR books about the Negro Leagues: *Bittersweet Goodbye: The Black Barons, the Grays, and the 1948 Negro League World Series* (2017); *The Newark Eagles Take Flight: The Story of the 1946 Negro League Champions* (2019); and the *Pride of Smoketown: The 1935 Pittsburgh Crawfords* (2020). Rick lives with his wife, Michelle, their three sons – Michael, Andrew, and Daniel – and their border collie-mix, Bailey, in the greater Houston area, where he teaches English at Wharton County Junior College's satellite campus in Sugar Land.

JP Caillault has been a professor of astronomy at the University of Georgia for 33 years. He joined SABR in 1984, when, as a Ph.D. student at Columbia University, he made his first SABR presentation to the Casey Stengel Chapter (NYC) at the Shea Stadium Diamond Club. He has since written articles for *Baseball Digest* and SABR's *Baseball Research Journal,* chapters for *Inventing Baseball: The 100 Greatest Games of the 19th Century* (SABR 2013) and *The Glorious Beaneaters of the 1890s* (SABR 2019), and two books on nineteenth-century baseball: *A Tale of Four Cities* (McFarland & Co., 2003) and *The Complete New York Clipper Biographies* (McFarland & Co., 2009). His presentation at the 2010 SABR National Convention in Atlanta was given the *USA Today Sports Weekly* Award for Best Poster Presentation. He is an avid collector of baseball cards, owning the complete set of Topps cards for every season dating back to 1957.

Ralph Caola is from Troy, New York, where he grew up playing baseball and listening to Yankees games with his father. After a lack of talent ended his collegiate baseball career, he played softball for 30 years. In 2003 he wrote a series of articles titled "Using Calculus to Relate Runs to Wins," which appeared in SABR's Statistical Analysis Research Committee newsletter, *By the Numbers.* He also wrote the SABR biographies of Bobby Bonds and Nomar Garciaparra. The retired engineer and businessman

now spends his summers in Troy and winters in Port Charlotte, Florida, playing tennis and golf.

A lifelong White Sox fan surrounded by Cubs fans in the northern suburbs of Chicago, **Ken Carrano** works as a chief financial officer for a large landscaping firm and as a soccer referee. Ken and his Brewers fan wife, Ann, share two children, two golden retrievers, and a mutual distain for the blue side of Chicago.

Alan Cohen has been a SABR member since 2010. He serves as vice president-treasurer of the Connecticut Smoky Joe Wood Chapter and is datacaster (MiLB First Pitch stringer) for the Hartford Yard Goats, the Double-A affiliate of the Colorado Rockies. His biographies, game stories, and essays have appeared in more than 40 SABR publications. Since his first *Baseball Research Journal* article appeared in 2013, Alan has continued to expand his research into the Hearst Sandlot Classic (1946-1965), which launched the careers of 88 major-league players. He has four children and eight grandchildren and resides in Connecticut with his wife, Frances, their cats, Morty, Ava, and Zoe, and their dog, Buddy.

Rory Costello, a lifelong Mets fan, nearly drove his mother's car off the road while listening to Game Six of the 1986 NLCS. He lives in Brooklyn, New York, with his wife, Noriko, and son, Kai.

Richard Cuicchi joined SABR in 1983 and is an active member of the Schott-Pelican Chapter. Since his retirement as an information technology executive, Richard authored *Family Ties: A Comprehensive Collection of Facts and Trivia about Baseball's Relatives.* He has contributed to numerous SABR BioProject and Games publications. He does freelance writing and blogging about a variety of baseball topics on his website, TheTenthInning.com. Richard lives in New Orleans with his wife, Mary.

Rich D'Ambrosio is an ardent Phillies fan. A lifelong resident of Philadelphia and a longtime Phillies season-ticket holder, he has been a member of the Connie Mack Chapter of SABR since 1997. Rich is a graduate of Temple University, La Salle University, and St. Joseph's University. He is an English teacher at St. Hubert Catholic High School for Girls in Philadelphia. Rich has contributed bios of Dick Allen and Larry Bowa to SABR. In addition to writing, Rich enjoys collecting Phillies memorabilia, the literary works of John Updike and William Faulkner, and Notre Dame football, which he worships from afar.

Scott Ferkovich is the answer to the trivia question, "Who wrote *Motor City Champs: The 1934-1935 Detroit Tigers*"? He has also edited or contributed to a seemingly endless lineup of SABR publications, including the classic *Tigers by the Tale: Great Games at Michigan and Trumbull*. A child of the '70s, he used to carry a shabby Mark Fidrych rookie card in his wallet, until somebody stole the wallet. Scott lives in Detroit, but asks that you please not alert the authorities.

James Forr is a recovering Pirates fan in the heart of Cardinals country. His book, *Pie Traynor: A Baseball Biography*, co-authored with David Proctor, was a nominee for the 2010 CASEY Award. He is also a winner of the McFarland-SABR Baseball Research Award and was a speaker at the 2019 Frederick Ivor-Campbell 19th Century Base Ball Conference.

Brian Frank is passionate about documenting the history of major- and minor-league baseball. He is the creator of the website The Herd Chronicles (herdchronicles.com), which is dedicated to preserving the history of the Buffalo Bisons. His articles can also be read on the official website of the Bisons. He was a contributor to and assistant editor of the book *The Seasons of Buffalo Baseball, 1857-2020*, and he's a frequent contributor to SABR publications. Brian and his wife, Jenny, enjoy traveling around the country in their camper to major- and minor-league ballparks and taking an annual trip to Europe. Brian was a history major at Canisius College, where he earned a bachelor of arts. he also received a juris doctor from the University at Buffalo School of Law.

Adrian Fung lives and works in Toronto. He joined SABR (Hanlan's Point Chapter – Toronto) in 2014 and has contributed several stories to SABR Games Project, mostly about memorable games in Blue Jays history, including some that are now part of SABR books. Adrian attended the 2019 SABR Black Sox Scandal Centennial Symposium and survived the Friday night deluge that washed away the scheduled doubleheader at Guaranteed Rate Field. In January 2020, at a Hanlan's Point Chapter meeting, he presented cases for how the 1919 Reds could have won a "clean" World Series as well as how Buck Weaver was unfairly treated. Adrian occasionally writes for the longest-running Pittsburgh Penguins fan blog,

the Pensblog, under the guise of his Twitter *nom de guerre* "PenguinsMarch."

Gregory Funk joined SABR in 1981 and serves on the steering committee for the Ted Williams Chapter in the San Diego area. He prepares tax returns and plays the organ for his living, but his passion has been baseball and its statistics, strategy, and trivia. He is lifelong Padres fan who has never missed attending a home opener.

Gordon J. Gattie is an engineer for the US Navy. His baseball research interests include ballparks, historical records, and statistical analysis. A SABR member since 1998, Gordon earned his Ph.D. from SUNY Buffalo, where he used baseball to investigate judgment performance in complex dynamic environments. Ever the optimist, he dreams of a Cleveland Indians-Washington Nationals World Series matchup, especially after the Nationals' 2019 World Series championship. Lisa, his wonderful wife who roots for the Yankees, and Morrigan, their yellow Labrador, enjoy traveling across the country to visit ballparks and other baseball-related sites. Gordon has contributed to several SABR publications and the Games Project.

Nate Gilman lives in the Milwaukee area with his wife and two children. Having graduated with a degree in print journalism, Nate fell into the world of enterprise software sales. As a lifelong baseball fan, he has looked for different ways to combine his passion for writing with his love of the game. While Nate has been a SABR member for several years, this is his first contribution to a SABR publication.

Steven Glassman is currently the Manor College director of sports information and an entertainment staff member/phanstormer for the Philadelphia Phillies. He has been a SABR member since 1994. Steven regularly makes presentations for the SABR Connie Mack Chapter. He wrote five SABR Convention articles, most recently "Padres' Near No-Hitters" (SABR 49). He also wrote a SABR Games Project article, "September 27, 1963: Houston Colt .45's start a lineup of all rookies." Steven graduated with a bachelor of science degree in sport and recreation management from Temple University. He was certified Microsoft Office Specialist in Word 2016 by Full Circle Computing. Originally born in

Philadelphia, Steven currently lives in Warminster, Pennsylvania.

Irv Goldfarb has written numerous articles, bios, and book reviews for various SABR publications since joining in 1999. He and his lovely wife, Mercedes, live in Union City, New Jersey, and their dog and two cats have since been updated to a dog and three cats! They are all Mets fans. Irv has worked at ABC Television for 20 years, but will be retiring in December 2020 to sell vintage comic books and write more articles.

William Grmek lives in Wickliffe, Ohio, and is a member of the Jack Graney Chapter (Cleveland) of SABR. He is a data analyst for Progressive Insurance and a lifelong Indians fan who grew up idolizing Buddy Bell, Joe Charboneau, and Cory Snyder.

Vince Guerrieri is a SABR member and Indians fan from Youngstown, Ohio (hometown of Jimmy McAleer, Bonesetter Reese, and Billy Evans). He's a journalist and author who's written for POLITICO, *Smithsonian*, *Ohio Magazine*, and *Popular Mechanics*, among others.

Michael Hanks, a long-standing member of SABR and the Baseball Hall of Fame, and his wife Linda provided digital media from his personal Topps baseball card collection.

Paul Hofmann, a SABR member since 2002, is the associate vice president for international affairs at Sacramento State University and a frequent contributor to SABR publications. Paul is a native of Detroit and a lifelong Tigers fan. In his free time, Paul enjoys reading and collecting baseball cards. He currently resides in Folsom, California.

Mike Huber joined SABR in 1996 and is currently chair of SABR's Games Project Committee. He started rooting for the Baltimore Orioles in the late 1960s and has stuck with the Birds through thick and thin, savoring moments like the July 2, 1995, comeback win against the Toronto Blue Jays. He enjoys researching and writing about rare events in baseball, particularly games in which batters hit for the cycle.

Ronnie Joyner is a graphic artist from Charlotte Hall, Maryland. Ronnie has created over 500 baseball player "bio-illustrations," most of which were published in *Sports Collectors Digest*, as well as other publications, over the last 25 years. He created 24 bio-illustrations for the Pittsburgh Pirates in 2016-17 which appeared in *First Pitch*, the team's gameday program. Ronnie's baseball writing has also appeared in SABR's *National Pastime*. In addition, he has co-authored autobiographies with former major league players Don Gutteridge, Virgil "Fire" Trucks, Frank "The Original One" Thomas, Bob Dillinger, and Ned Garver. Ronnie also spends his weekends as a singer/guitarist/songwriter for Flea Bops, a Maryland rockabilly band with whom he has been a member since 1992.

Russ Lake lives in Champaign, Illinois, and is a retired college professor. The 1964 St. Louis Cardinals remain his favorite team, and he was distressed to see Sportsman's Park (aka Busch Stadium I) being demolished not long after he had attended the last game there on May 8, 1966. His wife, Carol, deserves an MVP award for watching all of a 13-inning ballgame in Cincinnati with Russ in 1971 – during their honeymoon. In 1994, he was an editor for David Halberstam's baseball book *October 1964*.

Kevin Larkin retired after 24 years as a police officer in his hometown of Great Barrington, Massachusetts. He has always been a baseball fan and has been going to minor-league and major-league baseball games since he was 5 years old. He has authored two books on baseball: *Baseball in the Bay State (*a history of baseball in the Commonwealth of Massachusetts) and *Gehrig: Game by Game* (an account of all of the major-league games played by his hero, Lou Gehrig. He has also co-authored *Baseball in the Berkshires: A County's Common Bond* along with James Tom Daly, James Overmyer, and Larry Moore. The book details a history of baseball in Berkshire County, where Larkin grew up. He has authored numerous articles for SABR and also recently has published on Legends On Deck, a list of who Larkin thinks are the top 100 Black Baseball/Negro League baseball players. Black Baseball and the Negro Leagues are a subject he really enjoys. Researching and learning about this great game are what drives him and he loves researching, reading, and writing about the game's history. He does fact-checking and hyperlinking for SABR, as well as writing biographies and game accounts, and according to him, is living the dream of writing and researching about the great sport of baseball.

Bob LeMoine grew up in Maine and has lived and died with the Red Sox for most of his life. He joined SABR in 2013 and has contributed to several SABR book projects. Having a love for both history and baseball, he usually contributes to most SABR book projects. Bob lives in Rochester, New Hampshire, and works as a high-school librarian and adjunct professor.

Len Levin is retired after a long career as a newspaper editor in New England. Currently he is the grammarian for the Rhode Island Supreme Court and copyedits their decisions. He also copyedits many of SABR's books, including this one. He lives in Providence.

Justin Mattingly covers Virginia politics and policy for the *Richmond Times-Dispatch*. He joined SABR in 2014 while a student at Syracuse University, where he studied journalism and political science. He lives in Richmond, Virginia, and is a member of SABR's Bud Metheny Chapter. While growing up in northern New York, he frequented Olympic Stadium in Montreal and has attended a game at every active major-league ballpark and seven others that have closed.

Madison McEntire is a structural engineer from Bryant, Arkansas. He has served as the president of the Brooks Robinson-George Kell SABR Chapter since its inception in 2004, self-published *Big League Trivia* in 2006, and has datacasted Double-A games for the Arkansas Travelers since 2010. He has been a Cubs fan since 1983, when his small hometown finally got cable TV. A native Arkansan and Arkansas Razorback fan since birth, Madison graduated from the University of Arkansas, where his son will be a freshman pitcher again in 2021 (thanks to COVID-19).

Bill Nowlin sat in the center-field bleachers at Fenway Park and took in the eight-run bottom of the ninth, the greatest comeback he ever witnessed in person. Born in Boston, living in Cambridge, he is one of the founders of Rounder Records and author or editor of very close to 100 books, mostly as a member of SABR.

Tony S Oliver is a native of Puerto Rico currently living in Sacramento, California, with his wife and daughter. While he works as a Six Sigma professional, his true love is baseball and he cheers for both the Red Sox and whoever happens to be playing the Yankees. He is fascinated by baseball cards and is currently researching the evolution of baseball tickets. He be-

lieves there is no prettier color than the vibrant green of freshly mown grass on a baseball field.

Dennis Pajot was born in Milwaukee, raised and schooled in Milwaukee, worked for and retired from the City of Milwaukee, still lives in Milwaukee. Happily or sadly, that says it all about Dennis.

Laura Peebles is a retired CPA, still writing and editing tax materials part-time for Bloomberg. She brings her writing and editing skills to SABR as an associate editor for the Games Story Project. Her other baseball project is writing rhyming game summaries of Washington Nationals games. She lives with her wife, two cats, and an ever-growing collection of baseballs in Arlington, Virginia.

Matthew Perry is a resident of Arlington, Massachusetts, and has been a SABR member since 2018. A lifelong fan of the Red Sox and the Braves, he enjoys researching and learning about baseball history in New England and has contributed to the SABR Games Project as a writer and copy editor. Matthew was published in *Worcester Magazine* about the city's National League History, and posts his other baseball research to his blog: massachusettsbaseballhistory. com/.

Alan Raylesberg is an attorney in New York City. He is a lifelong baseball fan who enjoys baseball history and roots for the Yankees and the Mets. Alan also has a strong interest in baseball analytics and is a devotee of baseball simulation games, participating both in draft leagues and historical replays

Carl Riechers retired from United Parcel Service in 2012 after 35 years of service. With more free time, he became a SABR member that same year. Born and raised in the suburbs of St. Louis, he became a big fan of the Cardinals. He and his wife, Janet, have three children and he is the proud grandpa of two.

Richard Riis is a writer, researcher, genealogist, and lifelong baseball fan who still remembers his first baseball card: Senators second baseman Chuck Cottier. He has contributed to 10 SABR books and co-authored the autobiography of former child star and close friend Pamelyn Ferdin. A New Yorker by birth, he lives today in central California.

Tom Ruane is a SABR member and the Vice President of Retrosheet. His baseball writing has appeared in *Total Baseball*, *The Baseball Research Journal*, and *The Big Bad Baseball Annual*, as well as on several websites. His fiction has appeared in several magazines, including *The Yale Review*, *The Southern Review*, and *The Carolina Quarterly*. He lives in Poughkeepsie, New York, with his lovely wife Eileen, where he works for a local computer company.

Tom Schott holds a Ph.D. in American history (LSU, 1978) and is a retired historian for the Air Force and Special Operations Command. He currently reads, writes, plays chess, and freelance-edits to stay busy.

Peter Seidel has been a member of SABR since 2014. A lifelong Yankee fan, Pete grew up a short ride from Yankee Stadium in southern Westchester County. After earning a master's degree from Harvard University, Pete relocated to the Dallas-Fort Worth area with his two children for his day job as business development executive for AT&T. Pete has contributed to several SABR books, starting with the Mike Sandlock book in 2016, as well as many articles for SABR's Games Project. Aside from being a diehard Yankee fan, Pete enjoys spending time with his teenage kids, bicycling, hiking, kayaking, and playing guitar in whatever spare time he has.

Andrew Sharp, a retired newspaper editor, began writing BioProject and Games Project essays in 2017. He grew up in the D.C. area as a fan of the original and expansion Senators. He lives in central New Jersey. A Mets fan for the 30-plus years Washington was without a team, he has been a fervent Nationals supporter since 2005. From 2007 through 2019, he charted minor-league games on a freelance basis for Baseball Info Solutions.

Mark S. Sternman attended Game Four of the 2008 ALCS and saw Tampa Bay beat Boston 13-4. As a fan of the Yankees who grew up in New York, Sternman appreciated witnessing this rout rather than the Red Sox comeback in the following game about which he wrote in this book.

Andrew Stockmann, a SABR member since 2017, is a student at Wichita State University pursuing a degree in sport management. He is from Liberty, Missouri, and grew up an avid Royals fan. Currently,

Andrew lives in Omaha, Nebraska, and is an intern for the Omaha Storm Chasers. This is his second contribution to a SABR publication.

Jim Sweetman's paternal great-grandfather emigrated from Ireland to work in the shipyards in Bristol, Pennsylvania, in the late nineteenth century, establishing the family's affinity for Philadelphia baseball. He remains a lifelong Phillies fan, despite growing up on the edge of the New York media market in central New Jersey and living for the past 30-plus years just outside Washington, D.C. Since 1994 he's operated broadandpattison.com, a website providing daily slices of Phillies history, for which he has conducted extensive reviews of contemporary press accounts. He holds bachelor's and master's degrees from Rutgers University and an MBA from James Madison University. He is a senior official with the US Government Accountability Office, where he manages efforts to evaluate the efficiency and effectiveness of government programs, primarily those dealing with information technology.

Bruce "Wicker" Thompson has been a SABR member since 2018. He is a graduate of the Connecticut School of Broadcasting, and completed a baseball analytics course from Sports Management Worldwide. He was an EMT, a former member of the Massena (New York) Fire Department and former captain of the Lake Placid (New York) Fire Department. He is also an official for the United States Biathlon Association and also served as co-chair for the New York State Biathlon. He is currently living in Terryville, Connecticut, with girlfriend Sarah and working for the utility company. In addition to this book's article, he has enjoyed working on SABR's media guide project.

Michael Trzinski is a resident of Port Edwards, Wisconsin, and has been a Brewers fan since 1970. He is married to wife Kelli and has three children, Corey, Bronson, and Emily, along with eight grandchildren. They have a black cat named Hudson, who thinks he is a dog. Michael has done freelance work, mostly for regional Wisconsin sports magazines. He is the co-founder, partner, and editor of the *Wisconsin Prep Hockey* website, covering Wisconsin high-school hockey since 2001. Michael works in logistics at a central Wisconsin chemical plant in order to pay the bills. A relative newcomer to SABR, Michael looks forward to doing more pieces for the baseball community to share. Check out his hockey website at Wisconsin Prep Hockey.

Joseph Wancho lives in Brooklyn, Ohio. He has been a SABR member since 2005. Currently, he serves as vice chair of the Baseball Index Research Committee.

Brian Williams began writing as a high-school sports stringer before launching a broadcast, writing, and voice-over career at age 15. He has performed radio play-by-play for PIAA state championship baseball and football as well as some minor-league baseball. After he built a new FM radio station with three partners, added an AM, and sold both in 2001, Brian switched gears to a career in medical equipment software, where he authored several articles for national trade magazines. Brian still writes and voices projects (brianwilliamscreative.com), and currently works with a middle-school emotional support team in Harrisburg, Pennsylvania.

Jim Wohlenhaus is a retired internal auditor who just likes baseball. His favorite team is the one closest to where he is at the time. Right now, that is the Colorado Rockies. He joined SABR in the 1970s, got disgusted when each new president moved the headquarters, and quit. He rejoined SABR in time to help with the SABR convention in Denver. He now lives on the Eastern Colorado prairie, having finally escaped a big city, and loves every minute. He is trying to determine why historically there has been little interest in town ball or semipro ball on the Eastern plains. Jim lives alone with a cat and a dog.

Gregory H. Wolf was born in Pittsburgh, but now resides in the Chicagoland area with his wife, Margaret, and daughter, Gabriela. A professor of German studies and holder of the Dennis and Jean Bauman Endowed Chair in the Humanities at North Central College in Naperville, Illinois, he has edited a dozen books for SABR. He is currently working on projects about Shibe Park in Philadelphia and Ebbets Field in Brooklyn. Since January 2017 he has been co-director of SABR's BioProject, which you can follow on Facebook and Twitter.

Allan Wood has been writing professionally for 40 years, as a sportswriter, music critic, and a general observer of politics. He is the author of *Babe Ruth and the 1918 Red Sox* and co-author of *Don't Let Us Win Tonight: An Oral History of the 2004 Boston Red Sox's Impossible Playoff Run* (with Bill Nowlin). He has contributed to eight books published by SABR and has been writing "The Joy of Sox" blog since 2003. He was born and raised in Vermont, enjoyed 2004 while living in New York City, and currently makes his home on Vancouver Island, in British Columbia, Canada.

Jack Zerby prefers low-scoring pitchers' duels, but couldn't resist the opportunity to write about a comeback game from a time – 1951 – when he was just starting to follow baseball. The Reds-Braves tussle he chronicled here kindled memories of some of his earliest baseball cards and the latter days of Boston as a National League franchise. Jack joined SABR in 1994 and, with colleague Mel Poplock, co-founded the Seymour-Mills chapter in southwest Florida. A retired attorney and estates/trusts administrator, Jack found his SABR niche with BioProject and Games Projects and writes, vets, fact-checks, and edits for both. He lives in Brevard, North Carolina, with his wife, Diana, a violinist.

SABR BioProject Team Books

In 2002, the Society for American Baseball Research launched an effort to write and publish biographies of every player, manager, and individual who has made a contribution to baseball. Over the past decade, the BioProject Committee has produced over 6,000 biographical articles. Many have been part of efforts to create theme- or team-oriented books, spearheaded by chapters or other committees of SABR.

THE 1986 BOSTON RED SOX:
THERE WAS MORE THAN GAME SIX
One of a two-book series on the rivals that met in the 1986 World Series, the Boston Red Sox and the New York Mets, including biographies of every player, coach, broadcaster, and other important figures in the top organizations in baseball that year. .
Edited by Leslie Heaphy and Bill Nowlin
$19.95 paperback (ISBN 978-1-943816-19-4)
$9.99 ebook (ISBN 978-1-943816-18-7)
8.5"X11", 420 pages, over 200 photos

THE 1986 NEW YORK METS:
THERE WAS MORE THAN GAME SIX
The other book in the "rivalry" set from the 1986 World Series. This book re-tells the story of that year's classic World Series and this is the story of each of the players, coaches, managers, and broadcasters, their lives in baseball and the way the 1986 season fit into their lives.
Edited by Leslie Heaphy and Bill Nowlin
$19.95 paperback (ISBN 978-1-943816-13-2)
$9.99 ebook (ISBN 978-1-943816-12-5)
8.5"X11", 392 pages, over 100 photos

SCANDAL ON THE SOUTH SIDE:
THE 1919 CHICAGO WHITE SOX
The Black Sox Scandal isn't the only story worth telling about the 1919 Chicago White Sox. The team roster included three future Hall of Famers, a 20-year-old spitballer who would win 300 games in the minors, and even a batboy who later became a celebrity with the "Murderers' Row" New York Yankees. All of their stories are included in Scandal on the South Side with a timeline of the 1919 season.
Edited by Jacob Pomrenke
$19.95 paperback (ISBN 978-1-933599-95-3)
$9.99 ebook (ISBN 978-1-933599-94-6)
8.5"x11", 324 pages, 55 historic photos

WINNING ON THE NORTH SIDE
THE 1929 CHICAGO CUBS
Celebrate the 1929 Chicago Cubs, one of the most exciting teams in baseball history. Future Hall of Famers Hack Wilson, '29 NL MVP Rogers Hornsby, and Kiki Cuyler, along with Riggs Stephenson formed one of the most potent quartets in baseball history. The magical season came to an ignominious end in the World Series and helped craft the future "lovable loser" image of the team.
Edited by Gregory H. Wolf
$19.95 paperback (ISBN 978-1-933599-89-2)
$9.99 ebook (ISBN 978-1-933599-88-5)
8.5"x11", 314 pages, 59 photos

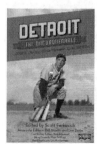

DETROIT THE UNCONQUERABLE:
THE 1935 WORLD CHAMPION TIGERS
Biographies of every player, coach, and broadcaster involved with the 1935 World Champion Detroit Tigers baseball team, written by members of the Society for American Baseball Research. Also includes a season in review and other articles about the 1935 team. Hank Greenberg, Mickey Cochrane, Charlie Gehringer, Schoolboy Rowe, and more.
Edited by Scott Ferkovich
$19.95 paperback (ISBN 9978-1-933599-78-6)
$9.99 ebook (ISBN 978-1-933599-79-3)
8.5"X11", 230 pages, 52 photos

THE TEAM THAT TIME WON'T FORGET:
THE 1951 NEW YORK GIANTS
Because of Bobby Thomson's dramatic "Shot Heard 'Round the World" in the bottom of the ninth of the decisive playoff game against the Brooklyn Dodgers, the team will forever be in baseball public's consciousness. Includes a foreword by Giants outfielder Monte Irvin.
Edited by Bill Nowlin and C. Paul Rogers III
$19.95 paperback (ISBN 978-1-933599-99-1)
$9.99 ebook (ISBN 978-1-933599-98-4)
8.5"X11", 282 pages, 47 photos

A PENNANT FOR THE TWIN CITIES:
THE 1965 MINNESOTA TWINS
This volume celebrates the 1965 Minnesota Twins, who captured the American League pennant in just their fifth season in the Twin Cities. Led by an All-Star cast, from Harmon Killebrew, Tony Oliva, Zoilo Versalles, and Mudcat Grant to Bob Allison, Jim Kaat, Earl Battey, and Jim Perry, the Twins won 102 games, but bowed to the Los Angeles Dodgers and Sandy Koufax in Game Seven
Edited by Gregory H. Wolf
$19.95 paperback (ISBN 978-1-943816-09-5)
$9.99 ebook (ISBN 978-1-943816-08-8)
8.5"X11", 405 pages, over 80 photos

MUSTACHES AND MAYHEM: CHARLIE O'S THREE TIME CHAMPIONS:
THE OAKLAND ATHLETICS: 1972-74
The Oakland Athletics captured major league baseball's crown each year from 1972 through 1974. Led by future Hall of Famers Reggie Jackson, Catfish Hunter and Rollie Fingers, the Athletics were a largely homegrown group who came of age together. Biographies of every player, coach, manager, and broadcaster (and mascot) from 1972 through 1974 are included, along with season recaps.
Edited by Chip Greene
$29.95 paperback (ISBN 978-1-943816-07-1)
$9.99 ebook (ISBN 978-1-943816-06-4)
8.5"X11", 600 pages, almost 100 photos

SABR Members can purchase each book at a significant discount (often 50% off) and receive the ebook edtions free as a member benefit. Each book is available in a trade paperback edition as well as ebooks suitable for reading on a home computer or Nook, Kindle, or iPad/tablet.

To learn more about becoming a member of SABR, visit the website: sabr.org/join

SABR BioProject Books

In 2002, the Society for American Baseball Research launched an effort to write and publish biographies of every player, manager, and individual who has made a contribution to baseball. Over the past decade, the BioProject Committee has produced over 2,200 biographical articles. Many have been part of efforts to create theme- or team-oriented books, spearheaded by chapters or other committees of SABR.

THE YEAR OF THE BLUE SNOW:
THE 1964 PHILADELPHIA PHILLIES
Catcher Gus Triandos dubbed the Philadelphia Phillies' 1964 season "the year of the blue snow," a rare thing that happens once in a great while. This book sheds light on lingering questions about the 1964 season—but any book about a team is really about the players. This work offers life stories of all the players and others (managers, coaches, owners, and broadcasters) associated with this star-crossed team, as well as essays of analysis and history.
Edited by Mel Marmer and Bill Nowlin
$19.95 paperback (ISBN 978-1-933599-51-9)
$9.99 ebook (ISBN 978-1-933599-52-6)
8.5"X11", 356 PAGES, over 70 photos

DETROIT TIGERS 1984:
WHAT A START! WHAT A FINISH!
The 1984 Detroit tigers roared out of the gate, winning their first nine games of the season and compiling an eye-popping 35-5 record after the campaign's first 40 games—still the best start ever for any team in major league history. This book brings together biographical profiles of every Tiger from that magical season, plus those of field management, top executives, the broadcasters—even venerable Tiger Stadium and the city itself.
Edited by Mark Pattison and David Raglin
$19.95 paperback (ISBN 978-1-933599-44-1)
$9.99 ebook (ISBN 978-1-933599-45-8)
8.5"x11", 250 pages (Over 230,000 words!)

SWEET '60: THE 1960 PITTSBURGH PIRATES
A portrait of the 1960 team which pulled off one of the biggest upsets of the last 60 years. When Bill Mazeroski's home run left the park to win in Game Seven of the World Series, beating the New York Yankees, David had toppled Goliath. It was a blow that awakened a generation, one that millions of people saw on television, one of TV's first iconic World Series moments.
Edited by Clifton Blue Parker and Bill Nowlin
$19.95 paperback (ISBN 978-1-933599-48-9)
$9.99 ebook (ISBN 978-1-933599-49-6)
8.5"X11", 340 pages, 75 photos

RED SOX BASEBALL IN THE DAYS OF IKE AND ELVIS: THE RED SOX OF THE 1950s
Although the Red Sox spent most of the 1950s far out of contention, the team was filled with fascinating players who captured the heart of their fans. In *Red Sox Baseball*, members of SABR present 46 biographies on players such as Ted Williams and Pumpsie Green as well as season-by-season recaps.
Edited by Mark Armour and Bill Nowlin
$19.95 paperback (ISBN 978-1-933599-24-3)
$9.99 ebook (ISBN 978-1-933599-34-2)
8.5"X11", 372 PAGES, over 100 photos

THE MIRACLE BRAVES OF 1914
BOSTON'S ORIGINAL WORST-TO-FIRST CHAMPIONS
Long before the Red Sox "Impossible Dream" season, Boston's now nearly forgotten "other" team, the 1914 Boston Braves, performed a baseball "miracle" that resounds to this very day. The "Miracle Braves" were Boston's first "worst-to-first" winners of the World Series. Refusing to throw in the towel at the midseason mark, George Stallings engineered a remarkable second-half climb in the standings all the way to first place.
Edited by Bill Nowlin
$19.95 paperback (ISBN 978-1-933599-69-4)
$9.99 ebook (ISBN 978-1-933599-70-0)
8.5"X11", 392 PAGES, over 100 photos

THAR'S JOY IN BRAVELAND!
THE 1957 MILWAUKEE BRAVES
Few teams in baseball history have captured the hearts of their fans like the Milwaukee Braves of the 1950s. During the Braves' 13-year tenure in Milwaukee (1953-1965), they had a winning record every season, won two consecutive NL pennants (1957 and 1958), lost two more in the final week of the season (1956 and 1959), and set big-league attendance records along the way.
Edited by Gregory H. Wolf
$19.95 paperback (ISBN 978-1-933599-71-7)
$9.99 ebook (ISBN 978-1-933599-72-4)
8.5"x11", 330 pages, over 60 photos

NEW CENTURY, NEW TEAM:
THE 1901 BOSTON AMERICANS
The team now known as the Boston Red Sox played its first season in 1901. Boston had a well-established National League team, but the American League went head-to-head with the N.L. in Chicago, Philadelphia, and Boston. Chicago won the American League pennant and Boston finished second, only four games behind.
Edited by Bill Nowlin
$19.95 paperback (ISBN 978-1-933599-58-8)
$9.99 ebook (ISBN 978-1-933599-59-5)
8.5"X11", 268 pages, over 125 photos

CAN HE PLAY?
A LOOK AT BASEBALL SCOUTS AND THEIR PROFESSION
They dig through tons of coal to find a single diamond. Here in the world of scouts, we meet the "King of Weeds," a Ph.D. we call "Baseball's Renaissance Man," a husband-and-wife team, pioneering Latin scouts, and a Japanese-American interned during World War II who became a successful scout—and many, many more.
Edited by Jim Sandoval and Bill Nowlin
$19.95 paperback (ISBN 978-1-933599-23-6)
$9.99 ebook (ISBN 978-1-933599-25-0)
8.5"X11", 200 PAGES, over 100 photos

SABR Members can purchase each book at a significant discount (often 50% off) and receive the ebook editions free as a member benefit. Each book is available in a trade paperback edition as well as ebooks suitable for reading on a home computer or Nook, Kindle, or iPad/tablet.
To learn more about becoming a member of SABR, visit the website: sabr.org/join

THE SABR DIGITAL LIBRARY

The Society for American Baseball Research, the top baseball research organization in the world, disseminates some of the best in baseball history, analysis, and biography through our publishing programs. The SABR Digital Library contains a mix of books old and new, and focuses on a tandem program of paperback and ebook publication, making these materials widely available for both on digital devices and as traditional printed books.

GREATEST GAMES BOOKS

TIGERS BY THE TALE:
GREAT GAMES AT MICHIGAN AND TRUMBULL
For over 100 years, Michigan and Trumbull was the scene of some of the most exciting baseball ever. This book portrays 50 classic games at the corner, spanning the earliest days of Bennett Park until Tiger Stadium's final closing act. From Ty Cobb to Mickey Cochrane, Hank Greenberg to Al Kaline, and Willie Horton to Alan Trammell.
Edited by Scott Ferkovich
$12.95 paperback (ISBN 978-1-943816-21-7)
$6.99 ebook (ISBN 978-1-943816-20-0)
8.5"x11", 160 pages, 22 photos

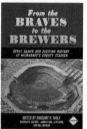

FROM THE BRAVES TO THE BREWERS:GREAT GAMES AND HISTORY AT MILWAUKEE'S COUNTY STADIUM
The National Pastime provides in-depth articles focused on the geographic region where the national SABR convention is taking place annually. The SABR 45 convention took place in Chicago, and here are 45 articles on baseball in and around the bat-and-ball crazed Windy City: 25 that appeared in the souvenir book of the convention plus another 20 articles available in ebook only.
Edited by Gregory H. Wolf
$19.95 paperback (ISBN 978-1-943816-23-1)
$9.99 ebook (ISBN 978-1-943816-22-4)
8.5"X11", 290 pages, 58 photos

BRAVES FIELD:
MEMORABLE MOMENTS AT BOSTON'S LOST DIAMOND
From its opening on August 18, 1915, to the sudden departure of the Boston Braves to Milwaukee before the 1953 baseball season, Braves Field was home to Boston's National League baseball club and also hosted many other events: from NFL football to championship boxing. The most memorable moments to occur in Braves Field history are portrayed here.
Edited by Bill Nowlin and Bob Brady
$19.95 paperback (ISBN 978-1-933599-93-9)
$9.99 ebook (ISBN 978-1-933599-92-2)
8.5"X11", 282 pages, 182 photos

AU JEU/PLAY BALL: THE 50 GREATEST GAMES IN THE HISTORY OF THE MONTREAL EXPOS
The 50 greatest games in Montreal Expos history. The games described here recount the exploits of the many great players who wore Expos uniforms over the years—Bill Stoneman, Gary Carter, Andre Dawson, Steve Rogers, Pedro Martinez, from the earliest days of the franchise, to the glory years of 1979-1981, the what-might-have-been years of the early 1990s, and the sad, final days.and others.
Edited by Norm King
$12.95 paperback (ISBN 978-1-943816-15-6)
$5.99 ebook (ISBN978-1-943816-14-9)
8.5"x11", 162 pages, 50 photos

ORIGINAL SABR RESEARCH

CALLING THE GAME:
BASEBALL BROADCASTING FROM 1920 TO THE PRESENT
An exhaustive, meticulously researched history of bringing the national pastime out of the ballparks and into living rooms via the airwaves. Every play-by-play announcer, color commentator, and ex-ballplayer, every broadcast deal, radio station, and TV network. Plus a foreword by "Voice of the Chicago Cubs" Pat Hughes, and an afterword by Jacques Doucet, the "Voice of the Montreal Expos" 1972-2004.
by Stuart Shea
$24.95 paperback (ISBN 978-1-933599-40-3)
$9.99 ebook (ISBN 978-1-933599-41-0)
7"X10", 712 pages, 40 photos

BIOPROJECT BOOKS

WHO'S ON FIRST:
REPLACEMENT PLAYERS IN WORLD WAR II
During World War II, 533 players made the major league debuts. More than 60% of the players in the 1941 Opening Day lineups departed for the service and were replaced by first-times and oldsters. Hod Lisenbee was 46. POW Bert Shepard had an artificial leg, and Pete Gray had only one arm. The 1944 St. Louis Browns had 13 players classified 4-F. These are their stories.
Edited by Marc Z Aaron and Bill Nowlin
$19.95 paperback (ISBN 978-1-933599-91-5)
$9.99 ebook (ISBN 978-1-933599-90-8)
8.5"X11", 422 pages, 67 photos

VAN LINGLE MUNGO:
THE MAN, THE SONG, THE PLAYERS
40 baseball players with intriguing names have been named in renditions of Dave Frishberg's classic 1969 song, Van Lingle Mungo. This book presents biographies of all 40 players and additional information about one of the greatest baseball novelty songs of all time.
Edited by Bill Nowlin
$19.95 paperback (ISBN 978-1-933599-76-2)
$9.99 ebook (ISBN 978-1-933599-77-9)
8.5"X11", 278 pages, 46 photos

NUCLEAR POWERED BASEBALL
Nuclear Powered Baseball tells the stories of each player—past and present—featured in the classic Simpsons episode "Homer at the Bat." Wade Boggs, Ken Griffey Jr., Ozzie Smith, Nap Lajoie, Don Mattingly, and many more. We've also included a few very entertaining takes on the now-famous episode from prominent baseball writers Jonah Keri, Joe Posnanski, Erik Malinowski, and Bradley Woodrum
Edited by Emily Hawks and Bill Nowlin
$19.95 paperback (ISBN 978-1-943816-11-8)
$9.99 ebook (ISBN 978-1-943816-10-1)
8.5"X11", 250 pages

SABR Members can purchase each book at a significant discount (often 50% off) and receive the ebook edtions free as a member benefit. Each book is available in a trade paperback edition as well as ebooks suitable for reading on a home computer or Nook, Kindle, or iPad/tablet.
To learn more about becoming a member of SABR, visit the website: sabr.org/join

Friends of SABR

You can become a Friend of SABR by giving as little as $10 per month or by making a one-time gift of $1,000 or more. When you do so, you will be inducted into a community of passionate baseball fans dedicated to supporting SABR's work.

Friends of SABR receive the following benefits:
- ✓ Annual Friends of SABR Commemorative Lapel Pin
- ✓ Recognition in This Week in SABR, SABR.org, and the SABR Annual Report
- ✓ Access to the SABR Annual Convention VIP donor event
- ✓ Invitations to exclusive Friends of SABR events

SABR On-Deck Circle - $10/month, $30/month, $50/month

Get in the SABR On-Deck Circle, and help SABR become the essential community for the world of baseball. Your support will build capacity around all things SABR, including publications, website content, podcast development, and community growth.

A monthly gift is deducted from your bank account or charged to a credit card until you tell us to stop. No more email, mail, or phone reminders.

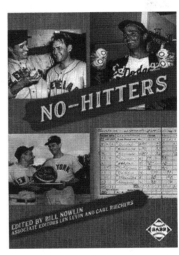

Join the SABR On-Deck Circle

Payment Info: _____Visa _____Mastercard

Name on Card: _____

Card #: _____

Exp. Date: _____ Security Code: _____

Signature: _____

- ○ $10/month
- ○ $30/month
- ○ $50/month
- ○ Other amount _____

Go to sabr.org/donate to make your gift online

Society for American Baseball Research

Cronkite School at ASU
555 N. Central Ave. #416, Phoenix, AZ 85004
602.496.1460 (phone)
SABR.org

Become a SABR member today!

If you're interested in baseball — writing about it, reading about it, talking about it — there's a place for you in the Society for American Baseball Research.

SABR memberships are available on annual, multi-year, or monthly subscription basis. Annual and monthly subscription memberships auto-renew for your convenience. Young Professional memberships are for ages 30 and under. Senior memberships are for ages 65 and older. Student memberships are available to currently enrolled middle/high school or full-time college/university students. Monthly subscription members receive SABR publications electronically and are eligible for SABR event discounts after 12 months.

Here's a list of some of the key benefits you'll receive as a SABR member:

- Receive two editions (spring and fall) of the *Baseball Research Journal*, our flagship publication
- Receive expanded e-book edition of *The National Pastime*, our annual convention journal
- 8-10 new e-books published by the SABR Digital Library, all FREE to members
- "This Week in SABR" e-newsletter, sent to members every Friday
- Join dozens of research committees, from Statistical Analysis to Women in Baseball.
- Join one of 70+ regional chapters in the U.S., Canada, Latin America, and abroad
- Participate in online discussion groups
- Ask and answer baseball research questions on the SABR-L e-mail listserv
- Complete archives of *The Sporting News* dating back to 1886 and other research resources
- Promote your research in "This Week in SABR"
- Diamond Dollars Case Competition
- Yoseloff Scholarships

- Discounts on SABR national conferences, including the SABR National Convention, the SABR Analytics Conference, Jerry Malloy Negro League Conference, Frederick Ivor-Campbell 19th Century Conference, and the Arizona Fall League Experience
- Publish your research in peer-reviewed SABR journals
- Collaborate with SABR researchers and experts
- Contribute to Baseball Biography Project or the SABR Games Project
- List your new book in the SABR Bookshelf
- Lead a SABR research committee or chapter
- Networking opportunities at SABR Analytics Conference
- Meet baseball authors and historians at SABR events and chapter meetings
- 50% discounts on paperback versions of SABR e-books
- Discounts with other partners in the baseball community
- SABR research awards

We hope you'll join the most passionate international community of baseball fans at SABR! Check us out online at SABR.org/join.

SABR MEMBERSHIP FORM

	Standard	Senior	Young Pro.	Student
Annual:	☐ $65	☐ $45	☐ $45	☐ $25
3 Year:	☐ $175	☐ $129	☐ $129	
5 Year:	☐ $249			
Monthly:	☐ $6.95	☐ $4.95	☐ $4.95	

(International members wishing to be mailed the Baseball Research Journal should add $10/yr for Canada/Mexico or $19/yr for overseas locations.)

Participate in Our Donor Program!

Support the preservation of baseball research. Designate your gift toward:

☐ General Fund   ☐ Endowment Fund   ☐ Research Resources   ☐ _____
☐ I want to maximize the impact of my gift; do not send any donor premiums
☐ I would like this gift to remain anonymous.

Note: Any donation not designated will be placed in the General Fund.
SABR is a 501 (c) (3) not-for-profit organization & donations are tax-deductible to the extent allowed by law.

Name _____

E-mail* _____

Address _____

City _____ ST _____ ZIP _____

Phone _____ Birthday _____

* Your e-mail address on file ensures you will receive the most recent SABR news.

Dues $_____

Donation $_____

Amount Enclosed $_____

Do you work for a matching grant corporation? Call (602) 496-1460 for details.

If you wish to pay by credit card, please contact the SABR office at (602) 496-1460 or sign up securely online at SABR.org/join. We accept Visa, Mastercard & Discover.

Do you wish to receive the *Baseball Research Journal* electronically? ☐ Yes   ☐ No
Our e-books are available in PDF, Kindle, or EPUB (iBooks, iPad, Nook) formats.

Mail to: SABR, Cronkite School at ASU, 555 N. Central Ave. #416, Phoenix, AZ 85004

10/19

Made in the USA
Middletown, DE
27 August 2021